ETHICS, LAW AND

M000192120

Ethics, Law and Society
Volume III

Edited by

JENNIFER GUNNING AND SØREN HOLM

Cardiff Law School, Cardiff University, UK

Routledge
Taylor & Francis Group

LONDON AND NEW YORK

First published 2007 by Ashgate Publishing

2 Park Square, Milton Park, Abingdon, Oxon OX14 4RN
711 Third Avenue, New York, NY 10017, USA

Routledge is an imprint of the Taylor & Francis Group, an informa business

First issued in paperback 2016

British Library Cataloguing in Publication Data
Ethics, law and society
   Vol 3
   1. Professional ethics 2. Law and ethics 3. Bioethics
   4. Social ethics 5. Human rights
   I. Gunning, Jennifer II. Holm, Søren
   174

Library of Congress Cataloging-in-Publication Data
Ethics, law and society / edited by Jennifer Gunning and Søren Holm.
   p. cm.
   Includes bibliographical references and index.
   ISBN 0-7546-7180-0
   1. Applied ethics. 2. Law. 3. Civilization. I. Gunning, Jennifer. II. Holm, Søren.

   BJ1581.2.E85 2005
   170--dc22

                                                                2005007651

ISBN 13: 978-0-7546-7180-0 (hbk)
ISBN 13: 978-1-138-25367-4 (pbk)

Contents

INTRODUCTION

PART I: BIOETHICS

PART II: ETHICS AND SOCIETY

List of Figures and Tables

Figures

Tables

List of Contributors

Dr Benjamin Capps is currently a Research Associate at the Centre for Ethics in Medicine, University of Bristol. During 2007 he was a Visiting Fellow at the Centre for Biomedical Ethics, at the National University of Singapore. Dr Capps is trained in applied genetics, law and philosophy (ethics in medicine). He completed his doctoral thesis in 2003 on European biotechnological regulation in stem cell science, and completed his postdoctoral studies in 2006 on the idea of procedural ethics in Enlightenment and contemporary political philosophy. Dr Capps was the principal researcher and author on the Ethics report for the Department of Trade and Industry's Foresight Project on 'Brain Science, Addiction and Drugs' in 2005. His research on the ethics of stem cell science and neuroethics has been widely published, and he has been invited to speak at a number of prominent international forums.

Cristiana Cianitto was born in Monza in 1975. She attended the Faculty of Law in the Università degli Studi in Milan, where she got her degree in 2000 and her PhD in 2005. Last year she won a fellowship in the same Faculty in order to carry on research about church and state relationships. She teaches Anglican Canon Law in the Faculty of Theology in Lugano, 'Master di diritto comparato delle religioni'. Her main fields of investigation are church and state relationships in the UK with particular attention to Anglican Canon Law and the British legal system in relation to religious issues; and hate crimes.

Luke Clements is a solicitor, a Professor in Law at Cardiff University and Associate Fellow of the Department of Social Policy and Applied Social Studies at the University of Warwick. He has taken many cases to the European Commission and Court of Human Rights on behalf of socially excluded people and written widely on social exclusion, particularly the rights of disabled people and Roma.

John Coggon is a Postdoctoral Fellow at Manchester Law School, having received his doctorate at Cardiff Law School. His doctorate focused on end-of-life issues. His other research interests include the interplay of law and ethics, and the use of abstract theories in law-making and judicial dicta.

Edgar Dahl is spokesman for the German Society for Reproductive Medicine. Trained in philosophy and biology, he specialized in bioethics and earned his PhD with a doctoral thesis on ethical issues in xenotransplantation. He has been a Visiting Fellow at the Centre for Human Bioethics at Monash University, Australia, the Hastings Centre in New York, and the Centre for Applied Philosophy and Public Ethics at the University of Melbourne, Australia. His research interests include moral philosophy, political philosophy, philosophy of law, philosophy of religion, evolutionary psychology, evolutionary ethics and bioethical issues such as physician-assisted suicide, preconception sex selection and human enhancement.

Ken Daniels is Adjunct Professor of Social Work at the University of Canterbury in Christchurch, New Zealand. He has been teaching, researching, writing and acting as a policy consultant on the psychosocial aspects of assisted human production for over 30 years. He has published over 100 papers and chapters, and his book, *Building a Family with the Assistance of Donor Insemination*, is used by parents around the world. He was Deputy Chair of the National Ethics Committee on Assisted Human Reproduction and is now Deputy Chair of the Advisory Committee on Assisted Reproductive Technology in New Zealand.

James Davey is a Lecturer at Cardiff Law School, specializing in insurance contract law and theory. He has held similar positions at the University of East Anglia and Birmingham University. He has published extensively on this topic, in the *Cambridge Law Journal*, *Journal of Business Law* and *Lloyd's Maritime and Commercial Law Quarterly*.

Mark Davies teaches at the Sussex Law School, University of Sussex. His research interests are primarily in the fields of professional negligence and conduct, education and the law, and science and law. He has published widely in these areas, with a particular focus on the professional conduct of lawyers and medical practitioners and the application of law to higher education. Recent projects include crisis and change in the self-regulation of medical practitioners and the changing regulatory climate for solicitors.

Professor Norman Doe is a Professor at the Law School, Cardiff University, and Director of its Centre for Law and Religion, and teaches public law and law and religion. He studied law at Cardiff, theology at Oxford, and for a doctorate at Cambridge. He has written books and articles on medieval law, ecclesiastical law, canon law, and church–state law. A barrister, he is a member of the European Consortium for Church and State Research and the Colloquium of Anglican and Roman Catholic Canon Lawyers. He was a member of the Lambeth Commission in 2003–2004.

Wybo Dondorp (1957), ethicist, is on the senior scientific staff of the Health Council of the Netherlands (The Hague). He is Scientific Secretary of the Council's Standing Committee on Medical Ethics and Health Law (since 1993) and has staffed committees preparing reports on several issues, including assisted reproduction, embryonic stem cells, and prenatal screening. His dissertation at the Free University Amsterdam (1994) was on virtue ethics. He taught ethics both in Amsterdam (Free University) and Rotterdam (Erasmus Medical Centre), where he also participated in research on reproductive choices and solidarity. He is a member of the Research Ethics Committee of the Erasmus Medical Centre in Rotterdam. Since September 2006 he has been Senior Research Fellow at Maastricht University, the Netherlands.

H. Martyn Evans is Professor of Humanities in Medicine at the University of Durham, and Principal of John Snow College at the University. He is joint editor of the Medical Humanities editions of the *Journal of Medical Ethics*. He has published (usually as H.M. Evans) variously on the aesthetics of music, ethics and philosophy of medicine, and the role of humanities in medical education. His current interests concern music and medicine; the role, nature and extent of humanities in medicine; and philosophical problems in medicine. When not being a philosopher, he is a musician (currently conductor and musical director of the University's Endeavour Orchestra) and, when time allows, a dinghy sailor. He is married with two sons; his wife Janet is a professional pianist.

Professor Philip Fennell is a Professor of Law at Cardiff Law School, Cardiff University where he teaches medical law, public law and human rights. He has published many articles on law and psychiatry. His book entitled *Treatment Without Consent: Law, Psychiatry and the Treatment of Mental Disorder since 1845*, was published by Routledge in 1996. Phil is a member of the Law Society's Mental Health and Disability Committee and was a member of the Mental Health Act Commission from 1983–89. In 2000 Philip lectured to the judiciary as part of the judicial training for the implementation of the Human Rights Act 1998. From November 2004 to March 2005 he served as specialist legal adviser to the Joint Parliamentary Scrutiny Committee on the Draft Mental Health Bill 2004. In November 2006 he was appointed specialist legal adviser to the Parliamentary Joint Committee on Human Rights for the Committee's scrutiny of the Mental Health Bill 2006. He regularly gives lectures to professional bodies on mental health law.

Dr Jennifer Gunning originally trained as a scientist; over the years she became an expert on the regulatory and legislative aspects of assisted reproduction, having provided advice both to the European Commission and the British government. She was secretary to the Voluntary (later Interim) Licensing Authority for Human In Vitro Fertilisation and Embryology, which regulated human embryo research and IVF before statutory regulation was introduced. Later she was seconded to the Department of Health to write a report on the comparative regulation of human IVF and embryo research for use while the Human Fertilisation and Embryology Bill was going through Parliament. Subsequently, she was involved in science policy, developing research assessment methodology and research ethics. A Visiting Fellow for six years at the Centre for the Analysis of Social Policy at the University of Bath, she is now a Senior Research Fellow in bioethics and law at Cardiff Law School and an independent consultant in bioethics and science affairs. From 2003–2007 Jennifer was Co-ordinator of the Cardiff Centre for Ethics, Law and Society (CCELS).

Natasha Hammond LLB, LLM is a Graduate Teaching Assistant at Cardiff Law School undertaking research on the legal and moral aspects of human embryonic stem cell research. Her interests include embryo research, cloning, biotechnology and bioethics.

Stephen Hogan is a Principal Lecturer in Marketing at Brighton Business School and has wide industry experience. Having gained a PhD in the area of marketing to children, he has published journal articles and presented conference papers with a particular focus on ethical issues in children's markets.

Professor Søren Holm is a medical doctor and philosopher. He is Director of the Cardiff Centre for Ethics, Law and Society and Professor of Medical Ethics (part-time) at the University of Oslo. He has written extensively on numerous topics in bioethics and the philosophy of medicine.

David Hunter is a Lecturer in Bioethics at the University of Ulster, Northern Ireland. Prior to this he lectured at Massey University, New Zealand in the Philosophy Department. David is the Alternative Vice-Chair for REC 1 Northern Ireland, and on his university's Research Ethics Committee. His main research interests are distributive justice, political theory and research ethics.

Gordon C. Jayson is a Professor of Medical Oncology at the Christie Hospital NHS Trust in Manchester, UK. Professor Jayson is a Principal Investigator in several Phase I trials of anti-angiogenic agents in which pharmacodynamic endpoints are incorporated, as well as Phase II/III trials in ovarian cancer at both national and international levels. His special interests are ovarian cancer and the development of anti-angiogenic drugs. He has an extensive laboratory programme focusing on the development of oligosaccharides as anti-angiogenic agents and further work on the validation of pharmacodynamic end points for anti-angiogenic agents. He is a reviewer for several international scientific journals and sits on the editorial board of the *British Journal of Cancer*.

Dr Ian Kenway is currently Director of the Centre for the International Study of Cyberethics and Human Rights (CISCHR), Honorary Research Fellow in Ethics and ICT at Cardiff University and Co-ordinator of CCELS. Previous positions have included Assistant Secretary of the Church of England's Board for Social Responsibility at Westminster, where he exercised a brief for legal affairs and edited its journal *Crucible* (1988–93), and Director of Studies at the Centre for the Study of Theology – later renamed the Centre for Theology and Society – at the University of Essex (1993–99). During 1999–2001 he was engaged in independent research in Southern Nevada in ethics and information and communication technologies. His interests include: internet governance, 'the digital divide', censorship and privacy issues, digital watermarking and the relationship between IT and public policy.

Dr Mairi Levitt is Deputy Director of CESAGen (ESRC Centre for Social and Economic Aspects of Genomics) at Lancaster University. Her research interests are in public understanding/perceptions of science, social and ethical implications of genetics and empirical bioethics. She is currently Principal Investigator on a project on 'Criminal Genes and Public Policy' (2006–2007). She is also researching children on the forensic database for the EU-funded INES project and working on a project in conjunction with NOWGEN (North West Genetics Knowledge Park) examining young people's ideas about human enhancement ('Making humans better?'). Recent publications include (with F. Tomasini, 2006) 'Bar-coded Children: Should Children be Included on the England and Wales National DNA Database?', *Genomics Society and Policy* 2: 1; and (with S. Weldon, 2005) 'A Well Placed Trust? Public Perceptions of the Governance of DNA Databases', *Critical Public Health* 15: 4, 311–21.

Professor Sheila A.M. McLean is the first holder of the International Bar Association Chair of Law and Ethics in Medicine at Glasgow University and is Director of the Institute of Law and Ethics in Medicine at Glasgow University. She has acted as a consultant to the World Health Organization, the Council of Europe and to individual States. She has published extensively in the area of medical law and is on the editorial boards of a number of national and international journals. She is a Fellow of the Royal Society of Edinburgh, has been awarded honorary Fellowships by the Royal College of Physicians of Edinburgh, the Academy of Medical Sciences, the Royal College of General Practitioners and the Royal Society of Arts. She has been awarded Honorary Doctorates in Law by the University of Edinburgh and the University of Abertay, Dundee. In 2005, she was awarded the first Lifetime Achievement Award at the Scottish Legal Awards.

Dr Javier Oliva studied Law at the University of Cádiz, where he obtained his first degree, LLM and PhD (cum laude and European distinction). After finishing his first degree, he became a Lecturer at the University of Cádiz (1996–2000) and a Research Fellow at the Centre for Law and Religion, Cardiff University (2001–2004). In this institution he taught public law, European Union law, and law and religion, amongst other subjects. He was appointed Lecturer at the University of Wales Bangor in 2004, where he is currently Head of Public Law as well as the Course Leader of Law with Modern Languages. He is also teaching on a part-time basis at University College London (UCL). Furthermore, he is a Research Associate at the Centre for Law and Religion (Cardiff University), the Convenor of the SLS Public Law section and the Book Review Editor of *Law and Justice*. His publications include the book *El Reino Unido: un Estado de Naciones, una pluralidad de Naciones*, (Granada: Comares, 2004).

Taiwo Oriola teaches intellectual property law on the LLM Commercial Law Module at Cardiff Law School. His research interests, in which he has extensive publications, include: intellectual property law, technology regulation, internet law and policy, and bioethics. He is currently researching liability, risk allocation, and modalities for award of damages for adventitious release of genetically modified organisms. Taiwo is a member of the International Society for Law and Technology (ISLAT), Anaheim, California, and a fellow of the Salzburg Seminar, Austria. He was a Visiting Fellow at the Max-Planck Institute for Intellectual Property Law, Munich, Germany, and the Max-Planck Institute for Comparative International Law, Heidelberg, Germany. He was also a Visiting Scholar at the Cegla Centre for Interdisciplinary Research of the Law, Buchmann Faculty of Law, Tel Aviv University, Israel, and a Research Scholar at the Faculty of Law, National University of Singapore. He was a recipient of the Erasmus Mundus Fellowship in Applied Ethics at the Ethics Institute, Utrecht University, Netherlands, and the Centre for Applied Ethics, Linkoping University,

Sweden. In June 2002, he participated in the Bioethics Institute Workshop, held at the University of Wisconsin-Madison, and organized by the United States National Agricultural Biotechnology Council. He was also an in-person attendee at the Internet Corporation for Domain Names and Assigned Numbers (ICANN) Public Meetings, held in Melbourne, Australia in March 2001.

Professor Stephen Pattison is Professor of Religion, Ethics and Practice at the University of Birmingham, having been Head of the School of Religious and Theological Studies at Cardiff University and previously having taught theology at the University of Birmingham, and health and social welfare at the Open University. An interdisciplinary scholar, he focuses on the way that theories, beliefs, values and practices intersect in contemporary life and practice, and has published extensively in healthcare ethics, practical theology and management studies. His latest books are (ed. with Roisin Pill), *Values in Professional Practice* (Oxford: Radcliffe, 2004), *The Challenge of Practical Theology* (London: Jessica Kingsley, 2007) and *Seeing Things: Deepening Relationships with Visual Artefacts* (London: SCM Press, 2007).

Carlos María Romeo-Casabona is Professor of Criminal Law at the University of the Basque Country, and Director of the Inter-University Chair BBVA Foundation – Provincial Government of Biscay in Law and the Human Genome, at the Universities of Deusto and of the Basque Country. He has a Doctorate in Law, a Diploma in Criminology and a Doctorate in Medicine. He is an author, co-author and editor of several books and numerous articles (220), published in seven languages. He is a founding editor of the reviews *Derecho y Genoma Humano/Law and the Human Genome* and *Perspectives of Law and the Human Genome* (both bilingual), as well as of the series *Library of Law and the Life Sciences* and *Studies in Criminal Law* (Comares Publishers). He has co-ordinated or participated in several national and European research projects. He is a member of the Spanish National Commission on Human Assisted Reproduction, of the Monitoring and Control Commission on the Donation and Use of Human Cells and Tissues, of the Committee of Bioethics (CDBI) of the Council of Europe, of the Ethics Committee of the Human Genome Organization (HUGO), Chairman of the Ethics Committee on Clinical Research of the Autonomous Community of the Basque Country and Adviser to the Spanish Minister of Health. He has received four Honorary Doctor in Law degrees from several Latin-American and Spanish universities.

Daniela Dornelles Rosa is a Medical Oncologist with great interest in basic, translational and clinical research in breast cancer and gynaecologic oncology. She works in a large women's public hospital in Southern Brazil, Hospital Fêmina. She obtained her Master of Science degree with a meta-analysis about cervix cancer. In her PhD thesis, she analysed several clinical aspects of patients with ovarian cancer treated at Christie Hospital NHS Trust UK, where she worked as a Research Fellow. From 2005 to 2006 she was a Clinical Research Fellow at Jules Bordet Institute, in Brussels, Belgium. Currently she is a Research Fellow of Paterson Institute for Cancer Research in Manchester, UK, being supported by CAPES (Coordenação de Aperfeiçoamento de Pessoal de Nível Superior), a foundation of the Brazilian government.

Sam Salek is Professor in Pharmacoepidemiology and Director of the Centre for Socioeconomic Research at the Welsh School of Pharmacy, Cardiff University, as well as being the Director of the internationally recognized Cardiff University/British Association of Pharmaceutical Physicians Postgraduate Course in Pharmaceutical Medicine. He is a member of a number of management and policy boards including the Centre for Applied Ethics, University of Wales. He is also a member of several national and international professional organizations, including honorary life membership of the British Association of Pharmaceutical Physicians; the Royal College of Physicians of the United Kingdom, Faculty of Pharmaceutical Medicine; and Professor of Pharmacy Practice, School of Pharmacy, Texas Tech University, USA. He speaks regularly at national and international scientific meetings and in the last decade he has given over 90 lectures related to his research areas. His main research interests are the development and clinical applications of health-related quality of life instruments. Examples of his developmental work are: United Kingdom Sickness Impact Profile (UKSIP); Renal Quality of Life Profile (RQLP); Community Dementia Quality of Life Profile (CDQLP); and palliative care specific quality of life instrument, the Cardiff Short Form McGill Quality of Life Questionnaire (MQOL-CSF). His areas of interest also include pharmacoepidemiology, pharmacoeconomics, drug safety evaluation and pharmacovigilance, drug profiling and patient knowledge, communication and patient information need, global pharmaceutical development and regulatory environment.

Judit Sándor is a Professor at the Faculty of Political Science, Legal Studies and Gender Studies of the Central European University (CEU), Budapest. In 1996 she received her PhD in law and political science. She was one of the founders of the first Patients' Right Organization ('Szószóló') in Hungary, she is a member of the Hungarian Science and Research Ethics Council, and also works at the Hungarian Human Reproduction Commission. In 2003 she was appointed as an expert for the Prime Minister's Advisory Committee on Human Genetics. She participated in different national and international standard-setting activities in the field of biomedical law. In 2004–2005 she worked as the Chief of the Bioethics Section at UNESCO. She has published six books in the field of human rights and biomedical law. Since September 2005 she has been a Director of the Center for Ethics and Law in Biomedicine (CELAB) at the Central European University.

Dr Win Tadd is Senior Research Fellow in the Department of Geriatric Medicine, Cardiff University. Win spent many years as a nurse and lecturer in the UK and Australia. In 1985 she graduated from the University of East Anglia with a BEd (Hons). In 1989 she was awarded a visiting scholarship to the Hastings Centre, New York and gained her PhD in applied ethics from Cardiff University in 1995. Her research interests now focus on the ethical aspects of ageing and care of older people and palliative care in dementia. She has co-ordinated two large EU-funded projects, on dignity and older Europeans, and information needs of older disabled people. She has published widely in healthcare ethics and recently completed a series of three books exploring the ethical dimensions of European nursing.

Dr Samarthia Thankappan is a Research Associate at the Centre for Business Relationships, Accountability, Sustainability and Society (BRASS) based at Cardiff University. Her work focuses on examining the changing dynamics within the supply chains of the food industry, and the emergence of alternatives to conventional food supply chains. Samarthia is involved in various projects that look at the consumption patterns affecting sustainable development.

Michael Thomson is Professor of Law, Culture and Society at Keele University. His research interests include healthcare law, law and gender, and law and literature. His particular focus has been the regulation of reproduction and the relationship between law and gender. The focus of his most recent work is masculinity and the legal regulation of the male sexed body. He is the author of *Reproducing Narrative: Gender, Reproduction and Law* (Aldershot: Dartmouth, 1998) and *Endowed: Regulating the Male Sexed Body* (Routledge, 2007).

Dr Peter Wells is a Senior Research Fellow in the Centre for Automotive Industry Research, which he joined in 1990, and a Lecturer in Logistics and Operations Management. He has a particularly wide knowledge of the components and materials supply industry and of automotive presswork, on which he is a noted expert. In recent years his interests in the automotive industry have become broader, such that Dr Wells is now a noted expert on materials choice for vehicle manufacturing, particularly in an environmental context. Other research interests include the distribution, retail and marketing of cars, and the history of car design. He has acted as a consultant to a number of private and public sector organizations, is a regular contributor to industry conferences, and has published widely on the industry. He has undertaken research throughout Europe, as well as the USA, Canada, Japan, China, South Korea, India, Mexico and New Zealand. In 2002 Dr Wells became a founder member of the ESRC-funded Centre for Business Relationships, Accountability, Sustainability and Society (BRASS) with a five-year programme to analyse the concept of Micro Factory Retailing. He is editor of *Automotive Environment Analyst*, and a member of the editorial board of the *International Journal of Innovation and Sustainable Development*.

Professor Guido de Wert (1959) is Professor in Biomedical Ethics at Maastricht University, the Netherlands. In 1999, he defended his thesis *Looking Ahead. Reproductive Technologies, Genetics and Ethics* at the Erasmus University, Rotterdam (cum laude). Guido de Wert is a member of the Health Council of the Netherlands, of the Ethics Committee of the International Stem Cell Forum, and of the Ethics Task Force of the European Society of Human Reproduction and Embryology. The main topics of his research interest concern the ethics of clinical and community genetics, reproductive medicine and stem cell research.

Acknowledgements

The production of this volume would not have been possible without the assistance of Matthew Davies, former Resource Manager of Cardiff Centre for Ethics, Law and Society, John Coggon and, last but not least, Sarah Kennedy, to whom we are indebted for ensuring that contributors' texts arrived on time and for her help in putting the volume together.

Jennifer Gunning
Søren Holm

List of Abbreviations

ACART	Advisory Committee on Assisted Reproductive Procedures and Human Reproductive Research (New Zealand)
ACEA	Association des Constructeurs Européens d'Automobiles
AD	Alzheimer's Disease
AHR	Assisted Human Reproduction
ANH	Artificial Nutrition and Hydration
ANT	Altered Nuclear Transfer
BAS	Belt Alternator System
BATNEEC	Best Available Technique Not Entailing Excessive Costs
BCIRG	Breast Cancer International Research Group
BICA	British Infertility Counselling Association
BMW	Biodegradable Municipal Waste
BRASS	Centre for Business Relationships, Accountability, Sustainability and Society, Cardiff
BTHA	British Toy and Hobby Association
CAPES	Coordenação de Aperfeiçoamento de Pessoal de Nível Superior
CARE	Christian Action Research and Education
CCELS	Cardiff Centre for Ethics, Law and Society
CCNE	French National Bioethics Council
CCS	Consumer Complaints Service
CDBI	Council of Europe Committee on Bioethics
CDQLP	Community Dementia Quality of Life Profile
CELAB	Centre for Ethics and Law in Biomedicine at CEU
CESAGen	Centre for Social and Economic Aspects of Genomics
CEU	Central European University
CHI	Commission for Health Improvement (UK)
CHRB	Convention on Human Rights and Biomedicine
CISCHR	Centre for the International Study of Cyberethics and Human Rights
COPA	Children's Online Protection Act (USA)
CORE	Comment on Reproductive Ethics
CVS	Chorionic Villus Sampling
DBA	Diamond Blackfan Anaemia
DOE	Dignity of Older Europeans Project
DoJ	Department of Justice (USA)
ECART	Ethics Committee on Assisted Reproductive Technology (New Zealand)
EDRI	European Digital Rights Campaign
ESC	Embryonic Stem Cells

ESRC	Economic and Social Science Research Council (UK)
EU	European Union
FAP	Familial Adenomatous Polyposis
FGM	Female Genital Mutilation
GIFT	Gamete Intra Fallopian Transfer
GMC	General Medical Council (UK)
HAS	Health Advisory Service (UK)
HFEA	Human Fertilisation and Embryology Authority
HGAC	Human Genetics Advisory Commission
HGP	Human Genome Project
HLA	Human Leucocyte Antigen
HOLP	Head of Legal Practice
HUGO	Human Genome Organization
ICANN	Internet Corporation for Domain Names and Assigned Numbers
ICN	International Council of Nurses
ICT	Information and Communication Technologies
ICTI	International Council of Toy Industries
INECART	Interim National Ethics Committee on Assisted Reproductive Technology (New Zealand)
ISLAT	International Society for Law and Technology
ISP	Internet Service Provider
IUI	Intra-Uterine Insemination
IVM	In Vitro Maturation (of Oocytes)
JHA	Ministers of Justice and Home Affairs Council (EU)
LATS	Landfill Allowances Trading Scheme
LDP	Legal Disciplinary Practice
LSA	Legal Services Authority
LSB	Legal Services Board
LSCC	Legal Services Complaints Commissioner
LSO	Legal Services Ombudsman
MCART	Ministerial Committee on Assisted Reproductive Technologies (New Zealand)
MDP	Multi-Disciplinary Practice
MHRA	Medicines and Healthcare Regulatory Agency
MQOL-CSF	Cardiff Short Form McGill Quality of Life Questionnaire
MSW	Municipal Solid Waste
NCCTG	North Central Cancer Treatment Group
NDNAD	National DNA Database (UK)
NECAHR	National Ethics Committee on Assisted Human Reproduction (New Zealand)
NHS	National Health Service (UK)
NICE	National Institute for Clinical Excellence (UK)
NMC	Nursing and Midwifery Council
NOWGEN	North West Genetics Knowledge Park
OLC	Office for Legal Complaints
OSS	Office for the Supervision of Solicitors

PGD	Preimplantation Genetic Diagnosis
PKU	Phenylketonuria
REC	Research Ethics Committee
RQLP	Renal Quality of Life Profile
RTAC	Reproductive Technology Accreditation Committee (Australia)
SAE	Serious Adverse Event
SC	Stem Cell
SCB	Solicitors Complaints Bureau
SCNT	Somatic Cell Nuclear Transfer
SDT	Solicitors Disciplinary Tribunal
SMMT	Society of Motor Manufacturers and Traders
SUV	Sports Utility Vehicle
UCL	University College London
UKSIP	United Kingdom Sickness Impact Profile
WIP	Waste Implementation Programme
WRAP	Waste Resources Action Programme
WSIS	World Summit on the Information Society

INTRODUCTION

Chapter 1

Introduction

Søren Holm and Jennifer Gunning

Ethics is no longer exclusively the domain of the 'professional' philosopher. Scratch an ethicist and you may find underneath a lawyer, or a scientist, a doctor, social scientist or IT specialist. Ethics has become an interdisciplinary field and part of everyday life, and has been taken up by the media in regular transmissions, such as the BBC programme 'The Moral Maze' and in regular newspaper columns such as the ethics columns in *The New York Times* (Randy Cohen) and *The Times* (Joe Joseph). Every day the media carry news items highlighting the ethical issues relating to government policies, business dealings, the environment, healthcare, education, ethnic minorities, war and so on across the whole range of human experience.

The series *Ethics, Law and Society* tries to tap into this current broad stream of ethical enquiry looking at topical issues as they arise and providing a more in-depth analysis than is usually available in the media. The chapters in this book originally appeared as papers on the website of the Cardiff Centre for Ethics, Law and Society (www.ccels.cardiff.ac.uk). For this volume they have been amended and revised as necessary.

The chapters in the first part of the book are all concerned with bioethics (or biolaw), one of the traditional core areas of applied ethics. A pervading topic in this part is human embryonic stem cell research, reflecting the recent high profile of this issue which is one that continues to excite discussion around the world. This part also addresses sex selection and research ethics.

The chapters in the second part of the book, 'Ethics and Society', cover the societal aspects of interventions such as assisted reproduction. The important issue of how we deal with the vulnerable elderly is the focus of one chapter, and the status of the human body in the constant quest to extend the biological limits of life is the subject of another.

The third part of the book analyses current issues in business and professional ethics; some of these are traditional issues in professional ethics, but others are quite new, not because they are not important or not worth analysing, but simply because they have been overlooked. The bicentenary of the abolition of the slave trade is currently being celebrated and one chapter looks at potential corporate liability for reparations arising from involvement in the slave trade. The issue of the human body also arises again in a chapter which challenges the fact that tissue donors are not allowed proprietary rights in products derived from their donated tissue.

The short commentaries in the fourth part of the book seek to provide deeper analysis of ethical issues that have hit the recent headlines. Topics range from the rapidly growing accumulation by the police of DNA profiles in the UK National

DNA Database, to tackling the problem of food waste. Recent legal judgements in the areas of end of life decision making and assisted reproduction also feature, along with a commentary on the new Italian assisted reproduction law. Items on restricting access to medicines in the treatment of cancer and Alzheimer's disease reflect the increasing difficulty of the National Health Service in providing treatment using the latest and more expensive drugs.

The aim of the book is that it should, as a whole, be attractive to anyone interested in the broader area of ethics. Necessarily, however, each of the chapters in the book focuses on a particular topic and is therefore of value primarily to readers interested in that topic. Nonetheless we hope that , as a compendium of current thinking across a range of issues, this volume will serve as a source of inspiration for further work and will encourage people to think beyond their normal disciplines.

PART I
BIOETHICS

Chapter 2

On Waving the Embryos Banner: Embryonic Stem Cell Research and Moral Reasoning in Recent Reports from the USA, the Netherlands and France

Wybo Dondorp and Guido de Wert

The prize for the most fascinating ethical literature of the last few years? A good candidate is the report of the American President's Council on Bioethics on 'Alternative Sources of Human Pluripotent Stem Cells'.[1] It tries to circumvent restrictions on public funding of stem cell research by seeking 'embryo-friendly' ways of obtaining embryonic (or functionally equivalent pluripotent) stem cells. By accepting the position that human embryos are worthy of full protection, but not joining in with the then familiar call for restricting research to adult or somatic stem cells, the report rings the bell for a new round in the debate on the acceptability of embryonic stem cell research. In this chapter, we take the report as a lead for discussing three requirements for a morally proper debate about the further regulation of this field: consistency of arguments, definitions that do not pre-empt moral questions, and the acknowledgement that there is more to the ethics of embryonic stem cell research than what may or may not be done to human embryos. Our discussion will also refer to argumentative strategies in recent reports from the Netherlands[2] and France,[3] both recommending a larger scope for embryonic stem cell research than current legislation would allow.

Introduction

Expectations are that, in the future, stem cells may serve as basic material for the culturing of all kinds of specialized restoration tissue: cardiac muscle cells for the

---

1 The President's Council on Bioethics (2005), *Alternative Sources of Human Pluripotent Stem Cells. A White Paper* (Washington DC: The President's Council on Bioethics).

2 Commissie evaluatie regelgeving (2006), Olsthoorn-Heim, E.T.M., De Wert, G.M.W.R. and Winter, H.B., *Evaluatie embryowet* (The Hague: ZonMw) reeks evaluatie regelgeving; 2006: 20.

3 Ministère de la santé et des solidarités (2006), Fagniez, P.L., 'Cellules souches et choix éthiques' (Paris: Ministère de la santé et des solidarités), available at: http://www.ladocumentationfrancaise.fr/rapports-publics/064000623/index.shtml.

repair of a damaged heart, dopamine producing cells limiting the effect of Parkinson's disease, and so on. There is, however, a problem: the most promising source of stem cells for regenerative cell therapy is human embryos.[4] Since it would seem that harvesting those embryonic stem cells inevitably entails the destruction of the embryo, the moral question arises whether it is acceptable to use (or create) human embryos for this purpose.

Even though not all individual members of the President's Council would personally reject the use of embryos, the report as a whole takes 'the strongly held belief of many Americans that human life, from its earliest stages, deserves our protection and respect' as a solid ethical norm. Stripping human beings bare of vital parts so as to be able to use these for the treatment of others, however urgent that treatment may be, is morally unacceptable. And embryos, according to this 'strongly held belief of many Americans', are as much human beings (persons) as the rest of us. So if we want those stem cells, we should find alternative ways of obtaining them. This is what the report is about: seeking to 'advance biomedical science while upholding ethical norms'.

What makes the report fascinating reading is the ingenuity with which it tries to avoid choosing between either forgoing the full scientific and therapeutic promises of stem cell research or giving up on the notion that the moral status of human embryos forbids their destruction. The council thereby breaches the stalemate in the debate about what types of stem cells the research should focus on. Whereas 'pluripotent' stem cells from human embryos seem to have the greatest potential for development, some promising results have also been obtained from 'multipotent' stem cells from tissues taken from adults (bone marrow, for example), aborted foetuses and umbilical cord blood.[5] Until now, adherents of the view that embryos are worthy of full protection argued that research should only use the latter type of cells ('adult' or 'somatic' instead of embryonic stem cells). Against this position, there is a broad scientific consensus that a multitrack approach is needed, which would also have to include the pluripotent type of stem cells derived from human embryos.[6]

Present sources of embryonic stem cells are surplus embryos left over from IVF or embryos that are specially created for the purpose. As left over embryos are abundantly available (even if new IVF procedures may lead to a significant reduction in the future), there would seem to be no need for creating any new ones. However, for scientific reasons (furthering the basic understanding of the field) and in view of optimizing future therapeutic applications, it is felt necessary to create embryonic stem cell sources through a cloning procedure called Somatic Cell Nuclear Transfer (SCNT).

---

4 Odorico, J., Zhang, S.C. and Pedersen, R. (2005), *Human Embryonic Stem Cells* (Abingdon: Garland Science/BIOS).

5 Henon, P.R. (2003), 'Human Embryonic or Adult Stem Cells: An Overview on Ethics and Perspectives for Tissue Engineering', *Advances in Experimental Medicine and Biology* 534, 27–45; Rogers, I. and Casper, R.F. (2004), 'Umbilical Cord Blood Stem Cells', *Best Practice & Research. Clinical Obstetrics & Gynaecology* 18:6, 893–908.

6 De Wert, G. and Mummery, C. (2003), 'Human Embryonic Stem Cells: Research, Ethics and Policy', *Human Reproduction* 18:4, 672–82; Health Council of the Netherlands, *Stem Cells for Tissue Repair* (The Hague: Health Council of the Netherlands, 2002/09E).

This involves transferring the nucleus of a somatic cell (when applied therapeutically, this would be a cell from the patient in question) into a donor oocyte from which the nucleus has been removed. As a result of this a one-cell embryo would be produced, which after culturing to the blastocyst stage, would then serve as a source of embryonic stem cells. It is hoped that, eventually, these could then be used for autologous cell therapy. 'Autologous', because the transplant material, created via the intermediate stage of an embryo, has been cultivated from cells taken from the patient him or herself. Although this explains the alternative name for SCNT: 'therapeutic cloning', that designation is better avoided.[7] It is confusing, firstly because the predicate 'therapeutic' refers to one of its envisaged applications rather than to the technique itself. And secondly, because the technique itself is still very much in the phase of fundamental research.

In the remainder of this section, we briefly present the four proposals discussed by the President's Council in its quest for sources of pluripotent stem cells that would be compatible with giving full protection to human embryos.

Direct Reprogramming

An appealing alternative for the present sources would be to obtain pluripotent stem cells through 'direct reprogramming' of somatic cells, without having to create an embryo as an intermediate stage. This is regarded, not only by the President's Council, but by several other commentators as well, as *the* alternative for the future.[8] As with SCNT, this technique should produce matching tissue type transplant material for autologous cell therapy, thereby avoiding rejection.

Work on direct reprogramming is still in the very early stages and much more research is required. A first line of approach is trying to understand how (in SCNT) the enucleated oocyte or substances in the ooplasma (the cytoplasm of the oocyte) reprogramme the somatic cell nucleus. Once it is known what mechanisms and substances are involved, one can try to imitate this in the laboratory via chemical induction. From the perspective taken by the President's Council, there is, however, a bump in this road. Even if much of the research can be conducted using animal material, it is hard to see how this approach could be further developed without having to create human embryos through SCNT at least at some stage of it. Another line of investigation might perhaps avoid that difficulty. This approach would involve transplanting a somatic cell nucleus, not into an enucleated oocyte, but into a human embryonic stem cell.[9] It appears that embryonic stem cells are capable of (at least partially) reprogramming somatic cells.

---

7 De Wert, G.M.W.R. (2001), 'Humane embryonale stamcellen als Heilige Graal', *Filosofie & Praktijk* 22:3, 34–56.

8 Ibid; Trounson, A. (2002), 'The Genesis of Embryonic Stem Cells', *Nature Biotechnology* 20:3, 237–8.

9 Tada, M., Takahama, Y., Abe, K., Nakatsuji, N. and Tada, T. (2001), 'Nuclear Reprogramming of Somatic Cells by In Vitro Hybridization with ES Cells', *Current Biology* 11:19, 1553–8; Do, J.T. and Scholer, H.R. (2004), 'Nuclei of Embryonic Stem Cells Reprogram Somatic Cells', *Stem Cells* 22:6, 941–9; Strelchenko, N., Kukharenko, V., Shkumatov, A.,

In order for this to qualify as 'embryo-saving', there should, as the council observes, be no doubt that direct reprogramming may not, inadvertently, produce totipotent rather than pluripotent cells. Whereas the latter have the ability to develop into all types of body tissue, they differ from totipotent cells in that they lack the ability of developing into a complete new organism. Embryonic stem cells are pluripotent, zygotes (one-cell embryos) are totipotent. Should direct reprogramming lead to totipotency, 'we would be back in the ethical soup from which this proposal was intended to provide an escape'.[10]

As direct reprogramming is still very much a hope for the more distant future, the question arises what other alternatives could be considered. In its report, the President's Council discusses three further proposals for obtaining pluripotent stem cells without moral pain. In each of these, the requirement that no human embryos are being 'created, destroyed or harmed' in the process would be satisfied in a different way.[11] Or at least, according to their proponents.

The Human Embryo as 'Living Stem Cell Donor'

If the harvesting of stem cells could be done in embryos at an earlier developmental stage, this might allow the embryo to stay alive and, after being transferred into a woman's uterus, grow into a child. The idea is to use separate biopsied blastomeres (embryonic cells in the cleavage stage of embryonic development), taken from the early embryo in the stage where it consists of around eight such cells, without thereby compromising the remaining embryo's potential to develop normally into a child. The embryo would thus serve as a 'living donor', leaving parental consent as the only remaining hurdle for this embryo-saving alternative.

For the developmental capacities of the embryo, the loss of one or two blastomeres makes no difference. At least that is what seems to follow from the experience with pre-implantation genetic diagnosis (PGD), in which the same biopsy procedure is used as part of reproductive care. In PGD, blastomere biopsy is performed in order to allow genetic testing for a disease the parents would not want to transmit to their children. The remaining six- or seven-cell embryo will only be placed in the uterus if the disease in question is not found in the cells. The only difference between PGD and the procedure under consideration is that, here, the cells would not be used as material for testing, but as a source of embryonic stem cells.

While the feasibility of obtaining embryonic stem cells from blastomeres was fully theoretical when discussed in the report, the procedure has since been

Verlinsky, O., Kuliev, A. and Verlinsky, Y. (2006), 'Reprogramming of Human Somatic Cells by Embryonic Stem Cell Cytoplast', *Reproductive Biomedicine Online* 12:1, 107–11.
    10 The President's Council on Bioethics (2005), op.cit.
    11 Ibid.

successfully tried, first in mice,[12] and more recently also using human embryos.[13] Whether blastomere-derived embryonic stem cells do indeed have the same potential as embryonic stem cells obtained in the later blastocyst stage of embryonic development is a question for additional research.

The Human Embryo as 'Post-mortem Stem Cell Donor'

Most embryos that spontaneously stop dividing ('cleavage arrest') do not resume development. While this is often due to chromosomal abnormalities, irreversibly arrested embryos may contain blastomeres with normal developmental potential. Should it be possible, on the basis of biochemical markers, to determine which embryos are irreversibly arrested, one might – according to a further proposal – consider their condition as the equivalent of 'brain death' in the context of cadaveric organ donation. Such 'organismically dead' embryos could then be used to derive embryonic stem cells. As the embryo would be already dead, no killing would be involved.

As the idea is presented in the report, IVF embryos that fail to resume normal development after cryopreservation and thawing qualify for being tested as either or not 'organismically dead'. Selection of suitable candidates could thus be conducted in the context of normal IVF procedures, and would not interfere with treatment apart from the need for parental consent. This consent is seen here as the equivalent of parents consenting to the excision of transplantable organs from their brain-dead child.

As in the former proposal, this approach requires harvesting embryonic stem cells from cleavage stage human embryos, because their developmental arrest leaves the usual stage for harvesting (after blastocyst formation) out of reach. This has now also been successfully tried.[14] Whether stem cells from the meant category of embryos (spontaneously stalled development) would be suitable for scientific or therapeutic purposes remains to be seen.

Altered Nuclear Transfer

The final proposal builds on the presupposition that only those products of fertilization or cloning that have the potential to develop into a human being are human embryos. This means that non-viable embryos are not embryos properly speaking. Since non-viability need not stand in the way of such entities being a suitable source of

12 Chung, Y., Klimanskaya, I., Becker, S., Marh, J., Lu, S.J., Johnson, J., et al. (2006), 'Embryonic and Extraembryonic Stem Cell Lines Derived from Single Mouse Blastomeres', *Nature* 439:7073, 216–19.

13 Klimanskaya, I., Chung, Y., Becker, S., Lu, S.J. and Lanza, R. (2006), 'Human Embryonic Stem Cell Lines Derived from Single Blastomeres', *Nature*, 23 August [Epub ahead of print].

14 Zhang, X., Stojkovic, P., Przyborski, S., Cooke, M., Armstrong, L., Lako, M., et al. (2006), 'Derivation of Human Embryonic Stem Cells from Developing and Arrested Embryos', *Stem Cells* 24:12, 2669–76.

embryonic stem cells, using non-viable embryos would conveniently circumvent the whole embryos problem.

But how can we be certain whether something that looks and develops as an embryo is in fact a non-viable 'biological artefact'? It has been suggested that SCNT embryos, or else the cybrid embryos resulting from interspecies SCNT, fall into this category. However, until it has been clearly established what entities are definitely non-viable, the moral implications of this for how they can be treated remain undecided. This is where genetic technology comes in. The idea is to deliberately create non-viable embryo-like artefacts, meant to serve as a source of embryonic stem cells. Altered Nuclear Transfer (ANT) is only one elaboration of that idea.[15]

ANT involves the introduction of a mutation in the somatic cell nucleus used in an otherwise normal SCNT procedure. This would lead to a defect in a gene that embryos need to successfully implant in the uterus, thus depriving them of the ability to further develop into a human being. If that ability is an essential element in the definition of an embryo, this implies that ANT products are not embryos at all, however embryo-like they may look and however normal their in vitro development may be. And as they are not embryos, neither would there be a moral problem with first creating and then destroying such entities in the process of stem cell harvesting.

In the wake of the council's report, ANT has already been successfully attempted in mice: the embryos (artefacts) developed normally into blastocysts, turned out to be suitable sources for stem cell derivation, whereas subsequent uterine transfer led to implantation failure.[16] Unlike the former two, this third proposal would have the advantage of allowing the full range of embryonic stem cell applications, including the derivation of patient-tailored cells for autologous tissue repair.

The Virtue of Consistency

The President's Council supports further scientific and conceptual research into each of these proposals, with the exception of the 'living stem cell donor' approach.[17] That is where we start our discussion. It would seem that the council gives good reasons for rejecting this proposal: as the embryo is supposed to further develop into a child, this future child should not be exposed to avoidable health risks if doing so is not in the child's best interest. But if these are indeed cogent arguments for rejecting blastomere biopsy in the 'living donor' proposal, the question arises whether the same reasons could not also be held against the same procedure if carried out in the context of PGD.

15 Hurlbut, W.B. (2006), 'Framing the Future: Embryonic Stem Cells, Ethics and the Emerging Era of Developmental Biology', *Pediatric Research* 59:4 Pt 2, 4R–12R; Snyder, E.Y., Hinman, L.M. and Kalichman, M.W. (2006), 'Can Science Resolve the Ethical Impasse in Stem Cell Research?', *Nature Biotechnology* 24:4, 397–400.

16 Meissner, A. and Jaenisch, R. (2006), 'Generation of Nuclear Transfer-Derived Pluripotent ES Cells from Cloned Cdx2-Deficient Blastocysts', *Nature* 439:7073, 212–15.

17 The President's Council on Bioethics (2005), op.cit.

What about PGD?

Since the procedure is the same, so are the risks. No serious harmful consequences have until now been found in children born after PGD, but insight into the long-term health effects is still lacking.[18] The council does not, however, consider this a reason for rejecting PGD. Instead, it says that many regard those remaining safety concerns as 'more than balanced by the desire of the couple to have their own biological child free from a specific genetic disease'. Secondly, as the council acknowledges, PGD is not for the benefit of the child-to-be. Only in the trivial sense of enlarging the chances of selection for the embryo that would grow into this specific individual, can the biopsy be said to be in the interest of the future child. The reason for undertaking the procedure, however, is the couple's interest not to give birth to a child with a serious disease. We would argue that this is as much a third-party interest as would be the case in the 'living donor' proposal, and not necessarily a weightier one.

Our point here is not that whoever accepts PGD would also have to give the green light to the 'living donor' proposal. In our view, a sufficient argument against that proposal is that there are alternatives (use of left-over or specially created embryos) that would not require the imposition of invasive procedures on embryos meant to be transferred to the womb. But the President's Council, at least for the sake of its argument, does not consider these alternative stem cell sources acceptable, since these would imply the destruction of human embryos. And that, it seems to us, leaves it without arguments for rejecting the 'living donor' proposal that would not also count against PGD.

How should this inconsistency be solved? Can we conclude that the President's Council is perhaps a bit too quick in rejecting this proposal? If no other sources of stem cells are morally acceptable, if the risks are indeed as small as they seem until now in PGD, and if the parents consent, why should the 'living donor' proposal be more of a problem than PGD? Following a similar line of argument, the researchers who recently proved the feasibility of using human blastomeres as stem cell sources have suggested that the council's objections can be overcome by limiting the procedure to embryos already for PGD.[19] If stem cell harvesting could be done without taking any additional cells,[20] neither would there be any risk in addition to those already accepted in the context of PGD.

But this fails to acknowledge that PGD itself is unacceptable for those holding that human embryos are to be treated as persons. There are two reasons for this, of which the council only mentions the first, but without giving the argument its due. This is what may be called the 'totipotency argument': we cannot be sure at what stage in early embryonic development separate human blastomeres have lost the ability to form a complete embryo, including the placental tissues needed for growing into a new individual ('totipotency'). Even if it is thought to be unlikely

---

18 Human Genetics Commission (2006), *Making Babies: Reproductive Decisions and Genetic Technologies* (London: Human Genetics Commission).

19 Klimanskaya, I., et al. (2006), op. cit.

20 Wade, N., 'New Stem Cell Method Avoids Destroying Embryos', *The New York Times*, 23 August 2006.

that human blastomeres are still totipotent at the eight-cell stage, there is no morally acceptable way of finding this out.[21] The uncertainty about this has implications for the moral status of these cells: it cannot be excluded that they are to be regarded as (the equivalent of) human embryos.[22]

The President's Council acknowledges this, calling it a 'possible source of concern'. Should blastomeres be totipotent, 'some would find destruction of that blastomere ethically objectionable'. That is a strangely weak way of putting it. If it cannot be excluded that the procedure would entail the creation and destruction of a new human embryo, this should be a decisive reason for rejecting blastomere biopsy (whether for stem cells or for PGD), at least for those who, like the President's Council in its report, regard human embryos as persons.

The second argument, not mentioned in the report but equally decisive, is that if embryos are to be treated as persons, they ought not to be subjected to a selection procedure aimed at allowing only healthy embryos to be transferred to the womb. From the moral perspective taken by the President's Council, the whole idea behind PGD is simply unacceptable. This also renders the proposal to only harvest stem cells in the context of PGD a non-starter. Instead of making the original 'living donor' proposal more acceptable, it actually makes it worse, at least in the eyes of those it was meant to win over to the cause of embryo-friendly stem cell harvesting.

What about IVF?

Let us now turn to the 'embryos as post-mortem donors' proposal. The council finds this ethically acceptable for further investigation in humans: 'it is difficult to see how dissecting spontaneously dead embryos can be said to harm them'. But this, of course, does not take away the question of how those embryos were first created and then died. According to the report, there is no problem with this if 'only those embryos are considered for use (…) that were originally created with reproductive intent' and if 'their prospective users have not deliberately killed them or neglected them so that they would die'. The report suggests that these conditions can be met in current IVF practice, including hyperstimulation and cryopreservation (following the proposal under consideration, 'organismically dead' stem cell donors are selected after cryopreservation and thawing).

But if embryos are persons, it is not enough that they should not be deliberately killed. Neither should they be exposed to procedures that, as the council acknowledges, 'knowingly increase the likelihood that many individual embryos will die or be discarded'. Moreover, if embryos are persons, the first condition ('created with reproductive intent') should be taken in a far stronger sense than current IVF

---

21 Solter, D. (2005), 'Politically Correct Human Embryonic Stem Cells?', *New England Journal of Medicine* 353:22, 2321–3.

22 Health Council of the Netherlands (1998), *IVF-related Research* (Rijswijk: Health Council of the Netherlands, 1998/08E); German National Ethics Council (2003), *Genetic Diagnosis Before and During Pregnancy* (Berlin: German National Ethics Council).

procedures allow.[23] It should be taken to mean not just 'created to contribute to the success of the couple's IVF treatment', but indeed 'created with the intent of having each resulting embryo implanted and letting it grow into a child'. But if that is what the condition means, IVF should not be conducted as it is now.

By accepting current IVF procedures, the council is again inconsistent. If the status of the human embryo is compatible with the weaker sense of 'reproductive intent' (allowing the creation of a larger number of embryos of which it is certain beforehand that many will not be given the chance to grow into a child), then neither can it pose a problem with regard to using surplus embryos as material for research or therapy, nor with regard to specially creating embryos for those purposes.[24] On the other hand, if embryos are persons, it is unacceptable to use them as a mere means to the ends or projects of others, be that stem cell-based research or therapy, or the reproductive projects of IVF couples.

Waving the Embryos Banner Comes at a Price

What can we conclude from the council's discussion of these two proposals? Whereas the council claims to uphold the 'ethical norms' of those 'many Americans' who regard embryos as persons, it does not seem to take this view very seriously. It fails to openly acknowledge that those same ethical norms not only preclude the creation or destruction of embryos as stem cell sources, but also forbid most if not all of current assisted reproductive procedures, including standard IVF and PGD. Since both proposals build upon these very procedures, it would have been clear from the start that this is not really going to lead to embryo-friendly stem cell sources. Why is the council not open about this? Why does it not honestly say, not only that if you want the omelette, there will be some breaking of eggs involved, but also that we already do and accept this breaking for quite some time? Is it from fear that those many Americans, if they find out what those procedures do to human embryos, will also turn against IVF and PGD? Or why does the council not do so itself, if it is indeed so deeply committed to the view that embryos are persons?

This is, of course, a highly politicized debate, not only in the United States, but also in Europe, where several countries are in the process of reviewing relevant legislation. But where does that leave ethics? In a recent commentary, supportive of the President's Council's report, it is said that 'most of us would agree that, in a pluralistic society, it is not unreasonable to assuage the moral reservations of a sizable minority'.[25] That may seem very democratic and ethical, but as the slightly paternalistic wording cannot fail to reveal, it is the opposite of taking moral arguments seriously.

---

23 Dondorp, W.J. and Bolhuis, P.A. (2002), 'Mitochondriale ziekten: celkerntransplantatie en de Embryowet', *Tijdschrift voor Gezondheidsrecht* 25:1, 2–9; Health Council of the Netherlands (2001), *Nuclear Transplantation in Cases of Mutations in Mitochondrial DNA* (The Hague: Health Council of the Netherlands, 2001/07).

24 Devolder, K. (2006), 'Creating and Sacrificing Embryos for Stem Cells', *Journal of Medical Ethics* 31:6, 366–70.

25 Snyder, E.Y., et al. (2006), op. cit.

Ethics is precisely about that: taking moral arguments seriously. In this debate it requires showing that the view of the human embryo presupposed in several widely accepted practices is one in which it is seen as having only limited moral worth. Only on that basis can there be no problem with using intra uterine devices (IUDs) even though these may prevent embryos from implanting, nor with creating surplus embryos in IVF, nor with accepting the possibility that PGD implies the creation of new embryos to be wasted in the procedure. In each of these practices embryos are used merely as means. If the ends in question, birth control and assisted reproduction (both for those with fertility problems and for couples at genetic risk), are regarded as worthy enough to justify this, then it would seem difficult to make a consistent case against using embryos for at least equally worthy ends (development of medical therapies) as are involved in embryonic stem cell research.

Our point here is that the 'ethical norms' upheld by the President's Council come at a price. One cannot both wave the embryos banner and have all the goods of IVF, PGD and embryonic stem cell research.

Definitions Matter

The final proposal in the President's Council's report, ANT, is perhaps the most ingenious, as it combines a deliberately narrow definition of what counts as a human embryo with advanced genetic technology. Genetic technology is designed to optimally exploit the distinction between embryos (to be regarded and treated as persons) and 'non-viable embryo-like artefacts' (to be used as material for research and therapy).

Here again, the political question is whether those concerned about human embryos receiving less than full protection could accept the reasoning. Otherwise, not much would be gained by it.[26] Already at the very meeting of the President's Council where the proposal was presented, the secretary of the American Bishops Conference, Mgr Doerflinger, expressed his reservations.[27] As he made clear, the fact that an embryo that started to develop normally will not survive because of some genetic defect does not make it less of an embryo in the view of the Roman Catholic Church. Nor would it in any way diminish its moral status. Being a human embryo, even if a non-viable one, it would still have to be treated as a human person.

---

26 Health Council of the Netherlands (2005), *Embryonic Stem Cells without Moral Pain?* (The Hague: Health Council of the Netherlands, 2005/07-01E); Devolder, K. (2006), 'What's in a Name? Embryos, Entities, and ANTities in the Stem Cell Debate', *Journal of Medical Ethics* 32:1, 43–8.

27 Zucker, H.A., Landry, D.W. and Hurlbut, W. (2004), 'Session 6: Seeking Morally Unproblematic Sources of Human Embryonic Stem Cells' (Washington DC: The President's Council on Bioethics), available at: http://bioethicsprint.bioethics.gov/transcripts/dec04/session6.html.

Non-viable, No Embryo, No Problem?

From an ethical point of view, the difficulty with the ANT proposal is that it solves a problem by defining it away.[28] Non-viable, then no embryo, then no problem. In ethical debate, definitions often have the important role of delineating the margins of what can meaningfully be discussed. Narrowing a definition may have the (sometimes intended) effect that questions or considerations that would otherwise be meaningful cannot even come up. Here, the question that is prevented from being asked is how we should regard the moral status of non-viable embryos. Do they or do they not deserve the same level of protection as do viable embryos? If not, what then should their status be? By making viability part of the definition, the ANT proposal not only prevents these questions from being asked; to the effect that 'no embryo' entails 'no other status than that of any human cell', an implicit answer is also given.

Interestingly, the narrow definition of a human embryo presupposed in ANT is the actual definition figuring in the Dutch and Belgian Embryos Acts. In the Dutch Act (2002), a human embryo is defined as: 'a cell or collection of cells with the capacity to develop into a human being'. The reason for this is not the wish to exclude non-viable embryos from consideration, but that these Acts are from the post-Dolly era. The wording was chosen to also include embryos created by other methods than fertilization. A Dutch predecessor Bill drawn up in the early 1990s still defined an embryo as 'the result of the fusion of human gametes prior to birth'. Similar definitions referring to the process of fertilization appear in German and British legislation dating from the same period.[29] The birth of the cloned sheep Dolly in 1997, suggesting that the same procedure could possibly also be used to create human embryos, led to additional legislation in those countries.

The explanatory memorandum to the Dutch Embryos Act gives the following comments on the present definition: 'Scientific progress has allowed embryos to be created in various ways. However, the degree of protection that an embryo enjoys depends not on how it is created, but rather on its capacity to develop into a human being.' But as some commentators were quick to point out, the new definition no longer covers non-viable embryos.[30] As a large percentage of IVF embryos are non-viable as a result of chromosomal abnormalities, this would indeed seem to constitute a serious gap. By literally outlawing such embryos, the definition allows that they can be subjected to treatments or interventions that may be undesirable, but against which no objections can be raised on the grounds of the Act.[31]

---

28 Health Council of the Netherlands (2005), *Embryonic Stem Cells without Moral Pain?* op. cit.

29 Morgan, D. and Ford, M. (2004), 'Cell Phoney: Human Cloning after Quintavalle', *Journal of Medical Ethics* 30:6, 524–6; German National Ethics Council (2004), *Cloning for Reproductive Purposes and Cloning for the Purposes of Biomedical Research* (Berlin: German National Ethics Council).

30 De Wert, G.M.W.R. (2001), op. cit; Dute, J.C. (2003), 'Toepassing van de genetica in het kader van wetenschappelijk onderzoek', in *Toepassing van de genetica in de gezondheidszorg* (Den Haag: ZonMw), 27–50.

31 Health Council of the Netherlands (2005), *Embryonic Stem Cells without Moral Pain?* op. cit.

This is also seen as a problem in the recent report by an ad-hoc scientific expert committee, drawn up on the government's request in view of the pending evaluation of the Dutch Embryos Act.[32] From the perspective of what the Act is meant to protect, there are 'sound arguments for a definition that encompasses all embryos'. The report recommends a reconsideration of the present definition in the light of this. The new wording would also have to be better fenced off against the absurd consequence of considering every body cell an embryo because it has the capacity of being turned into one through the application of advanced technology.[33] A tentative formulation, meant to both include non-viable embryos and rule out the latter interpretation, was suggested in an earlier report by the Dutch Health Council: 'the fertilised oocyte, or any other functionally equivalent cell, and the whole of cells that develops from it prior to birth'.[34] The inclusion of non-viable embryos does not necessarily imply that such embryos should enjoy the same degree of protection as do viable ones.[35] But a broader definition of this kind does appear to be necessary in order to even raise the question of whether the former category of embryos deserves protection, and if so to what extent.

The main issue for the current evaluation of the Dutch Act is whether or not to allow the creation of embryos for other purposes than pregnancy. This would include, but not be limited to, applications of SCNT. Whereas legislation in the United Kingdom, Belgium and Sweden allows this, other European countries have Acts that either completely forbid the use of embryos for research, or only allow the use of leftover embryos from IVF. The Netherlands is a special case among the latter countries. The Embryos Act contains a ban on the creation of embryos for research or therapy, but also the provision that this ban shall lapse on a date to be determined within five years after the coming into force of the Act (2002), thus effectively turning the ban into a moratorium.

Moreover, the Act already contains regulations that, after lifting of the ban, will apply to the use of embryos especially created for research or therapy. This construction was chosen to provide a basis for making a proviso when ratifying the Convention of the Council of Europe on Human Rights and Biomedicine (Oviedo Convention), article 18.2 of which explicitly forbids the creation of embryos for research. Making a proviso at this point would allow maximum flexibility for national legislation.

At the time of drafting the Act, the reason for not yet allowing the creation of embryos for research or therapy was not a matter of strong moral convictions. Following on earlier Health Council reports, the explanatory memorandum makes clear that from a moral point of view, there is no big difference between using leftover IVF embryos for research or creating new ones for the purpose.[36] Rather, the feeling was that society was not yet ready to go beyond accepting the use of spare

32 Commissie evaluatie regelgeving (2006), op. cit.

33 De Wert, G.M.W.R. (2001), op. cit.

34 Health Council of the Netherlands (2005), *Embryonic Stem Cells without Moral Pain?* op. cit.

35 De Wert, G. and Mummery, C. (2003), op. cit.

36 Health Council of the Netherlands (1998), *IVF-related Research*, op. cit.

embryos. This was expected to change as a result of further scientific developments and public debate on the issue.

The recent evaluation report now recommends proceeding to lift the ban.[37] Doing so is deemed necessary for scientific reasons, whereas there are no compelling moral reasons for maintaining it. The authors also refer to shifting views in other European countries, showing a tendency toward more liberal legislation.

No Fertilisation, No Embryo, No Problem?

An interesting development in this connection is the recent French Fagniez report on 'Stem cells and ethical choices'.[38] This was drawn up by a parliamentary mission in preparation for the 2009 revision of the French Bioethics Act of 2004. As does the Dutch report, it calls for a legalisation of SCNT. But the route toward this is distinctively different.

Without providing a formal definition, the current French Act forbids the creation of embryos for research or therapy. The Fagniez report does not question this interdiction insofar as it refers to creating embryos through fertilization. The report recommends to limit the scope for embryo research to the use of leftover IVF embryos (now formally forbidden, but allowed under a five-year moratorium of the relevant provision). Since research using spare embryos is not at odds with the ban in article 18.2 of the Oviedo Convention (forbidding the creation of embryos for research), the report concludes that France should without hesitation proceed to ratify the Convention. But it also recommends lifting the prohibition on 'therapeutic cloning', or SCNT.

How can these recommendations be reconciled? How can France commit itself to banning the creation of embryos for research and also give the green light to SCNT? The answer is, again, in the definition. When the Oviedo Convention was drafted, in the years prior to Dolly, the word 'embryo' in article 18 could only be taken to refer to the result of fertilization. According to the Fagniez report, it is at least undecided whether that should be different in the post-Dolly era. Whereas some argue that the ban also applies to the creation of embryos through SCNT, others disagree, either by pointing to the low viability of SCNT products, or by holding on to a definition in terms of embryos being the result of fertilization.

The report here discusses the example of two other Latin countries, Spain and Portugal, that are traditionally strongly committed to giving a large measure of protection to the embryo, but that are now in the process of rapid social change. Since 2005, a new Spanish Act allows research using leftover IVF embryos, and a similar revision of more conservative legislation is under discussion in Portugal. Moreover, in Spain, a recent Bill calls for legalization of SCNT and there is growing support in Portugal for also going that far (we derive this information from the Fagniez report). Since both countries have already ratified the Oviedo Convention (whereas Holland and France have until now only signed it), any revisions of their

---

37 Commissie evaluatie regelgeving (2006), op. cit.
38 Ministère de la santé et des solidarités (2006), op. cit.

national legislation in this field would have to comply with the ban in article 18.2. However, this is not regarded as standing in the way of current efforts to legalize SCNT. According to the French report, the reasoning for this refers to 'the natural distinction between an embryo issued from two gametes and an embryo brought about by nuclear transfer'.[39]

Without explicitly endorsing this distinction, the Fagniez report observes that the precise meaning of 'embryo' in the relevant article of the Oviedo Convention is far from clear. Legally, according to international treaty law, states would not be bound by provisions the meaning of which was not sufficiently clear at the time of adoption. In view of all this, the report concludes that by ratifying the Oviedo Convention, France would still be able to legalize SCNT.

What to say about this? Politically, this may be a smart move, clearing away a difficult obstacle to what is felt as a necessary modernization of the law. Whereas the reasoning will probably not convince the religious right, these groups are politically far less influential in countries such as France and Spain than they are in the United States. Moreover, it would allow these countries to keep a high moral profile on embryo protection (holding on to the ban on creating embryos for research), while yet being able to reap all the potential benefits of SCNT. If this is found convincing by parliaments and public, we may see a considerable change of scene in the coming years. Paradoxically, the outcome may be that SCNT is more easily legalized in traditionally less liberal countries than may be the case in the Netherlands, where the Embryos Act leaves no doubt that products of SCNT are embryos.

From the perspective of the advancement of (medical) science, this larger scope for SCNT would of course seem welcome. However, the outcome is disappointing in that it would still not be allowed to create embryos for research. In fact, the reasoning of the Fagniez report leads to writing this commandment in stone. As has been made clear all along in the Dutch debate, there are other reasons besides applications of SCNT that would require lifting the ban.[40] This would include evaluating the feasibility and safety of new techniques aimed at improving IVF, a type of research for which spare embryos are not always suitable material.[41] Such research is important as it may contribute to lessening the burdens and risks of IVF for the women involved. The further development and safe introduction of in vitro maturation of oocytes (IVM) is a good example of this.[42]

Ethics, finally, is the losing side here. As in the ANT proposal endorsed by the President's Council, a moral problem is solved by defining it away. If SCNT products

39 Ibid.

40 Commissie evaluatie regelgeving (2006), op. cit; Health Council of the Netherlands (1998), *IVF-related Research*, op. cit.

41 De Rycke, M., Liebaers, I. and Van Steirteghem, A. (2002), 'Epigenetic Risks Related to Assisted Reproductive Technologies: Risk Analysis and Epigenetic Inheritance', *Human Reproduction* 17:10, 2487–94.

42 Hovatta, O. (2004), 'Cryopreservation and Culture of Human Ovarian Cortical Tissue Containing Early Follicles', *European Journal of Obstetrics, Gynecology, and Reproductive Biology* 113: Suppl. 1, S50–S54; Picton, H.M., Danfour, M.A., Harris, S.E., Chambers, E.L. and Huntriss, J. (2003), 'Growth and Maturation of Oocytes In Vitro', *Reproduction (Cambridge, England) Supplement* 61, 445–62.

are not embryos, then neither could creating them pose a problem in terms of their moral status. Whereas the ANT proposal defines the embryo in terms of its capacity to develop into a human being, the Fagniez report implies that only products of fertilization would qualify for the title. But whereas the American definition at least contains an argument as to why embryos (if only viable ones) should be protected, the reasoning in the French report leaves us completely without a clue. If SCNT products, even though – given the chance – they might develop into a human being, do not deserve the same protection as do human embryos, then why is it that human embryos are being protected in the first place?

At the occasion of an earlier round of revision of the French Bioethics Act, the National Bioethics Council (CCNE) argued that, precisely from the perspective of what the Act aims to protect, SCNT products must indeed be embryos.[43] There may be political reasons for now denying this, but doing so comes at the price of undermining the ethical consistency of (this chapter of) the Bioethics Act. More specifically, the recommendations of the Fagniez report effectively block a proper debate about what is the real issue here. This is not whether SCNT products are embryos, but what arguments there are for sustaining the distinction between research using spare embryos (allowed) and creating embryos for research or therapy (banned).[44]

The Oocytes Problem

Finally, the emphasis in this whole debate is still very much on what may or may not be done to human embryos. However, if there is indeed a tendency in a growing number of countries to move towards legalizing the creation of embryos for research or therapy, the question of how to obtain the necessary oocytes would certainly deserve more attention.[45] The facts are that, even if the efficiency of SCNT can be enhanced, many oocytes will be needed for every successful attempt at deriving embryonic stem cells. Also, given the burdens and risks of oocyte donation, the scarcity that already exists in the context of assisted reproduction is expected to make itself more sharply felt where oocytes for research are concerned.

The problem here, of course, is not just practical but also, or even primarily, moral. On the one hand, respect for women's autonomy entails allowing them to make an informed decision about whether or not to serve as an oocyte donor. On the other hand, compensation that would amount to 'undue inducement' or soliciting donors in dependent positions (for example, IVF patients) may undermine this freedom. Women should not in any way be pressured into donating oocytes for research.[46] The scandal of the recent Korean stem cell fraud, where donors were paid large sums of

---

43 National Consultative Ethics Committee (CCNE) (2001), *Opinion on the Preliminary Draft Revision of the Laws on Bioethics* (Paris: CCNE) 67.

44 Health Council of the Netherlands (1998), *IVF-related Research*, op. cit; Devolder, K. (2006), op. cit.

45 Picton, H.M., et al. (2003), op. cit.

46 German National Ethics Council (2004), op. cit.

money and dependent junior researchers were recruited as 'volunteers', has shown that this is indeed a genuine concern.[47]

Internationally, the Korean affair has prompted efforts at drawing up guidelines that would both protect women and allow researchers to share material without having to worry about the morality of its origins.[48] A matter of ongoing discussion is whether compensation should only be for direct expenses (as recent American guidelines prescribe), or might also include a figure for time, effort and inconvenience (as allowed by draft guidelines of the International Society for Stem Cell Research).[49] In this connection, an important concern is also that a globalized oocyte trade may victimize many poor and illiterate women in developing countries.[50]

With regard to SCNT eventually becoming applicable for cell therapy, it can be speculated that women might be more willing to donate if their oocytes could enable treatment of a loved one suffering from a serious disease, rather than just for research. But it is obvious that this would not ease all concerns about pressure and exploitation. Moreover, as long as treatments cannot yet be offered, there is a danger of donation being provoked by a 'therapeutic misconception': the illusion that this might indeed help a relative or a friend in need.[51] This should be a further reason for not using the term 'therapeutic cloning'.[52]

In the Shadow of the Embryos Banner

The emphasis given to the embryos issue in much of the ethical debate about stem cells stands in the way of appreciating the implications the new technology may have for women.[53] As one of the members of the President's Council recalls: 'All of the other considerations, including the troubling issues related to the use of human eggs, seemed to be more matters of prudent regulation than disagreement over principle.' However, the few and very general remarks that the report devotes to those 'troubling issues' immediately bend away from concrete consequences for women back to concerns about how commodification of oocytes would further 'a dehumanized and utilitarian view of human beginnings'.[54] Back, that is, to the embryos issue again.

It is at least one-sided that the American report fails to also stress the importance of research into, and ethical debate about, alternative sources of oocytes. If it is felt

---

47 Cyranoski, D. and Check, E. (2005), 'Clone Star Admits Lies over Eggs', *Nature* 438:7068, 536–7.

48 Check, E. (2006), 'Ethicists and Biologists Ponder the Price of Eggs', *Nature* 442:7103, 606–7.

49 Hyun, I. (2006), 'Fair Payment or Undue Inducement?', *Nature* 442:7103, 629–30.

50 Dickenson, D. (2004), 'The Threatened Trade in Human Ova', *Nature Reviews Genetics* 5:3, 167.

51 Magnus, D. and Cho, M.K. (2005), 'Ethics. Issues in Oocyte Donation for Stem Cell Research', *Science* 308:5729, 1747–8.

52 Commissie evaluatie regelgeving (2006), op. cit.

53 Dickenson, D. (2005), *The Lady Vanishes: What is Missing from the Stem Cell Debate* (London: Birkbeck ePrints).

54 The President's Council on Bioethics (2005), op. cit.

morally important that stem cell research and therapy should be 'embryo saving', it is no less important that the promise they bring should be freed from raising concerns about the treatment of oocyte donors. In order to achieve this, several options have been proposed in the literature.[55] Here again, 'direct reprogramming' would be an appealing solution, as it would allow the creation of pluripotent stem cells without any oocytes needed. Other options that have been suggested comprise the use of animal oocytes, the creation of oocytes from embryonic stem cells, and in vitro maturation (IVM) of donated immature oocytes.

The latter option would appear to be less far beyond the horizon than some of the other, still highly theoretical, solutions. It would also be least perfect, as it still relies on the willingness of women to undergo vaginal punction in order to allow the harvesting of oocytes. But it would already make a considerable difference if hormone stimulation, the most risky and burdensome part of present donation procedures, could be replaced by IVM. Currently, IVM seems feasible only with fully grown oocytes.[56] Should it become possible to both grow and mature oocytes in vitro from a much earlier stage of development (primordial follicles), then this would open up new sources of donor oocytes for SCNT (such as ovaries removed during surgery, ovaries of deceased women or girls, or even ovaries of aborted foetuses) that would not raise the concerns presently connected to the procedure.

The recent Dutch and French reports both stress the importance of these attempts at finding alternative sources of (donor) oocytes.[57] However, in the Fagniez report, this leads to a tension between encouraging IVM for donation while leaving the blockade in place that prohibits research into the further development and safe introduction of that same technique in IVF, research that would involve the creation of embryos through fertilization rather than SCNT. Since no good reasons are (or can be) given for banning the creation of research embryos while allowing SCNT, this raises the question of whether women's interests are being taken as seriously as the report suggests. Here again, it is clear that waving the embryos banner is not without moral implications.

Protecting Oocyte Donors from Harm

Since no satisfying alternative for the use of human oocytes is readily available, it remains of great importance to have regulations in place that would protect donors from harm. The Dutch evaluation report stresses that if the present ban on creating embryos for research is indeed lifted, this should be accompanied by strengthening of the position of oocyte donors.[58] Proposed measures include risk-limiting professional guidelines (for example, limiting the number of hormone treatments a

---

55 Health Council of the Netherlands (2005), *Embryonic Stem Cells without Moral Pain?* op. cit; Solter, D. (2003), 'New Paths to Human ES Cells?', *Nature Biotechnology* 21:10, 1154–5.

56 Picton, H.M., et al. (2003), op. cit.

57 Commissie evaluatie regelgeving (2006), op. cit; Ministère de la santé et des solidarités (2006), op. cit.

58 Commissie evaluatie regelgeving (2006), op. cit.

donor is allowed to undergo, prescribing the use of only mild stimulation, excluding women who still have a desire for children of their own) and additional regulations concerning meaningful informed consent and donor control (for example, allowing donors to pronounce upon the specific kinds of research for which their oocytes may be used). With regard to the issue of compensation for more than direct expenses, the report recommends further discussion. Finally, global justice requires international efforts aimed at protecting potential oocyte donors in developing countries.

Conclusion

An honest debate about the morality of human embryonic stem cell research requires facing rather than circumventing the ethical issues involved. We have shown that the report by the President's Council fails to meet this requirement. Its reasoning is partly inconsistent (where its alternatives build on techniques that should be no less problematic for those maintaining that embryos are to be regarded as persons), partly evasive (where it simply defines the problem away). We found the latter strategy also in the French Fagniez report. Against these approaches, we have argued that accepting IVF and PGD implies a view of human embryos which would already allow using or creating them as a source of stem cells. We have called for the freeing of the ethical debate in this field from its political captivity. Lowering the embryos banner, as is done in the Dutch report, also makes room for seeing more clearly the importance of other relevant aspects, including the interests of oocyte donors.

Chapter 3

Bioethics, Procedural Ethics, and Misrepresentation in the Stem Cell Debate

Benjamin Capps

Introduction

The stem cell (SC) debate is an issue characterised by scientific scepticism. The controversy is driven by the culturally determined and unsubstantiated character of scientific assumptions and facts, which are used as justifications for the various – typically conflicting and often incompatible – comprehensive doctrines that make up the pluralistic nature of democratic communities. In the SC debates, mutually incompatible ideas about right or wrong research conduct have been illustrated by seemingly irresolvable normative conflict regarding the status of human embryos. However, answering descriptive questions – requiring interpretation and the balancing of evidence – may provide answers that permit political compromise. This partly explains why, in various national and international policy-making fora, the SC debates have often focused on the scientific possibility of using alternatives to controversial research (and the ethical implications), rather than resolving metaphysical (ontological) questions.

According to John Rawls, political stability requires a process of dispute resolution which produces a consensus outcome that is acceptable to most as a political solution.[1] In this regard, the validity of various policy options has depended in part on the availability of reliable means to filter scientific facts and to present justifiable and coherent arguments for policy consumption. This raises the question as to whether political resolution necessarily requires a procedural turn to find 'compromise solutions'. Like many liberal moral–political theories, a procedural turn is central to the Rawlsian Theory of Justice as a solution to political conflict; however, procedural ethics is also criticised as justifying unacceptable intrusions into personal freedom for the sake of a majority's happiness. Furthermore, controversies in the recent SC debates have emphasised that the mere establishment of mechanisms for conflict resolution does not 'solve' complex issues; and indeed they are open to abuse which can be used to distort deliberative democracy.

---

1 Rawls, J. (2005), *Political Liberalism*, Expanded Edition (New York: Columbia University Press).

In this chapter, I develop an argument defending procedural ethics, and show that it is part of the wider picture of political liberalism built upon a social contract. I suggest a conception of justice which prescribes an authoritarian government that tends towards neutrality between competing doctrines, and thereby emphasis is placed on free political participation and the protection of fundamental civil and political rights. Finally, to put this argument in context, I argue that the policy decisions regarding scientific evidence and SC research made in the UK were justified on the grounds of the evaluative procedures employed. The SC controversy has many distinguishable fronts; however, in this chapter I concentrate on the contentious destruction and cloning of human embryos for the purpose of deriving SC, to look at the interpretive use of scientific data that is used to justify polemic argument for and against embryo research.

The Stem Cell Controversy

SCs are premature and phenotypically indistinct cells that can differentiate into at least one other functional cell.[2] These cells may have significant impact on a number of aspects of technological and medical advancement, but especially in the clinical aspects of regenerative medicine. They can be isolated from various human sources including in vitro fertilised and cloned embryos (called embryonic stem (ES) cells), aborted foetuses (embryonic germ cells), cord blood, and somatic 'adult' organs and tissues.[3]

The fundamental claim of the 'Dignitarian Alliance' is that deriving ES cells and the prospect of 'therapeutic' cloning oversteps a moral line.[4] These acts are unacceptable, even if they may lead to potential therapies that improve or extend the lives of many individuals, because they compromise a notion of 'human dignity'.[5] However, their critical appraisal of ES cell science has also been taken to a second front, by exposing the limits of the embryo research and therapy on the grounds of scientific evidence, while championing the merits of SCs found in other, less controversial sources. Conversely, pro-science proponents (again generalised) argue that, in spite of the moral status of the embryo (if it has a moral status at all), the

---

2 Thomson, J., et al. (1998), 'Embryonic Stem Cell Lines Derived from Human Blastocyts', *Science* 282, 1145–7.

3 Solter, D., et al. (2003), *Embryo Research in Pluralistic Europe* (Berlin Heidelberg: Springer-Verlag).

4 Such a generalisation risks simplifying the arguments offered for opposing embryo research and cloning technology. However, the view of the 'Dignitarian Alliance' is one typified by conservative and cautious (prohibitive) policies; Brownsword, R. (2003), 'Bioethics Today, Bioethics Tomorrow: Stem Cell Research and the "Dignitarian Alliance"', *Notre Dame Journal of Law, Ethics and Public Policy* 17, 15–51.

5 A view typically expressed by so-called 'pro-life groups', such as Comment on Reproductive Ethics (CORE): 'Regardless of potential benefit, we must reject outright any research which results in the deliberate destruction of human life'; Josephine Quintavalle (2004), BBC News, available at: http://news.bbc.co.uk/go/pr/fr/-/1/hi/programmes/if/4038281. stm; published and accessed: 15 December 2004.

potential for unprecedented therapeutic advancement renders it unjustifiable to not support (or at least tolerate) embryo research: they claim that scientific evidence demonstrates that ES cells are the best, if not the only, means of effectively transposing SC science into the clinic.

The moral conflict has therefore turned to questions of scientific scepticism, and a focus on the possibility for discriminatory critical evaluation. The scientific uncertainty has fuelled the ethical controversy, leaving various communities, including policy makers, to struggle over the complex scientific questions. This has galvanised and dismantled ethical opinions, instigated new alliances and factions, and offered up novel ethico-political 'solutions', such as using 'embryo-like-artefacts' in place of 'normal' embryos.[6] As the possibility of normative resolution fades, resolving these issues of scientific 'fact' has become critical. Contemporary arguments have therefore moved away from metaphysical and religious opposition, to be predominated by accusations (and evidence) of experimental errors and unsound results, clinical misrepresentation and sham claims of 'miracle cures'. It is claimed by both sides that evidence has been subject to questionable rhetoric and exaggerated reporting, and advisory and political bodies have been accused of being infiltrated by partisans and deliberately using biased 'experts' and selective evidence to promulgate pre-set agendas.

Procedural Ethics and Political Regulation

The controversial nature of ES cell research highlights the 'pressure' that is evident in democratic societies, consisting of diverse personal and community values, to formulate rules to limit otherwise unrestricted actions in the field of biotechnology.[7] In Europe, there is a long history of inter-personal and community conflict generated from biotechnological 'progress';[8] and the resulting state of anxiety has resulted in (paternalistic)[9] local and regional frameworks of oversight to detect and minimise misuse,[10] install confidence in the goals of science, and purge the moral unease that is seeming intractably linked to it.[11] Procedural frameworks have therefore developed

---

6 Murray, T. (2005), 'Will New Ways of Creating Stem Cells Dodge the Objections?', *Hastings Center Report* 35, 8–9.

7 For a discussion at the EU level, see Capps, B. (2002), 'The European Union and Stem Cell Research: A Turnaround on Policy Regarding Human Embryo Research', *Legal Ethics* 5, 18–23; and for a global perspective, see Beyleveld, D. and Patterson, S. (2004), 'Globalisation and Human Dignity: Some Effects and Implications for the Creation and Use of Embryos', in Brownsword, R. (ed.), *Global Governance and the Quest for Justice Volume 4 Human Rights* (Oxford: Hart Publishing) 186–202.

8 Caplan, A. (ed.) (1992), *When Medicine Went Mad: Bioethics and the Holocaust* (Totowa, New Jersey: Humana Press).

9 Kennedy, I. and Stone, J. (1990), 'Making Public Policy on Medical-Moral Issues', in Byrne, P. (ed.), *Ethics and Law in Health Care and Research* (Chichester: Wiley) 81–103.

10 Reverby, S. (ed.) (2000), *Tuskegee's Truths: Rethinking the Tuskegee Syphilis Study* (Chapel Hill: University of North Carolina Press).

11 For example, Ontario Law Reform Commission (1985), *Human Artificial Reproduction and Related Matters* (two volumes), quoted in Kennedy, I. and Grubb, A. (2000), *Medical*

to address the 'regulatory challenge' of creating effective, legitimate, and optimal policies. The sometimes-elaborate nature of these frameworks – for example, involving a number of specialised advisory bodies – is indicative of the difficulty of assessing the unresolved scientific facts in light of complex moral disagreements.[12]

Procedural ethics concerns how societies can justify holding individuals bound to the larger political–legal regime, often begrudgingly or against their better judgements. The proceduralists' fundamental claim is that toleration for particular moral positions and worldviews can be legitimately limited for the sake of a stable social society, but at the same time they likewise disavow moral tyranny. They therefore '… justify what they do by principles and rules that ought – or so it is maintained – to be found acceptable by any clear-sighted person seeking fair terms of social cooperation for a population of presumptively free and equal persons holding diverse and conflicting conceptions of the good'.[13] How can procedural frameworks, which subject individuals to regimes of *positive legal ordering* and coercive compliance with majority-accepted rules, be justified?

Many contemporary libertarian theories have in common the purpose of binding individuals to a central cause that benefits them all equally. The first significant attempt to achieve this was by Thomas Hobbes; he wanted to create a social contract that could emancipate individuals from a lawless and disorganised socio-political state, into one in which reason creates a system of just law. He achieved this by describing a hypothetical 'state of nature', in which agents are '… saddled with the constant need to watch, distrust, anticipate, and get the better of others, and to protect themselves by all possible means'.[14] Rationally, every agent wants to escape this situation on the grounds of self-preservation, and for Hobbes this was only possible through a social contract enforced by the will of an absolute sovereign (whether it be a univocal monarch or system of government). This created a Commonwealth and a stable legal system that would benefit everyone equally, even if they were forced into things that they (sometimes) objected to.

The relevance of Hobbes' project to this discussion is that the hypothetical state of nature still exists in the form of – often subtle – antagonism between conflicting comprehensive doctrines competing for superiority. Not all of these doctrines can coexist as political solutions; but equally, society cannot turn to *laissez faire* doctrines, because scientific progress causes anxiety due to past abuses and future (potentially catastrophic) risks. Self-regulation fares no better, since no agent can reasonably expect to comprehend the effects of their own or anyone else's actions, and ignorance or malicious motivations could lead to unacceptable and incompatible laws of self-preservation, and which look more to private benefit than to that of the

---

Law 3rd Ed. (London: Butterworths) 1215–16: '… the pervasive notion in many circles is that the dictates of medical science, when followed to their logical extremes, will lead inexorably to horrors hitherto characterised as fantasy or science fiction' (p. 1216).

12 Rein, M. (1978), *Social Science and Public Policy* (London: Penguin Education).

13 Michelman, F. (2003), 'Constitutional Legitimation for Political Acts', *Modern Law Review* 66, 1–15, p. 1.

14 Hobbes. T. (1642; 1998), *On the Citizen*, Tuck, T. and Silverthorne, H. (eds) (Cambridge: Cambridge University Press) 11.

community. There are many examples of where biotechnology potentially threatens individual or community welfare, and calls for Hobbesian measures of preservation. The threats vary in the kind of harm, the severity and scale of the harm, and the possibility of that risk materialising. In this regard, SC science represents the threat of, or actual harm, for example, to those that oppose the technology on moral or religious grounds, or those that are exposed to dubious therapies found in regulatory havens.[15]

At this point I turn my attention to the type of rule-making institution that is required; and I leave Hobbes, since there arise considerable concerns in creating absolute power in any sovereign. Avoiding the possibilities of tyrannical government requires a representative government – themselves bound by the obligations of the social contract which protects 'life, liberty and estate'[16] – and the division of power.[17] This latter point is important because without it, representation could become skewed to particular interests.

Thus we have the necessary arguments to justify establishing a constitutional government. It is bound by the constitution (the social contract) that 'postulates how it ought to operate, and makes declarations about the purposes of the state and society and the rights and duties of citizens'.[18] It resolves disputes by providing a framework of rules of permissible and impermissible conduct, and therefore must establish institutions that can carry out these regulatory functions. At its heart, therefore, is a procedural turn which optimises deliberation between political, cultural and philosophical representatives. They are then able to discuss and analyse the available information, air opinions and explore options,[19] with the government then able to make an informed public declaration on the course of policy.

Opponents of proceduralism point out that dissenters of a given public policy must compromise their integrity; fundamentally, their concessions make them culpable of the 'ethical betrayal' of their own fundamental convictions, because they must 'stand aside' to publicly sanctioned but immoral acts.[20] However, procedural ethics can shift focus by separating the moral grounding of the procedural *process* from the substantive *outcome*. Such a separation depends upon finding *constitutional*

---

15 Aldhous, P. (2000), 'Panacea, or Pandora's Box?' *Nature* 408, 897–8.

16 Locke, J. (1689; 1967), *Two Treatises of Government*, Laslett, P. (ed.) (Cambridge: Cambridge University Press) especially Second Treatise, Chapter Two.

17 Marsilus of Padua, *Defensor pacis (The Defender of Peace)* (1324; first published in English, New York, 1951). A. Gewirth. trans. and ed. Edition consulted, 1980 (Toronto: University of Toronto Press) 48–9.

18 De Smith, S. (1973), *Constitutional and Administrative Law* 2nd Ed. (London: Penguin) 18.

19 While public opinion can identify areas of social agreement or disagreement, it should not be used to establish ethical norms '... or [as] a substitute for reasoned argument about alternatives open to policy makers'; Campbell, A. (2005), 'Public Policy and the Future of Bioethics', *Genomics, Society and Policy* 1, 86–91, 90–91.

20 Finnis, J. (1999), 'Natural Law and the Ethics of Discourse', *Ratio Juris* 12, 354–73, 365–8.

consensus on the basic principles that are part of democracy's very nature.[21] Rawls described these principles as being part of the political process necessary to allow individuals to support a particular conception of justice while not compromising their moral, religious or philosophical views as a whole.[22] Thus, a fair procedural model would make possible substantive compromise – which is more broad and deep than that seen in constitutional consensus – through 'end-state' analysis on the grounds that 'overlapping consensus' can be achieved.[23] Thus, proceduralism is not merely a 'method of avoidance',[24] but an exercise in democratic compromise for the sake of substantive political decision making, and thereby social stability.

Establishing an optimal procedural model will normally require constructing at least three interrelated levels. The first level 'filters' opinions and evidence to establish those arguments that are fit for policy consumption; in doing this, opinion may be sufficiently narrowed to advocate a 'discriminatory moral position'.[25] The second level is responsible for authorship of public policies. In the political setting, second level procedures also facilitate critical debate and (peaceful) dissent; input is expected from level one, as well as acknowledging international commitments and the restraints of national security. Policies are finally subject to a third level of adjudication, which incorporates appropriate mechanisms of review,[26] amendment[27] and oversight,[28] and primarily ensures the protection of civil and political rights. If these procedures are consented to – which is assumed on an individual level by simply participating in the democratic process – individuals are committed (to a point) to supporting policies as binding.[29] The result is a coherent policy which

---

21 Besson, S. (2005), *The Morality of Conflict: Reasonable Disagreement and the Law* (Oxford: Hart Publishing) 257–84.

22 Rawls, op. cit., note 1, 133–72 and 421–33.

23 For a discussion of the separation thesis, see Kuflik, A. (1979), 'Morality and Compromise', in Pennock, J. and Chapman, J. (eds), *Compromise in Ethics, Law, and Politics* (New York: New York University Press) 38–65, who claims that such a separation is misleading; and Habermas, J. (1996), 'Reply to Symposium Participants: Habermas on Law and Democracy: Critical Exchanges', *Cardozo Law Review* 17: 1477–1557, who offers support for the 'democratic pluralist' view.

24 Michelman, op. cit., note 13, 6–8.

25 Dworkin, R. (2004), *Taking Rights Seriously: New Impression with a Reply to Critics* (London: Duckworth) 248–52.

26 The French 1994 'Bioethics' laws provide for their revision and re-examination by Parliament every five years (Article 21 of Law 94-654).

27 Under Schedule 2(3) of the Human Fertilisation and Embryology Act 1990, the Secretary of State can introduce new regulations through both Houses with a view to the '... authorisation of projects of research which increase knowledge about the creation and development of embryos, or about disease, or enable such knowledge to be applied'.

28 Established under section 5 of the 1990 Act, the HFEA is responsible for licensing embryo research and provides for oversight of permissible research activities under Schedule 2.

29 Otherwise, participation would conceal intentions of non-compliance to objectionable outcomes, and would render the entire process pointless (and without methods of dispute resolution, the inevitable conflicts of the 'state of nature' would prevail). Thus, the procedural principles (such as trust and goodwill) would fail from the outset, making open debate

cannot be reasonably rejected because: (1) it acknowledges reasonable disagreement on the matter; (2) it incorporates important elements of any personal positions; and (3) it respects as many different reasonable positions as any workable alternative.

Procedural Regulation and Oversight: The Paradigm of UK Policy Making

In the formulation of the present UK policy on SC research, the constitutional model of proceduralism has been effectively deployed. Policy makers (second-level) have been informed by numerous reports (first level); the most important being the Warnock Report (1985),[30] the Human Genetics Advisory Commission-Human Fertilisation and Embryology Authority Report (1998),[31] the 'Donaldson' Report (2000),[32] and the House of Lords Expert Committee Report (2002).[33] These reports offered philosophical appraisal, scientific analysis, and invited public consultation. Ongoing monitoring of the ethical and scientific developments, and ad hoc policy making, is provided by the Human Fertilisation and Embryology Authority (HFEA), a statutory licensing body created under the Human Fertilisation and Embryology Act 1990 (hereafter the 1990 Act).

The issue of SC research has been debated extensively in Parliament in both Houses, firstly leading up to the 1990 Act, and secondly, in amendments to that Act, ending up as the Human Fertilisation and Embryology (Research Purposes) Regulations 2000;[34] thus providing ample opportunity for MPs to be lobbied by interested parties.

---

redundant, and decision making would have to resort to undemocratic or autocratic systems which have significant shortfalls; Rawls, op. cit., note 1, 56–7; Waldron, J. (1999), *Law and Disagreement* (Oxford: Clarendon Press) 113–14. This is not the only means of justifying civil obligation on the grounds of consent; however, a detailed discussion is beyond the scope of this chapter. See Watt, E.D. (1981), 'Rousseau Réchaufée – Being Obliged, Consenting, Participating, and Obeying Only Oneself', *Journal of Politics* 43, No. 3, 707–19.

30 Warnock, M. (1985), *A Question of Life: The Warnock Report on Human Fertilisation and Embryology* (Oxford: Oxford University Press).

31 HGAC-HFEA (1998), *Cloning Issues in Reproduction, Science and Medicine* (London: Department of Trade and Industry).

32 Department of Health (2000), *Stem Cell Research: Medical Progress with Responsibility* (London: Department of Health).

33 House of Lords Select Committee (2002), *Stem Cell Research – Report*, HL 83(i) (London: HMSO).

34 Subsequent to debates leading up to the 1990 Act, in 2000 the debates turned specifically to the issue of SC research, including the concerns of human cloning: *House of Commons Hansard Debates* 17 November 2000, 19 December 2000 and 29 November 2001; *Lords Hansard Debates* 22 January 2001, 26 November 2001 and 5 December 2002.

Lastly, the policies of the government have been challenged by judicial review at the highest level,[35] including a string of cases challenging the decisions made by the HFEA.[36]

The result has been that ES cell research – controversially also including creating embryos specifically for research by any means – is permitted on the grounds that it is 'necessary and desirable'[37] for high-ranking goals, and that alternative ethical objections are not sufficiently compelling to outweigh the potential benefits. For a licence to be issued, research must satisfy the criteria of the proportionality principle (that is, the destruction of the embryo should serve important and worthwhile goals and purposes) and subsidiarity principle (that is, research on embryos should only be conducted if no other suitable alternatives exist).[38] However, both the necessity and desirability claims lie in the gathering of reliable scientific evidence and expert review. According to the UK's legislation, on the one hand, if the claims that somatic SC research offers a better means of achieving therapeutic results, then controversial research is no longer necessary and therefore will be automatically prohibited; on the other hand, while evidence supports continued ES cell research, embryo research is justified.

Scepticism and Procedural Ethics

The majority of criticism that the UK SC policy has drawn has come from the 'Dignitarian Alliance'. This is perhaps not surprising, since the UK is one of a handful of states that represent the most liberal regard to embryo and therapeutic cloning research. The defence of the UK policy therefore tends to be taken up by pro-science protagonists, who clearly have most to benefit from the current permissive situation. Critics have taken two approaches: firstly, they normatively argued that the UK policy directly harmed the rights of embryos and violated natural laws of commodification. However, in a secular and pluralistic society, such a tack was unlikely to succeed. The second approach therefore, was to dismantle the justness of the procedural model. They therefore turned their attention to objections to the seemingly further liberalisation of biotechnology on the basis of evidence; in essence, the procedural mechanisms had failed because they were biased towards liberal policies and a permissive interpretation of the science, and overseen by individuals who did not acknowledge the sceptical claims of the 'Dignitarian Alliance'.

One of these claims was that scientific misrepresentation (perhaps unknowingly) had been used to sway government policy. Biased interpretations and the misrepresentation of facts, the critics argued, raised specific concerns of the validity

---

35 For example, on the question of the competency of the HFEA to regulate therapeutic cloning, see *R. (on the application of Quintavalle) v Secretary of State for Health* [2001] EWHC Admin 918 [2001] 4 All E.R. 1013; [2002] QB 628; [2003] UKHL 13.

36 Brownsword, R. (2004), 'Regulating Human Genetics: New Dilemmas for a New Millennium', *Medical Law Review* 12, 14–39.

37 Schedule 2 (1)(3) of the 1990 Act.

38 De Wert, G., et al. (2002), 'Ethical Guidance on Human Embryonic and Fetal Tissue Transplantation: A European Overview', *Medicine, Health Care and Philosophy* 5, 79–90.

of the government's policies and the ability of advisory institutions to offer non-partisan opinions; their concerns would be dramatically illustrated by the public accusations, and eventually confirmation, of scientific misconduct of the South Korean scientist, Hwang Woo Suk.[39]

There are a number of ways that misrepresentation can creep into procedural frameworks. Often they are far more subtle and concealed than deliberate misconduct. For example, selective or seditious membership of advisory bodies can hijack the debate and render its neutral operation doubtful. Thus, membership and the use of experts can impact upon the ability to represent a coherent philosophical view in light of scientific findings, leading to questions of consistency in methods of deliberation and outputs. Such a criticism was levelled at the President's Commission on Bioethics in the US. This advisory body allegedly contributed to the 'political distortion of biomedical science' by using delaying tactics, misleading communication and misrepresented evidence, to bias the final report towards the benefits of less controversial – and presidentially supported – science.[40] In the UK, the 'stacking' of committee membership has been alleged because the HFEA has a specific remit to license embryo research, thus there is an implied acceptance of the legitimacy of destroying embryos, and no one openly opposed to such research could be a member.[41]

Misrepresentation in UK Bioethics?

How seriously should these criticisms of the UK policies be taken? If such claims could be verified, then proceduralists would face a daunting task in making a justificatory case for the UK policies. After all, the basis of any defensible procedural solution is to show that policies are rooted in decisions made openly, in good faith, and based on a truthful representation of the available facts. Reports that are available to government ministers should espouse rationally defensible and non-contradictory arguments. Furthermore, proceduralism requires review and accountability, thus removing uncertainty and maximising trust.[42]

So was it the case that science was misrepresented in the UK debates? It seems unlikely for a number of reasons. Firstly, at the reporting level, all advisory bodies provided effective consultation and drew on a wide area of expertise, including

39 Vogel, G. (2006), 'Picking Up the Pieces after Hwang', *Science* 32, 516–17.

40 Blackburn, E. (2004), 'Bioethics and the Political Distortion of Biomedical Science', *New England Journal of Medicine* 350, 1379–80.

41 Representations from CORE questioned the accountability and transparency of the HFEA, and specifically how biased (unelected and delegated) membership leaves little scope for 'pro-life' views to be aired; House of Commons Science and Technology Committee (2005), *Human Reproductive Technologies and the Law: Fifth Report of Session 2004-2005. Volume II: Oral and Written Evidence*, HC-7-II (London: The Stationery Office) Ev 83–Ev 93.

42 O'Neill, O. (2002), *Autonomy and Trust in Bioethics* (Cambridge: Cambridge University Press) 134–5.

scientists with adult SC expertise.[43] Some alleged that the bodies employed a tactic of specifically framing the consultations so that they were able to implicitly exclude certain points of view or reduce their impact.[44] However, it is clear that dissenting views to the UK policy were expressed and reflected in the various reports (and evidence), and powerful lobbying groups, such as CORE, were privy to the various exchanges, and therefore one cannot claim that they were not taken into account.[45] (Although the weight given to them in the final committee opinion may not be so easily established.) No reports limited their remit so as to exclude wider, and perhaps fundamental, ethical questions, such as the status of the embryo. Their conclusions never strayed far from the basic premise of the Warnock Report – that the embryo only had a status of 'respect' – but they offered additional contextual and moral appraisal, rather than a mere duplication of the previous ethical reasoning.[46] Appointments tended to be transparent and based on merit, and were, to a degree, representative of ethical, legal and scientific expertise and UK socio-cultural outlook. Although the representative *membership* of certain committees may be limited, a number of declared views were present; and realistically, not all opinions *can* be represented outside a (not unproblematic) referendum.[47] Ultimately, the impact of such bodies is limited because, as Singer points out, such committees would have to have binding rule-making authority (which they do not) for them to seriously threaten democratic processes.[48]

Secondly, at the level of government policy, the debates in the Houses of Commons and Lords were published in Hansard, and it is evident that representatives of both sides were actively present. Again, it can hardly be said that opponents to the liberal position were not privy to the debate, and therefore could not contest the justification for the eventual policy. The debate was not one-sided or biased towards the further liberalisation of current policy, even though the government openly did not support a conservative 'Dignitarian' view.[49] Indeed, the crux of the debate was whether current embryo research laws should be amended to allow ES cells to be used for the

---

43 Department of Health, op. cit., note 32, s. 1.5; House of Lords, op. cit., note 33, s. 121.

44 If a committee on SC research is only asked to consider *new* ethical issues in SC research/therapy, that is, not the fundamental status of the embryo, this might exclude certain lines of reasoning/discussion, or implicitly suggest that such issues have already been solved.

45 Brownsword, R. (2002), 'Stem Cells, Superman, and the Report of the Select Committee', *Modern Law Review* 65, 568–87.

46 Department of Health, op. cit., note 32, s. 1.4; House of Lords, op. cit., note 33, Ch. 4.

47 O'Neill, op. cit., note 42, 173. There may have been a perceived lack of participation in the stages of public consultation, but this does not necessarily illustrate a failure in procedural mechanisms, but more likely a degree of apathy on the part of the public.

48 Singer, P. (1988), 'Ethical Experts in a Democracy', in Rosenthal, D. and Shehadi, F. (eds), *Applied Ethics and Ethical Theory* (Salt Lake City: University of Utah Press) 149–61.

49 Department of Health (2000), *Government Response to the Recommendations Made in the Chief Medical Officer's Expert Group Report*, Cm 4833; and (2002), *Government Response to the House of Lords Select Committee Report on Stem Cell Research*, Cm 5561 (London: The Stationery Office).

purposes of regenerative medicine; as things stood, ES cell research was possible, but only for purposes of fertility, congenital disease, miscarriage, contraception or genetic illness. The evidence presented and used was the *state-of-the-art* at that time, and included the airing of 'Dignitarian' opinions through membership of the bodies themselves, or as expert or lay representation to the advisory bodies and committees (including ethicists, theologians and 'adult' SC scientists).

Some argued that there was a lack of time to consider the complexity of the scientific and ethical issues which contributed to a limited consideration of conservative views; others suggested that the policy process had been rushed so that the research could proceed without further delay, and that the new regulations would lead to a sudden and substantial increase in embryo research. But it should be pointed out that the debates concerning embryo research have effectively been ongoing since the 1980s, and the more recent issue of SC research had, since 1998, been considered at length in various public, expert and governmental fora.[50] The 1998 Report unequivocally recommended that, on the basis of the potential for therapeutic advancement using ES cells, the current law be extended; but the government did not rush to implement the recommended changes, instead preferring to commission another report.[51] Furthermore, a government moratorium on HFEA licensing of ES cell research was in place during the House of Lords' Select Committee reporting.[52] There was no sudden influx of applications to the HFEA for embryo research licences – there were two applications immediately subsequent to the House of Lords' Report[53] – nor a disquieting rise in licences granted annually, suggesting that the new law would not open the flood gates.[54]

Finally, the courts were called to action on issues of legality. In the case of legal review, specific *questions of law* had to be answered (such as the status of the cloned embryo). They had to do this while addressing the concerns that the courts alone *should not* determine policy, thus limiting themselves to a law-*interpreting* role,[55] or fill gaps in government policy, since questions here should be sent back to Parliament

---

50 See Yvette Cooper, House of Commons 19 December 2000, op. cit., note 34, col. 211 and 212; Lord Hunt of King Heath, House of Lords 22 January 2001, op. cit., note 34, col. 21.

51 HGAC-HFEA, op. cit., note 31; Department of Health, op. cit., note 32.

52 Stewart, A. (2001), 'Lords Pass Regulation on Stem Cell Research, but Government Agrees Delay', *Public Health Genetics Unit*, 24 January, at: http://phgu.org.uk/ecard?link_ ID=874. Accessed 7 November 2006.

53 Dickson, D. (2002), 'New Regulations Give UK the Lead in Stem Cell Work', *Nature Medicine* 4, 315.

54 As of August 2002, the HFEA had received 141 applications for research licences, of which 136 were granted (on embryos and gametes); between August 2002 and August 2003, eight licensed research projects that related to ES cells and one to parthenogenesis were issued (HFEA, *11ʰ* (2002) and *12ʰ* (2003) *Annual Report and Accounts*, London: HFEA). As of August 2005, 19 licences were ongoing regarding ES cell research (*14ʰ Annual Report and Accounts 2004–2005*, London: HFEA). Between April 2005 and May 2006, 17 ES cell-related licences were issued (*15ʰ Annual Report and Accounts 2005–2006*, HC 1444, London: The Stationery Office).

55 Kennedy and Stone, op. cit., note 9.

for clarification or new laws.[56] The government policy was therefore significantly scrutinised,[57] and ultimately (rightly or wrongly)[58] justified on legal grounds.

If there was little at fault with the procedures, then were there concerns with regard to the evidence used? In this regard, there are clearly difficulties in procedural mechanisms, since all levels are vulnerable to misleading information, and may be defeated by a lack of evidence, by lack of time, or by lack of expertise to access evidence.[59] In light of this, there have developed two distinct readings of the SC scientific evidence: (1) that which favours adult SCs; and (2) that which promotes a 'dual track' approach.

The 'Dignitarian Alliance' has forcibly argued that not only is embryo research not necessary, but that present science (and presumably foreseeable developments in the science) demand concentrating on adult and cord blood SC. These latter SCs, it was argued, have not only be clinically *proven*,[60] but there is also scientific evidence to demonstrate that ES cells are inherently unsafe – '[o]ne rarely hears of the dangers associated with this kind of [ES] cell'[61] – and that we should be sceptical as to the 'vague prospect' of drastic opportunities in ES cell therapy.[62]

The present SC controversy is subject to a degree of scientific uncertainty, and this limits our deliberations to subjective claims. However, pro-science advocates have been keen to approach the debates with a more balanced view, typified in the Report of the House of Lords' Select Committee. In this report it was argued: 'the evidence from the great majority of scientific and medical research organisations, and the experts on adult stem cells whom we consulted, did not support that view [of adult research surpassing or making obsolete ES cell research]'.[63] They concluded that 'adult stem cells and ES cells [should not been seen] as alternatives but as complementary pathways to therapy'.[64] They further noted that 'it is probable that scientific advances from embryonic stem cell research will be necessary to understand how to make greater use of stem cells derived from adult tissue'. Thus:

> Although almost all the scientists who gave evidence to us were excited by recent studies on adult stem cells, most sounded a note of caution: many of the published studies are still open to multiple interpretations or require replication; and there are many crucial scientific issues to be resolved.[65]

---

56 Brownsword, (2004) op. cit., note 36.

57 At one point leading to 'emergency' legislation, with the (some claim rushed) enactment of the Human Reproductive Cloning Act 2001.

58 Morgan, D. and Ford, M. (2004), 'Cell Phoney: Human Cloning After *Quintavalle*', *Journal of Medical Ethics* 30, 524–36.

59 O'Neill, op. cit., note 42, 142.

60 Press release from CORE, 14 December 2004, available at: http://www.coreethics. org.

61 Ibid.

62 Habermas, J. (2003), *The Future of Human Nature* (Cambridge: Polity Press) 20.

63 House of Lords, op. cit., note 33, s. 3.16.

64 Ibid.

65 Ibid, s. 3.15.

This position was also taken by the 'Donaldson' Report, and together the reports showed a willingness to make recommendations in light of what is scientifically known (and unknown) regarding the risks and limitations of all sources of SC, and to not encourage or hasten a binding political decision regarding the science until the answers are known. Much of the evidence on both sides requires confirmation as to its validity; but not to confirm whether scientists are deliberately misleading policy makers, but as part of a process of research scrutiny.[66]

Conclusion

This chapter has been concerned with how procedural mechanisms *can* work to unravel scientific uncertainty within the practical limits of community disagreement. While not intending to disavow pluralism, public policy positions have to be taken with regard to regulating controversial developments in biotechnology. The concern is that this must take place where at the same time there is moral and scientific uncertainty. The questions addressed here were of the justification for procedural ethics in light of scientific misrepresentation, and not whether the utilitarian–consequentialist position of advisory bodies and government was morally defensible. How can it be ensured that decision-making bodies and individuals with responsibilities to make policy are doing so with truthful and unbiased representations of the scientific evidence? How do we assure that, as much as possible, such decisions are made independently of political ends or internally biased to the detriment of community participation? Was the 'Dignitarian' anti-embryo research position and its moral underpinnings given a chance to be aired under a fair process of consultation and deliberation?

To analyse the effectiveness of procedural ethics in one specific area – scientific misrepresentation – I have highlighted the concerns and criticisms of those that oppose the present UK system of policy establishment. This assessment shows that the procedural model used by the UK in the SC debates successfully provided a fair framework for open and free dialogue, rational employment of applied ethics, and consistent analysis of the 'facts'. On balance, the decisions made were in good faith and fully justified, and furthermore, no voices were excluded from *all* parts of the procedural process.

The 'Dignitarian' criticisms should be taken seriously, as they point to the dangers of relying purely on 'expert' opinion, since the interpretation of 'facts' can reasonably differ between individuals, and value solutions do not emerge from facts but from the values that are brought to those facts. Furthermore, I do not necessarily reject any calls for the UK system to be overhauled in light of their concerns, especially in light of the concerns that the organisation of the HFEA contributes to suspicions regarding its members' expertise and objectivity.[67] This has knock-on effects for public trust in such bodies, and certainly highlights concerns as to how close to political processes

---

66 Cook, G. (2004), 'From Adult Stem Cells Comes the Debate', *Boston Globe*, 1 November.

67 The licensing remit of HFEA does raise specific concerns, since this gives it considerable power to determine how the HFE Act is deployed, but as such it is not a democratically elected body. See House of Commons Science and Technology Committee, op. cit., note 41.

such bodies should operate. Emphasis should therefore be placed on the use of wide and declared expertise, ensuring that the reasoning behind policy decisions is made clear and transparent, and supported by evidence that demonstrates the level of critical appraisal at that time, and a willingness to utilise procedural mechanisms to review and amend policies in light of progress.

The case of Hwang has been used by some to emphasise that the scientific limitations of ES cells have been hidden from public scrutiny.[68] However, occurrences such as those in South Korea emphasise the importance of procedures to detect fraud, misconduct and misrepresentation. Criticism may be directed at the peculiarities of the South Korean incident, and specifically at the role of competition for funding in encouraging 'success', and the South Korean government's attitude to oversight which allowed Hwang to carry out his work in a regulated, but laxly enforced, environment.[69] In this regard, it is unlikely that such events, including donor exploitation and misrepresented findings being published in a major peer-reviewed journal, could occur unnoticed in the UK. The political oversight framework is adapted to detect misconduct and corruption at the research level through independent monitoring (Research Ethics Committees) and licensing (HFEA). However, the knock-on effects of the incident to UK science must be acknowledged. Hwang's published research certainly should be reassessed, and if necessary retracted from the evidence used. Thoroughness probably requires that the hundreds of text citations of Hwang's work which appear in many scientific journals should also be re-investigated, possibly leading to a reappraisal of some of the specific licences issued by the HFEA.

To date, there are still no scientifically proven clinical applications using stem cells in regenerative medicine. This suggests that not only was the 'dual track' approach advanced in UK policy justified, but also shows that medical progress requires the backing of credible science, and therefore procedural filters remain important to expose scientific misrepresentation and to identify dubious claims of medical success. The latter point of scientifically questionable, and possibly harmful, treatment claims, which are normally only found in regulatory havens, emphasises that a tight authoritative grip is justified in regulating stem cell science.

Procedural ethics commits one to rational deliberation in important matters of public policy. I have argued that justifiable policy should be based on sound scientific evidence. In this assessment, communities should expect reasonable disagreement on matters of fact, and therefore political resolution requires fair and equal methods of deliberation. This should be proceduralised to filter cases of scientific misrepresentation, and to identify opinions suitable for policy consumptions. By maximising individual participation, communities are justified in promoting their own interests over those that are personal. Ultimately, this requires one to consent to political rules as binding, even when one disagrees with (some of) them as a matter of personal values.

---

68 Editorial (2006), 'Ethics and Fraud', *Nature* 439, 117–18.

69 Scanlon, C. (2006), 'South Korea Probes Stem Cell Trails', BBC News: http://news.bbc.co.uk/1/hi/sci/tech/4639992.stm. Accessed on 23 January 2006.

Chapter 4

Ethical, Legal and Social Issues Related to Cell Therapy

Carlos M. Romeo-Casabona

Introduction

One of the great challenges of humanity has been to achieve a permanent source of tissues to be used in order to cure degenerative diseases. In the last years, scientists have discovered that the characteristics of certain cells could in turn derive from them others that are suitable in the treatment of these and other diseases. These cells, known as stem cells (SC), could inaugurate a new and revolutionary therapy (cell therapy) and medicine (regenerative medicine).

As we shall see throughout this work, cell therapy, and the previous research needed in order for it to become an efficient and safe achievement for medicine, entails certain problems, and not only of a scientific nature. For instance, the unresolved matter of the recognition of the freedom of scientific research and its reconciliation with the respect of other interests involved, the safety of society and the rights of the patients who undergo these new therapies in their research stage, in the first place. The most intense debates that are now taking place are probably those centred on the moral lawfulness of using human embryos as a source of stem cells (ESC). For the moment, we do not seem to have reached an international consensus, not even at the European level, as can be seen by the disparity in the legal solutions and regulations.

The Obtaining of In Vitro ESC: The So-called Ethical and Legal Status of the Embryo

The current problems in regards to the use of ESC is centred on the ethical and legal valuation of the use of such as a material or means of research and experimentation and which is not destined for treatment on specific patients. Each of the sources for the obtaining of human embryonic stem cells involves its ethical and legal reflection. Anyway, in order to better understand both, it is necessary to previously look into a very complex matter, that is, the ethical and legal status of the embryo. This will be very briefly looked at in the following.

The first matter which must precede the design of a possible ethical – and legal – status of the human embryo is whether this embodies any value that is worthy of recognition, and therefore of protection. Within the ideological and ethical plurality in the existing Western societies, there has been a proposal to identify an ethical civics based on human rights that will allow the compilation of shared ethical values. We can notice that we have different approximations to the value of the embryo in our society.

One of these states that the life of the embryo embodies a personal value, in that there already exists a potential person from the moment of fertilization, irremissibly aimed to be so in the act. Therefore, the embryo must be afforded the same protection as that offered to a natural person, elevating all its vital phases as part of its faculty and as a titleholder of rights. This is a modification that could be done without difficulties, as it is a juridical creation. However, other specialists have reminded us that this modification would have a difficult placing, both because of the attributes that have been conferred in an almost universal form in time and space to such legal categories, as well as because of its own operation in relation to prenatal life. Added to the former would be the fact that it would not coherently reflect the legal values that have been traditionally projected on prenatal life and to those which particularly have been more recently profiled on the embryo in vitro.

From a very different perspective, the close relation that exists between the prenatal life and that of the mother is highlighted. As a consequence, the protection of the prenatal life should not exceed the will of the mother, at least until the foetus reaches extra-uterine viability. Along the same lines, a precision has been made in that the embryo in vitro should not be afforded any special protection if other superior individual or collective interests collide with it. That is, the embryo would not be the holder of such rights, in so much as it does not embody any interest worthy of protection. This criterion does not seem to find constitutional backing in some European legal systems (that is, Germany and Spain).

Finally, there are varieties of positions, which we could probably label as intermediate, that have in common the assumption that the embryo in vitro has value and deserves a special respect, but that this value is counter-weighable to other values. This last is the opinion of the Spanish Counselling Committee on Ethics in Scientific and Technical Research. According to it, the shared values in relation to the human embryo could be the following: (1) the respect for human life from the embryo stage, meaning that the human life deserves from that moment on a special respect that is not given to other living beings; (2) the intrinsic value of trying to ease human suffering through research aimed towards this easing; (3) the value of the freedom of research, always when it does not contravene the human rights, that is, always when there is an awareness that the technical power does not match the ethical; and (4) the value of freedom, and therefore, its defence; in this case, the freedom of the affected couple and therefore, the need to ask for their consent, after providing sufficient information.

A significant number of European legal systems do not accord to either the nasciturus (implanted embryo and human foetuses) or the embryo in vitro the status of a person or of a titleholder of rights and obligations, which is indeed recognized after birth. Nonetheless, there is also an acceptance that the law must provide adequate mechanisms of protection to the prenatal human life, and specifically to the life of the embryo in vitro, in so far as it is a form of human life and could lead to the birth of a human being. Likewise, there is a consideration that the law must additionally guarantee that the embryo in vitro will not be the object of interventions that could place in danger the integrity or identity of the new being.

This is without prejudice to the fact that there could be a weighing of the opportunity to admit specific exceptions – also debated – for the benefit of the individual themselves or for third parties, in this last instance in the event that such a fertilization project cannot be undertaken. The lack of personality of the nasciturus and of the embryo in vitro does not mean that they should be understood without exception as mere objects of rights and therefore as objects subject to appropriation. This is because they enjoy and should enjoy other different and superior privileges to those afforded to other parts of the human body that are separate from it. In this manner, the conflicts that could be posed in relation to the embryo in vitro should be resolved applying the legal principle of weighing all the interests involved.

After looking at these presuppositions, we can go on to study the problems raised by the creation of embryos in order to obtain their ESC.

The Use of SC from Supernumerary Embryos

In a reproductive setting, there has been a preference for the interest of the well-being of the sterile woman (thereby avoiding subjecting the woman to a process of obtaining ova every time that the doctor tries for her to become pregnant) over the risk of having surplus embryos (if the option is to obtain an abundant number of ova at one time, which in turn creates as many embryos, which could be frozen for successive reproductive attempts). That is, in those legal regulations that have decided so, the interests of the woman patient are more valuable than those of the embryo, even if this entails the risk that they could not be used for the initial reproductive purpose.

Then the question that arises is what to do with these 'surplus' embryos. Notwithstanding what the applicable legislation may say about these matters, the only possibilities would be:

a) To use these embryos in the fertility of couples different from the couple who originated them. Nonetheless, for different reasons, it has been shown that this possibility does not use all the available cryopreserved embryos.

b) To destroy them once the maximum cryopreservation period allowed by law has been reached. Some backers of this approach have proposed, in order to smooth it, to unfreeze these embryos and to let nature follow its course, which, as is easily deduced, precisely leads to its destruction.

c) To use them in research, adding a set of requirements that could have various degrees of restrictiveness. This last option ties with the matter that is being expounded in this chapter.

Comparative law shows a great disparity of solutions. Some states (Belgium, Spain, Finland, Greece, the Netherlands, the United Kingdom and Sweden) have authorized research with supernumerary embryos and therefore have allowed the obtaining of their ESC, although establishing a time limit in relation to the moment of the creation of such embryos (Spain, 2003). On the contrary, other states (Germany, Austria,

Denmark, France, Ireland, Iceland and Italy) have opted for a rigorous prohibition, even under criminal sanction. Nonetheless, some states have authorized the import and use of ESC under certain conditions (Germany, 2002) while others have opted for a moratorium (France, 2004). Finally, an even smaller number of states (Portugal) do not have a specific regulation in relation to research on human embryos.

European Law

Within the European framework, as there has not been a wide consensus in this area, the Council of Europe has adopted a solution that is more or less open and a compromise, in the Convention on Human Rights and Biomedicine (CHRB) of 4 April 1997. Nevertheless, this was one of the matters that led to a great number of discrepancies and probably the most relevant cause why some of the most representative European states still have not signed or ratified the Convention (the Federal Republic of Germany and the United Kingdom, while it is still pending ratification in France and Italy, though for different motives in each).

The Convention could not be totally foreign to the possibility of using embryos for research, in order to advance knowledge of the biological processes that are associated with the beginning of human life, with fertilization, with the human genome, with the passing of time and in order to treat the diseases of other individuals (regenerative medicine through the use of ESC). In accordance with article 18:

> Research on embryos 'in vitro'.
> 1. Where the law allows research on embryos in vitro, it shall ensure adequate protection of the embryo.
> 2. The creation of human embryos for research purposes is prohibited.

As shall be shown in the following, the content of this important precept is not easy to determine, in reference to which one should not forget that it is the first to regulate research with embryos in vitro in international law. Nonetheless, this is a decisive matter in order to be able to weave in the European sphere some meeting points from such a precept and from others which I will refer to further in this work, none of which, by the way, deal with the embryo in vivo.

The Reach of Authorization to Research with Embryos

In accordance with article 18.1 of the CHRB, research with human embryos in vitro is allowed. In relation to this matter, we must clarify four principal issues:

i)   Which are the embryos that the Convention allows experimentation on;
ii) What type of research is permitted, particularly if it may or may not be destructive;
iii) The normative drafting procedure that must be followed by the states in this field; and
iv) The relative guarantees that must be afforded to the embryo.

There is no doubt that the literal meaning of article 18.1 of the CHRB leads to the conclusion that research with human embryos in vitro is permitted. However, it is also true that the creation of these embryos for the purpose of researching with them (article 18.2) is expressly prohibited. Therefore, in order to be able to give material content to this legal provision, which could apparently seem contradictory (paragraph 1 in relation to paragraph 2), we must find out which could be those embryos that, not having been created for experimentation, have been created with other lawful objectives and can later be destined for research. These can be no other than the embryos obtained in relation to medically assisted procreation techniques; that is, that they were created for the purpose of helping a couple to have descendants, and after, as an ensuing fact, such an objective was frustrated.

Types of Research Allowed on the Embryo In Vitro

It is not an easy matter to answer which type of research is allowed within the framework of the Convention. There are several alternative interpretations that are compatible between them. The first is whether research on the embryo could be invasive or not. In the first part of this alternative it could lead to its direct destruction (if it entails substantial alteration of the biological structure of the embryo, in such a way that it is no longer capable of continuing the process of cell division) or indirect destruction (when the manipulated embryos are discarded for their procreative use). The second interpretation is that the research works to the direct benefit of the embryo itself or, on the contrary, serves for the general interest of the progress of science or of third parties. If one adopts the first criteria, only invasive experimentation (more so if it was destructive) could place in danger the continuity of the embryo. But even if the research was not invasive, the risks that it could entail for the embryo would not be justified by attending to the general interest or that of third parties. Therefore, we must immediately exclude those hypotheses that claim that the research is aimed towards the benefit of the embryo. This is neither a requisite that is mentioned in the Convention nor implies a guarantee, as it makes reference to the objective of the research (that it should be to the benefit of the embryo). If it were to be invasive (destructive) it would be a contradiction, as it would not benefit the embryo due to the hazards that it could entail. Then, we must conclude that the research must be aimed towards the general interest or to the benefit of third persons, establishing the issue as to whether the nature of the experimentation is invasive or not.

In order to establish the reach of research with human embryos, we must take into account several extremes. In the first place, doubt arises whether the word 'research' could mean non-invasive actions (for example, merely observational).In paragraph 2 of article 18, the word must have a wide meaning, as the prohibition of creating embryos in vitro for research must necessarily make reference to both non-invasive as well as invasive interventions. The latter, it must not be forgotten, can entail the destruction of the embryo. As the latter are more threatening for the embryo, it would not make sense that they would only prohibit harmless interventions for the embryo. If this were so, for systematic coherence, the word research (or recherché, experimentación in official Spanish translation) must have the same meaning as in paragraph 1 of the aforementioned article.

The chapter that is dedicated to research as a whole strengthens the previous considerations. In this chapter, the same terms mentioned earlier are used and the principles are aimed both towards the assurance of the establishment of a record of an informed consent by the subject who is undergoing the experimentation or by a duly authorized third party on his or her behalf, as well as towards the justification of the risks of the research and that they are taken into account with the expected benefits of such research, which means the acceptance that this could be invasive for the subject (though in this case, obviously not 'destructive').

On the other hand, the express regulation of this matter (that of paragraph 1 of article 18) would not have been necessary in the Convention if the said regulation had been limited to non-invasive research on the embryo, as seen by the more general principles that the Convention as a whole deals with (it would have been enough to postpone this matter to a future protocol on the embryo; this is not so with article 18.2, as its importance justifies its presence in the Convention). On the contrary, the background of this legal provision, which is reflected in the diverse drafts that were created during its proceedings, highlights that the discussion was centred on the authorization or prohibition of the research with embryos in vitro. As previously noted, in the end, the adopted solution was one of compromise.

In any case, it must be recognized that the Convention does not provide any more explicit guidance in this respect.

A Matter of Law

The first paragraph of article 18 establishes that the member states to this Convention may authorize by law the research on human embryos. That is, it is up to the decision of the states whether to authorize or prohibit such an activity. This means that the citizens (and the scientists in particular) cannot directly make experimentations with human embryos in vitro on grounds of the Convention, but rather will be subject to their applicable legislation. If we assume the position that is favourable to experimentation, the states would only have the imposition of the obligation that the law ensure an adequate protection of the embryo, or in other words, the law must include some form of guarantee that can satisfy this mandate.

This way, we find ourselves with two formal or external guarantees. This is done in order to require that the executive power establish this matter by law through dispositions that will regulate this matter, which demands its passing through and approval of Parliament, thereby allowing the establishment of majorities that are sufficient in accordance with what the internal legislation requires. At the same time, it excludes the pretension to unilaterally regulate by the executive power through norms that have an inferior rank to that of law. Therefore, this reservation of law is projected in the authorization and regulation of research on embryos in vitro as well as with the guarantees that must be set for an adequate protection of the embryo in relation to the acts of experimentation, which we shall look at next.

Guarantees Aimed towards an Adequate Protection of the Embryo

From the moment in which the embryo is used for research, its later use for human reproduction is discarded and thereby leads to its destruction. This in turn makes the definition of which could be these guarantees not an easy task. The CHRB makes exclusive reference in paragraph 1 to the surplus embryos from assisted procreation techniques, and by definition also means that the possibility that they could be destined for any parental or procreative project has also been excluded. Therefore, it lacks sense that such guarantees would be directly aimed at protecting each embryo in particular, for as we have previously stated, destructive experimentation on embryos is not prohibited. In consequence, it must necessarily mean a set of indirect guarantees on the protection of embryos in vitro in general, but not specifically of each embryo. These could consist, for example, in that the research is really scientifically justified based on the expected relevant results (for example, for human health), in that other research procedures have previously been exhausted, in that there are no other alternatives without having recourse to human embryos (which does not mean the recognition of the preference of research with adult SC, as these are methodologically different lines of research), in that the number of these is the minimum possible, in that they do not develop beyond a specific period under the pretext of the demands of the research (for example, more than 14 days), and so on. On the other hand, notice how the CHRB does without a distinction between viable and non-viable embryos – independently of what should be understood by these terms at present – an allusion that is likewise left in the hands of the member states.

The Creation of Human Embryos for Research Purposes

The second section of article 18 of the CHRB clearly establishes a prohibition: the creation of embryos in vitro for research purposes. Although this pronouncement is more forceful than that of the first section that makes reference to the establishment of adequate guarantees, it is a matter that must be the object of discussion by the international community, as the limits of this precept do not seem to be very well defined. On the other hand, against the demands to provide a broad legal protection to the embryo in vitro, to which this section of article 18 would give a fulfilled – but partial – response, there is a wide sector of the scientific community that does not resign itself to this restriction, as it considers it a serious slowing down of its research needs or aims.

In any case, the prohibition of article 18.2 makes reference only to the creation of embryos in vitro for research, independent of the nature and the aims of such research. However, this must be clarified.

The Prohibition to Create Embryos In Vitro for Industrial or Commercial Purposes

The CHRB also does not mention anything about the lawfulness or unlawfulness of creating embryos in vitro for other purposes, be it industrial (pharmacological or cosmetic) or commercial.

The question that must be raised, then, is whether these practices should be understood as allowed, through the application of the general legal principle that that which is not expressly prohibited by law must be consequently understood as permitted. In accordance with this principle, we should also conclude that the creation of embryos for other purposes is also permitted, such as for therapeutic purposes using embryonic material (ESC) in direct benefit of the persons. On the other hand, although the CHRB has not explicitly made a pronouncement, it is evident that the creation of embryos in vitro in the context of the use of the diverse techniques of assisted procreation, that is, for reproductive purposes, is in conformance with the Convention. In reference to the latter, article 18.1 provides for research with embryos in vitro, otherwise it could never come into play. This is independent of how one conceives the legal framework of this experimentation, as noted earlier, specifically with the use of the supernumerary embryos of the said techniques.

Anyway, some of these provisional conclusions do not seem satisfactory for several reasons. At first glance, it is not so clear that the creation of human embryos in vitro for the above stated purposes is lawful, at least in relation to some of them. In fact, article 18 as a whole, and in particular the second section, would have little use for achieving a real – though not absolute – protection of the human embryo in vitro, if there were not an obstacle by the CHRB to create such embryos for industrial purposes, given the purely commercial object that they would entail (besides the possible repercussions of the benefits to consumers). This final purpose would not sit well with the spirit of the general principle of prohibition of financial gain from the human body (article 21 of the CHRB).

However, the exclusion of the lawfulness of the act of creating embryos for industrial or commercial purposes within the Convention could only be done through a systematic approach that dealt with the Convention as a whole. This approach would have to include the Protocols, if need be, and not be exclusively based on article 18. It is already known that the protection of this article would be insufficient and non-satisfactory, as seen from a point of view of restrictiveness and concretion. We believe that we can deduce a set of valuation principles on the human embryo in vitro, when analysing the prohibition of human reproductive cloning in both the Convention and the Protocol as one. This could constitute the basis of its legal status, pending its development and concretion through a new Protocol.

Article 1 of the CHRB states as its purpose the protection 'of the dignity and identity of all human beings and guarantee everyone, without discrimination, respect for their integrity and other rights and fundamental freedoms with regard to the application of biology and medicine'. Although this clause does not make an explicit pronouncement on whether the embryo in vitro is a title-holder of these rights, it seems that only the person is a holder of such, as deduced from the Preamble. It states 'the need to respect the human being both as an individual and as a member of the human species and recognising the importance of ensuring the dignity of the human being', without prejudice to the fact that this is usually considered an open matter which is left to the criteria of the states. However, as we know, there is no doubt that the embryo is also within the scope of protection of the Convention as it offers an explicit protection of the embryo in vitro in article 18 and indirectly or implicitly in articles 13 and 14. Although the embryo in vitro does not legally seem to be a person – at least in accordance with the majority of European legal systems – it would objectively be the holder of a wider protection than that which could be extracted only from article 18.

On the other hand, the transcendental article 2 establishes that 'the interests and welfare of the human being shall prevail over the sole interest of society or science'. Although the reach of this legal provision is not very clear, it excludes at least the subordination of the human being to the exclusive interest of society or of science, that is, to merely general and abstract interests. Once again, to determine what must be understood by the term human being is problematic, specifically if it also includes the embryo in vitro. We could consider Article 18.2 as an expression or concretion of this legal provision, in such a way that it would mean that the creation of embryos merely for the purpose of experimentation would require the CHRB to unduly put the interests of embryos before other general interests. For similar reasons, one can also assert that the creation of embryos for industrial or commercial purposes would contravene the Convention beginning with article 2, with the help that article 18 seems to provide. In fact, the satisfaction of these objectives would involve, according to the Convention, giving priority to the exclusive interests of society or science, in a similar manner to what happens with experimentation.

The Lawfulness of the Creation of Embryos for Therapeutic Purposes

Along the same discussion lines, the last hypothesis that we must study is that of the creation of embryos in vitro for the use of their cells to treat the diseases of specific persons. Two observations must be made. First, now we are not facing general or abstract interests, but rather facing specific persons who have serious pathologies that cannot be cured through other means. Second, as a general rule, the therapeutic purpose deserves a higher value than that of research, and therefore it is usually subjected to fewer restrictions than the latter. Something similar happens with the CHRB, as it is enough to compare the legal provisions established in articles 5 and the following (consent and private life) with the requisites established in articles 15 and the following (on human research). However, it must not be forgotten that the case at hand is not about healing the embryo, but a third party. Likewise it must not be forgotten that the experimentation with embryos is not in their interest, as was previously established, and it is indeed permitted by the CHRB in certain situations, as previously noted. The issue we want to highlight is only the worth that the therapeutic action deserves in itself (and in its case, preventive), and its priority in relation to the acts of research, also in relation to it. In conclusion, while industrial and commercial purposes would be prohibited due to the reasons noted earlier, in spite of its omission in the literal text of the CHRB, the same conclusion could not necessarily be reached in relation to the treatment of people with embryos created in vitro for that purpose; that is, where the vital interest of specific human beings is at stake and not exclusively other more general interests.

In accordance with this interpretation, it could be understood that the Convention has set the interest of the embryo before the collective interest (in reference to the promotion of certain sectors of research and other industrial activities). However, the Convention has placed the health and the life of specific persons (article 2 of the Convention, 'Primacy of the human being') before the embryo. Therefore, this interpretative proposal, which could have great importance in the future, is that the Convention neither prohibits in article 18.2 nor in the Convention as a whole the creation of embryos with the direct or immediate purposes of either improving the health or saving the life of a person. It does not matter what may be the technical procedure used for obtaining the embryo, as this is an activity that is radically different to that of experimentation.

This conclusion means that the authorization to create embryos in vitro for therapeutic purposes would be left open to the member states of the CHRB that so desire (via legislation, in a manner similar to that established in article 18.1), although it is true that it would not be authorized for research purposes, even if it was in relation to those possible treatments. This last reflection presents paradoxes and limitations (embryos cannot be created for research on a specific disease, but can be created to treat it). This reflection would require the finding of other ways (for example, with supernumerary human embryos) until they reach the phase of experimental use on human beings (the so-called therapeutic experimentation, used correctly in this context). Nonetheless, the latter would in turn be subject to the general legal demands provided for the clinical tests. Therefore, we understand that the frequently called 'therapeutic' cloning (really of research) would be prohibited, in that it is presently aimed towards research in a laboratory. However, it could be authorized through a law of any member state of the CHRB that would so desire once it really was therapeutic for a person.

Finally, it must be noted that article 26.1 of the CHRB exceptionally allows the introduction of certain restrictions to the exercise of rights and the dispositions of its protection. However, this must be done always when provided by law 'and are necessary in a democratic society in the interest of public safety, for the prevention of crime, for the protection of public health or for the protection of the rights and freedoms of others'. None the less, the Convention immediately points out that such restrictions 'may not be placed on Articles 11, 13, 14, 16, 17, 19, 20 and 21' (article 26.2). As can be noted, article 18 does not appear in this last listing, which means that the dispositions of protection that article 18 has on the embryo can be subject to restriction, always assuming, of course, that there is a concurrence of the premises that appear in the close list of the aforementioned article 26.1.

Is Nuclear Transfer – Therapeutic Cloning – Prohibited?

The thesis that will be defended consists in that no matter what may be the legal concept of the embryo that can be deduced from the CHRB, or even besides it, so-called 'therapeutic' cloning has not been regulated either by the Convention or by the Additional Protocol on the Prohibition of Cloning Human Beings. It has not been prohibited, so therefore there would not be an obstacle to its regulation as a permissive technique, always being respectful of the protective spirit of article 18.

The first interpretative premise consists in that the CHRB did not aim at that time to evaluate in any case whatsoever the techniques of human cloning. This was a matter that consciously and deliberately was left aside for a later development through the approval of additional protocols. Therefore, the reference to the embryo must be understood to mean the biological being that is the result of fertilizing. The considerations that may fall on the biological being created through cloning techniques (basically, through nuclear transfer) would come from what is established in the Protocol on Cloning. This first Additional Protocol clearly makes reference to human reproductive cloning, but does not want to make an explicit pronouncement on non-reproductive cloning. This is a matter that is open to the free disposition of the states, as I will try to show in the following.

In fact, this affirmation comes from certain commentaries that are made in the narrative recitals of the Additional Protocol and especially in its Explanatory Report. In the narrative recitals of the Preamble of the Protocol, there is already a clear focus on what is the centre of the immediate and urgent concern, as there is reference to the need to prohibit cloning due to a fear of the 'instrumentalization of human beings ... contrary to human dignity' and to the 'serious difficulties of a medical, psychological and social nature that such a deliberate biomedical practice might imply for all the individuals involved'. That is, there is an emphasis on the rejection of reproductive cloning. The Explanatory Report is very clear on this:

> 3. Deliberately cloning humans is a threat to human identity, as it would give up the indispensable protection against the predetermination of the human genetic constitution by a third party.

The Protocol aims to avoid, in any case, the creation of an 'identical' being to another human being who existed previous to him or herself (space–time identity) due to a fear of a predetermination of the same. This would mean a hindrance to the freedom of this individual, and in sum to the free development of his or her personality. However, when we try to evaluate the content of this Protocol in relation to the nuclear transfer technique, the issue is not so clear. To begin with, the Explanatory Report of the Protocol recognizes that 'there are different views about the ethical acceptability of cloning undifferentiated cells of embryonic origin'.

The aforementioned paragraphs, that are presented in those documents as a positive contrast to the rejection of reproductive cloning, would permit a deepening in the idea that the use of the cloning techniques (such as nuclear transfer) would not be within the scope of application of the Protocol, if undertaken in a strict biomedical context and if they do not seek to create a human being. Or, at least, it provides the states with the freedom to adopt such an interpretation.

The next matter derived from the Additional Protocol on Reproductive Cloning is with regard to what should be understood by the term 'human being', as this is applicable to 'any intervention seeking to create a human being'. That is, if the resulting biological being of the nuclear transfer is a human being, then we must conclude that such technique will be prohibited. If it is not so, then it would not be prohibited, at least according to this Protocol. However, the Protocol avoids openly pronouncing itself on the meaning of 'human being', as happened with the Convention, leaving now, as they did then, the freedom to the states to define in their internal legislation what they consider as a human being.

This is stated so in the Explanatory Report of the Protocol:

6. (…) it was decided to leave it to domestic law to define the scope of the expression 'human being' for the purposes of the application of the present Protocol.

In accordance with this faculty, the Kingdom of Holland has manifested that, in compliance with the application of this Protocol within their state, the term human being will be interpreted as that exclusively referring to an individual human, for example, to a human being already born. It is clear that with this interpretation, an internal disposition that would authorize therapeutic cloning would not be contrary to the Protocol, as the resulting biological being would not be a human being, and therefore, an identical 'human being' to another would not have been created. This would only occur if there was an allowance for a latter development that would result in the birth of an individual human.

In this way, if a human being is only the person or the embryo 'in uterus', then the creation of cloned embryos in vitro would not be prohibited, and in the specific case of 'therapeutic' cloning, as the result is neither a human being, nor is the aimed finality – by definition – to create a human being.If these biological beings that are created by nuclear transfer are understood to be 'embryos', then their creation would indeed be prohibited in accordance with article 18 of CHRB, for coherence reasons, as we must remember that according to article 3 of the Protocol, the substantive articles of such 'shall be regarded as additional articles to the Convention and all the provisions of the Convention shall apply accordingly'.

In sum, in order to authorize the techniques of nuclear transfer without being contrary to the Convention, we would have to understand that neither is the cloned biological being in vitro a human being, nor that the creation of such is the end purpose (otherwise, the creation would be prohibited by the Protocol), but it is not an embryo in the sense of the Convention (as in such case, its creation would be prohibited by itself).

In any case, it is clear that the Convention does not include within this prohibition nuclear transfer, be what may be the purpose of such. That is, if a specific Protocol does not look into a matter due to its excessive complexity at present, as it is clear happens with 'therapeutic' cloning, then the Convention, which is more general and previous to the aforementioned Protocol, also cannot (or does not want) to prohibit it. In coherence with this interpretation, it would not make much sense to state that something that is not specifically prohibited by a specific regulation, which completes the Convention in a specific field, is indeed prohibited by making a very strict interpretation of the Convention.

On the other hand, we must not forget some of the characteristics of conventional international law (that is, the law of Treaties), which are of surmount importance in this matter. The Treaties of international law are a voluntary act whereby the states that become parties to such are bound – I insist, voluntarily – to a set of obligations that are derived from the corresponding treaty. Legally, this is an act of sovereignty of the states, specifically an act of voluntary limitation of its own sovereignty. This voluntary limitation must be understood as an exceptional act, without prejudice to the fact that this is quite frequent in the current international setting. As a consequence, any broad interpretation of the content of a Treaty or Convention, or of any part of such, which goes beyond the obligation that a specific state voluntarily undertook at the moment of adhesion to such, can entail an additional limitation to its non-consented sovereignty and, therefore, be contrary to Conventional law.

As a summary of the reflections in the earlier paragraphs, a joint interpretation of the CHRB and the Additional Protocol is possible on reproductive cloning that would allow us to reach the conclusion that cloning, in any of its forms, is not regulated –prohibited – by the first; that non-reproductive 'therapeutic' cloning has no room in the Protocol; and that the question of the legitimacy of this last has been postponed for a future and, at the moment incomplete, Additional Protocol that is specific on the human embryo.

Bibliography

Advisory Committee on Ethics of Scientific and Technical Research, Ministry of Science and Technology (2003), *Report on Stem Cell Research* (Madrid).

Commission Staff Working Paper (2003), *Report on Human Embryonic Stem Cell Research* (Brussels: Commission of the European Communities).

Council of Europe (1998), Explanatory Report: *Additional Protocol to the Convention on Human Rights and Biomedicine on the Prohibition of Cloning Human Beings* (Strasbourg).

Eser, A. and Koch, H-G. (2004), 'La investigación con células troncales embrionarias humanas. Fundamentos y límites penales', *Revista de Derecho y Genoma Humano / Law and the Human Genome Review*, 20, 37.

Romeo-Casabona, C.M. (2002), *Los genes y sus leyes* (Bilbao-Granada: Comares).

Romeo-Casabona, C.M. (2002), 'Embryonic Stem Cell Research and Therapy: The Need for a Common European Legal Framework', *Bioethics*, 16, 6.

Romeo-Casabona, C.M. (2005), 'La cuestión jurídica de la obtención de células troncales embrionarias humanas con fines de investigación biomédica. Consideraciones de política legislativa' (Bilbao-Zaragoza: Informe a la Ministra de sanidad y Consumo) Agosto.

Steering Committee on Bioethics (CDBI) (2003), *The Protection of the Human Embryo In Vitro* (Strasbourg: Council of Europe).

Chapter 5

Boy or Girl: Should Parents be Allowed to Choose the Sex of Their Children?

Edgar Dahl

For centuries, couples have been trying to influence the sex of their children by myriads of dubious tricks. Italian men were biting their wife's left ear during intercourse to beget a daughter and their right ear to sire a son. Swedish men were hanging their pants on the left bedpost to father a girl and on the right one to father a boy. German woodcutters were taking an axe to bed and then chanting: 'Ruck, ruck, roy, you shall have a boy!' or 'Ruck, ruck, raid, you shall have a maid!' Needless to say, all these old wives' tales turned out to be a forlorn hope.[1]

Sex selection is now a reality. Thanks to MicroSort®, a new technology currently being tested in an FDA-approved clinical trial, parents will soon be able to choose the sex of their children prior to conception. MicroSort® allows separation of the sperm that produce a boy from the sperm that produce a girl. The separated sperm can then be used for artificial insemination. If a couple would like to have a son, the woman will be inseminated with male-producing sperm only; if a couple would like to have a daughter, the woman will be inseminated with female-producing sperm only. Given that not every attempt at artificial insemination results in a pregnancy, couples will have to undergo an average of three to five cycles of insemination. Each attempt will cost about £1,250 sterling. All expenses incurred must be covered by the couple undergoing treatment.[2]

It will probably take another two or three years until the safety and efficacy of MicroSort® has been properly established. Given the current results – at 3.4 per cent, the incidence of congenital malformations in babies conceived after MicroSort® is similar to that in the general population[3] – there is virtually no doubt that the technology will get the approval of the US Food and Drug Administration. If so, fertility centres around the globe may apply for a sublicence to use MicroSort® and to offer their own service for preconception sex selection.

---

1 Thompson, J.M. (2004), *Chasing the Gender Dream* (Imperial Beach: Aventine Press).

2 Schulman, J.D. and Karabinus, D.S. (2005), 'Scientific Aspects of Preconception Sex Selection', *Reproductive BioMedicine Online*.

3 Stern, H.J., et al. (2003), 'MicroSort Babies 1994–2002: Preliminary Postnatal Follow-Up Results', *Fertility and Sterility* 76, 54.

To prevent British fertility specialists from offering MicroSort® for social reasons, the Human Fertilisation and Embryology Authority (HFEA) recently advised the government of the United Kingdom to enact a law prohibiting sex selection for any but the most serious of medical reasons.[4] Great Britain will not be the first Western society outlawing non-medical sex selection. In 1990, Germany passed its notorious Embryo Protection Act making social sex selection a criminal offence punishable by one year's imprisonment.[5] In the Australian state of Victoria, the sentence is even harsher. According to section 50 of the Infertility Treatment Act of 1995 doctors performing sex selection for non-medical reasons face up to two years' imprisonment.[6]

Is there any valid justification for criminalizing social sex selection and for sentencing a doctor to jail for, say, helping the parents of three boys to finally conceive a girl? I do not think so – at least not in a Western liberal democracy.

Modern Western societies are pluralistic societies. They consist of individuals devoted to differing religious views and, consequently, to differing moral views. Hence, in modern societies there will always be irresolvable differences over fundamental ethical issues. If a government tries to impose a particular morality upon its citizens, social conflict is inevitable. To avoid social tension and to deal with the moral pluralism of its citizens, the politics of modern societies ought to be based upon a 'presumption in favour of liberty': each citizen should have the right to live his life as he chooses so long as he does not infringe upon the rights of others. The state may interfere with the free choices of its citizens only to prevent serious harm to others.

The presumption in favour of liberty has at least three important implications. Firstly, the burden of proof is always on those who opt for a legal prohibition of a particular action. It is they who must show that the action in question is going to harm others. Secondly, the evidence for the harm to occur has to be clear and persuasive. It must not be based upon highly speculative sociological or psychological assumptions. And thirdly, the mere fact that an action may be seen by some as contrary to their moral or religious beliefs does not suffice for a legal prohibition. The domain of the law is not the enforcement of morality, but the prevention of harm to others.[7]

With this in mind, let us turn to some of the most common objections to sex selection and see whether they provide a rational basis for outlawing it.

---

4 Human Fertilisation and Embryology Authority (2003), *Sex Selection: Options for Regulation* (London: Paxton House).

5 German Embryo Protection Act of 1990, *Reproductive BioMedicine Online* 6, 91–3 (2003).

6 Infertility Treatment Act 1995, Victoria, Australia, Section 50, 43.

7 Hart, H.L.A. (1963), *Law, Liberty, and Morality* (Stanford: Stanford University Press); Taylor, R. (1973), *Freedom, Anarchy, and the Law* (New Jersey: Prentice-Hall); Grey, T.C. (1983), *The Legal Enforcement of Morality* (New York: Knopf); Lyons, D. (1984), *Ethics and the Rule of Law* (Cambridge: Cambridge University Press); Feinberg, J. (1984), *Harm to Others: The Moral Limits of the Criminal Law* (New York: Oxford University Press); Dworkin, G. (1994), *Morality, Harm, and the Law* (Boulder: Westview Press); Epstein, R.A. (2002), *Principles for a Free Society: Reconciling Individual Liberty with the Common Good* (Reading: Perseus Publishing).

A constantly recurring objection to sex selection is that choosing the sex of our children is to 'play God'. This religious objection has been made to all kinds of medical innovations. For example, using chloroform to relieve the pain of childbirth was considered contrary to the will of God as it avoided the 'primeval curse on woman'. Similarly, the use of inoculations was opposed, with sermons preaching that diseases are 'sent by Providence' for the punishment of sin and it is wrong of man to escape from such divine retribution. Since even fundamentalist Christians ceased to regard the alleviation of pain and the curing of diseases as morally impermissible, it is hard to take this objection seriously. What was once seen as 'playing God' is now seen as acceptable medical practice. More importantly, the objection that sex selection is a violation of 'God's Law' is an explicit religious claim. As Western liberal democracies are based on a strict separation of state and church, no government is entitled to pass a law to enforce compliance with a specific religion. People who consider the option of sex selection as contrary to their religious belief are free to refrain from it, but they are not permitted to use the coercive power of the law to impose their theology upon all those who do not share their religious worldview.[8]

Some are opposed to sex selection because they have the feeling it is somehow 'unnatural'. Like the objection that choosing the sex of our children is playing God, the claim that sex selection is not natural most often expresses an intuitive reaction rather than a clearly reasoned moral response. That a particular human action is unnatural does in no way imply that it is morally wrong. To transplant a heart to save a human life is certainly unnatural, but is it for that reason immoral? Surely not! Thus, if we have to decide whether an action is morally right or wrong, we cannot settle the issue by asking whether it is natural or unnatural.

A more serious objection to sex selection is based on the claim that medical procedures ought to be employed for medical purposes only. Flow cytometric sperm separation, it is argued, is a medical technology designed to enable couples who are at risk of transmitting a severe sex-linked genetic disorder to have a healthy child. In the absence of a known risk to transmit a serious X-linked disease, there is simply no valid justification for employing flow cytometric sperm separation. This is a familiar objection in debates over novel applications of genetic and reproductive technologies. However, as familiar as it may be, it is certainly not a persuasive one. We have already become accustomed to a medical system in which physicians often provide services that have no direct medical benefit but that do have great personal value for the individuals seeking it. Given the acceptance of breast enlargements, hair replacements, ultrasound assisted liposuctions and other forms of cosmetic surgery, one cannot, without calling that system into question, condemn a practice merely because it uses a medical procedure for lifestyle or child-rearing choices.[9]

A related objection insists that offering a service for social sex selection constitutes an inappropriate use of limited medical resources. Again, if offering face-lifts is not considered to be a misallocation of scarce medical resources, it is

---

8 Dahl, E. (2003), 'Procreative Liberty: The Case for Preconception Sex Selection', *Reproductive BioMedicine Online* 7, 380–84.

9 Ethics Committee of the American Society for Reproductive Medicine (2001), 'Preconception Gender Selection for Nonmedical Reasons', *Fertility and Sterility* 75, 861–4.

hard to see how offering sex selection can be considered a misallocation of scarce medical resources. Moreover, by implying that every time a patient gets a nose-job another patient misses out on a bypass betrays a severely distorted conception of economics. If at all, this argument may apply to a state-run socialist economy based on a Five-Year Plan, but certainly not to a private-run capitalist economy based on a free market. Just as a chef opening up a fancy restaurant offering French cuisine does not deprive us of our daily bread, so a doctor opening up a fertility centre offering sex selection does not deprive us of our basic healthcare. Provided their businesses are set up privately and their services are paid for privately, they do not take away from anyone.

Perhaps the most powerful objection to sex selection is that it may distort the natural sex ratio and lead to a severe imbalance of the sexes, as has occurred in countries such as India, China, and Korea.[10] A surplus of men and a shortage of women, some sociologists have predicted, will invariably cause an enormous rise in enforced celibacy, homosexuality, polyandry, prostitution, molestation, rape and other sex-related crimes.[11] However, whether or not a drastic distortion of the natural sex ratio poses a real threat to Western societies is, of course, an empirical question that cannot be answered by mere intuition, but only by scientific evidence. For a severe sex ratio distortion to occur, at least two conditions have to be met. First, there must be a significant preference for children of a particular sex, and second there must be a considerable demand for sex selection services. The available empirical evidence suggests that neither condition is met in Western societies. According to representative social surveys conducted in Germany, the United Kingdom and the United States, the overwhelming majority of couples desires to have an equal number of boys and girls – usually two children, one boy and one girl.[12]

For instance, when asked 'If given a choice, would you like to have only boys, only girls, more boys than girls, more girls than boys, or an equal number of boys and girls?', 1 per cent of Germans stated that they would prefer to have only boys, 1 per cent only girls, 4 per cent more boys than girls, 3 per cent more girls than boys, 30 per cent as many boys as girls, and 58 per cent said they had no preference

---

10 Mudur, G. (2002), 'India Plans New Legislation to Prevent Sex Selection', *British Medical Journal* 324, 385; Chan, C.A.W., et al. (2002), 'Gender Selection in China: Its Meanings and Implications', *Journal of Assisted Reproduction and Genetics* 19, 426–30; Sen, A. (2003), 'Missing Women – Revisited', *British Medical Journal* 327, 1297–8; Hudson, V.M. and den Boer, A.M. (2004), *Bare Branches: The Security Implications of Asia's Surplus Male Population* (Cambridge: MIT Press).

11 Etzioni, A. (1968), 'Sex Control, Science, and Society', *Science* 161, 1107–12; Guttentag, M. and Secord, P.F. (1983), *Too Many Women? The Sex Ratio Question* (Beverley Hills: Sage Publications); Warren, M.A. (1985), *Gendercide: The Implications of Sex Selection* (Totowa: Rowman & Allanheld); Singer, P. and Wells, D. (1985), *The Reproduction Revolution: New Ways of Making Babies* (Oxford: Oxford University Press); Vines, G. (1993), 'The Hidden Costs of Sex Selection', *New Scientist*, 1 May; Bailey, R. (2004), 'Sexing Babies: Will Sex Selection Create a Violent World Without Women?' *Reason Magazine*, 6 October.

12 Dahl, E. (2005), 'Preconception Sex Selection: A Threat to the Sex Ratio?' *Reproductive BioMedicine Online* March 10: Suppl. 1,116–18.

whatsoever.[13] Similarly, in the UK 3 per cent preferred only boys, 2 per cent only girls, 6 per cent more boys than girls, 4 per cent more girls than boys, 68 per cent an equal number of boys and girls, and 16 per cent did not care about the sex of their future children.[14] And, finally, in the US 5 per cent preferred only boys, 4 per cent only girls, 7 per cent more boys than girls, 6 per cent more girls than boys, 50 per cent the same number of boys and girls, and 27 per cent simply did not mind the sex of their offspring.[15]

As we know all too well, there is often a yawning gap between what people say and what they actually do. However, demographic research does indeed confirm the stated preference for a so-called 'gender balanced family'. Couples with two boys and couples with two girls are more likely to have a third child than couples with one boy and one girl – suggesting that parents with children of both sexes are much more content with their family composition. This distinct trend towards a balanced family has not only been observed in Germany, the UK and the US, but also in Canada, Italy, Spain, Sweden, Belgium, Austria, Switzerland and the Netherlands.[16]

Even more instructive than social surveys and demographic research are data collected by so-called gender clinics. Worldwide, there are already about 75 fertility centres that offer some method of sperm sorting followed by artificial insemination. According to the leading gender clinic, the MicroSort Unit of the Genetics and IVF Institute in Fairfax, Virginia, well over 90 per cent of couples seeking social sex selection are parents who already have two or three children of the same sex and long to have just one more child of the opposite sex.[17]

In conclusion, the widespread fear of a sex ratio distortion seems to be unjustified. The existing empirical evidence suggests that a readily available service for preconception sex selection will have only a negligible societal impact and is highly unlikely to cause a severe imbalance of the sexes in Western societies.

Although the threat of a sex ratio distortion is potentially the most troubling problem, it is also a problem that is easily resolved – namely by limiting the service for sex selection to the purpose of 'family balancing'. If access to sex selection were restricted to parents having at least two children of the same sex, then helping them to have a child of the opposite sex would, if at all, only marginally alter the balance of the sexes.[18]

---

13 Dahl, E., et al. (2003), 'Preconception Sex Selection for Non-Medical Reasons: A Representative Survey from Germany', *Human Reproduction* 18, 2231–4.

14 Dahl, E., et al. (2003), 'Preconception Sex Selection for Non-Medical Reasons: A Representative Survey from the United Kingdom', *Human Reproduction* 18, 2238–9.

15 Dahl, E. and Brosig, B. (2006), 'Preconception Sex Selection Demand and Preferences in the United States', *Fertility and Sterility* Volume 85, 2, 468–473.

16 Hank, C. and Kohler, H-P. (2000), 'Gender Preferences for Children in Europe: Empirical Results from 17 Countries', *Demographic Research* 2, 1–21.

17 Fugger, E.F., et al. (1998), 'Birth of Normal Daughters After MicroSort Sperm Separation and Intrauterine Insemination, In-Vitro-Fertilization, or Intracytoplasmic Sperm Injection', *Human Reproduction* 13, 2367–70.

18 Pennings, G. (1996), 'Family Balancing as a Morally Acceptable Application of Sex Selection', *Human Reproduction* 11, 2339–45.

Another frequently advanced objection claims that sex selection is 'inherently sexist'. For example, the feminist philosopher Tabitha Powledge argues that, 'we should not choose the sexes of our children because to do so is one of the most stupendously sexist acts in which it is possible to engage. It is the original sexist sin.' Sex selection, she continues, is deeply wrong because it makes 'the most basic judgment about the worth of a human being rest first and foremost on its sex'.[19] However, this argument is deeply flawed. It is simply false that all people who would like to choose the sex of their children are motivated by the sexist belief that one sex is more valuable than the other. As we have seen, almost all couples seeking sex selection are simply motivated by the desire to have at least one child of each sex. If this desire is based on any beliefs at all, it is based on the quite defensible assumption that raising a girl is different from raising a boy, but certainly not on the belief that one sex is 'superior' to the other.

A further common objection concerns the welfare of children born as a result of sex selection. Thus, it has been argued that sex-selected children may be expected to behave in certain gender-specific ways and risk being resented if they fail to do so.[20] Although it cannot be completely ruled out, it is highly unlikely that children conceived after MicroSort® are going to suffer from unreasonable parental expectations. Couples seeking sex selection to ensure the birth of a daughter are very well aware that they can expect a girl, not some Julia Roberts; and couples going for a son know perfectly well that they can expect a boy, not some Hugh Grant.

Last but not least, there is the widely popular objection that sex selection is the first step down a road that will inevitably lead to the creation of 'designer babies'. Once we allow parents to choose the sex of their children, we will soon find ourselves allowing them to choose their eye colour, their height, or their intelligence. This slippery slope objection calls for three remarks. First, it is not an argument against sex selection, but only against its alleged consequences. Second, and more importantly, it is based on the assumption that we are simply incapable of preventing the alleged consequences from happening. However, this view is utterly untenable. It is perfectly possible to draw a legal line permitting some forms of selection and prohibiting others. Thus, if selection for sex is morally acceptable but selection for, say, intelligence is not, the former can be allowed and the latter not. And third, the slippery slope argument presumes that sliding down the slope is going to have detrimental, if not devastating, social effects. However, in the case of selecting offspring traits, this is far from obvious. What is so terrifying about the idea that some parents may be foolish enough to spend their hard-earned money on genetic technologies just to ensure that their child will be born with big brown eyes and black curly hair? I am sorry, but I cannot see that this would herald the end of civilization as we know it.

---

19 Powledge, T. (1981), 'Unnatural Selection: On Choosing Children's Sex', in Holmes, H.B. and Hoskins, B.B. (eds), *The Custom-Made-Child: Women-Centred Perspectives* (New Jersey: Humana Press) 193–9.

20 Davis, D.S. (2001), *Genetic Dilemmas: Reproductive Technology, Parental Choices, and Children's Futures* (New York: Routledge).

Since it cannot be established that preconception sex selection would cause any serious harm to others, a legal ban is ethically unjustified. However, that sex selection ought not to be prohibited does not preclude regulating its practice. For example, to limit sex selection services to licensed centres subject to monitoring by health authorities seems entirely appropriate. This would not only guarantee high scientific standards and high quality professional care, but it would also enable detailed research on possible demographic consequences and thus allow action if – contrary to expectations – significant imbalances were to develop.

Chapter 6

Bad Science Equals Poor, Not Necessarily Bad, Ethics

David Hunter

Abstract

In this chapter I discuss the often made claim that 'bad science is bad ethics'. This claim is typically used by Research Ethics Committees to justify rejecting scientifically problematic research projects on ethical grounds. However, I will show that while a piece of research being scientifically poor does make it ethically problematic, this is not always good grounds for an ethics committee to reject it. In particular I will draw a distinction between morally bad and morally poor research and argue that the role of an ethics committee is to enforce morally satisfactory behaviour and encourage morally excellent behaviour. This being the case, I claim that ethics committees ought to reject morally bad research, but not reject morally poor research.

Introduction

One of the implicit roles of Research Ethics Committees (RECS) both in the National Health Service (NHS) and in the university sector is to ensure high-quality science. While this role is not explicit, it is implied by the requirements for research projects to receive a satisfactory independent peer review before being seen by an NHS research ethics committee.[1] Likewise the Economic and Social Science Research Council's (ESRC) Research Ethics Framework also indicates this.[2]

Presently in the UK, ethics committees are not considered to have an explicit remit to provide a scientific review of applications. NHS Research Ethics Committees specifically are not supposed to base their judgement on the basis of the scientific quality of an application but solely to focus on ethical issues:

---

1 Department of Health (2001), *Governance Arrangements for NHS Research Ethics Committees*, July, 23. Accessed on 11 December 2006 at: http://www.dh.gov.uk/assetRoot/04/05/86/09/04058609.pdf.

2 Economic and Social Science Research Council (2005), *Research Ethics Framework*, available at: http://www.esrc.ac.uk/ESRCInfoCentre/Images/ESRC_Re_Ethics_Frame_tcm6-11291.pdf.

The Research Governance Framework makes it clear that the sponsor is responsible for ensuring the quality of the science.

Thus, protocols submitted for ethical review should already have had prior critique by experts in the relevant research methodology, who should also comment on the originality of the research. It is not the task of an REC to undertake additional scientific review, nor is it constituted to do so, but it should satisfy itself that the review already undertaken is adequate for the nature of the proposal under consideration.[3]

There are two principal reasons for RECs not having this remit. First, these applications should have received scientific review elsewhere, so this would be a case of double handling. Secondly, ethics committees are not well constituted to performing scientific review; they are, for example, unlikely to have more than one or two members familiar with the particular research methods and paradigms of a specific piece of research. This often makes it inappropriate for an ethics committee to make scientific comment, as they do not have the requisite expertise. Indeed it has been argued that, with the increasing amounts of social science research in the NHS and the use of research methodologies such as qualitative research, ethics committee membership needs to be adjusted to include expertise within this research paradigm.[4] Some ethics committees deal with this by providing ethical requirements, but only making suggestions with regard to the relevant science.

Nonetheless there is a principle which is often used to bridge the gap between scientific review and ethical review. This principle is that bad science is bad ethics; in other words that there is something morally wrong about carrying out bad science.[5] This sort of view is expressed by Angus Dawson and Steven Yentis in their forthcoming paper 'Contesting the Science/Ethics Distinction in the Review of Clinical Research'.[6] While I agree that there *are* cases where to allow certain bad science to go ahead would be morally objectionable, I do not think that these examples show that ethics committees should *always* rule against research which they construe as bad science.

For the purposes of this chapter, bad science is research which is methodologically unsound. By this I mean that there is a fundamental flaw in the design, that is, the research cannot answer the question it intends to answer. That said, it should be recognised that bad science comes in many guises and degrees; for example,

---

3 Department of Health (2001), *Governance Arrangements for NHS Research Ethics Committees*, July, 23–4. Accessed on 11 December 2006 at: http://www.dh.gov.uk/assetRoot/04/05/86/09/04058609.pdf.

4 Dawson, A. (2006), 'A Messy Business: Qualitative Research and Ethical Review', *Clinical Ethics* 1:2, 114–16; Ramcharan, P. and Cutcliffe, J.R. (2001), 'Judging the Ethics of Qualitative Research: Considering the "Ethics as Process" Model', *Health Social Care Community* November, 9:6, 358–66.

5 Department of Health (2005), *Research Governance Framework for Health and Social Care* 13. Accessed on 11 December 2006 at: http://www.dh.gov.uk/assetRoot/04/12/24/27/04122427.pdf.

6 Dawson, A. and Yentis, S. (forthcoming), 'Contesting the Science/Ethics Distinction in the Review of Clinical Research', *Journal of Medical Ethics*.

perfectly sound questionnaires can be used to carry out bad science if the participant selection is biased, or if too much is claimed from the results.

Bad science with human participants (or animals) is clearly ethically problematic; it imposes costs and potentially risks on the participants without much likelihood of any benefit. While it is unquestionable that doing research which is bad science is not morally excellent, it might be questioned whether ethics committees are obliged to enforce moral excellence or merely a moral minimum.

A distinction is commonly drawn between moral obligation and moral excellence.[7] While this distinction is hotly debated in some circles, and arguably rejected by at least one major theory of ethics (consequentialism), it is usual to recognise a difference between what we ought to do and what is superogatory, that is, those things we could do, which it would be better to do, but which are not morally obligatory.[8] The reasoning behind this distinction is straightforward; there are many things we could do which would be good, but to require people to do these things would be very burdensome (for example, giving most of our money to charity, spending our days patrolling the streets to help little old ladies cross the road, and so on).[9]

The corollary of this is that there are at least two sorts of moral wrongs: (i) actions that it is morally obligatory to avoid, and (ii) actions which it would be morally better but are not obligatory to avoid. In the title of this chapter I have deemed this distinction as one between morally bad and morally poor. This distinction is not discussed much in the literature but is a natural outcome of making the distinction between acts which are morally obligatory and those which are superogatory.[10]

Once this distinction is made, then it is clear that establishing that bad science is morally objectionable is not sufficient to show us that Research Ethics Committees should always reject research which is bad science. Instead two further questions need to be addressed: (1) Whether scientifically bad research is morally bad or simply morally poor? (2) What is the role of the Research Ethics Committee, and whether in particular it is required to enforce a standard of moral excellence or a moral minimum?

---

7 Rachels, J. (2000), *The Elements of Moral Philosophy* (New York: McGraw Hill College Division).

8 Hershenov, D.B.A. (2002), 'Puzzle about the Demands of Morality', *Philosophical Studies* February, 107(3), 275–89.

9 I am not suggesting that a modicum of these sorts of activities is not morally obligatory, just that doing these activities full time, even though that may produce overall the greatest amount of good, is not obligatory.

10 Since on a plausible account of ethics, it cannot be morally bad to fail to do superogatory acts, but it may be morally poor. The distinction drawn here is similar to that drawn between the minimally decent Samaritan and the good Samaritan in Judith Jarvis Thomson's famous 1971 article, 'A Defense of Abortion', *Philosophy and Public Affairs* 1:1, 47–66.

Is Scientifically Bad Research Morally Bad or Morally Poor?

Case 1

A researcher wishes to study whether a particular drug will aid diabetics. This drug imposes some significant risks of liver failure on the participants, but the researcher argues that the benefits outweigh these potential costs. Unfortunately, the study is over-ambitious and flawed, the researcher has little chance of achieving power within the time-frame of the available funding, the drug is contra-indicated against being used in combination with diabetes and the evidence presented to the committee that this may be of benefit to diabetics relies on flawed assumptions.[11] To add insult to injury, the placebo selected for use by the researcher is a sugar pill, with no consideration of either the issues involved in giving diabetics sugar pills or how this is likely to remove the blindness of the trial.[12]

Case 2

A small-scale questionnaire-based study is intended to be carried out to investigate people's preference for fizzy or non-fizzy drinks. Again it is unlikely that the research will achieve power, and this time the questionnaire design is flawed such that the answers to the questions being asked will not be useful to answer the overall research question.

In the first case it seems clear that the poor nature of the science of this study does mean that it is morally bad. This is because the participants are being put at serious risk, without any possibility of the research actually answering the set question.[13]

In contrast, the research in the second case, while not ideal, poses no serious risk of harm, despite being scientifically weak. Moreover, the cost to the participants in terms of time is minimal and the risks are no higher than getting cut by paper filling out the questionnaire.

Ruling out this research on the grounds of poor science seems obstentious and nit-picky. While one could not question that the research is ethically poor because of the poor science, it is a genuine question as to whether or not the research ought to be prevented because of this.

---

11 Power in this context is a statistical term: a piece of research has power if its results can be relied on as generalisable rather than just being a characteristic of this particular research population.

12 In a typical clinical trial the study is described as double blinded if neither the researcher nor the participants at the time know who is getting the placebo and who is getting the treatment. This is done to minimise the effects on the participants of psychological beliefs of the effectiveness of the new treatment, and to prevent the researcher from reporting results based on biased observations; Hunter, D. (2006), 'Placebos, and Moral Perils for Participants', *Research Ethics Review* 2:2, 71–2.

13 Obviously in practice the ethics committee here ought to ask for more evidence about the efficacy of the proposed treatment and require the study to be reformed to achieve power, rather than simply reject it.

This, however, leaves us with a puzzle; it seems that the answer to the question as to whether scientifically poor research is ethically bad or just ethically poor is an unresolved question. The answer depends on just how bad the science is when weighed against the likely costs, benefits and possible risks for the participants.

To explore this question, we must first explore why scientifically bad research might be morally objectionable.

Norms of Science

While science is commonly seen as objective and impartial, the process of science has certain built-in ethical norms.[14] In particular there is a commitment to both seeking the truth and not claiming anything beyond what the data can support.[15] Scientifically poor research will clearly violate the first commitment and, depending on how and if it is disseminated, may violate the second commitment as well. While this may be ethically objectionable, it may not yet tell us whether it is either ethically bad or ethically poor. I am inclined to think, though, that it is more likely to be merely poor than bad. There are two reasons for thinking this is the case. First, there is a spectrum of bad science which ranges from hopelessly poorly constructed projects, which could never answer the study question, to well-designed projects that either due to constraint in resources, such as finances, or constraint in scope, such as being part of a relatively short (one-year) research degree, are unlikely to enrol enough participants to achieve a properly powered study. It would seem that even if the first sort of scientifically bad research is seen as ethically bad, it is hard to see the second set as anything but merely ethically poor, and perhaps not even that. Secondly – and relatedly – there are often ways to improve the science of even scientifically valid projects significantly by various ethically dubious means, for example, making the information sheet less transparent in order to increase enrolment in the study or by designing studies as 'opt out' rather than as 'opt in'. If the commitment to the norms of science had great moral weight, such that failing in this commitment was ethically bad, then we might consider that attempts to increase the quality of the science might outweigh other ethical considerations and so should be allowed, even if they involve some unethical means. So while upholding the norms of science is important, some of the time its importance will be such that bad science is ethically bad, but in other cases it may merely be ethically poor.

Indirect Harms

Following on from the concern about the norms of science is a concern about the possible indirect harms of allowing bad science to proceed. These concerns are most prominent if the research is published or if a change in a treatment or in how healthcare professionals interact with their clients results because of the research. This is because

---

14 Macrina, F.L. (2005), *Scientific Integrity: Text and Cases in Responsible Conduct of Research* 3rd Edition (Washington DC: ASM Press).

15 Merton, R.K. (1938), 'Science and the Social Order', *Philosophy of Science* 5, 321–37.

the publication would be misleading and these changes are at least unwarranted and potentially harmful.[16] There are two things to be said here. First, not all or even much research turns out to be hugely influential; the chances of prominent publication are dependent on the results, something that an ethics committee is not well placed to judge. Furthermore researchers may well not be intending to publish their research in a formal way, for example, if it is part of a student research project. Secondly, even well-constructed, rigorous research can be abused by claiming conclusions not properly justified by the results.[17] Finally of course, Research Ethics Committees are not the final guardians against the publication of bad research. Journals themselves review research submissions with typically rigorous peer review processes and if there were any doubt about a submission's scientific integrity it ought to be rejected.[18] So again, while this seems morally problematic, it is not clear either that the Research Ethics Committees are well suited to deal with this problem, or whether, indeed, this is always going to be morally bad rather than merely morally poor.

Risks/Costs to Participants for No Gain

As well as indirect risks, there may of course be direct risks or costs to the research participants from being enrolled in research projects which involve bad science. This particular problem is twofold. First, much research involves some risk or cost for the participants. This is typically considered 'ethical' because the participants agree to take these risks and bear these costs, and because the costs are seen as outweighed preferably by benefits. Preferably the participants themselves will reap these benefits but, if not, then significant benefits to others may outweigh reasonably insignificant risks or costs for the participants.[19] Clearly if scientifically a project does not stack up, the risks/costs will still be present but the potential benefits will not. Secondly, additional risks or costs might be imposed on participants because of the poor science. For example, it may be possible to enrol far fewer research participants, or the research could be constructed or conducted in a different, less risky fashion. This is clearly morally objectionable and sometimes definitely morally bad. These include times when significant risks or costs are imposed on the research participants. Not all

---

16 Note though that the changes could still be beneficial as the researcher may have chanced upon a right answer despite not actually having evidence supporting the answer, and the present treatment may well be no more scientifically well supported than the new treatment and may do more harm than the new treatment or procedure.

17 Kohn, A. *Abusing Research*. Accessed on 11 December 2006 at: http://www.alfiekohn. org/teaching/research.htm.

18 This is not to say of course that this always occurs or that very important journals do not get it very wrong on occasion. We need look no further than the recent Korean stem cell scandal for a reminder of this: 'Disgraced Korean Cloning Scientist Indicted', *New York Times*, 12 May 2006; Council of Science Editors, *White Paper on Promoting Integrity in Scientific Journal Publications*. Accessed on 11 December 2006 at: http://www.councilscienceeditors. org/editorial_policies/whitepaper/entire_whitepaper.pdf.

19 Department of Health (2005), *Research Governance Framework for Health and Social Care* 8. Accessed on 11 December 2006 at: http://www.dh.gov.uk/ assetRoot/04/12/24/27/04122427.pdf.

research, however, will impose these sorts of serious risks or costs. For example, it is hard to see the serious risks or costs that an anonymous five-minute questionnaire about your preferences in terms of a particular fizzy drink is likely to impose, even if the study is poorly designed.[20] So while some of the time this is an excellent reason for ethics committees to reject a research proposal, (that is, when it is morally bad) at other times when no significant risks or harms are posed by the research, it will be merely morally poor, not bad.

Waste of Resources

Finally, bad science could be considered morally objectionable because it represents a waste of scarce resources that could be better used elsewhere. Many resources are used in the process of research: finances, tissue samples, willing participants and so on. In each case the resources used are scarce.[21] Clearly, the waste of millions of pounds' worth of funding in a particular badly designed research project would be morally bad. In contrast, it would seem that a smaller-scale waste of resources, such as what might occur in a badly designed student project, while still morally objectionable, would only be morally poor.

So we have established two things. First, bad science is morally objectionable. Secondly, bad science may be either morally bad or morally poor depending on the details of the case. As of yet this does not tell us what a research ethics committee ought to do, since we need to know whether an ethics committee ought to enforce moral excellence or simply moral satisfactoriness.

If a committee's role is to enforce moral excellence, then it ought to reject all research that is scientifically bad, since it is morally objectionable. If, on the other hand, its role is to enforce moral satisfactoriness, then it will reject those projects which are ethically bad, but allow those which are ethically poor.

Role of the Ethics Committee

It is common for frameworks to insist that committees work to the highest moral standards, in other words that they are enforcing moral excellence.[22]

However, there are reasons to be sceptical about whether this is what happens, or indeed whether it is what ought to happen.

1.   Many (even scientifically well-constructed) research projects are not morally excellent in every particular. There are two ways this occurs. First, there are commonly

---

20 I am not suggesting here that, as a class, questionnaire-based research is necessarily low risk. Clearly it would be possible to do very risky research in this manner, for example, on the experience of rape victims, on suicide or arguably on the identification of transplant recipients with their new organ.

21 Spilker, B. and Cramer, J.A. (1992), *Patient Recruitment in Clinical Trials* (New York: Raven Press).

22 Department of Health (2005), *Research Governance Framework for Health and Social Care* 2. Accessed on 11 December 2006 at: http://www.dh.gov.uk/assetRoot/04/12/24/27/04122427.pdf.

trade-offs between different ethical principles in the conduct of research. Secondly, it is often the case that, while the minimum requirements of these principles are lived up to, the highest ideals of these principles are rarely achieved.

With regard to the first concern, the trade-offs between different moral principles such as beneficence and non-maleficence, or autonomy and beneficence, become problematic because in the case of non-consequentialist accounts of moral excellence, it is hard to justify the claim that something is morally excellent if it involves trade-offs.[23] On consequentialist grounds 'moral excellence' would typically be simply bringing about the best outcome. On at least some other views, there is something regrettable about having to trade off between principles. Though this is sometimes necessary, 'moral excellence' would involve respecting all of the important moral principles.

With regard to the second concern, research projects often only minimally satisfy moral principles such as those important in Beauchamp and Childress's four-principles approach: autonomy, beneficence, non-maleficence and justice.[24]

One example of this would be justice. Many international guidelines suggest, in regards to the provision of post-trial care, that it would be best if this was provided but it is not required.[25] It seems clearly the case that the provision of post-trial care would be morally best. Thus when post-trial care is not provided, it is possibly morally acceptable but still far less than morally excellent.

Likewise, in the UK, the NHS presently refuses to provide insurance or guarantees for non-negligent harm which results from being involved in research.[26] One might think that if this were provided, both in terms of justice and non-maleficence, this would be at least better, if not, perhaps, obligatory.

If we were to insist on moral excellence, these research projects, along with those that are scientifically poor, ought to be rejected by ethics committees. In other words, moral excellence is too high a standard to which research should be held.[27]

---

23 Beauchamp, T.L. and Childress, J.F. (2001), *Principles of Biomedical Ethics* 5th ed. (New York: Oxford University Press).

24 Ibid.

25 Post-trial care in this context means providing for the healthcare needs of research participants and, particularly if the tested treatment is effective, providing the treatment for the research participants in both the active and the control arms of the study; Nuffield Council on Bioethics (2002), *The Ethics of Research Related to Healthcare in Developing Countries*. Accessed on 11 December 2006 at: www.nuffieldbioethics.org/fileLibrary/pdf/errhdc_fullreport001.pdf.

26 NHS R&D Forum, Primary Care Working Party (2005), *Indemnity Arrangements within Primary Care – Who is Responsible for What?* January. Accessed on 11 December 2006 at: http://www.rdforum.nhs.uk/workgroups/primary/indemnity_arrangements.doc.

27 It might be said that my argument relies on a false dichotomy between moral excellence and a much more relaxed account of moral satisfactoriness. We could alternatively hold research to a high, but not excellent, moral standard. I think this is fair point; however, as soon as we move from an account based on moral excellence, then some morally poor research, perhaps less than according to my account, will be permissible.

2.   As political theorists and ethicists are now well aware, we face a difficulty in getting any particular theory accepted and adopted on a national level. This is the problem of moral pluralism, namely that few countries' citizens share one moral theory and point of view. In contrast, in most countries there is a plurality of alternative and contradictory moral standpoints adopted by members of that country.[28] As such most present political theories aim to be supportable by several broad moral standpoints. Typically they aim to achieve consensus between different potentially opposing viewpoints. In the context of research ethics and identifying moral excellence, there is a similar problem. Unless we adopt just one moral theory, giving an account of moral excellence seems problematic since, almost definitionally, what one theory claims is morally excellent, other theories will not consider morally excellent and may well consider morally problematic.

But adopting one moral theory seems hard to justify given the fact of moral pluralism.

In contrast, achieving consensus between different ethical theories on what might be considered morally satisfactory is much easier (though of course still difficult). Plausible moral theories tend to converge on what ought to be definitely avoided, because otherwise they will tend to be rejected.[29]

In other words, viable moral norms in a pluralist society require consensus, and consensus is much easier to achieve in terms of morally bad issues than in terms of which issues are merely morally poor.

3.   In general we avoid legally enforcing moral excellence and often even morally satisfactoriness. Take, for example, a famous case, the Kitty Genovese case. Kitty Genovese was murdered while 38 individuals heard or saw suspicious events taking place.[30] Of those 38 people, none aided Kitty, nor did they even contact the authorities. Nonetheless legally, they did nothing wrong. What seems particularly outrageous about this example was that they did not even take the minimally inconvenient step of contacting the authorities. In most legal constituencies, there are only minimal legal duties to aid, despite it being morally excellent to intervene and aid in these situations.[31]

While many practices may be seen as morally objectionable, such as being rude, lying, and so on, only a few morally objectionable actions are seen as serious enough to warrant criminal proceedings. In other words, typically in law, only those morally objectionable actions that might be seen as morally bad are legislated against.[32]

---

28 Rawls, J. (1996), *Political Liberalism* (New York: Columbia University); Crowder, G. (2002), *Liberalism and Value Pluralism* (New York: Continuum).

29 Rachels, J. (2000), *The Elements of Moral Philosophy* (New York: McGraw Hill College Division).

30 Thomson, J.J. (1971), 'A Defense of Abortion', *Philosophy and Public Affairs* 1:1, 47–66.

31 Ratcliffe, J.M. (ed.) (1966), *The Good Samaritan and the Law*, New York:Anchor Books.

32 This is, of course, only one account of the justifications for particular laws; another alternative popular view in legal philosophy is that laws are not based on enforcing morality at all, instead they are simply a means to allow us to live together peacefully. While I do not

So it would seem that it would be unusual for ethics committees to hold researchers to a standard of moral excellence. Likewise other professionals, while held to the high moral standards of their professions, are not held to a standard of moral excellence. Instead, again they are required to behave satisfactorily, not excellently.[33]

Conclusions

Committees ought to enforce moral satisfactoriness, but encourage moral excellence. This means that if the poor quality of the science of a particular project means that it is morally bad, then an ethics committee ought to reject it because it does not meet the criteria of moral satisfactoriness. If, however, a project is scientifically bad such that it is only morally poor, then the committee ought not to reject the project, at least on those grounds. However, they should suggest to the applicant that there are scientific deficiencies in their project in order to give the applicant the chance to avoid, on a voluntary basis, morally poor behaviour of which they may well not be aware.

---

hold this view myself, I also do not think that it is incompatible with my overall point, namely that ethics committees ought not to enforce moral excellence.

33 This may not be immediately obvious, but consider this example. Which of these two is more morally excellent? (1) The doctor who carries out his job competently and well. (2) The doctor who carries out her job competently and well, but does it only charging just enough so that she can live well enough to be able to carry out her job well, thus saving money for the healthcare system and allowing more money to be devoted to the provision of other healthcare. It seems, assuming *ceteris paribus*, clearly the second doctor is more morally excellent, and so if we expected doctors to be morally excellent, we would expect them to behave like the second doctor, which we clearly do not.

PART II
ETHICS AND SOCIETY

Chapter 7

Dignity and Older Europeans

Win Tadd

Introduction

Ethical issues involving older people have recently come to the fore. This is not surprising as ageing of the population is a universal phenomenon affecting both developed and developing countries. By 2020, the numbers of people aged 80 years and over in Europe is predicted to be between 6 and 8 per cent of the total[1] and by 2050, over 100 million people in Europe will be over 65 years of age, with those over 80 years rising to 48 million. Such demographic changes throw into dramatic relief a number of profound questions which affect all aspects of life at a variety of levels: individual; family; society; economics; medicine; health and social care. For example, what, if anything, do we owe older people as individuals or societies? How do we determine a just distribution of resources between the generations? How do we decide about life-sustaining treatments in old age? What authority should be placed on advance directives? What constitutes successful ageing or for that matter, a good death? How should we treat people with dementia? What value should be placed on quality of life? How should we conduct research with older people? How can we ensure that services for older people promote important moral values such as autonomy, dignity and respect?

Within the confines of this chapter, clearly it will not be possible to address all of these issues and therefore I wish to focus attention on the topic of dignity in the care of older people, drawing on research undertaken as part of an EU-funded project between 2002 and 2004.[2]

The right to, and the need for, dignity is frequently cited in policy documents relating to the health and social care of older people.[3] In the UK, the *NHS Plan* (DoH, 2000) uses the term on a number of occasions (Chapter 15 is entitled 'Dignity,

---

1 Butler, R.N. (1997), 'Population Aging in Health', *British Medical Journal* 315, 1082–4.

2 The Dignity and Older Europeans project (contract number QLG6-CT-2001-00888) was funded by the European Commission, DG Research, Directorate E: Biotechnology, Agriculture and Food, under FP5, Quality of Life Programme.

3 Department of Health (2000), *The NHS Plan* (London: HMSO); Department of Health (2001a), *National Service Framework for Older People* (London: HMSO); Department of Health (2001b), *Caring for Older People: A Nursing Priority* (London: HMSO); Department of Health (2006), *A New Ambition for Old Age* (London: HMSO); Brazinová, A., Janská, E. and Jurkovi, R. (2004), 'Implementation of Patients' Rights in the Slovak Republic', *Eubios Journal of Asian and International Bioethics* 14: 90–91; Ministry of Health and Social Affairs, Sweden (1997), *Health and Medical Services*.

security and independence in old age') and the *National Service Framework for Older People* explicitly mentions dignity in relation to person-centred care.[4] More recently, the UK national director for older people presented the next steps for the Framework in a report entitled *A New Ambition for Old Age*.[5] The report describes how some staff demonstrate deep-rooted negative attitudes and behaviours towards older people and it concludes that much more is to be done if all older people are to receive care which is humane and dignified. As a first step, the Department of Health has established a Dignity in Care initiative to ensure all older people are treated with dignity when using health and social care services. This initiative is intended to create a zero tolerance towards violations of dignity in any care setting.

A similar emphasis is placed on dignity in other European countries. For example, the government of the Slovak Republic adopted a *Charter of Patients' Rights*[6] which states that the 'right of patients are based on the right for human dignity, self-determination and autonomy' and in Sweden, the (1996) Health Act[7] states that 'Care shall be given with respect for the equal value of all human beings and for the dignity of the individual'.

Dignity is also expressed as an important value in professional codes[8] and declarations of human rights.[9] Yet concerns about the standards of care for older people abound.[10] Although many older people are able to pursue their interests through better education and financial and physical well-being, for others the last years of life are devastated by chronic illness, disability or dementia, increased dependence and a reduced quality of life. A major issue therefore for many European societies is how to ensure that older people can live out their days with dignity.

Why dignity, one might ask? There is some evidence to suggest that positive health and social outcomes result when people feel more valued and respected; are involved in care decisions; maintain a positive self-regard; and are able to exercise direction over their lives.[11] In circumstances where cure is not an option, it seems

---

4 Department of Health (2001a), op. cit.

5 Department of Health (2006), op. cit.

6 Brazinová, A., Janská, E. and Jurkovi, R. (2004), op. cit.

7 Health Act (1996), Stockholm: Law decided by the Riksdag, 786.

8 International Council of Nurses (2000), *Code of Ethics for Nurses* (Geneva: ICN); Nursing and Midwifery Council (2004), *Code of Professional Conduct* (London: Nursing and Midwifery Council).

9 United Nations (1948), *The Universal Declaration of Human Rights*, adopted and proclaimed by General Assembly resolution 217 A (111) of 10 December 1948 (Geneva: The Office of the High Commissioner for Human Rights); Council of Europe (1997), *Convention for the Protection of Human Rights and Dignity of the Human Being With Regard to the Application of Biology and Medicine: Convention on Human Rights and Medicine* (Strasbourg: European Treaty Series No. 164).

10 Baggott, R., Allsop, J. and Jones, K. (2004), *Speaking for Patients and Carers: Health Consumer Groups and the Policy Process* (Basingstoke: Palgrave) 270–71; Tadd, W. and Bayer, A. (2001), 'Dignity as Feature of Complaints by Elderly People', *Age and Ageing* 30, 40.

11 Kenny, T. (1990), 'Erosion of Individuality in Care of Elderly People in Hospital – an Alternative Approach', *Journal of Advanced Nursing* 15, 571–6; Bensink, G.W., Godbey,

even more appropriate that care with dignity should become the standard. If this is not the case, then it has serious implications for human well-being, as well as an economic cost, as distressed and dissatisfied relatives may vent their displeasure by initiating formal complaints which require costly investigation and resolution.[12] Further, once dignity is put on the back-burner, there is a danger that neglect and disregard will become the norm and staff morale will plummet, as they themselves are 'brutalised' by 'uncaring' systems.[13] Such consequences have been routinely uncovered in investigations into patient abuse.[14] All this suggests that the perception of patients as people possessing dignity is of the utmost importance in practice and considerations of dignity appear to be a central element in the provision of high quality care.

Dignity, however, is a complex concept that is difficult to define, and without clarification of what the concept entails, aspirations to recognise, respect and promote the dignity of individuals within the daily reality of care giving are not only subject to wide variation, they are also toothless and in danger of degenerating into mere slogans.[15] It is somewhat surprising therefore that relatively little research has been undertaken to explore the meaning of dignity, especially in the case of the most vulnerable populations for whom cure is not possible. Some analysis of the concept and its importance for nursing has been undertaken[16] but systematic evidence as to how those providing care for older people see dignity, or how they promote dignified

K.L., Marshall, M.J. and Yarandi, H.N. (1992), 'Institutionalized Elderly: Relaxation, Locus of Control, Self-esteem', *Journal of Gerontological Nursing* 18, 30–38; Brillhart, B. and Johnson, K. (1997), 'Motivation and the Coping Process of Adults with Disabilities: A Qualitative Study', *Rehabilitation Nursing* 22, 249–52; 255–6; Ranzijn, R., Keeves, J., Luszcz, M. and Feather, N.T. (1998), 'The Role of Self-perceived Usefulness and Competence in the Self-esteem of Elderly Adults: Confirmatory Factor Analysis of the Bachman Revision of Rosenberg's Self-esteem Scale', *Journal of Gerontology: Psychological Sciences* 53B, 96–104; 'Dignity in Health Care: Reality or Rhetoric', *Reviews in Clinical Gerontology* 12, 4; Walsh, K. and Kowanko, I. (2002), 'Nurses' and Patients' Perceptions of Dignity', *International Journal of Nursing Practice* 8, 143–51.

12 Tadd, W., Dieppe, P. and Bayer, T. (2002), 'Dignity in Health Care: Reality or Rhetoric', *Reviews in Clinical Gerontology* 12, 1–4.

13 Health Advisory Service 2000 (1998), *Not Because They are Old* (London: HAS); Department of Health (2001b), op. cit; Tadd, W. and Bayer, A. (2001), op. cit.; Baggott, R., Allsop, J. and Jones, K. (2004), op. cit.

14 Commission for Health Improvement (2003), *Investigation into Matters Arising from Care on Rowan Ward*, Manchester Mental Health & Social Care Trust (London: HMSO).

15 Van Hooft, S., Gillam, L. and Byrnes, M. (1995), *Facts and Values: An Introduction to Critical Thinking for Nurses* (Sydney: Maclennan and Petty).

16 Pokorny, M.E. (1989), 'The Effects of Nursing Care on Human Dignity in the Critically Ill Adult', unpublished PhD thesis, University of Virginia; Söderberg, A., Gilje, F. and Norberg, A. (1997), 'Dignity in Situations of Ethical Difficulty in Intensive Care', *Intensive Critical Care Nursing* 13, 135–44; Shotton, L. and Seedhouse, D. (1998), 'Practical Dignity in Caring', *Nursing Ethics* 5:3, 246–55; Gallagher, A. and Seedhouse, D. (2002), 'Dignity in Care: The Views of Patients and Relatives', *Nursing Times* 98:43, 38–40; Haddock, J. (1996), 'Toward a Further Clarification of the Concept "Dignity"', *Journal of Advanced Nursing* 29, 924–31.

care, is limited.[17] Even in palliative care, which has a considerable literature on 'death with dignity', and where the goal is 'achievement of the best quality of life for patients and their families',[18] 'dignity remains a poorly defined and unexplored concept'.[19] This is despite the fact that requests for euthanasia and/or physician-assisted suicide are often rooted in concerns for the person's dignity.[20] Similarly, physicians often cite loss of dignity as a reason for acceding to patients' requests for assistance with suicide or for euthanasia.[21] Studies on dignity in palliative care have usually been small scale (with the exception of Chochinov's work) or they have relied on professionals' views of what constitutes dignified care or a dignified death.[22] The Dignity and Older Europeans (DOE) project sought to remedy some of these deficits.

---

17 Seedhouse, D. and Gallagher, A. (2002), 'Undignifying Institutions', *Journal of Medical Ethics* 28:6, 368–72; Woolhead, G., Calnan, M., Dieppe, P. and Tadd, W. (2004), 'Dignity in Older Age: What do Older People in the United Kingdom Think?' *Age and Ageing* 33, 165–70.

18 World Health Organization (1990), *Cancer Pain Relief and Palliative Care* (Geneva: WHO).

19 Enes, S.P.D. (2003), 'An Exploration of Dignity in Palliative Care', *Palliative Medicine* 17, 263–9.

20 Back, A.L., Wallace, J.I., Starks, H.E. and Pearlman, R.A. (1996), 'Physician Assisted Suicide and Euthanasia in Washington State: Patient Requests and Physician Responses', *Journal of the American Medical Association* 275, 919–25; Emanuel, E.J., Fairclough, D.L., Daniels, E.R. and Clarridge, B.R. (1996), 'Euthanasia and Physician Assisted Suicide: Attitudes and Experiences of Oncology Patients, Oncologists and the Public', *Lancet* 347, 1805–10; Van der Maas, P.J., Van Delden, J.J.M., Pijnenborg, L. and Looman, C.W.N. (1991), 'Euthanasia and Other Medical Decisions Concerning the End of Life', *Lancet* 338, 669–74; Van der Maas, P.J., Van der Wal, G., Haverkate, I., et al. (1996), 'Euthanasia, Physician Assisted Suicide and Other Medical Practices Involving the End of Life in the Netherlands 1990–1995', *New England Journal of Medicine* 335, 1699–1705; Meier, D.E., Emmons, C.A., Wallenstein, S., Quill, T., Morrison, R.S. and Cassel, C.K. (1998), 'A National Survey of Physician Assisted Suicide and Euthanasia in the United States', *New England Journal of Medicine* 338, 1193–1201; Kissane, D.W., Street, A. and Nitschke, P. (1998), 'Seven Deaths in Darwin: Case Studies under the Rights of the Terminally Ill Act, Northern Territory, Australia', *Lancet* 352, 1097–1102; Chin, A.E., Hedburg, K., Higgindon, G.K. and Fleming, D.W. (1999), 'Legalized Physician Assisted Suicide in Oregon – the First Year's Experience', *New England Journal of Medicine* 340:4, 577–83; Sullivan, A.D., Hedberg, K. and Fleming, D.W. (2000), 'Legalized Physician Assisted Suicide in Oregon – the Second Year', *New England Journal of Medicine* 342, 598–604; Ganzini, L., Nelson, H.D., Schmidt, T.A., Kraemer, D.F., Delorit, M.A. and Lee, M.A. (2000), 'Physicians' Experiences with the Oregon Death with Dignity Act', *New England Journal of Medicine* 342:8, 557–63.

21 Van der Maas, P.J., et al. (1991), op. cit.; Meier, D.E., et al. (1998), op. cit.; Ganzini, L., et al. (2000), op. cit.

22 Turner, K., Chye, R., Aggarwal, G., Philip, J., Skeels, A. and Lickiss, J.N. (1996), 'Dignity in Dying: A Preliminary Study of Patients in the Last Three Days of Life', *Journal of Palliative Care* 12:2, 7–13; Gamlin, R. (1998), 'An Exploration of the Meaning of Dignity in Palliative Care', *European Journal of Palliative Care* 5:6, 187–90; Street, A. and Kissane, D. (2000), 'Dispensing Death, Desiring Death: An Explanation of Medical Roles and Patient Motivation during the Period of Legalised Euthanasia in Australia', *Omega*:

Overview of the DOE Project

The study was cross-cultural, involving older people, health and social care professionals and young and middle-aged adults from the UK, Spain, Slovakia, Sweden, France and Ireland, and was multidisciplinary involving nurses, philosophers, sociologists, psychologists, clinicians, health service researchers and non-governmental organisations. It lasted three years, from 2002 to 2004, and was divided into three phases:

- Phase 1 involved a review of the philosophical and professional literature from which a model of human dignity was developed.
- Phase 2 involved the empirical elements where data from 265 focus groups involving 1320 participants in six European countries was qualitatively analysed.
- Phase 3 involved refinement of the model and development of the educational materials and policy and service recommendations for the care of older people in Europe.

Although a full account of the study is beyond the remit of this chapter, detailed versions of the methodology can be found in Calnan and Tadd;[23] of the philosophical model in Nordenfelt,[24] and Nordenfelt and Edgar;[25] and of the findings in Bayer, Tadd and Krajcik,[26] Arino-Blasco, Tadd and Boix-Ferrer,[27] and Stratton and Tadd.[28]

In this chapter, I would like to explore some of the findings that focus on healthcare for older people from the perspectives of older people and professionals, before considering some of the implications.

Journal of Death and Dying 40: 1, 229–246; Chochinov, H.M. (2002), 'Dignity-conserving Care: A New Model for Palliative Care – Helping the Patient Feel Valued', *Journal of the American Medical Association* 287:17, 2253–60; Chochinov, H.M., Hack, T., Hassard, T., Kristjanson, L.J., McClement, S. and Harlos, M. (2002a), 'Dignity in the Terminally Ill – a Cross-sectional Cohort Study', *The Lancet* 360, 2026–30; Chochinov, H.M., Hack, T., McClement, S., Kristjanson, L.J. and Harlos, M. (2002b), 'Dignity in the Terminally Ill: A Developing Empirical Model', *Social Science & Medicine* 54, 433–43; Enes, S.P.D. (2003), 'An Exploration of Dignity in Palliative Care', *Palliative Medicine* 17, 263–9.

23 Calnan, M. and Tadd, W. (2005), 'Dignity and Older Europeans: Methodology', *Quality in Ageing – Policy, Practice and Research* 6:1, 10–16.

24 Nordenfelt, L. (2004), 'The Varieties of Dignity', *Health Care Analysis* 12:2, 69–81; Nordenfelt, L. (2003), 'Dignity and the Care of the Elderly', *Medicine, Health and Philosophy* 6:2, 103–11.

25 Nordenfelt, L. and Edgar, A. (2005), 'Dignity and Older Europeans: The Four Notions of Dignity', *Quality in Ageing – Policy, Practice and Research* 6:1, 17–21.

26 Bayer, T., Tadd, W. and Krajcik, S. (2005), 'Dignity and Older Europeans: The Voice of Older People', *Quality in Ageing – Policy, Practice and Research* 6:1, 22–9.

27 Arino-Blasco, S., Tadd, W. and Boix-Ferrer, J.A. (2005), 'Dignity and Older Europeans: The Voice of Professionals', *Quality in Ageing – Policy, Practice and Research* 6:1, 3–36.

28 Stratton, D. and Tadd, W. (2005), 'Dignity and Older People: The Voice of Society', *Quality in Ageing: Policy, Practice and Research* 6:1, 37–45.

Older People's Views of Dignity in Care

A large proportion of the discussion among the focus groups with older participants in each country concerned dignity in care. Worryingly, most participants found it easier to speak of their experiences of indignity than of those where their dignity had been enhanced.

Family Care

Many types of care were discussed, including family care, acute care, long-term residential care and care at the end of life. Understandably the majority of participants preferred to be cared for by a loving family; however, for many this was not possible, either because their children had moved away or both partners had to work, leaving them unable to care for their ageing parents. Most participants decried this state of affairs, believing that European societies were both consumerist and individualistic, which resulted in many older people being reliant on external agencies for any care they required. For example:

> "What was the old mindset? Take care of your parents at home! The thing is that now young people have tons of work. And now a TV, now a car ... We used to do without anything!" (UK patient)

Some participants were 'shared' among their children, spending three months with one child and a similar period with another, or husbands and wives were separated with one going to one child and the other to another, while others recognised that there was no room for them.

> "When they pack you off from one home to the next ..."

> "That doesn't seem dignified, to go from one child's house to another in 'shifts'?"

> "No, not at all."

> "They make you feel like a ball. Like they were taking you in out of obligation." (Spain)

> "They would take me to stay in their flat if they could, but the children have a computer there and books and the flat is too small for the whole family." (Slovakia)

Older participants also recognised that governments need to do more to ease the economic and physical burdens for families who choose to care for their elderly relatives. When family care is not possible, nursing homes or some form of residential care are often the only alternatives. Most older participants wished to be involved in decisions to enter long-term care and many participants found the thought of being forced into residential care particularly abhorrent.

> "Now this person needs someone to care for them. What happens to people who don't have anyone?" 6.1: "Off to the nursing home."

"I think that a lot of people, at least 80%, when they find themselves like that, they'd prefer to be dead." (Spain)

"The prospect of being 'shoved' into a nursing home by family members and being 'forgotten' is still feared by some older people." (Ireland)

"One thing I have noticed here is that most people I know didn't come on their own decision. At one moment in their life, independent of their age and independent of being fit or not, ... it has been their family, their close relatives, their children who decided for them." (France)

Dependence and Independence

A major concern of all the participants was loss of independence which, together with increasing dependence, was one of the harder adjustments they faced.

"I am healthy for my age. I pray not to be dependent. I have pity for all who must rely on the help of other people. I pray for sanity." (Slovakia)

"I don't mind dying but ... I'm terrified of getting in the situation where I can't look after myself." (UK)

Whether because of physical or mental impairment, dependence was viewed as being utterly humiliating and in all centres participants expressed a fear of becoming a burden on either their families, or the state, as they found this prospect shameful. Participants also acknowledged that there were degrees of dependence, which affect a person's experience of dignity. When disability or frailty was such that intimate care would be necessary for the rest of one's life, then dignity was difficult to maintain. For this reason the attitude of older people towards increasing dependence and infirmity was important. If people remained positive regardless of their disability, then participants claimed they could better retain their dignity.

"When I've lost my faculties I would rather die. Because I should not be a burden for society, and certainly not a nuisance for my family." (Spain)

Attitudes of Carers

Such feelings could also be either ameliorated or exaggerated by the attitudes of family members and carers. When negative attitudes were displayed, feelings of uselessness and lack of value were heightened.

"Well they hounded me enough. Not now ... well they probably will pop up again some time but you just feel you are a burden. I felt a complete burden, that I should stay in hospital forever or just fade away ... that my useful days were over, it was condescending, patronising." (France)

Some participants believed that when care-givers demonstrated positive attitudes towards dependent old people, this was an expression of the regard in which they were held, in other words, a concrete demonstration of value.

"... When you feel that they treat you with loving care, affection, attention, gentleness, it makes you feel good. It makes you feel like a human being." (Spain)

"The nursing staff up here work very, very hard. They do. But I always find time to talk to them or they to me and they have always treated me with dignity, it didn't matter whether they were just passing, you were acknowledged and you were treated like the person you are". (Ireland)

Long-term Care

Although participants did not relish the thought of long-term residential care, most acknowledged that for many people there was no alternative. However, recognition, by staff and relatives, of the impact that such a move could have on an older person's experience of dignity was vital. Some participants from residential care spoke of the growing isolation they experienced and how even after accepting and adapting to changes in their lives, they were acutely aware of just how different their circumstances were. Long-term care frequently meant owning little, being away from friends, losing autonomy and the ability to control very ordinary aspects of daily life, all of which affected their experience of dignity.

"I think that's the thing about going into a home isn't it? You can't do what you want ... Set times for meals and at 6'o'clock would you like to be told 'Get out of bed now, come on because we haven't got time!'" (UK)

Another major concern was that once they entered formal care situations, they would cease to be treated as individuals and would simply become invisible.

"The old people now are invisible." 11.44: "They have no time for you, once you get old you're finished." (Ireland)

"It is hard to change or adapt. You are away from your home. Your friends are gone. That is what I find hard. I can't get out or move about. The visitors get fewer the longer you are away." (France)

"Because they are places where they park them like cars. They park them and leave them there, parked." (Spain)

When people had no relatives, they felt even more vulnerable in long-term care as they had no one to advocate for them. This was seen as a major disadvantage.

"That you don't dare express your fears or worries, that you'd like to know more about your illness, or whatever. Then no they don't treat people with dignity there, because the person can't act on all his needs, at that time. A person who isn't allowed to act on his feelings and hopes, and with the difficulties he has at that time, isn't acting as a person." (Spain)

"It has to be someone who ... by your side, who says things clearly, a relative or someone..." 12.1: "... but as long as he [her brother] was vigorous, and he could check up things and talk to the personnel, my sister-in-law had it much better than she had after he passed away." (Sweden)

Most participants recognised that entry into long-term care often followed a diagnosis of dementia and this was a particular worry for many older people.

"Alzheimer's takes away your self-worth and independence and you get no respect from others. I guess it's inevitable you lose all your dignity." (Slovakia)

"If you should end up like a cabbage, you're deprived of all dignity and all self-respect and ... that must be the worst possible experience – I hope I die before I get there." (Spain)

"If I have no self-consciousness any more, if I can't understand, I'm not living any more. This is a terrible situation, not being able to act appropriately." (Ireland)

Involvement in Decision-making

Whenever possible, older participants wanted to retain some control over decisions about their care.

"It's not very dignified if young people come along and say you shouldn't do this and you shouldn't do that. I mean they should give us the dignity of making our decisions while we are able to do so." (Ireland)

The choices older people made about their care were thought to be directly related to the amount of information made available to them.

"We weren't asked or told anything, we were just told to get out of bed." (Ireland)

"I'm one of those who don't want anything hidden from me. Let me say it another way: I have cancer. I've had cancer surgery, and I knew it before anyone else. Because I opened the letter. I didn't want them to hide anything from me." (Spain)

"And then I also noticed letters would arrive from authorities and decisions had been taken concerning me without me taking part. Who is representing me, acting in my place – who am I?" (Sweden)

Access to Care

Older participants believed that access to care was unjustly distributed and that ageism was rife within health and social care. In relation to long-term care, the fact that in many countries older people were expected to pay for care was particularly distressing. Participants complained that the lack of equity was evidence of how they were marginalised and devalued by society. They also claimed that acute care for older people was given a much lower priority than care for other sectors of society, which again emphasised the lower value placed on older people and damaged their experience of dignity.

"Society seems to want you to become helpless. If you need a knee replacement or a hip replacement that would improve your quality of life and make you a younger older person if you like, but you are at the bottom of that list … they just leave them to get worse and worse." (UK)

It was also claimed that general practitioners or community physicians denied older people access to sophisticated medical treatment and they recounted their experience of being asked, "What do you expect at your age?" when complaining of symptoms. This was not what participants wanted to hear. They wanted their conditions to be taken seriously.

Dignified Care

The attitude of staff was an essential ingredient of dignified care. By demonstrating the importance and value placed on older people, staff instill will and hope and enhance both the dignity of the person and that of the staff member. Kindness, politeness and a willingness to listen were qualities that older participants cherished in professionals. Ensuring privacy, asking permission to perform examinations and providing information and physical contact were also important in respecting dignity.

"And they touch you. Physical contact is very important. That person becomes closer through physical contact. A bond is established." (France)

Undignified Care

Most participants gave many examples of how they, or someone close to them, had been the recipient of undignified care. Often this was a result of insufficient staffing or other resources, so that old people ended up being 'warehoused' in overcrowded facilities where personalised care was impossible.

"And you see again at night, they're short staffed in these nursing homes and she has been told, 'Wet the bed, it's easier to change the bed than get the hoist.'"

"Well I've heard that."

"That's disgraceful isn't it?"

"This is where the pads come in, isn't it? It is easier to put pads and pants on people than to go and take them to the toilet."

"She was told that."

"So people become incontinent when actually they needn't be."

"What they have done now is catheterise her to save the hoisting, which again is wrong, isn't it?"

"Because at least when they are hoisted they are moved ... you see the pressure is taken off. But if they have a catheter in, they don't move them. They sit in a chair or they lie in a bed and they don't move." (UK)

Block treatments such as being told when to use the toilet and rough treatment sometimes bordering on physical abuse were examples of care that deny the individual dignity.

"I've seen caregivers who didn't treat certain people in a dignified manner. Once one came in with a list to check who had to go to the toilet. People don't have to go to the toilet by list. They have to go when they need to. Someone asked her to take them. She looked at the list and said, 'It's not your turn.' How do you like that? Does that person have dignity or not? That's not treating someone with dignity." (Spain)

"I spend my nights crying. If you saw my arms. Three nights ago ... They took me and my arms hurt and they do everything to me ... 'Turn around,' (order given in an impatient tone), like an animal. You can't turn around, you can hardly move." (Slovakia)

Many participants recognised that, although some staff displayed poor attitudes and shouted and swore at older people, or ignored their requests to use the toilet and such like, often it was the impoverished environments that made it difficult for carers to treat them in a dignified manner.

"Here I see, as far as dignity's concerned, that there's a lack of staff to care for the needs that exist." (Spain)

"They mashed her tablets up in part of her dinner like they do to the dog you know. I mean that, that's not on is it, it's just not on. That's the most undignified thing I've ever seen" (UK)

Lack of privacy, resulting in embarrassment, shame and humiliation, diminished the dignity of many participants. Washing, dressing, using the toilet, were all cited as examples of care that should be undertaken privately. Mixed sex wards and shared rooms were disliked and older women particularly hated having intimate aspects of personal care performed by male carers.

For many participants, one of the worst experiences involved being treated as an object, as, for instance, when nurses or doctors performed interventions and totally ignored the person's existence.

"I went into this particular specialist and he had an assistant, instead of talking to me, he was writing all the time, I could have been an elephant. He said 'Take her in there and tell her to strip down' and I just said, 'Am I invisible?'" (Ireland)

For others, unthinking and uncaring health professionals left people feeling shameful. Exposing parts of the body when being hoisted out of bed was a commonly cited example of how dignity is compromised on a daily basis.

"I don't know about that when I was in Hospital X, I felt very embarrassed on the hoist and I used to say 'can I cover myself up' and they just pulled your nightie down over you but the back view was wide open to anybody ... well when I say anybody, like the male nurse would help you and I was so embarrassed about that." (UK)

Disrespectful communication practices were also frequently cited, especially the manner in which older people were addressed. The majority of participants disliked being called by their first names or by pet names such as 'dear' or 'love', which were even more humiliating and patronising.

> "He was one of those sorts of dignified man, marvellous mind and he had to go into hospital towards the end of his life and he did tell me when I went in to see him once, he couldn't stand this business of 'Come on love', you know this sort of carry on ... that just wasn't his language." (Ireland)

> "Why don't patients complain? First of all they don't want to be thought stuffy. But also patients recognise their vulnerability, and will bend over backwards not to offend the people in whose hands they find themselves. This fact is documented. When asked to give thought to issues of dignity and psychosocial matters you may think title is a minor expression of dignity, but it is perhaps one of the few left to people struggling to maintain that dignity in the face of paralysis or incontinence." (UK)

Using first names as a matter of course was seen as a sign of disrespect and inappropriate in the healthcare setting. Most participants believed the use of first names signified a close relationship, which they did not have with the majority of health professionals, although some participants who were in long-term care preferred being called by their first names, a fact which seems to reinforce the significance of relationship. For most of the participants, the practice of routinely calling people by their first names emphasised the inequality in professional/client relationships and reinforced their helplessness by making them feel like children. The majority felt it would be a mark of some respect to at least ask about the preferred mode of address as this affords choice, rather than assuming that people do not mind how they are referred to.

In addition to being ignored, other examples of denigrating communication practices included being spoken to as if one was deaf or stupid and being patronised by being spoken to as a child might be.

> "There is another kind of not respecting dignity, that isn't as severe, in little details ... Like laughing at someone when they've said the wrong word, because when we get older we drift from one subject to another." (Spain)

> "I'm thinking of a patient who had difficulty in walking and was always sitting in a wheelchair when we went down to the city to buy new clothes. Especially when we were buying clothes ... the shop assistant addressed me, over her head!" (Sweden)

Undignified care emphasised the vulnerability of older people, often by stressing the unequal power relations between health professionals, especially doctors, and patients. Older participants felt particularly vulnerable in such situations due to their reluctance to complain for fear of retribution in the form of poor care. One of the most significant ways in which such powerlessness is heightened is either through a lack of involvement in decision making about care, or in the way that older people are coerced, or at least persuaded, to accept whatever professionals suggest as the best course of action. This was particularly evident when treatment involved new technologies and at the end of life.

Death with Dignity

A frequent comment was that palliative care facilities were often denied to older people, a fact well recognised in the research literature.[29] Dignified treatment was seen as especially important when someone was dying. Ensuring that the person was pain free, washed, in a clean bed and clothes, allowed privacy and provided with human contact, were all central to dignified care at the end of life.

"I remember when my husband died, right at the end, he was a very proud man and he was very ill and they knew he was going to die that night. A nurse came and she was a real hard sort of nurse and my friend said, 'Can we wash him and put him into his clean pyjamas?' She said 'Oh don't put him in clean pyjamas, he is not going to be here much longer.' I said to the nurse 'It's his dignity, I want him washed and changed', that's dying with dignity isn't it? It's all respect." (UK)

"I thought what the nurses did was wonderful ... They put her in the prettiest little nightgown, washed her and powdered her ... made sure she had clean sheets and everything and lots of love and care." (Ireland)

The opinions of participants varied most on individual rights at the end of life, although these differences were thought to be individual and not necessarily related to the major religious practices of the individual countries. Some with especially strong religious beliefs were against euthanasia; however, many people felt that going to extraordinary lengths to keep someone alive was a form of 'therapeutic cruelty', especially when people suffered with dementia or what they saw as an unbearable degree of dependence, such as being unable to move, communicate or eat independently.

Generally, older participants felt they should have the right to choose the manner of their death and that aggressive medical treatment at the end of life should be regulated. Many thought that medical technology had gone too far in prolonging life. Living wills were seen as an important tool in ensuring 'death with dignity', although many were concerned that these would be ignored.

"Having my dignity maintained by being able to make those choices about how I should die. I had no choice about being brought into the world but I hope and want a choice about how I should depart from it." (UK)

"The living will is very important, because now there's a trend, with all the improvements that exist, to prolong people's lives and sometimes it's worthless. So, if there is a person who, when lucid, was able to say what they wanted if that time came, I think it's a good idea that they are listened to." (Spain)

---

29 Ahmed, S. and O'Mahoney, M.S. (2005), 'Where Older People Die: A Retrospective Population-based Study', *Quality Journal of Medicine* 98, 865–70.

"Surely we will die, but for that we should have the right to decide, too often you don't die at the time you would like to." (France)

Professionals' Views of Barriers to Dignified Care

Professionals, most of whom spent more than 70 per cent of their time caring for older people, expressed divergent views of them, some calling them 'ugly', 'smelly', 'childlike', 'helpless' and 'disgusting', while others found them 'fascinating to listen to', 'gentle', 'rewarding' and 'challenging clinically'. The effect that these descriptions have on the professionals' care-giving would make an interesting study in itself.

Regardless of their views of older people, most of these participants saw dignified care as 'person-centred', 'empowering', 'courteous' and 'capable of meeting individual needs'. On the other hand, they described undignified care as 'brutal', 'humiliating', 'narrow in focus', 'reliant on routine', 'made people invisible', and 'disempowering'.

Professional participants identified many barriers to dignified care such as the lack of human, financial and material resources, their own attitudes to routine, and the lack of guidance on promoting dignity. Only a few participants had had the opportunity to discuss dignity or dignified care during their professional education.

Individual and Humane Care

Emotional care was not high on institutional agendas, sometimes even being frowned upon, and personal care was given a low priority in some institutions.

"There's just not a lot of time, it's not really ... it's frowned upon if you sit down and talk for too long."

"We don't usually have time to do that, it's the time factor ...

"But to be honest, if you sat down and talked you would be asked to go and do something else." (Healthcare assistants, UK)

"At a nursing home, often the person gets cancelled out. People seem to stop being themselves. There are nursing homes where everyone has to wear a gown. Please, tell me what for! People want to dress as they like or do their own thing, no?" (Spain)

"There is no time to sit down and talk to them, for instance. It would be wonderful to do that once, perhaps in the morning when they are having breakfast." (Nursing assistant, Sweden)

Resources

Lack of resources and the consequences of this for the care of older people were also emphasised.

"If only you didn't have to struggle all the time to get things, access things for patients, access equipment, access tests, the whole journey would be a better experience for patients. I think people operate under huge pressure and when people operate under huge pressure it's very easy to de-personalise the people that you are dealing with, it's very easy to focus on problems rather than people." (Geriatrician, UK)

"No, we tried to realise it [individualised care], but then you need some money and more staff."

"And the problem with this work is, that there is a big discrepancy about what you find and what ought to be." (Nurse, France)

"The elderly are forgotten, if you are working with younger people you get all the resources, all the money, you get grants for this, that and the other, but if you are working with the elderly you have to fight for everything." (Doctor, Slovakia)

Heavy and unremitting workloads left staff feeling they provided an inadequate service.

"I worked with 28 acutely ill people, and had lots of work, but you did it with all your loving care ..., and you left with your head high, it fulfilled you. Then, working in Geriatrics and also having 28 patients I leave with the feeling that you are better the faster you do the work. How you do it doesn't matter. And feeling like you work in a factory, that the more output you produce, the more you are appreciated." (Nurse, Spain)

"If you really did it properly, like really dignified, to get people out of bed and get them washed it can take up to an hour. I think that is why it [dignity] does get pushed to the bottom of the list." (Physio assistant, UK)

Impossible and impoverished environments, sometimes for even the most basic requirements, were highlighted, together with the callous attitudes of some staff members.

"When you have to care for 55 patients who all have dementia and there are only 2 nursing aides and one nurse..." (Nurse, France)

"It is a question of selection. You have to choose who will be provided with clean linen." (Nurse, Slovakia)

"I don't know how many of us could use a commode knowing that others were just outside the curtain." (Doctor, Ireland)

"There was a woman who had a convulsion. She had a brain tumour. I was changing her dressings, because they were quite soiled. And a doctor said, 'Why are you changing her dressings? She's going to die soon anyway.'" (Nurse, Spain)

Routine

Although many participants deplored routine, they appeared to accept unquestioningly that it was necessary to complete heavy workloads; however, some recognised that there was much they could do personally to reduce this barrier. For instance, by simply remembering that those they cared for were persons with a history and an individual identity, other than 'resident' or 'patient'.

"You know exactly what to do, you change the nappy and wash the old person. And it's just a matter of routine, you do it and you actually forget that it's a person lying there." (Nurse, Sweden)

"I don't know whether people get almost blasé about the fact that they are dealing with people in a vulnerable state all the time and they forget how that person may be feeling about it." (Physio assistant, UK)

"When you stop and look at residents and begin to say 'housewife', 'father', 'farmer', 'city counsellor', 'legal secretary', 'ward sister' – that sometimes works for me to remind me that these were people like me a few years ago, doing certain things ... and we need to be careful that because they are old not to lump them together under one title. They are still the 'ward sister retired', 'the judge retired', 'the city counsellor retired'. That is a preservation of dignity to see them as people." (Ireland)

Participants believed that routines also led to professionals taking over and engendering dependence in people who were previously capable of fulfilling the activities of daily living.

"Most of them who come into a nursing home, they may be walking and doing things for themselves but what I have observed is that we take them to be old and they need to be helped and we help them so much without thinking. We dress them up in the morning and then they stop dressing themselves. They would get out of bed on their own, but we help them and then they stop helping themselves. We need to give them the chance to do what they are able to do and that will keep them going. They just need to be encouraged and they will do it themselves." (Ireland)

"I think it is too easy to give up for them ... As I say there is not enough stimulation and also some people just do everything for them. Whereas if they were given the opportunity to keep themselves independent they would." (Care assistant, UK).

For professionals, the dignity of moral stature was particularly relevant as the barriers and systems in which they worked impacted on how they viewed themselves, their self-respect and professional integrity. This was especially so when resources and institutional practices prevented them from providing care of a standard and quality they felt was appropriate.

"I was visited by a doctor, a representative of the health insurance company, who asked me why I prescribed drugs for the elderly and did not think of young patients who would not get appropriate treatment because of old people." (GP, Slovakia)

The Media

The depiction of care for older people and of the professionals providing it, in the media and in the perceptions of other colleagues, also impacted negatively on many individuals' perception of their professional identity.

> "And we already talked about this, it affects our dignity, I think it touches our dignity as professionals. Even when you can hear the pain of the people, you hide in the institution. It is so badly perceived, as if because the institution is bad, so the carers working in the place are bad."

> "We are nearly forced to ... we are nearly hidden, the nursing help and the nurse ... In a systematic way I feel attacked as a professional in relation to the fact that I'm working in a nursing home ..." (Nurses, France)

> "It is horrible ... These pictures in the media are so ... Sometimes you feel guilty although you know that you do your best at your job." (Nursing assistant, Sweden)

> "Yes they say: 'It must not be easy every day, I grant you, I wouldn't do your job.' It is demeaning in comparison with emergency service ..."

> "And when you work in a nursing home that means that you are not able to do anything else. Elsewhere you are considered as incompetent. No! (For me) It's a choice!" (Nurses, Spain)

Discussion

Concerns by researchers that participants would find it difficult to discuss dignity or that it would have little meaning to them were unfounded. None of the participants expressed any difficulty in speaking about dignity and for older people in particular, it was relevant and salient to their lives. It is also clear that for many older people and especially those who are frail and vulnerable, their dignity (and human rights) appears to be violated on a daily and systematic basis. In many cases this was the result of besieged professionals trying to cope with unrealistic workloads, sometimes in unthinking and mechanistic ways.

Rather than being a 'useless' concept which 'means no more than respect for persons or their autonomy'[30] dignity appeared to be a rich and round concept for participants in this study. Although respect and autonomy featured highly in participants' accounts, dignity also entailed other notions which are particularly germane to the care of older people, including the meaning of care, justice, equality, recognition and personal identity, as well as respect and autonomy.

Societal perceptions about the need for care, especially on an ongoing basis, appear to have acquired evaluative connotations, which reflect on both the recipient and care-giver. The idea that increasing old age (which many of us are now able to look forward to) may also result in the need for care appears to threaten the experience

---

30 Macklin, R. (2003), 'Dignity is a Useless Concept', *British Medical Journal* 327, 1419–20.

of dignity. Potential recipients of care feared being a burden, and expressed shame at being in need of assistance or being dependent, so that not requiring care seems to have become a measure of individual dignity. This view of care being predominant in Western communities was evidenced by Keith et al.[31] in a study comparing American and Chinese communities. Whereas older Americans were concerned that they did not become dependent, the Chinese elders hoped they had raised children who would take care of them (p. 260).

Providing continuing care for older people is also seen as routine and relatively undemanding, requiring only basic training, and Thompson[32] argues that this is not simply a reflection of a lack of understanding, but instead reflects a more deeply ingrained negative and dismissive attitude towards older people, resulting in ageism, dehumanisation and a denial of dignity. Indeed, health and social care services for older people have been typically described as 'Cinderella services'. The irony is evident when we consider that a policy ideal for older people in many European societies is the provision of dignified care.

For many of today's older people, the provision of care was institutionalised within the framework of modern welfare states and distributed according to need. Until the last 20 to 30 years, 'free' care of a certain standard was guaranteed for all, in many European countries. Population ageing and diminishing resources, however, have resulted in many older people being required to either pay for long-term care, or at least certain aspects of it, including home or social care, or accept 'public' care of a reduced standard, when compared to that offered in private facilities. For many, this is viewed as another way in which they are devalued in society and subjected to unequal treatment. It is also a way in which older people are isolated and marginalised from the mainstream, all of which adds to a loss of dignity. When added to the unequal access to acute care, this perceived lack of justice in healthcare amounts to indignity.

Recognition of individuals as being worthy of respect, rather than being unproductive and a drain on resources, was clearly important; however, recognition of individual worth was also manifested in the way in which professionals communicated with older people. Older people wanted to be appreciated for what they had achieved in their lives, and the contribution they had made to family and society. For professionals also, public recognition of their special skills was important.

Acknowledgment of individuality was an important part of the dignity of personal identity. Being seen as someone with a history and relationships, someone who had been where their carers were today, was also important. This meant that being treated in ways that were sympathetic to their personal history was essential to being treated with dignity.

Although older participants emphasised the importance of participation and involvement in decisions about their care, there are negative consequences of the

---

31 Keith, J., Fry, C.L. and Ikels, C. (1990), 'Community as Context for Successful Aging', in Sokolovsky, J. (ed.), *The Cultural Context of Aging: Worldwide Perspectives* (New York: Bergin and Garvey Publishers) 245–61.

32 Thompson, N. (1995), *Age and Dignity: Working with Older People* (London: Ashgate Publishing Group).

current emphasis on autonomy, personal choice and freedom in both healthcare ethics and policy development. Over two decades ago, Callahan[33] warned that '[a]utonomy should be a moral good, not a moral obsession. It is *a* moral value, not *the* moral value.'

Pullman[34] also argues that an ethical framework based solely on considerations of autonomy assumes that the *highest* good is to maintain independence, and that dependence is a harm. Such a focus results in automatic failure for both frail older people and those caring for them. While for the majority of older people who are not frail, the primacy of autonomy may be rightly placed, for many individuals, however, the reality is that, physically and mentally, they will become more dependent, and care-givers must provide increasingly extensive care.

When value is placed solely on autonomy, we need to consider the impact on the most severely dependent persons, such as those in the final stages of dementia. Too high an emphasis on autonomy can lead to such people being viewed as 'minimal human beings' requiring only 'minimal moral consideration'.[35] Instead we should acknowledge that the severely demented person still has a basic moral worth, regardless of whether they are capable of exercising autonomy. Just existing as a human being confers a fundamental value (*Menschenwürde*), which ought to demand our moral attention.

When the dignity of frail older people is given centre stage, this not only protects all of their interests, but also exerts a moral force, even though all autonomy and experience of personal dignity is lost.

Conclusion

Dignity appears to be a fruitful concept for further research, especially in relation to services for the care of older people. A focus on dignity would require us to consider the dignity of both the cared for and the carer, especially their dignity of moral stature. Caring itself would acquire a greater moral value as it would recognise the intrinsic value of caring as an activity that expresses interdependence and the common dignity we all share as human beings, and emphasise the humanity of both carer and the frail older person.[36]

It is respect for *Menschenwürde* that demonstrates our care and concern for frail older people, such as those who are at the end of their life, or those with severe dementia, and it is our response to their inherent moral worth that enhances and expresses our own dignity. In the words of one older participant:

"It is in care that human dignity is consolidated. You feel more valued, when someone takes care of you. It is a demonstration of love and that gives dignity."

33 Callahan, D. (1984), 'Autonomy: A Moral Good, Not a Moral Obsession', *The Hastings Centre Report* 14:5, 40–42.

34 Pullman, D. (1999), 'The Ethics of Autonomy and Dignity', *Canadian Journal of Aging* 18:1, 26–46.

35 Van Hooft, S., et al. (1995), op. cit.; Pullman, D. (1999), op. cit.

36 Ibid.

Chapter 8

Guidelines for Embryo Donation for Reproductive Purposes in New Zealand: A Child/Family Approach

Ken Daniels

Introduction

Developments in cryopreservation techniques in assisted human reproduction (AHR) have led to increasing numbers of embryos being 'held in storage'. There are now an estimated 400,000 frozen embryos in the United States of America[1] and Nachtigall[2] (Schieszer, 2003) says that about 50,000 new frozen embryos are accumulating in that country each year. In New Zealand it has been estimated that there are between 5,000 and 7,000 frozen embryos being stored.[3] Couples with embryos in storage are faced with challenging questions over what to do with their 'spare' or 'surplus' embryos. Depending on the policy and legislative frameworks in different jurisdictions, they may have the choice of 'discarding' or donating them. If the decision is made to donate, then a further choice may be between donating to an infertile couple/individual, or donating for research purposes. Bankowski, et al.[4] have argued that a further option is available, namely the 'choice of inaction, simply maintaining the embryos in their current state of cryostorage'. De Lacey[5] points out however that there may be policy limits regarding the length of time embryos can be stored, and in the case of Australia and the United Kingdom, storage cannot exceed ten years. In Denmark the storage limit is two years. Continued storage can best be described as a response that delays making a choice between use for the couple's own family extension, discarding or donating.

---

1 Hoffman, D.I., Zellman, G.L., Fair, C.C., Mayer, J.F., Zeitz, J.G., Gibbons, W.E., Turner, J. and Thomas, G. (2003), 'Cryopreserved Embryos in the United States and their Availability for Research', *Fertility and Sterility* 79, 1063–9.

2 Schieszer, J. (2003), 'Couples' Feelings Mixed about Extra Embryos', Reuters, available at: http:www.reuters.co.uk/newsArticle.jhtml?type=healthNews&storyID=361345 1&section=news. Accessed on 22 October 2003).

3 National Ethics Committee on Assisted Human Reproduction (2004), *Guidelines for the Practice of Embryo Donation for Reproductive Purposes* (Wellington: Ministry of Health).

4 Bankowski, B.J., Lyerly, A.D., Faden, R.R. and Wallach, E.E. (2005), 'The Social Implications of Embryo Cryopreservation', *Fertility and Sterility* 84, 823–32.

5 De Lacey, S. (2005), 'Parent Identity and "Virtual children": Why Patients Discard rather than Donate Unused Embryos', *Human Reproduction* 20, 1661–9.

The policy and/or legislation regarding available options does not and cannot deal with the personal considerations and dilemmas of couples as they seek to reach a decision on what is a significant and disturbing issue for them.[6] This chapter acknowledges, but does not address, these personal dilemmas, focusing instead on the policy guidelines that have been developed in one particular country. These guidelines provide the framework within which it is expected many of the personal dilemmas can and will be examined. Following a discussion of some of the macro policy issues impacting on a consideration of embryo donation for reproductive purposes, a brief overview will be given of policy development in AHR in New Zealand. This provides the context for the discussion of the recently established guidelines, guidelines that are very firmly based on a child/family approach and which are likely to be regarded as radical.

Policy Considerations in Embryo Donation for Reproductive Purposes

The field of AHR has seen a proliferation of policy and legislation designed to manage new developments in appropriate ways. What will be obvious from a review of the international legislation and policy is that there is a great deal of variation in what is regarded as 'appropriate ways' and embryo donation is no exception in this respect.

Policy formation in embryo donation for reproductive purposes is likely to be influenced by ethical and pragmatic considerations. Ethical considerations are likely to include the status of the embryo, the welfare of the future child, informed consent and commercialisation/commodification issues. Pragmatic considerations are likely to be influenced by arguments concerning supply and demand – there are surplus embryos and some parents wish to donate their embryos to other couples who, without a donated embryo, would not be able to have children. Infertile couples' need for a child is therefore met through embryo donation.[7] Those persons holding strong moral views regarding the status of the embryo may support donation for reproductive purposes, as this enables embryos to be implanted, thus avoiding destruction/discarding. The guidelines discussed in this chapter have their foundation in both ethical and pragmatic considerations.

Embryo donation for reproductive purposes also raises issues concerning the appropriate policy sector that should be responsible for advising on, implementing and monitoring the practice of embryo donation. Traditionally it has been the health sector that has assumed responsibility, presumably on the basis that the embryos were created with the assistance of medical technology and that cryopreserved embryos are stored in health facilities. Recent developments in the USA are suggestive of a

---

6 Ibid; Nachtigall, R.D., Becker, G., Friese, C., Butler, A. and MacDougall, K. (2005), 'Parents' Conceptualization of their Frozen Embryos Complicates the Disposition Decision', *Fertility and Sterility* 84, 431–4.

7 Newton, C.R., McDermid, A., Tekpetey, F. and Tummon, I.S. (2003), 'Embryo Donation: Attitudes toward Donation Procedures and Factors Predicting Willingness to Donate', *Human Reproduction* 18, 878–84; Lee, J. and Yap, C. (2003), 'Embryo Donation: A Review', *Acta Obstetrica Gynecologica Scandinavica* 82, 991–6.

possible move for embryo donation to be 'managed' by the welfare sector rather than, or as well as, the health sector. These developments include the use of the term 'embryo adoption', rather than embryo donation. Adoption has always been managed by the welfare sector. The US Congress has allocated a total of more than $3 million to promote 'embryo donation' and most of this has been channelled to Nightlight Christian Adoptions and its Snowflakes Embryo Adoption programme. The Director of Snowflakes says embryo donation is basically adoption nine months earlier.[8]

A reproductive technology and adoption lawyer warns of 'language creep' in this area and suggests that this may reflect a more sinister agenda concerning the status of the embryo arguments. While the moral and political issues are important (and the matter of considerable debate, at least in the USA), there are also other issues arising from a welfare perspective that may be useful to consider. Any such consideration, however, is not likely to be easy, because as Brandon and Warner[9] pointed out some 30 years ago, the health and welfare sectors do not find it easy to understand or work with each other in the adoption field. If a continuum is constructed for creating and building families in different ways, gamete donation could be placed at one end of this continuum and adoption at the other end. Gamete donation is managed by the health sector and adoption, as stated, by the welfare sector. The issue regarding embryo donation is where it is placed on this continuum. It is clearly not the same as egg or sperm donation, as neither of these can lead to the birth of a child on their own. Embryos are established entities which, given appropriate conditions, can lead to the birth of a child. In this sense they are more than gametes but less than a living child, in that appropriate conditions are still needed. The debates concerning the status of the embryo highlight differing viewpoints regarding this latter point.[10]

From a policy perspective, the question arises as to what knowledge and models are best drawn on for managing this relatively new area, and is this knowledge and the models drawn from the health or welfare sectors. The guidelines discussed in this chapter are based on a recognition that embryo donation for reproductive purposes should be managed by the health sector, but that the professionals most involved in working with the adult parties will use a model that is heavily influenced by a concern for the psychosocial (welfare) needs of the donating couple, the future child and the family of which he/she will be a part. Counsellors, with their specialised knowledge of and skills in the psychosocial area, therefore become the key professionals to manage embryo donation for reproductive purposes within the AHR team in New Zealand. Their task is to combine a health and welfare perspective, but given that their basic professional orientation is a welfare rather than health one, this is likely

---

8 Weale, S. (2003), 'What Happens to All those Frozen Embryos?' *The Guardian* 12 June, London; Crockin, S. L. (2005), 'How do you "Adopt" a Frozen Egg?' (Massachusetts: *The New York Times*) available at: http://www.boston.com/news/globe/editorial_opinion/oped/articles/2005/12/04/how_do_you_adopt_a_frozen_egg.

9 Brandon, J. and Warner, J. (1977), 'AID and Adoption: Some Comparisons', *British Journal of Social Work* 7, 335–41.

10 Robertson, J.A. (1995), 'Ethical and Legal Issues in Human Embryo Donation', *Fertility and Sterility* 64, 885–93.

to dominate their interventions with the donating and recipient couples. It should be noted that the term 'welfare' is very general, but is being used in the context of this chapter to refer to the well-being of individuals, families and communities. Clearly health is one dimension of well-being, but it is only one dimension.

Policy Development in Assisted Human Reproduction in New Zealand

Like most Western countries in the late 1970s and early 1980s New Zealand was confronted with how to 'manage' developments in AHR – most notably in vitro fertilisation – that were proving so newsworthy. In 1984 a very influential grouping of organisations, the Royal Society of New Zealand, the New Zealand Law Society, the Medical Council of New Zealand, the Medical Research Council of New Zealand and the Medical Association of New Zealand requested the government to appoint a Standing Committee to consider the legal, moral and social issues arising from in vitro fertilisation, artificial insemination by donor, and related problems in biotechnology.[11] The government responded in 1985 by producing an issues paper entitled *New Birth Technologies*.[12] This paper had been prepared by an official in the Law Reform Division of the Department of Justice and was heavily influenced by the thinking in two overseas reports, the Waller Committee[13] and the Warnock Report.[14] Daniels and Caldwell[15] have described the public response to the issues paper as 'muted', there being only 164 submissions received. The government decided to adopt a 'wait and see' approach and established an inter-department monitoring committee 'to act as a repository of information to monitor the issues associated with artificial birth technology, and advise ministers as required'.[16]

The first specific New Zealand legislation relating to AHR was the Status of Children Amendment Act (1987)[17] which in effect established that offspring conceived as a result of donated gametes and the donors who provided those gametes had no legal rights or responsibilities to each other. This meant, for example, that

---

11 Royal Society of New Zealand (1985), 'Issues Arising from In Vitro Fertilisation, Artificial Insemination by Donor and Related Problems in Biotechnology', *New Zealand Medical Journal* 98, 396–8.

12 Department of Justice (1985), *New Birth Technologies. An Issues Paper on AID, IVF, and Surrogate Motherhood*, Department of Justice (Law Reform Division), New Zealand Government.

13 Waller, L. (1983), *Report on Donor Gametes in IVF* (Australia: The Committee to Consider the Social, Ethical and Legal Issues Arising from In-vitro Fertilisation).

14 Department of Health and Social Security (1984), *Report of the Committee of Inquiry into Human Fertilisation and Embryology*, (London, HMSO).

15 Daniels, K.R. and Caldwell, J. (2002), 'Family Law Policy and Assisted Human Reproduction', in Henaghan, M. and Atkin, B. (eds), *Family Law Policy in New Zealand* 2nd edition (Wellington: LexisNexis Butterworths).

16 Department of Justice (1986), *New Birth Technologies. A Summary of Submissions Received on the Issues Paper*, Department of Justice, (Law Reform Division), New Zealand Government.

17 New Zealand Government (1987) Status of Children Amendment Act (Wellington: Government Printer).

when donated sperm was used, the mother's husband or partner became the legal father of the child provided only that he gave his consent to the procedure.

In 1993, the Minister of Health – most previous policy work had been undertaken by the Department of Justice – established the Interim National Ethics Committee on Assisted Reproductive Technology (INECART). This initiative occurred as a result of concerns being expressed by the regional health ethics committees that there needed to be a national approach to the issues that were emerging in the field of AHR. In 1995 INECART was reconstituted as the National Ethics Committee on Assisted Human Reproduction (NECAHR). NECAHR was established under the Health and Disability Services Act 1993[18] to provide for ethical review in AHR and to advise the Minister of Health on ethical issues relating to AHR. It was also required to develop protocols and guidelines relating to ethical aspects of AHR for use by the service providers.

In that same year, 1993, the Minister of Justice appointed a two-person Ministerial Committee on Assisted Reproductive Technologies (MCART) to examine what was happening in New Zealand, to gather relevant information and to report to the Minister 'with options on the ways ahead for New Zealand in this field'[19] (Ministerial Committee on Assisted Reproductive Technologies, 1994). The committee's main recommendation was that a council on assisted human reproduction should be established and its tasks would include the preparation of codes of practice and guidelines to assist providers, consumers and the general public. The government, on the advice of an official committee, did not proceed with the establishment of a council.

For the ten years of its existence, NECAHR was the only government-appointed body with an overview of developments in AHR. While in name it was an ethics committee, in many areas its activities included policy considerations. Daniels and Caldwell[20] described NECAHR as a de facto policy committee.

In 2004 the Human Assisted Reproductive Technology Act[21] was passed. This comprehensive legislation has the following purposes:

a) to secure the benefits of assisted reproductive procedures, established procedures, and human reproductive research for individuals and for society in general by taking appropriate measures for the protection and promotion of health, safety, dignity, and rights of all individuals, but particularly those of women and children, in the use of these procedures and research:

b) to prohibit unacceptable assisted reproductive procedures and unacceptable human reproductive research:

c) to prohibit certain commercial transactions relating to human reproduction:

---

18 New Zealand Government (1993) Health and Disabilities Services Act (Wellington: Government Printer).

19 Ministerial Committee on Assisted Reproductive Technology (1994), *Assisted Human Reproduction: Navigating our Future*, Department of Justice, New Zealand Government.

20 Daniels, K.R. and Caldwell, J. (2002), op. cit.

21 New Zealand Government (2004), Human Assisted Reproductive Technology Act (Wellington: Government Printer).

d) to provide a robust and flexible framework for regulating and guiding the performance of assisted reproductive procedures and the conduct of human reproductive research:

e) to prohibit the performance of assisted reproductive procedures (other than established procedures) or the conduct of human reproductive research without the continuing approval of the ethics committee:

f) to establish a comprehensive information-keeping regime to ensure that people born from donated embryos or donated cells can find out about their genetic origins.

The principles on which the Act is based are:

a) the health and well being of children born as a result of the performance of an assisted reproductive procedure or an established procedure should be an important consideration in all decisions about that procedure:

b) the human health, safety, and dignity of present and future generations should be preserved and promoted:

c) while all persons are affected by assisted reproductive procedures and established procedures, women, more than men, are directly, and significantly affected by their application, and the health and well being of women must be protected in the use of these procedures:

d) no assisted reproductive procedure should be performed on an individual and no human reproductive research should be conducted on an individual unless the individual has made an informed choice and given informed consent:

e) donor offspring should be made aware of their genetic origins and be able to access information about those origins;

f) the needs, values, and beliefs of Maori should be considered and treated with respect:

g) the different ethical, spiritual, and cultural perspectives in society should be considered and treated with respect.

The Act lists prohibited and regulated activities, establishes an ethics committee and the activities requiring approval of that ethics committee, and also establishes an Advisory Committee on Assisted Reproductive Procedures and Human Reproductive Research (ACART). One of the functions of ACART is to issue guidelines and advice to the ethics committee and to keep such guidelines under review. As a result policy considerations and ethical review will be separated and managed by two different committees. It will be ACART that will in time review the guidelines on embryo donation for reproductive purposes which this chapter discusses.

The 2004 legislation also provides for the recording, keeping and sharing of information between donors of donated embryos or donated cells and donor offspring. Offspring, on reaching the age of 18, may access information concerning the identity of their donor. Provision is also made for donor offspring to have access to identifying information concerning siblings, once all parties have reached the age of 18. Donor offspring who are 18 or over may consent to disclosure of identifying information to the donor.

The guidelines on embryo donation for reproductive purposes was one of the last pieces of policy/ethical development that NECAHR completed. The background to the guidelines' development was that in 2002 a service provider (clinic) had sought approval from NECAHR to begin an embryo-donation programme. It was necessary for the clinic to seek ethics committee approval to meet the requirements of the professional self-regulation system that operates jointly between New Zealand and Australia.[22] In responding to the clinic, NECAHR had to first decide if embryo donation for reproductive services should become a treatment option. Having made the decision in conjunction with the Minister of Health that it should be, NECAHR prepared a consultation document which included draft guidelines, and distributed this to interested parties for comment. On the basis of the feedback received and further consideration of the issues, guidelines were prepared and submitted to the Minister of Health. The Minister approved the guidelines in 2005.

Guidelines for Embryo Donation for Reproductive Purposes in New Zealand[23]

Ethical Issues

The guidelines begin with prefactorial emphasising that the welfare of any child who may be born as a result of embryo donation is a particularly important ethical consideration. The document goes on to say:

Some of the key issues arising in relation to the welfare of children indicate:

- the need to minimise the harm to any offspring that might be born after embryo donation
- the need for those children to know and be able to access information about their genetic origins, including about the existence of any siblings from the same genetic parents.
- The principle of free and informed consent is regarded as essential to guard against pressure being placed on the people to donate their embryos (for example by clinics and families) and against people later regretting having donated their embryos. It is important that both those donating the embryo and those receiving the embryo are fully informed about the psychological, social and ethical aspects of embryo donation prior to giving consent to proceed with embryo donation (National Ethics Committee on Assisted Human Reproduction, 2005b).

The focus on the welfare of the child recognises that it is the potential child who is the most vulnerable party in embryo donation. While there has been considerable debate

---

22 Fertility Society of Australia (2005), *Code of Practice for Centres Using Assisted Reproductive Technology*, Reproductive Technology Accreditation Committee.

23 National Ethics Committee on Assisted Human Reproduction (2005b), *Guidelines on Embryo Donation for Reproductive Purposes*.

about how the 'welfare of the child' can be provided for,[24] or even what the phrase means, there is recognition that it is parents who are the primary providers for the welfare of their children. The role of the state is to provide requirements on and conditions for the parents, both donating and receiving, that ensure that they are as well informed and prepared for this kind of family-building as possible. Part of this information and preparation means looking ahead to the needs of the growing person – and not just to a baby. Such a looking ahead will include an active consideration of the need for the child to know and be able to access information about their genetic origins. This relates not just to their genetic parents, but also to knowing about the existence of any siblings from the same genetic parents. There is growing evidence, and mostly anecdotal at this point,[25] that many young people conceived as a result of donated gametes are as interested in meeting half siblings as they are the person who donated their gametes to enable the conception to occur. In developing the guidelines, NECAHR was very mindful of the well-established policy and practice (for the last 12–15 years) of clinics only recruiting gamete donors who were prepared to be identified to offspring in the future, should this be desired by the offspring. The committee was also aware of the provisions for information-sharing being considered by the select committee and now incorporated in the Human Assisted Reproductive Technology Act.[26]

It is the focus on the centrality of the welfare of the child, as provided for within the context of the two families, that lies behind my description of the guidelines as being based on a child/family approach. The relationship between the two sets of parents is crucial to the management of 'the need for those children to be able to access information about their genetic origins…'. I would suggest that this focus means that the clinic team is involved in much more than treating infertility and managing surplus embryos. The clinic is in effect treating infertility and building families.[27] The guidelines include the requirement that service providers apply to the Ethics Committee on Assisted Reproductive Technology (ECART) for approval on a case-by-case basis. This mechanism is designed to ensure that the guidelines have been followed and that the ethical requirements, especially as they relate to the future child, have been met.

The guidelines are divided into six sections:

- Guidelines relating to donor couples
- Guidelines relating to recipients
- Guidelines relating to both donor couples and recipients
- Guidelines relating to counselling
- Approval processes
- Reporting requirements for providers

---

24 Daniels, K.R., Blyth, E., Hall, D. and Hanson, K.M. (2000), 'The Best Interests of the Child in Assisted Human Reproduction: The Interplay between the State, Professionals, and Parents', *Politics and the Life Sciences* March, 47–58.

25 Daniels, K. and Meadows, L. (In Press), 'Sharing Information with Adults Conceived as a Result of Donor Insemination', *Human Fertility*.

26 New Zealand Government (2004), op. cit.

27 Daniels, K. (2004a), *Building a Family: with the Assistance of Donor Insemination* (Palmerston North, NZ: Dunmore Press).

Guidelines

For the purpose of this discussion, four areas/themes that are embedded in the guidelines are highlighted and discussed. All of the specific guidelines fall within these four areas; consent, requirements, engagement of donors and recipient/s, and counselling.

Consent Clearly, without the wish of couples to donate a surplus embryo, there would be no embryo donation. Service providers are required to inform patients whose treatment may lead to surplus embryos that embryo donation for reproductive purposes is an option open to them. This knowledge is to be provided when they are seeking treatment. While it is one thing to provide this information, it is another matter for couples to appreciate the significance of the information. They, after all, are almost certainly preoccupied with the creation of embryos that they will use for themselves. The possibility of surplus embryos may seem like a luxury to them. For those couples who currently have surplus embryos, there is a requirement on the service provider that such couples be informed that embryo donation to others is now possible. This will involve contacting patients, if this is possible, and consideration will have to be given as to how to manage the embryos of those who cannot be contacted. Because of continuing charges for storage, however, it is expected that most couples will be contactable.

The guidelines specify that clinics are not to pressure potential donor couples to donate. The fact that donating couples and recipient/s are to be seen by separate counsellors is one of the mechanisms designed to avoid potential conflict in this area. For a clinic, the donating couple have received their treatment and have been successful. For a recipient/s, they are currently 'in treatment' and the clinic has the potential to assist, if the surplus embryos in storage could be used. In such circumstances, the desire and means to assist those who are suffering from infertility may be powerful drives. Such drives, however, must not lead to pressure being exerted on potential donor couples.

If, after application to and approval from ECART, there are any variations in the agreed terms, then the alteration/variation has to be resubmitted to ECART, thus limiting the power of the professional to make independent decisions.

Donor couples have the right to withdraw from the donation or change the agreed terms of donation at any time until the embryos have been transferred to the recipient woman, but donating couples must be advised that the embryos may not be able to be refrozen if they decide to withdraw from the arrangement after the embryos have been thawed.

Written consent is required from all parties and a formal record of such consents must be kept by the provider. If one partner of the donating couple is deceased, embryo donation may only proceed if prior written consent from the deceased person exists.

Providers must inform donors and recipients of the requirements regarding information sharing under the Human Assisted Reproductive Technology Act[28]

---

28 New Zealand Government (2004), op. cit.

so that the giving of consents is fully informed. These requirements, as discussed earlier, make it very clear to parents that they are expected to share with any children born the nature of their conception. The requirement for donors and recipient/s to meet before agreeing to embryo donation is likely to ensure that this happens. While legislation does not require parents to share the information concerning the nature of the conception with any children, parents are left in no doubt as to the views of government and professionals on this central matter.

Requirements   The guidelines detail a number of requirements relating to the practice of embryo donation for reproductive purposes as well as requirements relating to the different parties.

It is only couples who have surplus embryos created from their own gametes, and intended for their own use, who may donate embryos to other people. Embryos created with the assistance of donated sperm or oocytes cannot therefore be donated. Two factors lie behind this requirement, potential confusion for the child and the implications for that child's welfare, and the need for the gamete donor to be involved in the counselling process involving the donating couple and recipient/s.

Donating couples may only embark on the donation process when at least two years have elapsed since they have decided their families are complete. They are also only allowed to donate embryos to one family. The time restriction is designed to ensure that 'hasty' decisions are not entered into, as it is such decisions, based on clinical experience, that are more likely to be regretted later. Only being able to donate embryos to one family recognises the intensity of the engagement process between the two families, both in the lead-up to donation and post-donation.

The grounds for using embryo donation have to be clearly established and must be based on medical conditions that prevent fertility occurring. Unexplained infertility that has not responded to other treatments is regarded as an acceptable medical condition. Providers have to be satisfied that the implanting of donated embryo/s would not pose any physical risk to the female recipient. Two restrictions apply to the embryos, namely that any embryo that has been subjected to procedures that carry any known risk, other than those normally encountered in IVF, cannot be used, nor can any embryo that is known to be affected by, or carrier of, a significant genetic disease be donated. 'Significant' is not defined, thus leaving professionals to adjudicate on this matter.

All treatment must be carried out in accordance with the Reproductive Technology Accreditation Committee (RTAC)[29] guidelines on embryo donation. RTAC is the professional monitoring system that operates in Australia and New Zealand. These guidelines include requirements relating to the medical screening of donor couples.

Service providers are required by the New Zealand Human Assisted Reproductive Technology Act (2004) to collect and keep information on the donor couple relating to date, place and country of births, height, eye and hair colour, ethnicity and in the case of Maori, the whānau, hapu and iwi and medical history considered significant of the donors, their parents and grandparents, their children and the reasons for donating. Both donors and recipient/s must be permanent residents of New Zealand

---

29 Fertility Society of Australia (2005), op. cit.

and this requirement exists to prevent persons travelling to New Zealand to undertake embryo donation.

Engagement of Donors and Recipient/s   A central component of the guidelines is that embryo donation occurs between two sets of adults who know each other, and have in effect 'selected' each other and made the decision that their planned action is in the best interests of the future child. This requirement of engagement and mutual selection and the process by which it is managed are based on a child/family approach and on some aspects of current adoption practice in New Zealand. A two-stage process is to take place. In the first stage, non-identifying profiles are to be completed by both potential recipient/s and donors. On the basis of these profiles and counselling, all parties will decide if they wish to proceed to the second stage which must involve one or more face-to-face meetings. For the potential recipient/s, information must be given to the provider for the profile to be drawn up, or they can complete their own. Potential recipients must approve any profile before it is passed on to potential donors. There are no specifications as to what is to be included in the profiles as this is to be left to the decision of the parties working in conjunction with counsellors. Providers, in passing on a profile to potential recipients, must also attach a copy of their criminal record. To do this, they have to apply to the Minister of Justice under the Privacy Act (1993)[30] for the records held on the Ministry of Justice's computer system. All personal identifying information on potential recipients' records (for example, names and addresses) are to be deleted. The criminal record may state either that there are no convictions or, if there are convictions, they will be listed. This provision is similar to the requirement relating to adoption in New Zealand which is designed to prevent persons with a criminal record, that might place the welfare of the child in jeopardy, being able to adopt. It is important to note that the information in the profile and the criminal record are supplied to the donating couple for them to decide if they wish to meet with the potential recipient couple.

The reverse also applies, in that if the donating couple wish to proceed to a meeting on the basis of the profile supplied, then they also have to provide a profile (without the criminal record) for the potential recipient couple to consider.

The process of engagement is to be managed by counsellors who are professionally qualified and there are extensive requirements regarding counselling in the guidelines.

Counselling   Both donating couples and recipient/s must be provided with implications counselling before entering the donation process.

The British Infertility Counselling Association (BICA) defines implications counselling as offering a service to clients to enable them to make a decision about whether or not to proceed with treatment. It is designed to provide space for clients to 'express or explore' issues. BICA says 'Implications counselling is about trying to help clients to focus on and explore a variety of issues which may directly or indirectly impact on them, their relationships, their family (including existing

---

30 New Zealand Government (2003), Privacy Act (Wellington: Government Printer).

children), friends and anyone else who may be affected by such treatment either in the present or in the future'.[31]

In embryo donation, implications counselling will also focus on a consideration of the implications of 'gifting' to another couple/individual an embryo that is the couple's 'creation'.[32] The embryo is of their 'making' and this embryo has the potential to become a child that they are likely to have some interaction with. There will also be the implications of the relationship between the siblings to consider.

The donor couple and the potential recipient/s are to have different counsellors who will not only provide implications counselling but also provide formal counselling once the decision has been made to proceed with embryo donation. In addition to separate counselling sessions for each party, counselling must include at least one session in which all the adult parties are involved. Both counsellors must be present at this joint session, which will be the first occasion on which the parties have met face to face.

In recognition that existing children, in the family of either the donor couple or the existing recipient/s, will be affected by the decision making of the adults, there is a requirement that such children should be included in the counselling sessions. This is to be on an age-appropriate basis. This requirement is also made in the guidelines on surrogacy in New Zealand.[33] The need for all public policies and practices in New Zealand to incorporate Maori (indigenous people) values has been a dominant factor in New Zealand's social and political development over the last 20 years.[34] This is very much in evidence in the field of AHR, and in embryo donation there is the requirement that counselling must be culturally appropriate. One specific way in which this is to occur is that whānau/extended family involvement should be provided for at the initial interview. This is because for many Maori, they would expect/wish to have their whānau/extended family with them for support and shared decision making. The guidelines recognise that the decision as to who to have present at the initial interview is one for the involved parties to make themselves.

Counselling is to be made available to the donors and recipient/s throughout the embryo donation process. Counsellors are required to furnish reports as part of seeking ethical committee approval. The reports (which are not to include the names of the parties) must indicate that certain matters have been discussed and, in the professional assessment of the counsellors, have been adequately understood. For the donor couple, these matters include: the reason for donating embryos; the

---

31 British Infertility Counselling Association (2004), *Implications Counselling for People Considering Donor-Assisted Conception* (Sheffield: British Infertility Counselling Association).

32 Bangsboll, S., Pinborg, A., Yding Anderson, C. and Nyboe Anderson, A. (2004), 'Patients' Attitudes towards Donation of Surplus Cryopreserved Embryos for Treatment or Research', *Human Reproduction* 19, 2415–19.

33 National Ethics Committee on Assisted Human Reproduction (2005a), *Guidelines for Non-commercial Altruistic Surrogacy using IVF as Treatment* (Wellington: Ministry of Health).

34 Daniels, K. (2004b), 'New Zealand: From Secrecy and Shame to Openness and Acceptance', in Blyth, E. and Landau, R. (eds), *Third Party Assisted Conception Across Cultures* (London: Jessica Kingley Publishers).

couple's feelings now, and feelings they may experience in the future, concerning the donation of embryos; the rights and needs of any child resulting from their embryo donation, and in particular the child's rights to access information about the donor couple and to contact them in the future; the issues associated with the process of selecting a recipient profile; the understanding that the recipient/s will be the legal parent/s of any resulting child; the possibility that the resulting child may be born with disabilities or genetic disorders; the possibility of legal termination of the pregnancy by the recipient/s. For the recipient/s, the matters include:

> the implications of accepting a donated embryo and therefore having a child that is not genetically related to them; the rights and needs of any child resulting from embryo donation and in particular, the child's rights to access information about the donor couple and initiate contact in the future; the possibility that the resulting child may be born with disabilities or genetic disorders; the possibility of legal termination of the pregnancy; the attitude of both parties (donor couples and recipient/s) to openness about the donation, especially with any resulting child.

For the joint session with donors and recipient/s, the matters include:

> the rights and needs of any child resulting from embryo donation and in particular, the child's rights to access information about their genetic origins and the implications of this for all parties; the donor couple and recipient'/s' understanding of each other's needs and wishes; the expectations and plans of all parties regarding ongoing contact and information sharing.

> Counsellors are also expected to follow the usual counselling practice of recording the family history of the donors and recipient/s. If there are issues that may affect the health and wellbeing of the recipient/s and donors and/or potential child, these must be referred to and discussed in the counselling report.

Conclusion

The guidelines and this chapter clearly indicate that counsellors are the key professionals involved in embryo donation for reproductive purposes. It is these professionals who are charged with providing a service that is based on the needs/interests/welfare of the two families, those donating and those receiving, and the children that link the families in a unique way. The New Zealand policy of information sharing concerning genetic origins means that children born as a result of embryo donation (and gamete donation) will grow up with the knowledge that they have two 'families'. The New Zealand guidelines have been developed to ensure, as far as it is possible, that the adult parties in these two families are as well prepared as possible for this form of family-building and that they are able to recognise and manage the issues and needs that will arise for the children as they develop. It is for this reason that the guidelines can be described as being based on a child/family approach.

Chapter 9

Assisted Reproduction and the Welfare of the Child

Sheila A.M. McLean

It is probably true that one of the most controversial provisions in the Human Fertilisation and Embryology Act 1990 is s. 13 (5); the 'welfare of the child' provision. Although everyone would doubtless agree that as a society we have obligations towards children, the insertion of this section into the Act has generated considerable academic debate and some professional concern. The section reads as follows:

> A woman shall not be provided with treatment services unless account has been taken of the welfare of any child who may be born as a result of the treatment (including the need of that child for a father) and of any other child who may be affected by the birth.

The Report of the Committee of Inquiry into Human Fertilisation and Embryology (Warnock Report),[1] which formed the basis of the UK legislation in the area of assisted reproduction, considered the question of how the welfare of the future child could be protected and concluded that 'hard and fast rules are not applicable...'[2] in this situation, preferring instead to leave the final access decision in the hands of the consultant. However, the Committee did:

> ... foresee occasions where the consultant may, after discussion with professional health and social work colleagues, consider that there are valid reasons why infertility treatment would not be in the best interests of the patient, the child that may be born following that treatment, or the patient's immediate family.[3]

Despite this, it can, however, be said that the Committee concluded relatively inconclusively. Their final recommendation on the welfare issue incorporates primarily an obligation that they sought to impose on consultants to provide a full explanation of their decision not to offer treatment.[4] Nonetheless, the Committee clearly envisaged that there might be occasions when doctors would be disinclined to offer treatment, based on grounds which were non-clinical.

---

1 Cmnd 9314 (1984) Report of the Committee of Enquiry into Human Fertilisation and Human Embryology, (London: HMSO).
2 Ibid, 12, para. 2.13.
3 Ibid, 12, para. 2.12.
4 Ibid., 12, para. 2.13.

As the Human Fertilisation and Embryology Bill made its way through the House of Lords, however, a more determined attempt was made to define eligibility for treatment services. Indeed, an amendment to the Bill, which would have restricted access to married couples, was defeated by only one vote.[5] The compromise that emerged in s. 13(5) was clearly less restrictive than this proposal, but nonetheless, as Lee and Morgan say, '[a]ssisted conception is to be, for the most part, for the married, mortgaged middle classes ...'.[6] Jackson agrees, saying that '... the purpose of this part of the Act is clear: it incorporates the political and moral belief that the heterosexual, two-parent family is the optimum, or even the only legitimate place to bring up children'.[7] Indeed, this vision of the 'normal' or appropriate family structure also influenced the Warnock Committee which concluded that '... we believe that *as a general rule* it is better for children to be born into a two-parent family, with both father and mother, although we recognise that it is impossible to predict with any certainty how lasting such a relationship will be'[8] (emphasis added).

Before evaluating the welfare provision in more depth, it is worth outlining how it has been interpreted by the Human Fertilisation and Embryology Authority (HFEA) which was established by the 1990 Act to oversee the provision of services covered by the Act. In its most recent Code of Practice[9] the HFEA provided the following guidance to licensed clinics:

> Treatment centres are expected to ensure that they have clear written criteria for assessing the welfare of any child or children which may be born or which may be affected by the birth of such child or children. Those criteria are expected to include the importance of a stable and supportive environment for any and all children who are part of an existing or prospective family group.[10]

The basis of the assessment of prospective parents must be 'fair' and should take into account:

i) The commitment to raise children
ii) The ability to provide a stable and supportive environment for a child/children
iii) Immediate and family medical histories
iv) The age, health and ability to provide for the needs of a child/children
v) The risk of harm to children including:
    a) inherited disorders or transmissible disease
    b) multiple births
    c) problems arising during pregnancy

---

5 For discussion, see Lee, R.G. and Morgan, D. (2001), *Human Fertilisation and Embryology: Regulating the Reproductive Revolution* (London: Blackstone Press) particularly 159–67.

6 Ibid, 164.

7 Jackson, E. (2001), *Regulating Reproduction: Law, Technology and Autonomy* (Oxford: Hart Publishing) 193.

8 Cmnd 9314/1984, op. cit., 11–12, para. 2.11.

9 *HFEA Code of Practice* (6th Edition), published January 2004, came into effect 1 March 2004.

10 Ibid, 3.3.

d) neglect or abuse
e) the effect of a new baby or babies upon any existing child of the family.[11]

Finally, guidance is given as to the nature and extent of the inquiries which clinics are required to conduct in order to make their evaluation. In their assessment of prospective patients, treatment centres are expected to:

i) Take medical and social histories from each prospective parent and see each couple together and separately
ii) Obtain the patients' consent to make enquiries of each of their GPs. Refusal by the patients, or either of them, to give such consent is a factor to be taken into consideration in the decision to provide treatment. In such circumstances, the treatment centre is expected to ask the patient's reason for the refusal and record the answer on the patient's medical records. In the absence of such consent, treatment centres are expected to seek to establish the identity of the patient(s) by appropriate evidence e.g. passport, photocard driving licence and birth certificate
iii) Once the relevant consents have been received from the prospective patients, ask the GP of both partners if he/she knows of any reason why the patient(s) might not be suitable for treatment and if he/she knows of anything which might adversely affect the welfare of any resulting child
iv) Where unsatisfactory responses or no responses to enquiries are received, obtain the further consent from the prospective patient(s) to approach any individuals, agencies or authorities for such further information as the centre deems to be required for a satisfactory assessment. (A response may be deemed to be unsatisfactory, for example, where prospective parents have had children removed from their care or committed a relevant criminal offence.) Refusal by the prospective parents or either of them to give such consent is a factor to be taken into consideration in the decision whether or not to provide treatment.[12]

In its consultation on the terms of the seventh edition of the Code, the welfare provisions are expressed thus:

The centre should take into account the welfare of any child who may be born as a result of treatment and of any other child who may be affected by the birth before providing any treatment service. Treatment services include any treatment (such as surgery or the administration of drugs) which is provided for the purpose of assisting women to carry children. In order to take the welfare of the child into account, the centre should consider any relevant information they receive in reaching their decision whether or not to provide treatment services.[13]

The revised guidelines repeat that '[t]hose seeking treatment are entitled to a fair assessment. The centre is expected to conduct the assessment with skill and care, and have regard to the wishes of all those involved.'[14] Taking account of the welfare of the child means that:

---

11 Ibid, 3.12.

12 Ibid, 3.20.

13 Available from the HFEA's website: http://www.hfea.gov.uk. Accessed on 4 December 2006.

14 Ibid.

... the centre should consider factors which are likely to cause serious physical, psychological or medical harm, either to the child to be born or to any existing child of the family. These factors include:

a) any aspect of the patient's (or, where applicable, their partner's) past or current circumstances which means that either the child to be born or any existing child of the family is likely to experience serious physical or psychological harm or neglect. Such aspects might include:
   i)   previous convictions relating to harming children, or
   ii) child protection measures taken regarding existing children, or
   iii) serious violence or discord within the family environment;

b) any aspect of the patient's (or, where applicable, their partner's) past or current circumstances which is likely to lead to an inability to care for the child to be born throughout its childhood or which are already seriously impairing the care of any existing child of the family. Such aspects might include:
   i)   mental or physical conditions, or
   ii) drug or alcohol abuse;

c) any aspect of the patient's (or, where applicable, their partner's) medical history which means that the child to be born is likely to suffer from a serious medical condition;

d) any other aspects of the patient's (or, where applicable, their partner's) circumstances which treatment centres consider to be likely to cause serious harm to the child to be born or any existing child of the family.[15]

In addition to these general considerations, specific reference is made to the situation where the child has no legal father; the proposed revised guidance exhorts that 'the centre should assess the prospective mother's ability to meet the child's/children's needs and the ability of other persons within the family or social circle willing to share responsibility for those needs'.[16]

Flesh has, therefore, been put on the bones of the Warnock Committee's original concerns and the rather vague legislative provisions. This does not, however, render the existence and value of the welfare provision uncontroversial, although Jackson suggests that its inclusion has 'gone largely unnoticed'.[17] Indeed, she continues that:

... the inclusion of a welfare principle was neither challenged nor defended. It was simply assumed to be self-evidently true that their future children's welfare ought to be taken into account before a couple is offered assistance with conception, and this assumption undoubtedly persists today.[18]

---

15 Ibid.
16 Ibid.
17 Jackson, E. 'Fertility Treatment: Abolish the Welfare Principle', available at: http://www.prochoiceforum.org.uk/irl_rep_tech_1.asp. Accessed on 1 August 2005.
18 Ibid.

Evaluating the Welfare of Future Children

The HFEA agrees that the welfare provision is a compromise; that 'a concern for the welfare of the child to be born as a result of the treatment should be one, but not the paramount, consideration to be taken into account before treatment is offered'.[19] While the fact that the future child's welfare is not to be the sole or paramount consideration is not as restrictive a provision as might have been enacted, the child's speculative welfare remains nonetheless a pivotal consideration. Moreover, for some the current provision does not go far enough. Some, for example, would argue that the welfare principle should be paramount, as it is in adoption legislation. CARE's[20] response to the recent (2005) HFEA consultation on the welfare principle argues, for example, that 'the welfare of the child should be one of the fundamental ethical concerns in fertility treatment' and criticises the HFEA for failing to give adequate guidance.[21]

On the other hand, others have been critical of the inclusion of this provision at all, arguing that it is tantamount to an unacceptable intrusion into the private decisions of individuals seeking to achieve what is generally regarded as a social good; namely, the birth of a child. In the House of Lords debates on the Bill, Lord Ennals, for example, said '[h]aving children is a private area of human affairs. I believe that it is really not for the state to decide who should or should not be allowed to bear children...'.[22] Moreover, it has been said that by its nature the legislative provision is 'incapable of distinguishing between adequate and inadequate parents'.[23] Not only, therefore, is the provision impossible to meet, it is also potentially discriminatory.

There is one further critique of its applicability in assisted reproduction that is hard to answer; namely – despite the HFEA's Code of Practice and the proposed revision to it – the question remains as to how it is possible to evaluate the likely welfare of a child yet to be conceived. On what criteria should this judgement be based, and from where would we pluck the principles on which it could be based? As has been said:

> ... if the birth of a child should always be a cause of celebration, how could you appeal to a future child's welfare in order to decide that his or her birth would not be something to be celebrated? If the law always treats conceiving a child as beneficial, how could it at the same time enjoin infertility clinics to weed out would-be-parents on the grounds that their child's conception would not be beneficial?[24]

---

19 HFEA (2005), *Tomorrow's Children: A Consultation on Guidance to Licensed Fertility Clinics on Taking in Account the Welfare of Children to be Born of Assisted Conception Treatment*, para. 2.1.

20 CARE (Christian Action Research and Education) describes itself as a mainstream Christian charity.

21 'Tomorrow's Children, Response from CARE to the HFEA Consultation on the Welfare of the Child', Transcript. The full report including the CARE reference can be found at <http://www.hfea.gov.uk/en/490.html>

22 House of Lords, Official Report, 6 February 1990, col. 789.

23 Jackson, transcript, op. cit.

24 Ibid.

Additionally, from a practical perspective, it is virtually impossible to identify welfare interests, as they will inevitably change with time. For example, the fact that a couple has a stable relationship at the time of seeking assistance is no guarantee that this will be the case when the child is born. Indeed, how can the welfare of a potential child ever be judged to be that it should not be born at all? Moreover, from a legal perspective, courts have consistently declined to engage in valuing life against non-existence, yet it appears that this is what we expect clinicians to achieve in making decisions about which couples or individuals should be permitted to become parents.[25]

The Need for a Father?

One of the factors required by law to be taken into account in the welfare judgement is the child's need for a father. This provision was undoubtedly designed to demonstrate support for the standard, heterosexual family unit, and thereby to discourage – if not disallow – single and lesbian parenting. Unsurprisingly, the insertion of this requirement into the welfare provision generated considerable heat. For some, such as the Warnock Committee which, as we have seen, expressed a preference for 'children to be born into a two-parent family, with both father and mother...',[26] it is self-evident that this is the situation most likely to create the environment best suited to bringing up children. For others, it is thinly disguised prejudice against single and gay people, seeking to prevent them from doing what others are permitted – even encouraged – to do; that is, becoming a parent.

So what would be the fears for children in families which lack a father? These can probably be split into two major parts: first are the possible social considerations, and second, where the single woman is lesbian, possible influences on sexual and psychological developments.

Social Considerations

Although the married, heterosexual family remains the ideal for many people, in fact the reality of the modern world is different. Golombok, writing in 2000, noted for example that 'more than 40 per cent of children find themselves in a single-parent family at some time during their school-age years'.[27] Like other authors, she agrees that children in one-parent families are 'less likely to do well at school and are more likely to develop psychological problems than children in two-parent families'.[28] O'Neill reports that single mothers:

- Are poorer

---

25 See the terms of the Congenital Disabilities (Civil Liability) Act 1976 (England and Wales); *McKay v Essex Area Health Authority* [1982] 2 All ER 771.

26 Cmnd 9314/1984, op. cit., 11, para. 2.11.

27 Golombok, S. (2000), *Parenting: What Really Counts?* (London: Routledge, reprinted 2001) 3.

28 Ibid, 13.

- Are more likely to suffer from stress, depression, and other emotional and psychological problems
- Have more health problems
- May have more problems interacting with their children[29]

She concludes, therefore, that:

> The weight of evidence indicates that the traditional family based upon a married father and mother is still the best environment for raising children, and it forms the soundest basis for the wider society.[30]

Golombok, on the other hand, while recognising that possible negative consequences may follow, suggests that it is not the absence of a parent *in se* that causes problems, but rather the social and other difficulties associated with single parenthood. She argues that '... what is clear is that the circumstances of single-mother families can be just as diverse as those of two-parent families, and it seems that it is the circumstances in which these families find themselves, rather than the absence of a parent, that matter most for the child'.[31] Thus, although there are signs that children in single-parent families may have certain disadvantages – indeed may even be more anti-social than others[32] – the level of risk to them (and others) is moot. Whether the limited information available is sufficient reason to deny single women the option of reproducing is moot and will certainly depend on the approach taken to reproduction and parenting. This will be returned to later in the chapter.

Sexual and Psychological Problems

It is evident that not only is there resistance to the deliberate creation of single-parent families, but there is also concern surrounding families when the single parent, or the partners to a relationship, are lesbian. The possibility of a child growing up with no male role model has caused anxiety, both about the child's socialisation and about its sexual orientation.

Golombok, et al., however, deduced from a study of children with lesbian parents that the parent–child relationship was positive and the children well adjusted.[33] Stevens, et al., conclude that the gender role development of pre-school children is typical even when there is no resident father figure.[34] Golombok also concludes that 'father absence appears to make little difference to sex-role development for either

---

29 O'Neill, R., 'Experiments in Living: The Fatherless Family', available at: http://www.civitas.org.uk/pubs/experiments.php. Accessed on 1 August 2005.

30 Ibid.

31 Golombok, op. cit., 13.

32 See O'Neill, op. cit.

33 Golombok, S., et al. (2004), 'Children with Lesbian Parents: A Community Study', *Developmental Psychology* 39, 20–23.

34 Stevens, M., Golombok, S. and Beveridge, M. (2002), 'Does Father Absence Influence Children's Gender Development? Findings from a General Population Study of Preschool Children', *Parenting: Science and Practice* 2, 47–60.

boys or girls....',[35] citing evidence that '... in both the UK and the USA, children from lesbian families have been found to be just as well adjusted as children from heterosexual homes'.[36] In fact:

> The gender identity of children raised by lesbian mothers was found to be in line with their biological sex. These children were not at all confused about their gender identity; the boys were quite sure that they were male, and the girls that they were female. Neither did the sons and daughters of lesbian mothers differ from the sons and daughters of heterosexual mothers in their preference for masculine and feminine toys, games and activities.[37]

As for sexual orientation, '[a]lthough children of lesbian mothers, particularly daughters, are more likely to consider the possibility of, and experiment with, same-sex relationships, the large majority of both sons and daughters of lesbian mothers identify as heterosexual when they grew up'.[38] Again, such evidence as there is suggests that sexual orientation is unlikely to be affected by being brought up in a same-sex relationship. Thus, even if one disapproves of such relationships, unless we approach parenting with firm – perhaps excessive – attention to the precautionary principle, it is not self-evident that the welfare of children is adversely affected by the sexuality of their family. In any event, disapproval of sexual orientation is scarcely an acceptable or appropriate basis on which to make significant inroads into people's liberties, backed by law and reinforced by society.

There are, of course, standard heterosexual families in which children are put at direct risk by their parents' behaviour, and it may be that similar patterns occur in single-parent or same-sex families. However, there does not appear to be a direct correlation between the kind of family unit in which children live and the inevitability of harm. One leading commentator in this area has concluded, therefore, that:

> It is no longer appropriate to assume that traditional families are good and non-traditional families bad for children. What matters most for children's psychological well-being is not family type – it is the quality of family life.[39]

Interestingly, one case stands out as an exception to the assertion that children have a need for a father; namely the case of Diane Blood.[40] It will be remembered that in this case, Mrs Blood arranged for sperm to be removed from her moribund husband with the express intention of seeking to use it to conceive following his death. For our purposes, what is important about this case is not the technicalities of the lawfulness or otherwise of the removal and storage of the sperm,[41] but is rather the

---

35 Golombok, op. cit., 21.

36 Ibid, 56.

37 Ibid, 54.

38 Ibid, 54.

39 Ibid, 104.

40 *R v Human Fertilisation and Embryology Authority ex parte Diane Blood* [1997] 2 All ER 687.

41 For a full consideration, see McLean, S.A.M. (1997), *Consent and the Law, Review of the Current Provisions in the Human Fertilisation and Embryology Act 1990, Consultation Document and Questionnaire* (London: Department of Health); McLean, S.A.M. (1998),

approach of both society and the law to her deliberate intent to create a child who would have no father. The Warnock Report specifically considered this situation and recommended that such pregnancies should be 'actively discouraged'.[42] In response, the government concluded that although 'many people are uneasy about this practice' it was not felt 'at present that this should be prohibited by law, although, obviously, it is not a practice which should receive active encouragement'.[43]

Of course, each of these comments preceded the passing of the 1990 Act, but Mrs Blood's case did not. It might, therefore, have been expected that it would have been concluded that the deliberate creation of an intentionally fatherless family would offend the welfare principle, just as much as any other case – for example, a single or lesbian woman – might. As Mrs Blood was in the event given permission to obtain treatment services overseas, it was not necessary for the UK's welfare provision to be invoked. Interestingly, however, there was considerable support for her desire to have children using her deceased husband's sperm. *The Times*, for example, criticised the HFEA's refusal to permit her to use the sperm as showing 'an unyieldingness that seems singularly inappropriate in this case';[44] *The Guardian* called its decision 'callous and pedantic'.[45] In addition, Bills were introduced in both Houses of Parliament, although they were subsequently withdrawn, which would have waived the written consent requirements in certain (unspecified) circumstances.[46] It may seem somewhat illogical that parliamentarians, many of whom will have voted in favour of the welfare provision, were so ready to abandon it in Mrs Blood's case.

Fitness for Parenting?

If the constraints intended by the welfare principle cannot be justified on the basis of the need for a father or the sexual orientation of the child(ren), are they justifiable on other grounds? In truth, is the real agenda not directly about the child to be, but rather about our judgement on prospective parents? Clearly, although it may be well nigh impossible accurately to evaluate the welfare of the future child in terms of the presence or absence of a father figure or the sexuality of the parents, it may be possible to make certain predictions based on other characteristics of the intending parents. As we have seen, the HFEA's Code of Conduct places considerable emphasis on this in its guidance to clinics. Certainly, we probably all know of people who we believe would be better not to have become parents, but that is a deduction usually

---

Review of the Common Law Provisions Relating to the Removal of Gametes and to the Consent Provisions in the Human Fertilisation and Embryology Act 1990 (London: Department of Health).

42 Cmnd 9314/1984, op. cit., 55, para. 10.9.

43 *Human Fertilisation and Embryology: A Framework for Legislation*, Cm 259/1987, para. 59 (London: HMSO).

44 *The Times*, 18 October 1996.

45 *The Guardian*, 4 October 1996.

46 Human Fertilisation and Embryology (Amendment) Bill (HL Bill 19, 1996); Human Fertilisation and Embryology (Consent) Bill (Bill 28, 1996).

drawn after the fact. In the case of assisted reproduction, of course, the conclusion as to welfare is sought before the child is even conceived.

In its consultation document, *Tomorrow's Children*,[47] the HFEA identifies a number of possible harms to children. These may be 'medical, physical, psychological or social'.[48] Medical harms, such as the transmission of genetic disease, are of no interest in this discussion, but clearly the others are. The HFEA describes physical harms as possibly arising when:

> ... either parent has a history of child abuse or neglect. They may have been convicted of a child-related offence or they may have had a child or children taken into the care of a local authority. A child may also be at risk of physical harm from a drug or alcohol addicted parent, either during the pregnancy or once the child is born.[49]

Psychological harm may be the result of growing up in a particular family structure, or may arise because of the family's general situation.[50] Finally, social harms may arise when:

> ... the care they receive from their parents is compromised. This might be because the parents are older, their health is impaired or the parents' relationship is unstable. Where there will be no legal father, a social harm could also be a lack of contact with male adult role models.[51]

Of course, each of these factors may well compromise a child's welfare, and society has in place mechanisms – social and legal – to offer protection for children who find themselves in such circumstances. However, neither of these has direct relevance to the unconceived. Social mechanisms cannot kick in until there is a person to protect, and, as Jackson points out, '... family law's protective function only applies to a child who already exists, and has no bearing upon a couple's choices prior to conception'.[52]

Some commentators, therefore, have suggested that the welfare of the child principle is not only a disguise for prejudice against people based, for example, on their sexual orientation, but is in reality a fitness for parenting test, reminiscent of the days when states believed that only the 'fit' should be allowed to reproduce. If so, they ask, then why should we confine ourselves to scrutinising people undergoing assisted reproduction; why not prevent others whom we believe to be potentially harmful to their future children from reproducing? Harris, for example, says:

> ... if we are serious that people demonstrate their adequacy as parents in advance of being permitted to procreate, then we should license all parents. Since we are evidently

---

47 HFEA (2005), op. cit.

48 Ibid, 2.3.

49 Ibid.

50 Ibid.

51 Ibid.

52 Jackson, E. (2001), op. cit., 195; see also *Re F (in utero)* [1988] 2 All ER 193.

not serious about this, we should not discriminate against those who need assistance with procreation.[53]

Of course, it may be objected that there is a difference between the two situations. Where people can conceive naturally, assessing their suitability to parent would involve policing the bedroom; something both practically and ethically unacceptable. This, it might be said, is not definitive when the activity being considered can be described as 'public' rather than 'private'; a commitment to respecting people's private choices – a commitment reinforced by the terms of the Human Rights Act 1998 – may not then apply. It might, therefore, be argued that whereas reproduction by sexual intercourse is essentially a private matter, once assistance is required to facilitate reproduction, it becomes a public matter and the state gains a right to impose restrictions. Even if this is so – and it is highly debatable – any limitations must be justified as proportionate to the consequence or harm sought to be avoided. In the absence of evidence that the inclusion of the welfare provision in the legislative framework is based on a realistic ability or reason to anticipate harm, it is difficult – if not impossible – to satisfy the proportionality argument. As Jackson argues, our reluctance to interfere with the procreative liberty of those who can conceive without assistance, and our enthusiasm for curtailing that same liberty in those who need help to conceive, means that 'the welfare of future children occupies a curious middle ground, in which it is always less important than fertile couples' bodily integrity and sexual privacy and more important than infertile couples' decisional privacy'.[54]

Indeed the recent report from the House of Commons Select Committee on Science and Technology agrees that the welfare provision is 'more akin to a "fitness for parenting" requirement, which was historically used to prevent certain "undesirable" groups from reproducing and is now widely rejected'.[55]

Nonetheless, the HFEA's consultation document recorded that many of those working in the area of assisted reproduction believe that the welfare of the child principle is useful. The document notes that '[m]ost respondents from staff working in clinics regard the welfare of the child assessment as an important part of clinical practice'.[56] Closer inspection of this review of clinics, however, also shows that clinics seldom turn patients down for treatment, which either means that virtually all of those presenting for treatment are the classic 'good' heterosexual patient in the ideal marriage (unlikely) or in fact that clinics do not regard the welfare of the child principle as being of major importance in practice. If so, its continued existence as part of the legislative framework and the decision-making process about access to treatment services must be in doubt on these grounds alone.

---

53 Harris, J. (2000), 'Rights and Reproductive Choice', in Harris, J. and Holm, S. (eds), *The Future of Human Reproduction: Ethics, Choice and Regulation* (Oxford: Clarendon Press) 5–37, 7.

54 Jackson, transcript, op. cit.

55 House of Commons Science and Technology Committee (2005), *Human Reproductive Technologies and the Law*, HC 7-1, 45, para. 93.

56 HFEA (2005), op. cit., para. 3.1.

The House of Commons Select Committee Report

There are, as we have seen, other reasons to doubt the soundness of the welfare principle. It has already been argued that it is vague and that it is not based on relevant evidence. There are, however, other strong arguments against retaining it which were canvassed by the House of Commons Select Committee on Science and Technology in its recent report, *Human Reproductive Technologies and the Law*.[57]

Describing the welfare of the child provision as 'contentious' and as having 'prompted widespread concerns of principle and practicality...',[58] the report aligns itself firmly on the side of those who oppose it as being discriminatory, disproportionate and disingenuous. The Select Committee's approach to the welfare principle is in part predicated on its avowed approach to assisted reproductive services in general. For the Committee, assisted reproduction is essentially standard medical practice and should be subject to minimal state regulation. This aspect of the report is based in large part on John Stuart Mill's rejection of state intervention unless it can be shown that failing to prevent certain behaviour will result in harm to others.[59] This approach predicts two conclusions. First, that the precautionary principle is inappropriate; rather those who object to certain practices should be required to establish that harm results. Second, in the case of welfare assessments carried out before conception, there is no 'person' to be harmed and therefore no basis to intrude into reproductive behaviour.

The report also notes that the welfare provision is unevenly applied:

> If one accepts that the welfare of the child provision is important and that the involvement of healthcare professionals justifies an erosion of liberty, logic would dictate that any professional intervention to overcome infertility or subfertility should be subject to the same standards. IVF is just one of a number of techniques that include ovulation induction, tubal and uterine surgery, surgical management of endometriosis, IUI and GIFT. Only with the last two is a welfare of the child assessment required, and only if donor sperm is being used. The exclusive requirement to consider the welfare of the child for fertility treatments where fertilisation takes place outside the woman or involves donated sperm is illogical. If the legislation aims to regulate the treatment of infertility or subfertility then it should cover all forms of interventions. If it wishes to do both then this needs to be clearly stated and justified.[60]

For the Select Committee no, or inadequate, justification for the legislative welfare provision could be found. The intrusion into individuals' reproductive decisions that may flow from it could not be supported. The report concluded therefore that the welfare provision 'discriminates against the infertile and some sections of society, it is impossible to implement and is of questionable practical value in protecting the interests of children born as a result of assisted reproduction'.[61] It should, accordingly, be abolished in its current form.

---

57 HC 7-1 (2005).

58 Ibid, 44, para. 91.

59 Mill, J.S. (1859) 'On Liberty'.

60 HC 7-1 (2005), 50, para. 105.

61 Ibid, 51, para. 107.

Even the Department of Health seems to have acknowledged the problems associated with the welfare principle. In its written evidence to the Select Committee, the Department noted that in its review of the provisions of the legislation it would need to pay attention to social change, saying:

> Changes in societal attitudes and developments in human rights legislation have taken place since the introduction of the Act, and the review will need to consider the extent to which the Act has kept pace with these. The Act is, for instance, framed in terms of heterosexual couples receiving assisted reproduction treatment. We will consider in the review of the Act, particularly through the public consultation exercise, the extent to which changes to the Act may be needed to better recognise the wider range of people who seek and receive assisted reproduction treatment in the 21st century.[62]

However, in her verbal evidence to the Select Committee, the then Parliamentary Under-Secretary of State for Public Health, Melanie Johnson, seemed to place even more importance on the welfare of the child provision than does the current law, declaring that 'the welfare of the child has to be the overriding main concern of anybody working in this area. The main overriding concern is the welfare of the child.'[63] Following subsequent questioning she said that 'the single most important factor is the welfare of the child'.[64]

This emphasis on the welfare provision may alter with changing government ministers, but it seems to reflect the presumption that welfare calculations are both feasible and desirable. Whether this position, or the more radical approach of the Select Committee, will dominate remains to be seen. A trend, however, seems to be emerging. Following the Select Committee's report and a consultation exercise carried out as part of the Department of Health's own review of the 1990 Act, the Minister of State for Public Health, Caroline Flint, gave evidence to the Select Committee on 12 July 2006.[65]

She specifically referred in that evidence to the welfare of the child provision saying:

> Before the consultation the view I was getting was that within the organised professions, the medical groups and others, was that there was a desire for this to be removed. Actually our consultation indicated that amongst the medical organisations, whilst they felt that there were some issues around it they thought that there should still be a need for that to be retained.[66]

Quite what the government will do with this information is unclear. Even if governments commit to using public opinion as the basis for strategy, as with all consultation exercises, those who respond can scarcely be taken as representative of the entire community. In the case of this consultation, the Minister explained that some 535 formal responses and submissions from about 100 organisations were

---

62 Memorandum from the Department of Health, Ev 195-200. Ev 197, para. 21.
63 Ev 185.
64 Ibid.
65 Available at: http://www.publications.parliament.uk. Accessed on 1 December 2006.
66 Ibid.

received. Nonetheless, under questioning from Bob Spink, MP, she conceded that the government was 'minded to retain a duty in terms of the welfare of the child to be taken into account', but also indicated that this might not include the need for a father, for which 'there is probably less of a case'.[67] Questioned by Evan Harris, MP, she seemed uncertain as to whether or not the use of the welfare principle to put a brake on same-sex couples being given access to assisted reproduction would legally amount to discrimination, although she agreed that this was a matter under active consideration.

Conclusion

The genesis of the welfare provision lies in a conservative approach to assisted reproduction and parenting, and in particular reflects concerns surrounding the leap into the dark that was made when assisted reproduction moved from science fiction to science fact. When the Warnock Committee was reporting, and when the Human Fertilisation and Embryology Bill was moving through its parliamentary stages, much was unknown about the safety of various forms of assisted reproduction. A commitment to the highest technical standards, and appropriate monitoring of emerging harms or risks, would have been intelligible. That the legislators went beyond that and moved into the realms of assessment of quality is perhaps unfortunate, albeit that it may also have been explicable in the face of uncertainty.

Things have moved on since then, however, and arguably even if there was a reason for the welfare of the child provision in the 1980s and 1990s, it is less easy to justify it in the early part of the twenty-first century. This is not a trivial matter. Although few intending parents are turned down for treatment – one notable exception being the case of *R v Ethical Committee of St Mary's Hospital (Manchester) ex parte Harriott*[68] – the welfare of the child provision's very existence can and should be evaluated on the basis of principle rather than on the frequency of its use. Arguably, any such principle should take account of the rights and interests of the intending parents, given that – unlike the speculative welfare of the future child – they are at least ascertainable. One such right can be found in the terms of article 8 of the European Convention on Human Rights, which was incorporated into UK law by the provisions of the Human Rights Act 1998. This right is, like many of the rights contained in the Convention, defeasible, but only on limited grounds; namely where this:

> ... is in accordance with the law and is necessary in a democratic society in the interests of national security, public safety or the economic well-being of the country, for the prevention of disorder or crime, for the protection of health or morals, or for the protection of the rights and freedoms of others.[69]

---

67 Ibid.
68 [1988] 1 FLR 512.
69 European Convention on Human Rights, article 8 (2).

It must be at least arguable that the welfare principle cannot be said to satisfy any of the permissible derogations from the basic right. Indeed, it has been described as 'an invidious and opportunistic invasion of infertile people's privacy'.[70] If it can thus be described, and if article 8 were deemed to be engaged by the welfare provision, it is likely also to run foul of the non-discrimination provision in article 14 of the Convention.

The final question, therefore, must be: what is the welfare provision for? If it is seldom invoked to deny access to treatment, and if it is based on little or no empirical evidence, its ethical status must be in doubt. In her evidence to the Select Committee on 12 July 2006, the Minister made it clear that her concern was that what was important was 'that the children are going to be, as far as we know, part of a loving family'.[71] However, as we have already seen, this is essentially an impossible challenge. The situation of a person or couple when they seek access to assisted reproduction is not immutable. The ability to offer a 'loving family' is equally difficult to predict and accurate measurements are unlikely to be developed.

Thus, there is no evidence that welfare predictions have any reliability; rather, they provide an opportunity for prejudice to creep into clinical decisions. It is generally unwise to include in legislation concepts which are difficult to define, readily open to subjective interpretation and not justified by evidence. The case of Diane Blood, already referred to, is also testimony to the ease with which such provisions can be discarded in the face of a sympathetic individual. Mrs Blood now happily has two healthy and much loved children and has written movingly about her experiences in a book, *Flesh and Blood: The Human Stories behind the Headlines*.[72] The welfare provision could have been used to prevent the birth of these children, and it is perhaps instructive that when confronted head-on by a forceful and intelligent media campaign by Mrs Blood, resistance to the deliberately created fatherless family waned considerably. Even Baroness Warnock supported her case, despite having previously and explicitly disapproved of such a situation arising. If the welfare provision is to be honoured more in the breach than in the practice, this surely puts one final nail in its coffin. To be sure the state has an obligation to protect the welfare of children. What it arguably does not have is the right to force superfluous, vague and discriminatory rules on those who merely seek to establish a family.

---

70 Jackson, transcript, op. cit.

71 Available at http://www.publications.parliament.uk/pa/cm200506/cmselect/cmstech/ 1308/6/071201.htm accessed on 15 August 2006.

72 Blood, D. (2004), *Flesh and Blood: The Human Stories behind the Headlines* (Edinburgh and London: Mainstream Publishing).

Chapter 10

Body Immortal[1]

Judit Sándor

'Sorry, but your soul has just died.'
Tom Wolfe[2]

The title evokes a widespread scientific ambition to extend the biological limits of life, but it also indicates that for law and ethics the status of the human body and body parts is never carved in stone. In this chapter I will mention numerous recognised and accepted, as well as still hotly debated, new technologies that have perhaps only one common element among them: they all serve to substitute for a disabled function in the body. I do not even try to provide an ethical assessment of the wide range of fundamentally different technologies such as pre-implantation diagnoses, embryonic stem cell utilisation or ICT implants, as each of them would deserve a separate and very detailed study. My goal is restricted merely to showing the effect of these new technologies on the legal concept of self-determination.

Transplanted organs, prostheses, ICT implants and stem cells serve as substitutions for disabled body parts and bodily functions, but they may also enhance certain corporal functions (such as the sense of hearing or seeing). Blood transfusion and organ transplantation are routine techniques today, but the establishment of stem cell banks and umbilical cord blood banks, as well as the practice of embryo selection, make it also possible to replace and 'repair' human cells, tissues, organs, and even body parts. Embryonic stem cells are self-renewing cell lines that give rise to all cells and tissues of the body. 'The potential for these cells is to allow permanent repair of failing organs by injecting healthy functional cells developed from them.'[3] Consequently, these technologies can contribute to the prolongation of the human life-span. Some of them are applied as routine procedures without significant ethical implications, while some other methods may evoke new ethical and legal dilemmas.

I think one of the most important questions that has to be asked is *in what sense and how far the principle of self-determination is applicable* in connection with artificial or organic body substitutes. In general, an individual has a right to decide what should happen to his or her body; consequently, implants may not be installed

---

1 The first draft of this chapter was delivered at the workshop of Public Understanding of Genetics held in Paris in June 2004.

2 Article by Tom Wolfe in *Forbes ASAP*, 2 December 1996, 210–19.

3 Okarma, T.B. (2001), 'Human Embryonic Stem Cells: A Primer on the Technology and Its Medical Applications', in Holland, S., Lebacqz, K. and Zoloth, L. (eds), *The Human Embryonic Stem Cell Debate* (Cambridge: MIT) 3.

and removed without the consent of the in vivo recipient. It is ethically more problematic when implants serve other functions beyond the ordinary replacement of a bodily function. Some implants, for instance, could be used to locate people or to obtain access to information stored in these devices.[4] In this case, the right to self-determination should encompass the right to control access to information that is stored in the implant.

The storage and the different uses of human body and body parts have recently become a central issue in ethics and legal debates. Expectations regarding the slowing down of aging and prolonging the arrival of death, diminishing suffering and reducing the cases of disability seem to have changed, at the very least, in those societies where scientific advances have flirted with the idea of stretching the boundaries and increasing the capacities of the human body. Expanding the human life-span has become a scientific project as it transformed from an object of utopian desire to mundane biotechnological bricolage. Recycling our biological building blocks and reprogramming our stem cells in place of the earlier surgical and biochemical treatment methods has made it possible to rebuild, quite literally, certain parts of our body.

These scientific advances invoke new questions concerning the philosophical relationship between the body and person. To what extent are we able to control and to make informed decisions on the extra-corporal or implanted parts of the body? Considering these bodily changes from ethical and legal perspectives, not only body images are affected but individual expectations and even personality rights may change.

The problems concerning stem cell utilisation involve even more complex decisions, as harvesting, cultivating, storing and using stem cells for future therapeutic purposes is a long and often ambiguous procedure.[5] Furthermore, in these procedures one could easily be a donor and recipient at the same time. Irrespective of what we believe about the body and mind, it is not only the time limits of our existence but also the spatial boundaries of our body that have become less determined.

Based on this, the following questions may be raised: is there any difference between self-determination concerning someone's medical treatment, and a decision concerning extra-corporal parts of the body? Consent to medical treatment is based on the legal principles of human dignity, privacy and self-determination, while decisions over stored gametes, embryos, and stem cells may also involve third-party interests (such as interest of the spouse, public health, protection of the embryo). States usually regulate the conditions for storage, control and disposal over embryos, cells, tissues: for instance, how many embryos can be transferred to the woman's body; how and to what purposes and from which sources stem cells can be harvested. Regulation is often justified by the fact that self-determination over stored, in vitro

---

4 'Ethical Aspects of ICT Implants in the Human Body', Opinion of the European Group on Ethics in Science and New Technologies to the European Commission, No 20, adopted on 16 March 2005.

5 Fletcher, J.C. (2001), 'NBAC's Arguments on Embryo Research: Strengths and Weaknesses', in Holland, S., Lebacqz, K. and Zoloth, L. (eds), *The Human Embryonic Stem Cell Debate* (Cambridge: MIT) 61–72.

parts of the human body involves the operation of huge cryopreservation centres and, in case of destruction, not personal injury but product liability or negligence shall be applied.

To understand the relevance of the legal and ethical dilemmas in harvesting parts of the body or cultivating cells to ourselves, to our relatives and to others, one should recognise a major legal distinction between persons and things. While things can be obtained, possessed or owned, property rights cannot be established on a person.

Dual Concept of the Human Body

When one thinks about a body part, a tissue, a hormone or a cell as material that can be the source for producing medicaments or be a subject of research and patenting, then it is the domain of property law. But one can think about the body as an integrated part of personhood and, as such, legally subject of personality rights or privacy. In the latter concept, the body cannot be directly accessed and property law is an inadequate way to describe that the body holds essential information that should be protected. Even if certain body parts are no longer integrated with the body, this characteristic of the body still remains.

Someone may cut the debate at this point by arguing that the human body inevitably encompasses the elements of both property and personality. One difficulty is, however, that in private law there is a sharp demarcation between *things* and *persons*. It is legally impossible to state that someone or something is both a thing and a person at the same time. This legal thinking on categorisation and the separation of things and persons goes back to Roman law.

Most of the contemporary civil codes dedicate separate chapters for persons and for things. Let me refer to an example of the contemporary distinction between persons and things. The Hungarian Civil Code does not define 'things' (*res*), only property. Instead, the Code simply states that 'anything that can be possessed may be subject of property law'.[6] According to the Commentaries to the Civil Code, the human body cannot be possessed and, consequently, it cannot be sold or purchased. On the other hand, some body parts and the cadaver can be subject of various contracts and be subject of donation.

Property rights encompass a bundle of different rights: right to use, right to enjoy, right to dispose, right to have, or right to possess (in Latin: *uti, frui, abuti, habere, possidere*). Property rights are used in relation to the body only when the tissues and cells are used to prepare another product, for example, blood, products, medicine or patentable cell lines.

Body as Part of Personhood: Personality, Privacy and Property Rights

The other possible alternative to express the legal rights over the body is to use the concept of *rights of personhood* and *privacy*. Privacy is a broad and ambiguous legal concept. Moreover, differences between the various legal systems are even more

---

6 Article 94(1) of the Hungarian Civil Code.

significant if we look at how they interpret the scope of privacy. Even within Europe people may have very diverse expectations of what should be regarded as private. Still, the notion of privacy is useful to describe personal expectations towards physical integrity, intimacy, and the interest to know information about someone's own body.

Although privacy is originally an Anglo-Saxon legal concept, it has recently gained widespread recognition in a variety of legal systems. In Hungary, legal norms that protect personality (*személyiségi jogok* or personality rights) function very similarly to privacy. Personality rights protect first and foremost human dignity and personal decisions, and the body only indirectly. This is so because the corresponding legal and ethical norms, as derived from respecting human dignity, presuppose bodily integrity. This is why torture and inhuman or degrading treatment are forbidden, but this is also why any research on living human beings is permitted only after the subject has expressed his or her consent to it. And this is why, in the practice of the last couple of decades, it is prohibited to initiate surgical interference without the written and informed consent of the human patient.

Hungarian criminal law enlists violation of the human body and misuse of body parts among special crimes: neither among crimes against property nor among the crimes against human beings.[7] In 1998 a completely new Title (Title II) was introduced that incorporated new crimes against the order of healthcare treatment and biomedical research and the violation of self-determination in healthcare. By creating a series of new types of crimes and placing individual self-determination in the centre, Hungarian law implicitly recognised various forms of individual self-determination that encompass rights on the temporarily stored and cultivated parts of the human body that exist outside of the body.

This extension is not a unique legal solution since, following the revolutionary discoveries concerning the human genome, most human tissues have also been widely regarded as carriers of personal data. As the right to self-determination is derived from the concept of human dignity (or right to privacy in the Anglo-Saxon version), no wonder that personal information may justify the extension of individual self-determination in considering what should be done with someone's body – even if some parts are temporarily (or permanently) not integrated in the human body but stored in liquid nitrogen for waiting reproductive or therapeutic destiny.

Special features of bodily integrity can be easily studied by looking at the laws on *consent*. Although the state may require individuals to undergo relatively minor intrusions into their bodies for the sake of general welfare (vaccination, blood test, X-ray examination of lungs), it may not require a person to donate his body, tissue or cell to preserve the life of another, even if the removal of a body part would pose little or no risk to the prospective donor and a family member would suffer serious harm or die without the donation.

---

7 Section 173/I(1) on the illegal use of the human body: 'The illegal access to human genes, cells, gametes, embryos, organs, tissues, cadavers or part of cadavers, as well as selling or in any way commercializing these body parts is punishable by up to 3 years of imprisonment.'

One of the classic cases on the dilemmas concerning the legal status of body parts detached from the body is *Moore v. Regents of the University of California*.[8] In this case, the California Supreme Court recognised the breach of fiduciary duties and lack of informed consent when doctors removed Mr Moore's spleen, but not the plaintiff's claim based on property law. Furthermore, the court ruled that the patented cell line was the product of invention owned by those who laboured to create it and not by Moore, who merely supplied the 'naturally occurring raw material'.[9]

While property law provides direct protection to the person's body and body parts, privacy and personality rights focus on the person and protect the person's body only indirectly.[10] The basic element both in privacy and property is the right to exclude unwanted interference by third parties. However, while the property law approach creates a fragmented relationship between the body and its owner, privacy and personality rights identify the body with the person and maintain the wholeness of the body. In the realm of property law, different treatments of body parts, cells and gametes can be envisioned, while in privacy law an abstract and more spiritual protection of the body may not be able to deal with different scenarios when body parts are temporarily stored and cultivated outside of the human body.

The uncertainty regarding the scope of property and privacy rights in the body is most evident in the reproductive field, in case of gametes and embryos. Issues of bodily integrity and boundaries of self-determination may arise when gametes, embryos, stem cells, umbilical cord blood samples or other genetic material samples are stored either for our own later use, or in the interest of other people, or for the purpose of scientific research. Stored gametes and embryos provide a hope to have children, but often when the couple already has a child due to assisted reproduction, the stored embryos become 'surplus'. These embryos may be donated or used for research, including stem cell research unless the national law prohibits it. Until the success of embryo transfer, rights over the embryos are very similar to the rights over one's own body. The life of the foetus is protected by special laws and from the moment of birth the law provides a protection equal to the rights of the person. It seems that the notion of 'potential personhood' is morally significant throughout the entire process from fertilisation until birth.[11]

The Body and its Boundaries

The problems concerning the boundary of the body, and thus self-determination, appear the most challenging when it has to be decided whether the stored gamete or embryo is intended to be used for the *reproduction of the self* or the stem cell, or other

---

8 *Moore v The Regents of the University of California* 793 P.2d 479 (Cal. 1990).

9 Mortinger, S.A. (1990), 'Comment: Spleen for Sale: Moore v. Regents of the University of California and the Right to Sell Parts of Your Body', *Ohio State Law Journal 51, 499*.

10 A similar approach can be observed in Thouvenin, D. (2001), ' La construction juridique d'une atteinte légitime au corps humain', *Recueil le Dalloz, Hors-Série au Recueil* 20, 24 May.

11 Tooley, M. (2001), 'Personhood', in Kuhse, H. and Singer, P. (eds), *A Companion to Ethics* (Malden: Blackwell Publishing) 117–26.

genetic material is to be utilised for *therapeutic purposes*, helping to cure the self or a family member. In these cases we could argue that exercising the right to self-determination over some genetic material outside the body of the self (and thus the genetic information contained in it) should be based on some form of informational self-determination. The stored sample, if it is not anonymous, contains important health data on the body of the self, even if it is displaced from that body. It could lead to disastrous consequences if these data are obtained by unauthorised agents. In the case of gametes and embryos, the rights and liberties associated with reproduction might be violated if, for example, due to inadequate storage the possibility of successful reproduction suffers harm together with the stored material. In case the embryo is transferred to some other couple than the genetic parents, due to some form of mismanagement or negligence, grave debates on paternity claims might occur, damaging the identity and family status of the newborn.

These instances of multiplying the body are only one step away from the practice of cloning whole bodies or certain bodily cells. These 'substitute bodies' or genetic 'spare parts' pose whole new challenges to the concept of self-determination. How far can someone exercise rights over harvested, stored, implanted parts of his or her body?

Issues regarding a person's right over his or her body so far have concerned medical or other interferences into the body, and not use of the body itself as a therapeutic tool. Thus, *the concept of a person's right over his or her body becomes doubled*: there is a right over the recipient body, on which the treatment is applied, and a right over the donor body, which is used in the therapy. One special characteristic of stem cell therapies is that the donor body and the recipient body are identical.[12]

Someone Else's Body as a Saviour Body: The Case of Saviour Siblings

It is an important legal and ethical question what interest may legitimise the therapeutic use of someone's body. Is it acceptable that an embryo is selected according to one of its specific characteristics, for example, to help a living but chronically ill sibling by bone marrow transplantation? This procedure presupposes that in the in vitro fertilisation process, one embryo is selected from many according to the specific biological characteristics that make it suitable to the already living ill sibling. According to a recent poll in the United States,[13] this type of embryo selection is viewed as acceptable by more people than the selection that intends to predetermine the sex of the child to be born.

Genetic testing and selection of embryos have been used already to make sure a baby will be a good match to donate blood or tissue to a sick brother or sister. In this case, even if the matching or saviour sibling is not used merely as a donor, the idea of creating a child for saving poses serious ethical problems. Although ethically this case is distinguishable from the case when a couple needs an in vitro embryo for

---

12 See also Faden, R.R., Dawson, L., Bateman-House, A.S., Mueller Agnew, D., Bok, H., et al. (2003), 'Public Stem Cell Banks: Consideration of Justice in Stem Cell Research and Therapy', *Hastings Center Reports* 33(6) (November–December 2003) 13–27.

13 A new report by the Genetics and Public Policy Center at Johns Hopkins University.

reproductive purposes, both techniques use selection with reference to the desire to help their already existing sick child. Here the desire to have a child is independent from the intent to instrumentalise the child, and selection plays only an additional criterion.

One of the most well-known saviour sibling cases is the American Nash case. Parents of a six-year-old female child with rapidly progressive bone marrow failure and myelodysplastic syndrome decided to have a saviour sibling for her. The technique that was used for the selection was pre-implantation genetic diagnosis. The child was born in August 2000. He is HLA-identical[14] to his sister. Three weeks after his birth, the sick child was treated with high doses of chemo-radiotherapy followed by the infusion of blood collected from her brother's placenta and umbilical cord after his birth.[15] She showed bone marrow recovery after four weeks.[16]

Diagnosed and Selected Body: Case of Pre-Implantation Genetic Diagnosis (PGD)

This technique involves the removal and genetic analysis of one or two cells from embryos created through in vitro fertilisation. PGD test results are used to select embryos that are transferred to a woman's womb to initiate pregnancy. While PGD was originally developed to prevent transmission of serious diseases, it has recently been used to pick embryos based on certain desired characteristics, such as sex or suitability for use as a tissue donor.[17] The boundaries of selection have become a controversial issue and, with the development of genetic research in this field, may provoke new problems.

Genetic enhancement should be differentiated from the embryo selection that serves the purpose of avoiding miscarriages and grievous diseases of the foetus.[18] According to Jürgen Habermas, the fact that some parents may determine certain

---

14 HLA stands for human lymphocyte antigen. It is genetically determined and is involved in cell self-identification and histocompatibility.

15 Susan Wolf points out correctly that a child created to be a donor is likely to have cord blood harvested at birth. If cord blood transplant fails, the question will immediately arise whether the donor child should undergo bone marrow harvest.

16 Wolf, S.M., Kahn, J.P. and Wagner, J.E. (2003), 'Using Preimplantation Genetic Diagnosis to Create a Stem Cell Donor: Issues, Guidelines and Limits', *Journal of Law, Medicine & Ethics* 31, 327.

17 McGee, G. (2000), *The Perfect Baby – Parenthood in the New World of Cloning and Genetics* (Boston: Rowman & Littlefield).

18 In 2003 the German National Ethics Council published a comprehensive opinion on genetic diagnosis before and during pregnancy, in which in the ethical assessment, as an argument against PGD, an objection was mentioned, that 'PGD sometimes calls into question the human individual's status as a person and turns him into an item of testable merchandise, because people could no longer conceive of themselves as free and equal if their characteristics did not develop naturally but were determined externally'. See German National Ethics Council (2003), *Genetic Diagnosis before and during Pregnancy: Opinion* (Berlin: Nationaler Ethikrat) 122.

characteristics of their future children by choosing certain features will create new relationships between the generations.[19]

I believe a new relationship between the person and the body may be generated by these new technological possibilities. We are starting to see our body and its 'building blocks' as more and more recyclable. To store blood, gametes and stem cells for future use has become an expectation of many health service consumers. And indeed, stem cell research may go in the direction of creating tissue banks. It is not yet clear who will contribute and who will benefit from these banks.[20] It is an equally grounded concern that in the near future elite medicine might be detached from the possibilities of mass treatment. It is obvious that therapeutic interferences using gene therapy and stem cells are currently very expensive and the access to them is very limited.

According to the ethical consensus in Europe (as it is represented by the Oviedo Convention), donors cannot ask for any reimbursement for their 'bodily contribution'. According to article 21 of the Convention, 'The human body and its parts shall not, as such, give rise to financial gain'. At the same time, healthcare therapies using these procedures are expensive and thus available only for the wealthier patients – storage is, in itself, very costly. Here a distinction should be made between public and private tissue banks. One special case of the latter is when umbilical cord blood is stored for the purposes of future medical assistance for the newborn and for the family. In this case the newborn baby can be considered as a donor, though as the blood in the umbilical cord is extra corporal, nevertheless it is regarded as blood that belonged to the baby.

Cloned Body

A confusion between genetic similarity and personal identity accelerated the debate on human cloning. Moreover, the integrated vision of body provoked even more exaggerated reactions as clones were imagined as copied human persons with not only identical genetic make-ups but with identical personalities.

Among all techniques, reproductive cloning seems to be so far the only unanimously prohibited intervention. However, it is not entirely clear what is the ethical foundation of such a limitation. Though reproductive cloning is prohibited by numerous legal instruments,[21] the desire to clone babies for reproductive purposes and often for substituting a deceased sibling appears in the news from time to time. In the case of reproductive cloning, not simply body parts and functions are to be

---

19 The argument is developed in Habermas, J. (2001), *Die Zukunft der menschlichen Natur: Auf dem Wege zu einer liberalen Eugenik* (Frankfurt am Main: Suhrkamp).

20 We might believe optimistically in a certain bodily solidarity. We know that umbilical cord blood banks might help children who are not members of the donor's family.

21 Article 11 of the *UNESCO Universal Declaration on the Human Genome and Human Rights* (adopted in 1997) states: 'Practices which are contrary to human dignity, such as reproductive cloning of human beings, shall not be permitted.' Furthermore, the Council of Europe adopted its *Protocol to the Convention on Human Rights and Biomedicine on the Prohibition of Cloning Human Beings* in 1997.

substituted but an entire human body, and this leads to the belief that in this way even a person can be substituted. The strongest argument against cloning is that it is an extremely risky, almost a trial-and-error, procedure that would involve unethical human experimentation leading to many wasted embryos and pregnancies. The clone, the opponents maintain, may suffer from severe disability. The problem with this position is that once technological advances reach a sufficient level of safety, these arguments cannot be applied any longer.

In addition to the arguments on safety, however, grave ethical concerns are raised against the instrumentalisation of human beings by using them as mere copies. According to the Universal Declaration on Human Genome and Human Rights, it is contrary to the principle of human dignity to clone people. But does dignity cover the genetic uniqueness of the individual? Once they are born, clones would deserve human dignity just as any other human beings living in the world. Social scientists would definitely disagree with the opinion that a copied human being is identical with the 'original'. Education, environment, personal history, inter-personal relations would make all clones different from each other.

Ethical dilemmas are also raised when a clone is demanded only to substitute someone. If a child is lost due to a tragedy, some families would like to clone a child. In these cases a reductionist view on person identifies a deceased child with a genetic copy. The reductionist view is unethical as it ignores personality, human dignity and consequently self-determination of persons to create their own, non-genetic identity.

Non-Commercialisation

Pharmaceutical and biotechnological companies have recently become interested in getting direct access to gene donors, to pregnant women (for instance, for umbilical cord blood), to prospective research subjects and to pharmaceutical product users. Whether we like it or not, healthcare has to operate under new circumstances where commercial actors contribute and seek the benefits of biomedical science, and patients, as consumers, seek healthcare and other biomedical services.[22]

The prohibition of making profit from the human body and its parts is stated by article 3 of the Charter of Fundamental Rights. It follows that the donation of organs, blood, stem cells, gametes, and so on, must not give rise to the reimbursement of the donors, apart from the justified compensation of costs.[23]

The legal claim for non-commercialisation and intellectual property law seem often in contradiction. Intellectual property law allows the establishment of patents on living organisms including even parts of the human body. There is a fear among the wider public related to the concept of the body as a carrier of information on the human being. However, the effects of patent law are often misinterpreted. Patents do not provide direct access to the individual nor do they create a legal access to the human body, only to the knowledge and information related to that body. A

---

22 Franceschi, M. (2004), *Droit et marchandisation de la connaissance sur les génes humaines* (Paris: CNRS).

23 See also the Oviedo Convention above.

patent provides the patent holder with protection, for a period of 20 years in general, against the commercial exploitation of the invention by others. Thus, a patent on some human biological material in itself does not alter the right to self-determination over the body.

We should mention here that European law deals laconically with this question. According to Council Directive 98/44/EC of 6 July 1998 on the legal protection of biotechnological inventions, and in particular its article 5 on the patentability of elements isolated from the human body, an organ, tissue, cell, gene, or other part isolated from the human body or otherwise produced by means of a technical process, including the sequence of a gene, may constitute an invention, even if the structure of that element is identical to that of a natural element.[24]

Conclusions

What follows then from these examples in which the human body and its parts are used for saving, curing and creating life and storing for research and future therapies? Should this area be more regulated? One fear that may motivate some regulation is the increasing danger of commercialising the human body. Gender issues are also implicated, as women are more exposed to the possibility of commercialised uses of their body: they carry saviour siblings, their eggs are used in various stem cell procedures. Moreover, the market of fear often targets women (especially pregnant women and women before delivery) to offer new medical technologies (even without proper research) to 'guarantee' the health of their children. Law in part reacts to the current social potential of science, but in addition it takes an overview of the basic ethical norms affecting future risks, basic rights and social values, health policy and scientific research, and then attempts to develop legal norms based upon these.

Legal changes have been much more limited than is warranted by the pressure for innovation emerging from science. Once a new technical or scientific development unfolds, legal thought is tending towards legal incorporation and analysis, rather than the development of new legal institutions. However, I do not agree with the widespread opinion that 'law always lags behind science'. What is a scientific novelty does not automatically require a brand new legal framework; no one urges, for instance, new traffic rules each time a new car, even if it introduces a revolutionary technical innovation, appears on the market. What does require regulation may well be based on a social and ethical assessment, and not all new legal instruments follow from scientific discoveries. Too early regulation without proper assessment may be as dangerous as leaving something unregulated for a certain time. If scientific advances require speedy normative responses, legal policy debates will become more and more isolated from a cultural and ethical elaboration of the concept of body. It seems that legal terminology may not easily overcome epistemological difficulties derived from the vague physical frontiers of the human body.

---

24 The Directive 98/44/EC of the European Parliament and of the Council of 6 July 1998.

Sometimes very risky and controversial scientific or technological inventions may require an urgent reaction, injunction or moratorium but not necessarily comprehensive regulation. Another way to avoid serious policy mistakes of responding to the pressure by too swiftly formulated regulations is the introduction of regular follow-up procedures in law.

Sometimes not the scientific invention itself but the ethical–social consequences of different inventions together require a change in legal policy. I believe that the consequences of biomedical advances on self-determination do call for a rethinking of legal policies and even the appropriateness of certain legal categories; self-determination over the in vitro elements of the human body does constitute such a case. While some elements of regulation should follow the logic of property law, some others, as genetic information creates a link between the person and the stored samples, require rights of persons. Furthermore, in the case of embryos, their special status serves as a model for regulation.

In order to develop a new legal framework, widely acceptable boundaries of different uses of the human body need to be established within the healthcare system. According to Tristam Engelhardt,

> the goal has been (so far) to find a culture-dependent border between those interventions that are truly medical (in that they respond to true diseases) and those that are not truly medical (in that they respond to conditions that are not true diseases, but merely dissatisfactions with elements of human conditions). Were such a border available, one could direct the energies of physicians and the resources of society toward addressing real medical needs and not face the prospect of a health care system without firm boundaries regarding what it is committed to treating.[25]

Though Engelhardt argues for a clear distinction between medical treatment and enhancement, the determination of which needs are medical and which are not is very dynamic in reality. What was considered a non-medical need 20 years ago, by now may well have become a truly medical need, such as the need for in vitro fertilisation. Nevertheless, I agree that defining boundaries is crucial in formulating regulative policies and developing the healthcare system. These boundaries may change as medicalisation reaches and encompasses new areas, but ethical assessment should be a routine part of licensing and authorising new technologies, as well as of determining the ways of access to them. As a response to the process of medicalisation, the claim for self-determination will be always present in policy debates. Moreover, some of these self-determination rights may survive the death of the person, and based on the act of donation in the lifetime of the donating person, his/her gametes, stem cells, organs may function in a new body. In this sense, the body becomes immortal, and the corresponding ethical dilemmas undying.

---

25 Engelhardt Jr., H.T. (2002), 'Germ-Line Genetic Engineering and Moral Diversity', reprinted in Sherlock, R. and Morrey, J.D. (eds), *Ethical Issues in Biotechnology* (Boston: Rowman and Littlefield) 513. Originally published in 1996.

Chapter 11

Masculinity, Reproductivity and Law

Michael Thomson[1]

Introduction

'Every woman he dares to sleep with bears his child. ... To be so fertile was a curse. To be so timid was a curse, as well.'

Jim Crace

The celebrated actor Felix (Lix) Dern, the focus of Jim Crace's novel, *Six*, is both hyper-fertile (a 'teeming alpha-male'[2]) and crushingly timid. Negotiating this central motif, Crace's novel maps out the actor's life. Chapters of Dern's life and Crace's novel reveal the six women he has loved. Whilst the actor is astonishingly potent and cannot escape the consequences of his love making, his emotional life is a failure, his six children unavoidable reminders.

Crace's novel provides an interesting starting point for a consideration of masculine corporeality and, more specifically, understandings of male reproductivity. Dern's experience of his potency is at odds with law's understanding of men and their reproductive bodies. Where historically legal discourse and practice has associated and tied women to their reproductivity, in law men have been comparatively distanced from this aspect of lived experience. This chapter considers the continued entrenchment of this difference in Anglo-American law. In particular, it briefly looks at two moments where the male reproductive body features (or fails to feature) in law. Firstly, the chapter addresses the legal regulation of workplaces that are seen as potentially damaging to reproductive health. Secondly, the legal regulation of routine neonatal male circumcision is considered.

The chapter starts by outlining Dern's imagined corporeality/reproductivity. Here it is argued that whilst Dern is very (traditionally) masculine in his sexual desires – indeed, we are frequently reminded of the rise and fall of our lead's penis and the various causes of this arousal – his experience of the consequences of acting on these desires is in many ways a feminised experience. Dern is constantly aware of, and limited by, the possible reproductive consequences of his sexual acts. Following from this, the chapter moves to outline how this model of a corporeal masculinity

1 The author would like to thank Ruth Fletcher, Marie Fox, Ambreena Manji and Sally Sheldon for their – as ever – insightful and helpful comments on an earlier draft. I am also very grateful for the research assistance provided by Nicola Barker and Julie McCandless. This assistance was partly funded by the AHRB Centre for Law, Gender and Sexuality.

2 Crace, J. (2003), *Six* (London: Penguin) 2.

is at odds with circulating ideas of the male body and its reproductive functions and possibilities. This is achieved through a consideration of the two brief case studies noted above.

Gender more than any other factor is central to the determination of health profile. Looking to law's engagement with the male (reproductive) body, the chapter asks for an ethical interrogation of the gendered body of healthcare law and policy. In particular, it looks at the need to question the way in which law replicates ideas concerning male corporeality that are circulating within wider discursive fields. Further, it is recognised that the incorporation of this imaginary anatomy embeds and normalises within the law the costs to male health that are the result of these understandings of masculinity and the male body.

Lix's Love

Crace's novel takes place in the 'once famous City of Kisses'.[3] The city is a romantic composite, a cityscape in flux; both generic and specific enough to respond to the reader's desires. The romantic title, City of Kisses, emerged from a *Life* photojournalism piece looking at 50 of the world's cities on one day. Dern's city, briefly emerging from a time of political repression, was revealed in a montage of kisses, erotic and otherwise. The signature image became an eroticised non-kiss: a woman in a Cuban beret applying a lipstick kiss to a glass of wine with her red mouth. In the glass, two men are reflected. Their own mouths are gaping and both are encircled – or consumed – by the kiss.[4] Reminiscent of many such iconic images, the photograph lived on in mass-produced posters.

Against this backdrop, the life of the 'fertile and flamboyant'[5] Lix unfolds. At its heart, it is a familiar tale of the pursuit of sex and love. The tale is of relationships, their incompleteness, and of mis/communication between the sexes. Yet in a number of ways our expectations are upset. The most obvious of these contradicted expectations concerns Lix's fertility. Whilst masculinity is often calibrated against a measure of potency (including impotency), we are drawn to what is understood as the more biological, and differently gendered, idea of fertility.[6] As already noted, Dern is unable to have sex without fathering a child. His experience is far removed from Giddens' 'plastic sexuality', the decentred sexuality that is freed from the needs of reproduction and is supposed to define modern relationships.[7] Each of his life's sexual and emotional partners have conceived and born a child. Dern's understanding of his sex life is in terms of his fertility and its consequences. This can be illustrated with a scene from our lead's life. At one point he contemplates an act of infidelity whilst

---

3 Ibid, 3.

4 Ibid, 7.

5 Ibid, 5.

6 Even though we are made very aware of his virility, we also see Dern as fertile rather than potent through our awareness of his timidity, which acts as counterpoise.

7 Giddens, A. (1993), *The Transformation of Intimacy. Sexuality, Love and Eroticism in Modern Societies* (Cambridge: Polity Press) 2.

out at breakfast with his third wife, a woman who had that prior night conceived his sixth child. Contemplating this act, Dern asks 'What harm in that?'

> The harm in that for him was the misfortune – was it truly a misfortune? – that every kiss produced a child. Remember? Fertile Lix had never slept with anyone without – eventually – a pregnancy. There always was an aftermath for him.[8]

And whilst Crace recognises that 'human biology is unequal in its distributions and rewards',[9] the formulation narrated here challenges (social) norms. Surveying the breakfasting women, Dern considers his possible fantasy companions. Of the many possibilities, he finally decides on an older woman who is 'oddly dressed, boy-haired and overdrawn as a cartoon':[10]

> How dare the over-fertile Lix take his *jolie laide* down to the beach …? Well, to all intents and purposes, that was not so problematic, he realized at once. Her age. Of course! He studied her again. Yes, in her fifties, certainly. Her fertile years long gone. Here was a woman he could safely cheat with, if he were the cheating kind. Perhaps that's why he'd felt so free in his imagination in her company. Whatever they might do, there'd be no child. It could be his first and only non-productive affair. Inconsequential sex![11]

Such awareness of fertility is, of course, more often associated with women. Indeed, literature is replete with stories of women's (generally) unsuccessful attempts to manage their fertility and men's disregard for the reproductive consequences of their actions. Dern challenges this, indeed, Dern questions the normal (clichéd?) triangulation of love, sex and gender. Watching Dern, Crace observes: 'Men fall in love more speedily and much more bodily than women.'[12] Indeed, in some ways Dern is more generally feminised in his physicality. This is seen in the cherry-sized and shaped birthmark on his face. This birthmark, like his fertility, makes him aware of his physicality, his bodily place in the world.

At the same time, the wider gender topography of Crace's world is very familiar. Dern is threatened by the female body, a fear translated to the city landscape. The City of Kisses – that city reduced to an image of a feminine and consuming mouth – is itself feminised, particularly in its leaky fluidity.[13] The City of Kisses, lying in the fold or embrace of a great European river, is prone to flooding. Whilst Dern enjoys it playfully at times (stranded at one point on the roof of his apartment building with his new wife, his youth and few cares) at others the flood is violent, consuming and destructive.

---

8 Crace, op. cit., 50.

9 Ibid, 29.

10 Ibid, 49.

11 Ibid, 51.

12 Ibid, 82.

13 Shildrick, M. (1997), *Leaky Bodies and Boundaries: Feminism, Postmodernism and (Bio)ethics* (London: Routledge).

Hegemonic Masculinities

As argued above, Dern's corporeality – his conspicuous fertility – is at odds with received understandings of men and their physicality. Whilst potency may be associated with masculinity, it is generally meant as that which is not impotent, rather than that which is fertile. In other words, men's bodies have historically been understood as sexed bodies rather than as reproductive bodies, and this is perhaps most clearly seen in the discussion of circumcision below. It is also illustrated with the example of the discourses around the erectile dysfunction drug Viagra and, in particular, its advertising. Here the focus is very much on images associated with a 'manly' masculinity – primarily a sporting, active masculinity – rather than foregrounding any procreative function.[14] This image of an active masculinity – sporting and potent – can be better understood by addressing Bob Connell's concept of hegemonic masculinity. In discussing this concept I want to foreground the place of masculine corporeality. In particular, I want to underline the role that specific models of the masculine body have within the hegemonic project. This will inform the subsequent discussion of law's masculine bodies.

Connell's theory is a reworking of Gramsci's idea of hegemony. Gramsci formulated the term in his attempt to understand class inequalities in democratic societies. Hegemony referred to 'the cultural dynamic by which a group claims and sustains a leading position in social life'.[15] Important within this model is the idea of consent. Ascendancy is maintained primarily through consent to the group's moral and intellectual leadership. Looking to Gramsci's formulation, Connell sought to map out the mechanisms through which inequalities in the gender order were reproduced. How are relationships of domination and subordination between men and between men and women routinely accepted? Hegemonic masculinity therefore becomes 'the configuration of gender practices which embodies the currently accepted answer to the problem of legitimacy of patriarchy, which guarantees (or is taken to guarantee) the dominant position of men and the subordination of women'.[16] Given the class and gender inequalities inherent in these relationships, Connell (and Gramsci) argued that the hegemonic group was never static, it was always contested and contingent. In other words, at different locations and at different times the hegemonic ideal is open to challenge from those whose practices conflict with the current hegemonic

---

14 See Thomson, M. (2006), 'Viagra Nation: Sex and the Prescribing of Familial Masculinity', *Law, Culture and the Humanities* 2:2, 259–83. Jennifer Harding's analysis of the media scare over environmental oestrogen levels challenges this assertion. Harding argues that the media-associated link to declining sperm levels revealed and relied upon an association between ideas of masculinity and potency/fertility. It is arguable, however, that this association is grounded in different ideas of emasculation. The oestrogen in the water supply is seen as the result of the widespread use of the contraceptive pill. Here men are seen as (further) emasculated by virtue of the technology that allowed women some control over their fertility. This physical 'emasculation' mirrors the (perceived) social emasculation that followed equality gains from the 1960s onwards. Harding, J. (1998), *Sex Acts: Practices of Femininity and Masculinity* (London: Sage).

15 Connell, R.W. (1995), *Masculinities* (Cambridge: Polity) 77.

16 Ibid.

structure. In short, hegemonic masculinity is the ideal expression of masculinity at a given place and time. Whilst Connell's work has moved towards attempting to identify *a* global hegemonic masculinity,[17] others have moved to question both the degree to which we can talk about *a* hegemonic masculinity and the extent to which masculinity/ies may be reduced purely to the sociological.

In terms of the first of these concerns, it is clear that Connell's concept recognises multiple masculinities. Connell constructs a model whereby a dominant masculinity is defined not just in terms of femininity but also various marginal, subordinate, and complicit masculinities.[18] Yet this tends to suggest *one* dominant masculinity, an increasingly problematic notion. The problems with this notion can be explained more clearly if we recognise that signifiers of masculinity may well vary in how they are played out in different cultural and class contexts:

> Social class positioning both constrains and enables certain forms of gendered social action and influences which ... behaviours are used to demonstrate masculinity. Demonstrating masculinities with fearless, high-risk behaviours may entail skydiving for an upper-class man, mountain climbing for a middle-class man, racing hot rods for a working-class man and street fighting for a poor urban man.[19]

Whilst the skydiver may have more economic and political power than the street fighter, these masculinities are nonetheless dominant within the context of their location. Whilst this helps to provide us with a more textured understanding of masculinity, it is also important to note the place of the physical – including the corporeal – in these different displays of, or claims to, hegemonic masculinities. In addition, it needs to be remembered that the collective effects of asserting masculinity are beneficial to all men even though the risks and rewards involved are unevenly distributed. This runs counter to the idea of a singular dominant masculinity and arguably has greater conceptual and analytical utility. A convincing critique of Connell's tendency towards a unitary hegemonic masculinity and some of its subsequent prolific usage has been forwarded by Tony Jefferson. Responding to the general concept of *a* hegemonic masculinity and Connell's recent focus on a global hegemonic masculinity, Jefferson asks whether there is only ever one hegemonic strategy at any given historical moment, or whether hegemonic masculinity is more contingent and context-specific, an idea that would accord with Connell's commitment to gender/masculinity as relational. Jefferson argues for recognition of multiple hegemonic masculinities, illustrating his position by focusing on the relationship between hegemonic and subordinate, complicit or marginalised masculinities in particular contexts. Again there is a focus – although to a lesser extent – on the physical:

> In school playgrounds up and down the country the masculinity that is hegemonic is more likely to be ... [a] physical, and anti-intellectual (but subordinate, in Connell's terms) masculinity ... [rather] than that of the computer 'nerd' or 'boffin'. Or, imagine Bill

---

17 Connell, R.W. (1998), 'Masculinities and Globalization', *Men and Masculinities* 1, 3.

18 Connell, *Masculinities*, op.cit., 78–9.

19 Courtenay, W.H. (2000), 'Constructions of Masculinity and their Influence on Men's Well-being: A Theory of Gender and Health', *Social Science and Medicine* 50, 1385, 1389.

Gates parachuted (alone) into Manhattan's Bronx district or Chicago's southside. Would being an ordinary-looking, bespectacled, white, middle-class, male 'carrier' of global, hegemonic masculinity count for much in the black-dominated public scenarios where a certain ostentatious stylishness and physical presence constitutes one visible, strong (but marginalized, in Connell's terminology) masculine standard?[20]

Having sketched out the theoretical lens through which I intend to read law's response to the male reproductive body, I now want to move on to look at the two regulatory case studies. Whilst one considers responses to possible reproductive harm and the other genital surgery, both explore the relationship between masculinity, reproductivity and our understandings of the male body.

Law and Men's Bodies

... the doing of health is a form of doing gender.[21]

So, what is the relationship between ideas of hegemonic masculinity and law's imaginary male body? The male body is frequently understood as 'phallic and impenetrable, as a war-body simultaneously armed and armored, equipped for victory'.[22] It is a bounded and safe body. It is the body of the liberal individual, public policy and law. To return to Gramsci, it is that which has enabled consent to the group's moral and intellectual leadership. Other bodies – permeable or penetrated – fall out with (and allow) the privileging of this hermetic imaginary body. In terms of the female body, Moira Gatens has argued that the female body is seen, and often 'lived', as an *envelope, vessel* or *receptacle*.[23] Women's bodies lack integrity; they are socially constructed as partial, dependent and lacking.[24] This lack of integrity or completeness is also associated with dangerousness, disease and pollution.

This section illustrates how this understanding of the male body is embedded in law. It also highlights the consequences for the protection of male health that flow directly from this. It is, however, worth stressing that this imaginary/hegemonic anatomy also has lived consequences in the male population ungoverned by these or other specific laws. Idea(l)s of impermeability and invulnerability – especially when these converge with other signifiers of masculinity – lead to negative health consequences. And it is easy to evidence this by reference to most standard health

---

20 Jefferson, T. (2002), 'Subordinating Hegemonic Masculinity', *Theoretical Criminology* 6, 63, 72.

21 Saltonstall, R. (1993), 'Healthy Bodies, Social Bodies: Men's and Women's Concepts and Practices of Health in Everyday Life', *Social Science and Medicine* 36, 7, 12.

22 Waldby, C. (1995), 'Destruction: Boundary Erotics and Refiguration of the Heterosexual Male Body', in Grosz, E. and Probyn, E. (eds), *Sexy Bodies: The Strange Carnalities of Feminism* (London: Routledge) 266, 268.

23 Gatens, M. (1989), 'Woman and Her Double(s): Sex, Gender and Ethics', *Australian Feminist Studies* 10, 33, 43–4.

24 Ibid.

indicators.[25] Whilst health is clearly multi-factorial, adjusted for race, age and economic factors, gender remains the single largest determinant of health profile.[26]

In general, law says more about its idea or understanding of male reproductivity and male reproductive health through its silences and absences than it does through any direct engagement. The lack of engagement is perhaps unsurprising given the normativity of the male body – particularly the white, middle-class male body:

> [W]hite middle-class male forms of embodiment … are largely unconscious and inarticulate. They tend to encode technologies of normativity that do not require the work of conscious performance. They constitute an unproblematic physicality in the body politic. They navigate social space – both public and private – unobstructed, un(re)marked. The policing of such a body is an accomplished fact of middle-class pedagogy which rarely calls for external reinforcement. It is this body that stands as the hegemonic body *par excellence*.[27]

Briefly outlined below are two specific regulatory issues. Firstly, I briefly consider the male body that has failed to populate industrial foetal protection policies. Secondly, and more directly, I consider the law's approach to routine male circumcision. Whilst the analysis illustrates, in part, the invisibility noted directly above, the purpose of these outlines is more to provide a sense of how, within this jurisprudence, a particular male body and reproductivity is narrated.

Foetal Protection Policies

Industrial foetal protection policies provide an interesting case study, casting light on the way in which responses to reproductivity are gendered. An issue that has largely escaped consideration (legal or academic) in the UK, the issue has been aggressively litigated and considered in the US. Ostensibly in the name of protecting foetal health, the policies act to exclude fertile women from the toxic workplace on the basis of potential adverse reproductive outcomes.[28] In the US this has concerned measures introduced by private corporations. In the UK the policies are both private and those contained in health and safety legislation. Whilst only one case has considered the legality of such policies in the UK,[29] there has been a raft of legal challenges in the US. This culminated in the Supreme Court decision in *International Union, United Automobile Workers v. Johnson Controls Inc.*[30] Johnson Controls had introduced a policy of exclusion from lead-affected areas for 'women who are pregnant or capable

---

25 Courtenay, op. cit.

26 Ibid.

27 Perkinson, J. 'The Body of White Space: Beyond Stiff Voices, Flaccid Feelings and Silent Cells', in Tuana, N. and Cowling, W. (eds), *Revealing Male Bodies* (Bloomington, Indiana University Press), 173–174.

28 It should also be noted that historically protective labour laws have selectively exaggerated the vulnerabilities of white women whilst generally ignoring the risks to women of colour. See Daniels, C. (1997), 'Between Fathers and Fetuses: The Social Construction of Male Reproduction and the Politics of Fetal Harm', *Signs* 22, 582.

29 *Page v Freight Hire (Tank Haulage Co.) Ltd* I.R.L.R 13 (1981).

30 499 US 187, 1991.

of bearing children'. The policy excluded 'all women except those whose inability to bear children is medically documented'. A number of women decided to be sterilised rather than lose their (relatively highly paid, unionised) jobs, incomes and benefits in an area of high unemployment. Ultimately, and following three separate cases affirming the legality of foetal protection policies in the Courts of Appeals,[31] the policies were recognised as sex discrimination and therefore unlawful under Title VII of the Civil Rights Act 1964.

It is not my intention to provide a detailed critique of these policies; rather I wish – briefly and in outline – to foreground the lack of articulation of male reproductive health concerns and consider the significance of this silence.[32] Again, the reasons for this are complex, interrelated and involve broader questions of gender politics. These policies must, for instance, have become more likely to be mobilised against a backdrop of increased female participation in previously male-dominated sections of industry (Johnson Controls, as one example, manufactures batteries). Indeed, this articulation must have become even more likely given the economic recession, a recession felt particularly hard in the manufacturing sector. Regardless of these multiple determinants, of interest here is the construction of reproductivity and vulnerability. Reproductive health becomes readable/determined against a backdrop of broader gender politics, as Thomas Laqueur informs: 'sex … is situational; it is explicable only within the context of battles over gender and power'.[33]

Whilst the effects on male reproductive health from occupational toxins have been known for decades, foetal protection policies almost exclusively target female employees.[34] Such policies generally provide for the blanket exclusion of fertile women of reproductive age. As many commentators have noted, these policies tend to assume reproductive intent in women and deny agency. At the same time they ignore or deny the reproductive interests of men. Women are excluded from areas of exposure and men retained where it is known that male exposure at these levels can cause reproductive health problems, including damage to the foetus.[35] Yet the policies do more than ignore male reproductive and wider health interests. The policies rely upon and contribute towards the construction of a particular masculine body; a safe and impenetrable body, one which is also distanced from reproduction. Unlike Felix Dern's body with its (to him, cursed) hyper-fertility, the body constructed here has

---

31 *Wright v. Olin* 697 F.2d 1182; *Hayes v. Shelby Memorial Hospital* 726 F.2d 1543 (11th Cir. 1984); *UAW v. Johnson Controls Inc.* 886 F.2d 871 (7th Cir. 1989).

32 For detailed commentary, see works cited in this section, and Annas, G.J. (1991), 'Fetal Protection and Employment Discrimination – The Johnson Controls Case', *New England Journal of Medicine* 325, 740; Draper, E. (1993), 'Fetal Exclusion Policies and Gendered Constructions of Suitable Work', *Social Problems* 40, 90; Thomson, M. (1996), 'Employing the Body: The Reproductive Body and Employment Exclusion', *Social and Legal Studies* 5, 243; and Thomson, M. (2002), 'Reproductivity, the Workplace and the Gendering of the Body (Politic)', *Law and Literature* 14, 565–94.

33 Laqueur, T. (1990), *Making Sex: Body and Gender from the Greeks to Freud* (Cambridge, Mass: Harvard University Press) 11.

34 For a discussion of the gendered reading of reproductive occupational hazards, see: Thomson, 'Reproductivity, the Workplace and the Gendering of the (Body) Politic', op. cit.

35 Ibid.

no reproductive interests and no reproductive risks. As with screening programmes, those not excluded – generally men – are assumed to be safe, resistant to harm. Here, these policies also engage with the wider discursive association that sees the female body as dangerous, susceptible and as a vector for damage to the foetus.

In line with industry, academic commentary has also largely ignored male reproductive interests. One of the few exceptions is seen with Sally Sheldon's consideration of the case of Donald Penney.[36] As Sheldon observes, in all the commentary that followed the actions of Johnson Controls and the subsequent litigation, little or no mention was made of Penney, a litigant in the case. Penney had complained that his request for a leave of absence in order to lower his blood lead level in advance of starting a family had been refused. Penney claimed sex discrimination. His claim was that he was prevented from availing himself of the health measures that were being imposed on female members of the workforce. As Sheldon concludes, male reproductive interests are '*explicitly denied* or trivialized, deemed unimportant relative to the male imperative of paid work'.[37]

As such, these policies provide an interesting insight into how the legal imagination understands and constructs the male (reproductive) body and male reproductive interests. Very different from Dern, this body is not imagined as reproductive. As elsewhere, the male body is figured as bounded, impermeable and resistant to harm. As Sheldon notes, male reproductive interests are also seen as secondary to the masculine imperative of paid labour. And these two features are interrelated. The male body is constructed as 'fit for purpose'. Unlike the dangerous or weak feminine body, the masculine body is built for the labour of the workplace, a form of labour that derives economic, political and social benefits. The policies help to generate the hegemonic ideal of masculine bodily superiority with its attendant advantages.

Circumcision[38]

Routine neonatal male circumcision has had a colourful but largely neglected history on both sides of the Atlantic. Interest in male circumcision emerged at the same time as interest was rekindled in now long-discredited sexual/genital surgery for women.[39] As such, male circumcision has considerably outlasted, particularly in the US, other forms of genital surgery. It is notable that whilst male circumcision has languished until very recently as a non-issue, female genital mutilation/modification (FGM) has become an international equality issue.[40] And whilst male circumcision

---

36 Sheldon, S. (2002), 'The Masculine Body', in Lee, E., *Real Bodies: A Sociological Introduction* (Basingstoke: Palgrave) 14–28.

37 Interestingly, as with his female colleagues, Penney's agency is also denied, 'He is refused the possibility of prioritizing his body's reproductive capacity over and above his ability to labour, as surely this prioritization is forced on his female colleagues.' Ibid, 17.

38 This section emerges from a much larger and ongoing project with Marie Fox looking at male circumcision and other genital surgeries.

39 Gollaher, D.L. (1994), 'From Ritual to Science: The Medical Transformation of Circumcision in America', *Journal of Social History* 5, 25.

40 It should also be mentioned that the very different public positions of these two types of procedure is, of course, related. Campaigners against FGM have distanced the procedure

is incomparable with the brutal extremes of FGM, it should be emphasised that there are many procedures that fall under this umbrella term. All are outlawed and yet a number are no more invasive (indeed maybe less invasive) than routinely performed male circumcision.[41] Whilst foetal protection policies clearly illustrate the way in which ideas of reproductivity are gendered, this is less immediately the case when looking at routine male circumcision. Circumcision is more evidently about the sexed male body. What needs to be foregrounded, however, is the extent to which human rights activists highlight the impact of FGM on reproduction. No such discourse exists within consideration of male circumcision. Again, it is a moment when male reproductivity and male reproductive interests are erased.

In terms of male circumcisions, the issues of pain and physical harm are rarely considered. Yet it is accepted that pain is experienced by the neonate.[42] In addition, while complication rates from routine circumcision are low, the chances of these complications being mutilatory, infective or haemorrhagic are high.[43] Indeed, it should be stressed that complications are potentially catastrophic, since death, gangrene, and total or partial amputation are known adverse outcomes.[44] Notwithstanding the experience of pain and the attendant risks (for no scientifically unequivocal benefit[45]), the procedure is generally accepted as legal.

Whilst the law has responded with increasingly inflexible and absolute prescriptions against FGM, male circumcision has been assumed to be legal or, in the case of some US states, has been legislatively exempt from statutes criminalising some cultural practices (such as scarification) and forms of child abuse.[46] These provide for the exemption of circumcision from laws that prohibit ritual abuse, and of ritual circumcisers from prohibitions on the unauthorised practice of medicine.[47]

In the United Kingdom the status of male circumcision is similar, if a little more complex. No statutory provision exists that directly or indirectly defines the

from male circumcision due in part to the desire not to analogise it with a form of genital cutting that is widely practised and accepted. It may also be distanced due to the increased evidence this may provide to charges of discrimination on the grounds of cultural practice. See Fox, M. and Thomson, M. (2005), 'A Covenant with the Status Quo: The New BMA Guidance on Male Circumcision', *Journal of Medical Ethics* 31, 463–9.

41	Ibid.

42	See Benatar, M. and Benatar, D. (2003), 'Between Prophylaxis and Child Abuse: The Ethics of Neonatal Male Circumcision', *American Journal of Bioethics* 3, 35, 37–8; and accompanying references: Warnock, F. and Sandrin, D. (2004), 'Comprehensive Description of Newborn Distress Behavior in Response to Acute Pain (Newborn Male Circumcision)', *Pain* 107, 242–55.

43	Williams, N. and Kapila, L. (1993), 'Complications of Circumcision', *British Journal of Surgery* 80, 1231–6; Gerharz, E.W. and Haarmann, C. (2000), 'The First Cut is the Deepest? Medicolegal Aspects of Male Circumcision', *BJU International* 86, 332–8.

44	Hodges, F.M., Svoboda, J.S. and Van Howe, R.S. (2002), 'Prophylactic Interventions on Children: Balancing Human Rights with Public Health', *Journal of Medical Ethics* 10.

45	See Fox and Thomson, 'A Covenant with the Status Quo?' op. cit.

46	For an analysis of the legal status of circumcision in the US, see Miller, G.P. (2002), 'Circumcision: Cultural-Legal Analysis', *Virginia Journal of Social Policy and the Law* 9, 497, 527.

47	Ibid.

legal status of the operation. Limited legal consideration does, however, exist that suggests a judicial acceptance or presumption of legality. In *Consent in the Criminal Law*,[48] the Law Commission was generally highly critical of the landmark House of Lords decision in *R v. Brown*, which criminalised the infliction of injury during consensual sado-masochistic sex. However, it endorsed an *obiter* comment by Lord Templeman, which lists male circumcision as an example of a deliberately inflicted, but apparently lawful, injury: 'Ritual circumcision, tattooing, ear piercing and violent sports including boxing are lawful activities.'[49] The Law Commission concluded that the lawfulness of male circumcision should be put beyond doubt.[50] Parliament has yet to do so, leaving open the question of routine circumcision's lawfulness.[51]

In addition to these statements, there are only two reported English cases on circumcision. In *Re J* a five-year-old boy lived with his mother, a non-practising Christian.[52] His father was a non-practising Muslim who, following a separation, lived elsewhere. The father wanted J to be circumcised in accordance with his faith/culture and in order to identify him with his father. The mother did not want the boy to undergo the operation. The Court of Appeal concluded that J should not be circumcised. It was believed that his 'essentially secular lifestyle' was unlikely to justify circumcising him for social reasons. Reaching this conclusion, the court avoided directly addressing the legal status of non-therapeutic circumcision. Rather, the court could simply reaffirm that the consent of both parents would be desirable.

This approach was recently followed in *Re S*. Here the Court of Appeal addressed a similar dispute.[53] A mother applied to the court for her eight-year-old son to be circumcised as a member of the Islamic faith. The application was opposed by the father. Here, the deciding factors were that the child had been brought up in a predominantly Jain household and the mother's primary motivation for seeking her son's circumcision seemed to be that her new husband was Muslim. Again, the best interest calculation did not engage with the fundamental question of whether it was in the best interests of the child to face the excision of healthy tissue, with the attendant risks and no demonstrable health benefit.

So, how can we understand the legal response to male circumcision? Lord Templeman brackets circumcision with activities that are generally only legal for consenting adults. Most notably, His Lordship aligns routine circumcision with violent sport, boxing in particular. More generally, male circumcision appears to be the only time at which we sanction the excision of healthy tissue for no demonstrable medical benefit and without the consent of the individual involved. Why should this be the case? Indeed, why should this be so when the criminalisation and eradication

---

48 Law Commission Consultation Paper 139, *Consent in the Criminal Law (1995)*.

49 *R. v Brown* [1993] 2 All ER 75, 78–9.

50 Law Commission, op cit., para. 9.3.

51 Per Lord Mustill in *Brown*, 109.

52 *Re J (A Minor) (Prohibited Steps Order: Circumcision), sub nom Re J (Child's Religious Upbringing and Circumcision) and Re J (Specific Issue Orders: Muslim Upbringing & Circumcision)* [2000] 1 FLR 571; [2000] 1 FCR 307; (2000) 52 BMLR 82.

53 *Re S (Children) (Specific Issue: Circumcision)* [2005] 1 F.L.R. 236.

of female circumcision has become a global issue? There are, as Marie Fox and I have argued elsewhere, a number of possible explanations for this position.[54] Within the context of this chapter there are two factors that should be foregrounded. The first, I would argue, takes us back to the discussion of the ideal body of hegemonic masculinity; that is the risk-free, invincible and impenetrable body. This would explain why the pain suffered by the neonate is routinely ignored and the risks downplayed.[55] Where risky behaviour and the endurance of pain can be seen as key indicators of masculinity – with the attendant costs this has for male health – routine circumcision can be understood as an early training in being a man. Whilst the risk of harm to women and female children is routinely exaggerated, harm to men is often downplayed or ignored.

The second factor that needs to be considered is the issue of the invisibility of male reproductive interests. As demonstrated in the consideration of foetal protection policies, whilst women are constructed as primarily reproductive actors, men's reproductivity and reproductive interests are frequently negated. Here men's interests are routinely put at risk, in part because of a failure to recognise these interests and in part because of law's imagined male body. This body is far removed from that narrated by Crace with its connectivity and place in the world.

Conclusion

> [I]f men could become pregnant, they would not be men (indeed no one would be a man as we understand the term), and to ask how abortion would be treated in so fundamentally different a world is to ask a question that is not subject to meaningful evaluation.[56]

Cass Sunstein's assertion is intriguing, engaging and deserves a far fuller analysis than I can afford it here. Whilst I do not wish to engage with the many problems and implications of the statement – including the sterile position regarding counterfactual inquiry that Sunstein adopts – I do want to 'jump off' from the association that is made between reproductive responsibility and gender. Whilst Sunstein is obviously addressing issues of US constitutional equality law, the gender axis along which reproductivity/reproductive responsibility is divided is clearly central to the case studies above. It is this form of division that meant Donald Penney was unable to limit his exposure to lead in advance of attempts to start a family. More generally, it is this division that foetal protection policies are predicated on. In terms of circumcision, the (almost exclusive) association drawn between women and reproductivity has contributed towards young boys lacking the same protection afforded young girls.

Yet is this changing? It is clear that men's interests in their reproductivity has shifted – or at least entered public discourse in a new way – in recent years.

54　Fox and Thomson, 'A Covenant with the Status Quo?' op. cit. See also Fox, M. and Thomson, M. (2005), 'Short Changed?: The Law and Ethics of Male Circumcision', *International Journal of Children's Rights* 13, 157.

55　Fox and Thomson, 'Short Changed?' op.cit.

56　Sunstein, C.R. (1992), 'Neutrality in Constitutional Law (With Special Reference to Pornography, Abortion, and Surrogacy)', *Columbia Law Review* 92, 1, 35, n. 129.

Circumcision, for instance, is emerging in the US as a new site of public awareness and concern. Men claiming the effects of the disputed Gulf War syndrome have alleged adverse reproductive effects and outcomes. The UK has seen a change in the law regarding donor anonymity, signalling, some would argue, a move against the historic detachment of men from their gametes. There does seem to be a changing male physicality and this has extended to the male reproductive body. Whilst Lix Dern's inability to have sex without consequence is far removed from contemporary lived experience, are we moving to a more feminised masculine reproductivity? If so, will this fold out to a more general reconsideration of the male body with its perceived invulnerability and safety? And, importantly, will this translate to legal change?

To close I want to return again to Donald Penney. Penney had an awareness of his reproductive body – a clear interest in his reproductive health. Yet this awareness and interest was elided both by the policies and within subsequent academic commentary. Yet, change might come, in part, through recovering the story of Penney and others. Narratives telling of men's awareness of their reproductive bodies and lives may act to challenge the circulating ideal of the hegemonic masculine body. Penney, Dern and others tell a story very different from the masculine body of law that leaves men's reproductive and sexed bodies unprotected. An interesting place to finish is with a 2004 study of fatherhood and HIV-positive heterosexual men. In their study, Sherr and Barry detail how HIV-positive heterosexual men are rarely given medical advice on reproduction. Yet the majority of the (relatively small) cohort felt that children gave meaning to life and a reason to live.[57] Nearly half of the men had considered having children, with only one in ten feeling that they were not ready for fatherhood.[58] At the same time they felt uninformed regarding the risks of transmission and the availability of techniques such as sperm washing. Significantly, most of the cohort considerably overestimated the risks of vertical transmission.[59] Such research again highlights how men's reproductive interests are frequently ignored. It also adds, however, to the potentially productive counter-narrative of men as reproductive actors and as aware of the sometimes fragile nature of their reproductive health and options.

---

57 Sherr, L. and Barry, N. (2004), 'Fatherhood and HIV-positive Heterosexual Men', *HIV Medicine* 5, 258–63.

58 Ibid, 260.

59 Ibid.

Chapter 12

Being Natural: An Exploration of the Natural in the Writings of Hans Christian Andersen

Søren Holm

Some of my best childhood memories revolve around the beach and the woods close to our family summerhouse. A lazy day in the dunes with an occasional dip in the sea, seeing a group of deer walk slowly through the forest, walking on a frozen lake in the winter, or fishing for cod on a cold autumn day; all of these experiences are indelibly imprinted in my memory and by thinking of them I can still conjure up a primeval feeling best described as a complex mixture of enjoyment, wonder and awe.

In literature we can find similar (but much more eloquent) descriptions of nature, but we can also find many novels and poems where the crueller side of nature plays a large role.

Many of us have a tendency to believe that if something is natural, it is therefore also good, and this idea pops up in many contexts: when we admonish other people to let their spoiled children run riot because it is 'only natural for boys of that age', when we talk about certain chemicals being natural and therefore presumably less dangerous, or when we discuss the ethical evaluation of 'unnatural' forms of procreation like test tube babies.

The question I want to explore in this chapter is connected to our use of ideas about the natural in ethics. I will explore this through the writings of one of the Danish authors that has written most about nature, the nineteenth-century writer Hans Christian Andersen. Most people know *The Ugly Duckling*, a (partly autobiographical) story about a young cygnet who is brought up in a ducks' nest, but whose nature eventually becomes apparent. This story gives a mainly positive account of nature, but this is by no means the case in all of Andersen's writing.

Here we will concentrate on two of the darker stories: *The Little Mermaid*[1] (1836) and *The Story of a Mother* (1848). Despite the fact that we now see Andersen as a fairy tale writer, he did not write his stories primarily for children and many of them are, if read in their original versions, clearly not nice bedtime stories. The not so hidden sub-text of this chapter is therefore also to get you, my dear reader, to go and

---

1 In its original, non-Disneyfied version.

read H.C. Andersen again, especially since 2005 was the bicentenary of his birth. You may well be surprised at what you find.[2]

Is Nature Ethical?

The most prominent school of thought in ethics that maintains that we can gain ethical wisdom from nature is natural law theory. Like all ethical theories it exists in many versions, but the most important version is that held by the Catholic Church. The main claim of natural law theory is that nature contains clues to how we ought to act. A proponent of natural law theory explains it in the following way:

> At the heart of tradition, however, is a conviction that creation is itself revelatory, and knowledge of the requirements of respect for created beings is accessible at least in part to human reason. This is what is at stake in the tradition's understanding of natural law. For most of its history, Catholic natural law theory has not assumed that morality can simply be 'read off' of nature, not even with the important help of Scripture. Nonetheless, what natural law theory does is tell us where to look; that is, to the concrete reality of the world around us, the basic needs and possibilities of human persons in relation to one another, and to the world as a whole. Looking (to concrete reality) means a complex process of discernment and deliberation, a structuring of insights, a determination of meaning from the fullest vantage point available, given a particular history that includes the illumination of Scripture and accumulated wisdom of the tradition. Hence, the intelligibility of 'realities' is not such that their meaning is immediately obvious. What is given to our understanding through experience is not only always partial, but it must always be interpreted. The limits, yet necessity, of this process account for many disagreements about specific matters, even within the faith community.[3]

Both of the H.C. Andersen stories we are going to look at here can be seen as an attempt to structure insights, determine meaning and discern the importance of nature and natural developments in the concrete lives of two different persons. Both stories also consciously play on the fact that such discernment must take place within the accumulated wisdom of a tradition. In the end they do, however, end up illustrating in a very clear way that nature is ethically ambiguous.

The Story of a Mother is the seemingly more simple of these two stories with a very simple linear plot. It is essentially a quest story about a mother whose child has been taken by Death. She pursues Death to get her child back, and has successively to sing all the songs she has sung to the child, press a thorn-bush to her breast, weep her eyes out (literally), and give away her beautiful hair to get the information that finally gets her into Death's hothouse before he has arrived with her child.

---

2   For reasons of copyright, all quotes are taken from the first almost complete English translation of Andersen's work by H.P. Paull (1872). This is not the best available translation, since it mainly relies on a German translation of Andersen and not on the original Danish texts. Better and more modern translations are, however, still under copyright.

3   Farley, M.A. (2001), 'Roman Catholic Views on Research Involving Human Embryonic Stem Cells', in Holland, S., Lebacqz, K. and Zoloth, L. (eds), *The Human Embryonic Stem Cell Debate* (Cambridge, MA: The MIT Press) 113–18, 114–15.

Finally Death arrives:

There rushed through the hothouse a chill of icy coldness, and the blind mother felt that Death had arrived.

"How did you find your way hither?" asked he; "how could you come here faster than I have?"

"I am a mother," she answered.

And Death stretched out his hand towards the delicate little flower; but she held her hands tightly round it, and held it fast at the same time, with the most anxious care, lest she should touch one of the leaves. Then Death breathed upon her hands, and she felt his breath colder than the icy wind, and her hands sank down powerless.

"You cannot prevail against me," said Death.

"But a God of mercy can," said she.

"I only do His will," replied Death. "I am his gardener. I take all His flowers and trees, and transplant them into the gardens of Paradise in an unknown land. How they flourish there, and what that garden resembles, I may not tell you."

"Give me back my child," said the mother, weeping and imploring; and she seized two beautiful flowers in her hands, and cried to Death, "I will tear up all your flowers, for I am in despair."

"Do not touch them," said Death. "You say you are unhappy; and would you make another mother as unhappy as yourself?"

"Another mother!" cried the poor woman, setting the flowers free from her hands.

"There are your eyes," said Death. "I fished them up out of the lake for you. They were shining brightly; but I knew not they were yours. Take them back—they are clearer now than before—and then look into the deep well which is close by here. I will tell you the names of the two flowers which you wished to pull up; and you will see the whole future of the human beings they represent, and what you were about to frustrate and destroy."

Then she looked into the well; and it was a glorious sight to behold how one of them became a blessing to the world, and how much happiness and joy it spread around. But she saw that the life of the other was full of care and poverty, misery and woe.

"Both are the will of God," said Death.

"Which is the unhappy flower, and which is the blessed one?" she said.

"That I may not tell you," said Death; "but thus far you may learn, that one of the two flowers represents your own child. It was the fate of your child that you saw, - the future of your own child."

Then the mother screamed aloud with terror, "Which of them belongs to my child? Tell me that. Deliver the unhappy child. Release it from so much misery. Rather take it away. Take it to the kingdom of God. Forget my tears and my entreaties; forget all that I have said or done."

"I do not understand you," said Death. "Will you have your child back? Or shall I carry him away to a place that you do not know?"

Then the mother wrung her hands, fell on her knees, and prayed to God, "Grant not my prayers, when they are contrary to Thy will, which at all times must be the best. Oh, hear them not;" and her head sank on her bosom.

Then Death carried away her child to the unknown land.

In this final section of the story, the natural is given two apparently conflicting interpretations. When asked how she has arrived so quickly, the answer 'I am a mother' suffices to explain both her sacrifices on the way and her ability to outrun Death. This immediate explanatory power of the nature of motherhood has also been used previously in the story to explain some of the individual sacrifices (for an exploration of this concept of motherhood see Holm, 1990[4]). The natural is thus used relatively directly as an explanation and justification for certain types of ethical actions (although motherhood is clearly a cultural and traditional concept as well).

In the further discussion between the mother and Death, this simple relation between motherhood and right action is, however, contested by Death. First by explaining that death is natural as well and fully understood to be so by their shared culture. Second by pointing out that her actions will impinge negatively on other mothers. And third by showing her that acting according to what is natural may lead to unpredictable consequences.

The second of Death's arguments is worth dwelling on because it essentially amounts to the observation that there is a possible inherent contradiction in acting according to nature, even nature fully interpreted through tradition, and so on. Nature does not take account of co-ordination problems, of what should happen if the naturally sanctioned acts of one moral agent are in conflict with the naturally sanctioned rights or role of another moral agent. Relying primarily on 'the natural' as a basis for our ethical thinking therefore leaves us without methods for resolving such conflicts.

The Little Mermaid is a much longer piece and has a much more complex storyline than *The Story of a Mother*. It is a coming-of-age story, a story about great and unrequited love, a tragic quest story and a morality tale. Here we will not be able to analyse all these aspects of the story, and will have to concentrate on Andersen's complex account of the relation between the natural, the cultural and the artificial as it is portrayed in the story.

The main protagonist, the little mermaid, is the youngest of six mermaid princesses and when we first meet her, she is presented in the following way:

---

4 Holm, S. (1990), 'The Mother–Child Relationship: A Tradition Recalled', *Ethics and Medicine* 6, 32–4.

Each of the young princesses had a little plot of ground in the garden, where she might dig and plant as she pleased. One arranged her flower-bed into the form of a whale; another thought it better to make hers like the figure of a little mermaid; but that of the youngest was round like the sun, and contained flowers as red as his rays at sunset. She was a strange child, quiet and thoughtful; and while her sisters would be delighted with the wonderful things which they obtained from the wrecks of vessels, she cared for nothing but her pretty red flowers, like the sun, excepting a beautiful marble statue. It was the representation of a handsome boy, carved out of pure white stone, which had fallen to the bottom of the sea from a wreck.

[…]

Nothing gave her so much pleasure as to hear about the world above the sea. She made her old grandmother tell her all she knew of the ships and of the towns, the people and the animals. To her it seemed most wonderful and beautiful to hear that the flowers of the land should have fragrance, and not those below the sea; that the trees of the forest should be green; and that the fishes among the trees could sing so sweetly, that it was quite a pleasure to hear them. Her grandmother called the little birds fishes, or she would not have understood her; for she had never seen birds.

We see that mermaid society and mermaid nature is different in many ways from human society and nature and we see that the little mermaid is peculiar in having a strong interest in what is above the water. This theme is reiterated many times in the story. Her older sisters and her wise, but proud, grandmother[5] are all interested in human affairs to some degree, but concentrate their attention on life as a mermaid.

The little mermaid is finally allowed to rise to the top of the sea on her fifteenth birthday and saves a beautiful prince from drowning. This makes her even more interested in human society:

And she remembered that his head had rested on her bosom, and how heartily she had kissed him; but he knew nothing of all this, and could not even dream of her. She grew more and more fond of human beings, and wished more and more to be able to wander about with those whose world seemed to be so much larger than her own. They could fly over the sea in ships, and mount the high hills which were far above the clouds; and the lands they possessed, their woods and their fields, stretched far away beyond the reach of her sight.

Andersen juxtaposes this description of the fascination with what others can do that I cannot do with a description of the Sea King's court ball – an event that no human being can experience – in order to show that the fascination of the unknown and the unknowable is simply that, a fascination, not a sound basis for evaluation. What the others have may not be better, but it may draw us anyway:

It is one of those splendid sights which we can never see on earth. The walls and the ceiling of the large ball-room were of thick, but transparent crystal. Many hundreds of colossal shells, some of a deep red, others of a grass green, stood on each side in rows,

---

5 '… on that account she wore twelve oysters on her tail; while others, also of high rank, were only allowed to wear six.'

with blue fire in them, which lighted up the whole saloon, and shone through the walls, so that the sea was also illuminated. Innumerable fishes, great and small, swam past the crystal walls; on some of them the scales glowed with a purple brilliancy, and on others they shone like silver and gold. Through the halls flowed a broad stream, and in it danced the mermen and the mermaids to the music of their own sweet singing. No one on earth has such a lovely voice as theirs.

Nevertheless the little mermaid persists in her belief that human life is extrinsically better, a belief that is strenuously denied by her grandmother. They discuss whether having an immortal soul (that is, an immortal soul being part of one's nature) is necessarily a benefit, and whether human biological nature (having legs) is better than mermaid biological nature (having a tail):

"If human beings are not drowned," asked the little mermaid, "can they live forever? Do they never die as we do here in the sea?"

"Yes," replied the old lady, "they must also die, and their term of life is even shorter than ours. We sometimes live to three hundred years, but when we cease to exist here we only become the foam on the surface of the water, and we have not even a grave down here of those we love. We have not immortal souls, we shall never live again; but, like the green sea-weed, when once it has been cut off, we can never flourish more. Human beings, on the contrary, have a soul which lives forever, lives after the body has been turned to dust. It rises up through the clear, pure air beyond the glittering stars. As we rise out of the water, and behold all the land of the earth, so do they rise to unknown and glorious regions which we shall never see."

"Why have not we an immortal soul?" asked the little mermaid mournfully; "I would give gladly all the hundreds of years that I have to live, to be a human being only for one day, and to have the hope of knowing the happiness of that glorious world above the stars."

"You must not think of that," said the old woman; "we feel ourselves to be much happier and much better off than human beings."

"So I shall die," said the little mermaid, "and as the foam of the sea I shall be driven about never again to hear the music of the waves, or to see the pretty flowers nor the red sun. Is there anything I can do to win an immortal soul?"

"No," said the old woman, "unless a man were to love you so much that you were more to him than his father or mother; and if all his thoughts and all his love were fixed upon you, and the priest placed his right hand in yours, and he promised to be true to you here and hereafter, then his soul would glide into your body and you would obtain a share in the future happiness of mankind. He would give a soul to you and retain his own as well; but this can never happen. Your fish's tail, which amongst us is considered so beautiful, is thought on earth to be quite ugly; they do not know any better, and they think it necessary to have two stout props, which they call legs, in order to be handsome."

Then the little mermaid sighed, and looked sorrowfully at her fish's tail. "Let us be happy," said the old lady, "and dart and spring about during the three hundred years that we have to live, which is really quite long enough; after that we can rest ourselves all the better."

This conversation shows how our specific frame of reference (our tradition and culture) determines our interpretation of the value of any specific aspect of nature. What is natural and thereby good and beautiful by mermaid standards is horrible and ugly by human standards. It also shows that it is very difficult to find a neutral point from which to judge. Our judgement on these issues is so bound to our concrete situation that there may not be any neutral vantage point.

We might perhaps now expect Andersen to propose a solution to the little mermaid's problem in technology,[6] in the artificial change of the natural state into a state that is more desired. But given the evaluative problem outlined just above, this path would be fraught with difficulty. What the little mermaid wants to achieve is not a better state of nature but just a different state, and as Andersen clearly implies, trying to change nature may not be possible without loss. In the story the technology that is applied is the technology of the sea witch, but in the description of the sea witch and her environment, we can clearly see the image of early industrial society:

> She now came to a space of marshy ground in the wood, where large, fat water-snakes were rolling in the mire, and showing their ugly, drab-colored bodies. In the midst of this spot stood a house, built with the bones of shipwrecked human beings. There sat the sea witch,…

[…]

> "I know what you want," said the sea witch; "it is very stupid of you, but you shall have your way, and it will bring you to sorrow, my pretty princess. You want to get rid of your fish's tail, and to have two supports instead of it, like human beings on earth, so that the young prince may fall in love with you, and that you may have an immortal soul."

[…]

> "I will prepare a draught for you, with which you must swim to land tomorrow before sunrise, and sit down on the shore and drink it. Your tail will then disappear, and shrink up into what mankind calls legs, and you will feel great pain, as if a sword were passing through you. But all who see you will say that you are the prettiest little human being they ever saw. You will still have the same floating gracefulness of movement, and no dancer will ever tread so lightly; but at every step you take it will feel as if you were treading upon sharp knives, and that the blood must flow. If you will bear all this, I will help you."

> "Yes, I will," said the little princess in a trembling voice, as she thought of the prince and the immortal soul.

> "But think again," said the witch; […] "if you do not win the love of the prince, so that he is willing to forget his father and mother for your sake, and to love you with his whole soul, and allow the priest to join your hands that you may be man and wife, then you will never have an immortal soul. The first morning after he marries another your heart will break, and you will become foam on the crest of the waves."

---

6 Andersen did, after all, write enthusiastically about steam trains elsewhere and predicted the airplane in his *In a Thousand Years*, where he also predicted the desire of Americans to see 'Europe in a week'.

"I will do it," said the little mermaid, and she became pale as death.

[…]

Then the witch placed her cauldron on the fire, to prepare the magic draught.

"Cleanliness is a good thing," said she, scouring the vessel with snakes, which she had tied together in a large knot; then she pricked herself in the breast, and let the black blood drop into it. The steam that rose formed itself into such horrible shapes that no one could look at them without fear. Every moment the witch threw something else into the vessel, and when it began to boil, the sound was like the weeping of a crocodile. When at last the magic draught was ready, it looked like the clearest water. "There it is for you," said the witch. Then she cut off the mermaid's tongue, so that she became dumb, and would never again speak or sing.

Not only does the little mermaid have to pay with her tongue, but the change in her nature will involve daily pain and a huge gamble on winning the love of the prince.[7] At the end of the story she loses this gamble as the prince marries another.

In this story, Andersen has presented the normative aspects of nature in a number of different ways and made clear that there is no possibility of reaching a single interpretation of the evaluative side of nature and the normative claims that nature makes on us. Even if we share a culture and a tradition, we may discern these claims in widely differing ways.

But for Andersen salvation is not to be found in technology either. Technology is literally a sharp double-edged sword, and those who use it to get their desires fulfilled risk having to pay a large price.

Recovering a Sense of the Natural?

From our reading of H.C. Andersen's two stories we have seen that we cannot derive ethical claims from descriptions of nature, even if we go through a complex process of discernment and deliberation. Nature is not revelatory in the way that natural law theory requires, but neither is technology necessarily liberating.

Is there any sense of nature we can recover that is both comprehensible and ethically important? It may be that the only ethical importance of nature is as a term used for describing the status quo ante before we add yet another human intervention. There is clearly no possibility of acquiring knowledge about an absolute state of nature, before any human action and before culture. All 'states of nature' are at the same time 'states of culture'. If nature is used as a description of the status quo, then it does not have any inherent goodness, but it does have some slight ethical importance anyway, in that we would need to be able to give reasons for why we want to move from this state to some other state, and those reasons would have to include ethical evaluation of the two states.

---

7 A state not that different from the side-effects of some of the more radical forms of cosmetic surgery performed today.

PART III
BUSINESS AND
PROFESSIONAL ETHICS

Genes for Sale: Ethical Reflections on Donors' Proprietary Rights in Human Genetic Derivatives

Taiwo A. Oriola

Introduction

The primary aim of this chapter is to examine the ethical externalities that underpin the legal methodology for allocation of proprietary rights in human genome products or derivatives. Throughout this chapter, all references to 'human genetic derivatives' refer to the legally commodifiable version of the human genome, that is, not the human genome as such, but the human genome as isolated from nature, and purified for medical and other scientific uses.

I will analyze critically the existing legal and ethical literature on the commodification of the human body and body parts. I will extrapolate my analysis to the ethical underpinnings of the ownership and commodification of human genetic materials and their derivatives, since the human genome is the critical determinant for the human body. My main task would be to demonstrate through descriptive and analytical argumentation how the law has excluded donors of human genetic derivatives from adequate remuneration and benefits-sharing in the market for commodification of human genetic derivatives.

While subjecting property allocation schemes in human genetic derivatives to ethical scrutiny, I will resort to relevant case law as case studies, in order to furnish my analysis with empirical data, evidencing the ongoing practice of human genetic materials donors' exclusion from benefiting from the commercialization of their genetic derivates.

However, a brief lay review of the technical nature of human genes, and the dynamics of academia and industry that drive human genetic engineering, is germane as a background for a better grasp of the central theme of this chapter.

Biotechnology is the art of using biological processes to intervene in nature through varied scientific techniques for the production of biological materials, services, or to achieve a desired result. The technique relies primarily on the manipulation of human, animal and plant genetic resources in the fields of medicine, animal genetics and plant agriculture respectively.[1] Moreover, genes could also be transferred across

---

1 For instance, genetic engineering techniques in agriculture usually involve the transference of certain desirable genetic traits from one plant species to another with a view

species barriers, such as from plants to animals and vice versa, with the aim of conferring certain desirable characteristics on the recipient of the exotic gene.[2]

Biotechnology is not entirely a new concept. It is said to be many centuries old, and has been used in the cross-breeding of farm animals and plants, yeast fermentation, and the use of micro-organisms for making bread, beer, wine, cheese, yoghurt, and so on. This ancient brand of biotechnology technique is often referred to as traditional biotechnology.[3] However, modern cutting-edge biotechnology is founded on molecular biology, and involves more sophisticated techniques of genetic modification, gene manipulation or gene shuffling, often between species and sometimes across species barriers as noted earlier.[4] This is otherwise known as genetic engineering technology, and it has been used extensively in the fields of medicine, agriculture and environment.[5] In the medical sphere, for example, genetic engineering technology is said to hold out promises for hitherto incurable diseases such as Alzheimer's, HIV/AIDS, gene therapy, and so on.[6]

In February 2001, the full sequencing of the human genome was completed. It was the culmination of concerted international efforts by geneticists, who in 1988 established the Human Genome Project (HGP).[7] The aims of the HGP were to unravel

---

to strengthening the plant's disease- or drought-resistance capability, or to improving yields in the recipient plant. See Oriola, T.A. (2002), 'Consumer Dilemmas: The Right to Know, Safety, Ethics, and Policy of Genetically Modified Food', *Singapore Journal of Legal Studies* (December), 514–73.

2　For example, scientists succeeded in genetically modifying cotton with a bacterial gene from *Bacillus thuringiensis*. The bacterium is known for making insecticidal chemicals. The resulting genetically modified cotton is known as BT cotton, and is resistant to cotton pests. The technique avoids the use of pesticides, and is said to be good for the environment. It is also a good example of gene transfer across species barriers, that is, from a bacterium, (a micro-organism) to a plant species. See Grace, E.S. (1997), *Biotechnology Unzipped: Promises and Realities* (Washington DC: Joseph Henry Press) 117–21.

3　See Reiss, M.J. and Straughan, R. (2001), *Improving Nature? The Science and Ethics of Genetic Engineering*, Canto edition (Cambridge: Cambridge University Press) 2.

4　See Grace, op. cit., note 2, 118; Hayes, R. (2000), 'Human Genetic Engineering', in Walker, C. (ed.), *Made Not Born: The Troubling World of Biotechnology* (San Francisco: Sierra Club) 80–98.

5　An example of an environmental use of genetic engineering was the genetically modified bacterium Pseudomonas. It was invented by a General Electric biochemist, Ananda Chakrabarty, for bioremediation of oil spills. See *Diamond v Chakrabarty* 447 U.S. 303 (1980). For a discussion, see generally Oriola, T.A. (2002), 'Ethical and Legal Issues in Singapore Biomedical Research', *The Pacific Rim Law & Policy Journal, Washington Law School* 11:3, 497–530.

6　See Grace, op. cit., note 2, 118; Morgan M.J. and Wallace, S.E. (2004), 'The International Human Genome Project: An Overview', in Brannigan, M.C. (ed.), *Cross-Cultural Biotechnology* (New York, Toronto and Oxford: Rowman & Littlefield Publishers) 15–23.

7　The Human Genome Project was led by a team of international scientists from the National Institutes of Health in the USA, and the Wellcome Trust in the United Kingdom. In May 1998, a private initiative led by Celera Genomics joined the race to map the human genome. The preliminary draft of the genome was simultaneously announced to the world by

or identify all the more than 30,000 genes in the human DNA; ascertain the sequences of the 3 billion letters comprising the human DNA; preserve the information in databases; fine tune tools for data analysis; transfer related technology to the private sector; and address the ethical, legal and social issues posed by the project.[8]

Unraveling the human genome has raised the vision of a personalized, modern cutting-edge healthcare delivery system.[9] It would, for instance, allow for the study of numerous human diseases at the genetic or molecular level. It is believed that over 4,000 genetic-related diseases stem from genetic mutations. Gene therapy could be used to correct genetic mutations, and possesses a promising prospect for reducing the incidence of inheritable diseases.[10] Furthermore, it is already possible to test for some genetic diseases prior to manifestation. For example, predisposition to breast cancer has been successfully diagnosed with genetic diagnostic tools.[11] Gene technology is also being used to manufacture pharmaceuticals and vaccines such as human insulin and growth hormone.[12]

However, the multifaceted uses of genetic technology in modern healthcare systems have arguably upped its commercial appeal cum potential, and precipitated a scramble for human genetic patents by scientists.[13] Proprietors of patents are vested

---

both parties on 26 June 2000. It is believed that the participation of the private biotechnology company sped up the pace of work and led to its early completion. See Hellstadius, A. (2002), *Gene Technology and the Law: A Guide to Intellectual Property Law and other Legal Aspects of the Use of Gene Technology* (Stockholm: Jure Bokhandel) 3–4.

8 See Hellstadius, op. cit., note 7, pp. 3–4. Significantly, scientists have been busy sequencing the genome of other organisms such as rats, the 1918 Avian flu virus, bacterium Escherichia coli, yeast, roundworm, fruit fly, and even mosquitoes. It is expected that the genetic information garnered from other organisms would help determine their usefulness or help understand their constitutions if they pose any danger to humans. Ibid.

9 Oriola, op. cit., note 5, 502.

10 See Hellstadius, op. cit., note 7, 9; Bruce, D.M. (2006), 'Moral and Ethical Issues in Gene Therapy', *Human Reproduction and Genetic Ethics: An International Journal* 12:1, 16–23; Woo, S.L.C. (1996), 'Gene Therapy: Beyond Genetic Diseases', in Rudolph F.B. and McIntire, L.V. (eds), *Biotechnology: Science, Engineering, and Ethical Challenges for the Twenty-First Century* (Washington DC: Joseph Henry Press) 72–87. For example, the first successful human gene therapy began on 14 September 1990, when a four–year-old girl was treated for Severe Combine Immunodeficiency (SCID). The genetic defect was caused by the absence of enzyme adenosine deaminase (ADA). She was injected with a normal ADA by gene transfer, and her immune system gradually reverted to normalcy. See Dronamraju, K.R. (1988), *Biological and Social Issues in Biotechnology Sharing* (Aldershot, England: Ashgate Publishing Company) 123–4.

11 For instance, Myriad Genetics, a US biotech company, holds the patent for testing for breast cancer genes, and charges rather exorbitantly for its services. See Rimmer, M. (2003), 'Myriad Genetics: Patent Law and Genetic Testing', *European Intellectual Property Review* 25:1, 20–33.

12 See Hellstadius, op. cit., note 7, 7.

13 See Sulston, J. (2002), 'Intellectual Property and the Human Genome', in Drahos, P. and Mayne, R. (eds), *Global Intellectual Property Rights: Knowledge, Access and Development* (New York: Palgrave Macmillan) 61–71.

with exclusive monopoly rights by law for a limited term of years, usually 20.[14] In the context of human gene patenting, owners of patents have exclusive proprietary rights over human genetic-related inventions for the duration of their patents.[15] Gene patenting has understandably precipitated a panoply of ethical and legal concerns in contemporary socio-legal discourses.[16]

Despite ethical and legal concerns, however, gene patenting is progressing inexorably. A recent estimate claims that at least 18.5 per cent of human genes are already covered by US patents.[17] Controversially and disturbingly, a significant part of human gene patents are no more than for mere gene discovery, as they fall below the patentability requirements threshold.[18] This practice, arguably in my opinion, is no more than gene sales, and contravenes national and international laws that forbid the commercialization of the human genome in its natural state. I shall expatiate on this point later in this chapter.

Significantly, despite the millions of dollars in profits raked in by industry, by reason of the commercialization of human genetic derivatives mainly via the instrumentality of the patent regime and other allied legislative constructs, donors of human genetic materials have no property rights in their genetic derivatives, and are not entitled to any remuneration or profits accruing from the commercialization of their genetic derivatives.

Although paragraph 132 of the explanatory note on article 21 of the Council of Europe Convention on Human Rights and Biomedicine provides that donors of human genetic materials could be entitled to limited compensatory awards, it explicitly rules out remuneration, while limiting the scope of compensation to mere out–of-pocket expenses and the cost of hospitalization incidental to the removal of donors' genetic materials. As I would argue later in this chapter, this is arguably inequitable, anomalous and ethically inappropriate.

---

14 See Article 28(1) of the Agreement on Trade Related Aspects of Intellectual Property Rights, Annex 1C to the Marrakesh Agreement Establishing the World Trade Organization (WTO), of 15 April 1994 (hereinafter referred to as the TRIPS Agreement).

15 See Article 28(1) of the TRIPS Agreement, op. cit.; Dutfield, G. (2003), *Intellectual Property Rights and the Life Science Industry: A Twentieth Century History* (Aldershot, England, Burlington, USA: Ashgate Publishing Limited) 151–73; Shiva, V. (2001), *Protect or Plunder? Understanding Intellectual Property Rights* (London and New York: Zed Books) 11–18.

16 See Weinberg, R.A. (2003), 'The Dark Side of the Genome', in Teich, A.H. (ed.), *Technology and The Future* (Toronto, London: Thomson Wadsworth) 187–99; Rothstein, M.A. (1996), 'Ethical Issues Surrounding the New Technology as Applied to Health Care', in Rudolph and McIntire (eds), *Biotechnology: Science, Engineering, and Ethical Challenges for the Twenty-First Century*, op. cit., note 10, 191–207.

17 See Pagan Westphal, S. (2005), 'Human Gene Patents Surprisingly High: A New Study Shows', *The Wall Street Journal* (14 October) B1.

18 For an invention to be patentable, it must be new, inventive, and capable of industrial application. See Soames, C. (2006), 'Grace Periods and Patentability', *Nature Reviews: Drug Discovery, The Science and Business of Drug Discovery and Development* 5:4, 275; Dutfield, op. cit., note 15, 162–3.

This anomaly was facilitated and fostered by two main factors. The first is the prohibition, with good reasons, of the commercialization of the human body, body parts, and the natural human genome, in national and international laws. Although illicit human body trade still thrives globally, there is, as yet, neither a parallel forum for trading in the human genome, nor an inclusive and open market for trading in human genetic derivatives. A fortiori, donors of human genetic materials lack the critical information mass and experience with which to negotiate adequate remunerative deals, should their genetic materials become commercially viable.

The second factor that facilitates the exclusion of donors from benefits is the scientific and juridical distinctions often made between human genetic materials in nature vis-à-vis human genetic materials isolated from nature, and tinkered around with on Petri dishes in scientific laboratories. While this distinction is functionally useful in prohibiting trade in the human genome in its natural state, it fosters property rights in human genetic derivatives, without specifying a list of possible claimants to ownership of human genetic derivatives. Such a list should ordinarily be non-exhaustive, and should comprise patent proprietors, entrepreneurs, investors, donors of genetic materials, licensees, donors of human genetic materials, and so on. This lacuna in the law arguably facilitates an easy override by industry of any potential remunerative or proprietary claims of donors in their genetic derivatives.

A fortiori, in the context of inclusiveness, the market in human genetic derivatives has failed and cannot self-regulate. I argue in this chapter that a legal construct of the market in human genetic derivatives is thus obliged to acknowledge and protect the interests of donors, as the weakest but indispensable players in the production chain of human genetic derivatives. This could be done by delimiting donors' legal role, duty, rights, and responsibilities, as an important player in an all-inclusive and open market in human genetic derivatives. In my opinion, it is therefore ethically imperative for authorities to intervene, and incorporate donors of human genetic materials into the benefit-sharing scheme concomitant to the commercialization of human genetic derivatives.

Article 4 of the UNESCO Universal Declaration on the Human Genome and Human Rights, and article 21 of the Council of Europe Convention on Human Rights and Biomedicine[19] are both antedated by a host of national juridical pronouncements that prohibit, and even criminalize, the commodification of the human body or body parts. There is thus unanimity of views in both the legislative and juridical spheres on when the human body or body parts could be objectified and commodified. It is when there is clear evidence of investments of time, money, skill, work, and so on, which preserved, modified or transformed the human genome, body or body parts, from its natural disposition, into a commodity object.

---

19 It provides that '... [T]he Human Body and its parts shall not as such give rise to financial gain.' See article 21 of the Council of Europe Convention for the Protection of Human Rights and Dignity of the Human Being with Regard to the Application of Biology and Medicine: Convention on Human Rights and Biomedicine (hereinafter Council of Europe Convention on Human Rights and Biomedicine), available at: http://conventions.coe.int/Treaty/EN/Reports/Html/164.htm. Last accessed on 24 April 2006.

Thus, in concert with the patent regime, juridical and legislative authorities would accord property rights in the human body, body parts or the human genome, upon evidence of purification, modification, isolation, preservation, investments, and so on. While there is nothing inherently wrong in this policy arrangement, the non-inclusion of donors of human genetic materials in the scheme of benefit-sharing constitutes a significant flaw in the legal regime for the commodification of human genetic derivatives.

Parts three and four of the chapter deal with the ethical and legal issues relating to renumerating donors of human genetic materials. Part one is entitled 'Of Goose and Gander: the Human Genome in its Natural and Derivative Forms.' The essence of my argumentation in this part is that 'what is good for the goose is also good for the gander.' If patent owners and other entrepreneurs could benefit from trading in human genetic derivatives, then donors of human genetic materials should also benefit.

Part two is entitled 'Who Owns Human Genetic Materials and their Derivatives?' In this part, I critically analyze the legal methodology for property rights allocation in the human body and body parts, in case law, patent law and a host of international treaties and conventions. With respect to human genetic derivatives, this part will show how the law is skewed in favor of corporations and big businesses at the expense of, and to the detriment of, donors of human genetic derivatives.

Part three of the chapter is entitled 'The Ethics of Conferring Property and Remunerative Rights on Donors of Human Genetic Materials.' I use three ethical principles, human dignity, Kantianism, and justice, as a composite ethical framework on the propriety of conferring of property rights on and remunerating donors of human genetic materials. The choice of my ethical framework is arbitrary and non-systematic. I do not, however, presume that it is the most appropriate bioethical framework to resolve the moral issues at hand. In fact, there can hardly be a satisfactory set of ethical theories that would automatically apply to any set of moral problems, as morality cannot be encoded in a set of rules. Indeed my choice was informed by the framework's regular recurrence in contemporary bioethical discourse on the commodification of the human body and body parts.

The chapter ends with the conclusion which sums up the central argument as well as the summary of key findings and recommendations.

Of Goose and Gander: The Human Genome in its Natural and Derivative Forms

In this section, I examine the scientific, legislative, and juridical distinctions usually made between the human genome in its natural and derivative forms. This distinction is significant because it is arguably the critical element for property rights allocation in the human genome. However, while the distinction recognizes property rights in human genetic derivatives, it is crucially mute on what legal rights the donors might have in their genetic derivatives. This has created a non-inclusive market in human genetic derivatives.

The Human Genome in Nature

Without doubt, genes are the critical determinant for all living organisms. They would instruct organisms to produce the requisite chemicals or proteins[20] that are crucial for survival, growth or continuity.[21] For example, the basic distinguishing physical features of human beings, ranging from the color or length of the hair, the color of the eyes, the color of the skin, to the height, are all dictated by the unique genetic blueprint or genetic information peculiar to each individual. This phenomenon is common to all living organisms and goes by the technical name of phenotype.[22]

Each individual's (or any organism's) phenotype is generated by their genotype, which is the aggregate sum of all their genes. The total sum of all genes in a living organism (genotype) would include both the coding genes and the non-coding genes. The coding genes are the genes that are known to actively instruct cells on which chemicals or proteins to produce to ensure growth, immunity, continuity and survival.

The non-coding genes have functions which scientists do not as yet fully comprehend or grasp, and they are often referred to as 'junk DNA'. It is the total sum of all genes (genotype) (comprising both the coding genes and the non-coding genes), in an organism that is known as the organism's genome.[23] In other words, every living species (human beings, plants and animals alike) has a genome. In scientific and juridical terms, the human genome is in its natural state when it is not isolated from nature or tampered with in any way. As noted earlier, article 4 of the UNESCO Universal Declaration on the Human Genome and Human Rights prohibits the commercialization of the human genome in its natural state.[24]

The Science of Genetic Modification

There are a variety of ways by which the human genes could be isolated from nature, and modified into a derivative form. Genetic engineering processes in all living species necessarily involve splitting apart or unzipping of the DNA double-stranded helix. The strands would thereafter be severed with a view to mapping the base sequences or to cut out and isolate a particular gene.

---

20 Proteins are of structural and functional importance. Examples are: collagen (found in bone and skin), keratin (makes hair and nail), fibrin (helps blood cloth), elastin (major parts of ligaments), hormones (control body functions), antibodies (fight infection), enzymes (help speed up chemical reactions in the body), and hemoglobin (carries oxygen in the blood). See Grace, op. cit., note 2, 21. According to Grace, every process and product in living cells depends on proteins. They do everything from activating essential chemical reactions, to carrying messages between cells, to fighting infections, to making cell membranes, tendons, muscles, blood, bone, and other structural materials. Ibid.

21 See Reiss and Straughan, op. cit, note 3, 1–5.

22 See Wei, G. (2002), *An Introduction to Genetic Engineering, Life Sciences and the Law* (Singapore: Singapore University Press) 45.

23 See Hellstadius, op. cit., note 7, 1–2.

24 See UNESCO Universal Declaration on the Human Genome and Human Rights, available at: http://unesdoc.unesco.org/images/0011/001102/110220e.pdf#page=47.

One of the methodologies for gene splicing is to heat up the DNA and break up the bonds between the base pairs. Another method involves using chemicals to break up the bonds between the base pairs. Cutting the DNA strands involves the use of certain bacteria enzymes. After the desired gene has been so isolated and cut out, copies of it could then be made where necessary.

Again bacteria plasmids are among a variety of tools used for copying desirable DNA strands or foreign genes, and fetching the DNA strands into a desired host.[25] This technique has been used to produce and replicate human hormones. For example, the DNA of E. Coli bacteria has been used to reproduce and replicate human insulin in large quantities, once human insulin genes have been spliced into the bacteria. The insulin is thereafter separated, crystallized, and deep-frozen under clean conditions, and made into the new inhalable insulin product, which can last for 24 hours after inhalation.[26]

Significantly, any human gene that is thus isolated from nature, or modified through biological processes, is perceived as a different product from its original form both by the courts and the scientific community, who have, over the years, piled up hundreds of patents on human genes, cell lines, genetically engineered tissue, organisms, and the recombinant DNA techniques.[27] Such human genetic derivatives are often therapeutically and diagnostically useful, and they include diagnostic tools for early diagnosis and treatment of diseases (notably breast cancer), genomic information for increasing gene therapy's efficiency, and so on.[28]

The juridical sanctioning of genetic derivatives as distinct products from their raw natural genetic pedigree was first propounded by courts in the United States in the landmark case of *Diamond v Chakrabarty*. Although it was a bacterial and not a human gene, the case is very relevant as it opens the subsequent floodgate for life patents. The US Supreme Court held inter alia, that a genetically engineered micro-organism is not a product of nature, but rather a product of a person's work, and thus is patentable.[29] The ethical propriety of this distinction, or patents on life per se, is

---

25 Plasmids are small circular pieces of bacterial DNA that can move from one bacterium to another. This movement allows a bacterium to get infused with the DNA from another bacterium. Another method for copying genes and transferring them into desired hosts is through bacteriophages, a variety of viruses that infect bacteria by injecting their DNA. The injected DNA would then replicate. See Wei, op. cit., note 22, 22–30.

26 The market for insulin products is immense due to the forecast increase in Type I and Type II diabetics worldwide. The pharmaceutical industry is cashing in on the insulin market. For instance, in early 2003, Aventis opened its new recombinant insulin plant in Frankfurt. It is estimated to be worth 150 million euros. See Aventis, 'Aventis Recombinant Insulin Plant, Frankfurt, Germany', available at: http://www.pharmaceutical-technology.com/projects/aventi. Last accessed on 24 April 2006.

27 See generally Warren-Jones, A. (2001), *Patenting rDNA: Human and Animal Biotechnology in the United Kingdom and Europe* (Oxford: LAWTEXT Publishing) 71–129; Rifkin, J. (1998), *The Biotech Century* (London: Victor Gollancz) 8–9.

28 See Haas, A.K. (2001), 'The Wellcome Trust's Disclosures of Gene Sequence Data into the Public Domain and the Potential for Proprietary Rights in the Human Genome', *Berkeley Technology Law Journal* 16, 145, 145–64.

29 See *Diamond v Chakrabarty* 447 U.S. 303 (1980).

well articulated in contemporary ethical and legal literature, and is well beyond the remit of this chapter.[30] However, it is ethically relevant to examine the distinction made between the raw human genome and its derivatives in the forms of vaccines, drugs, or other forms of therapeutic products, not least because the distinction is critical for property rights allocation in human genetic derivatives, and sometimes in the human genome itself, via dubious patents on mere gene discovery.[31]

While individuals cannot legally trade in their genes, industry freely trades and barters in genes and genes products. In fact, industry is obsessed with the appropriate methodology for allocation of genetic proprietary rights amongst its members, with a view to boosting funding for research in the human genome.[32] On the contrary, scant regard is given by law, and the industry, to a possible modality for equitable sharing of financial benefits accruing from the flourishing trade in genetic derivatives with donors of raw genetic materials.

Effects of the Legal and Scientific Distinctions between the Human Genome and its Genetic Derivatives

As noted earlier, juridical, legislative and scientific distinctions between the human genome and its derivatives facilitate proprietary rights and a market in human genetic derivatives such as therapeutic drugs, genetic diagnostic tools, genetic information, and so on. However, while the distinction creates a legal market in human genetic derivatives, it fails to specify what legal interest, if any, the donors of human genetic materials could have in their genetic derivatives.

Thus, the legal market in human genetic derivatives is non-inclusive. This lacuna in the law, of necessity, compels an inquiry into the ethics of the methodology for property rights allocation in human genetic derivatives.

The exclusionary nature and inequity in the market for human genetic derivatives is exemplified by a US patent on the cell line of a Papua New Guinean. The US Department of Health and Human Services and the National Institutes of Health filed patent applications on the human T-cell line of a Papua New Guinean in 1995. The cell line was unique because, despite its infestation with a variant of human T-cell leukemia virus, it did not cause leukemia, and was therefore of great research interest. Most significantly, the cell line was deemed potentially useful in treating or diagnosing patients infected with human T-lymphotropic virus type 1, which is commonly associated with adult leukemia.[33]

---

30 For a discussion of the ethics of patents on life, see Albright, M., 'Life Patents and Democratic Values', in Krimsky, S. and Shorett, P. (eds), (2005) *Rights and Liberties in the Biotech Age: Why We Need a Genetic Bill of Rights* (New York: Rowman and Littlefield Publishers, Inc.), 29–39; King, J. and Stabinsky, D. 'Life Patents Undermine the Exchange of Technology and Scientific Ideas', in Krimsky and Shorett, ibid, 49–55; Holtug, N. (2001), 'Creating and Patenting New Life Forms', in Kuhse, H. and Singer, P. (eds), *A Companion To Bioethics* (Oxford: Blackwell Publishing) 206–14.

31 See Albright, op. cit., note 30, 29–39.

32 See Haas, op. cit., note 28, 147.

33 See Senituli, L. (2003), *Biopolicy and Biopolitics in the Pacific Islands*, an occasional paper of the Edmond Institute (Washington, Edmond Institute) 1–6. Note that the patent has

While the patented cell line had obvious medical advantages, its huge commercial potential for patent proprietors was sacrosanct. Ironically, while profits were guaranteed for the patent owners, there was no reciprocal arrangement of any remunerative benefits for the Hagahai donor of the blood samples used for the patented cell line.

In this context, it is pertinent to pose the following relevant, albeit rhetorical questions: could there have been a 'human T-cell line' without the blood samples of the Hagahai people? If the law could facilitate the commercialization of the 'human T-cell line' and not the original blood samples from where it sprung, why could the law not make room for adequate remuneration of the Papua New Guinean who donated the blood samples? Is it morally acceptable to leave the donor unremunerated? These questions will be answered in part three below.

Who Owns Human Genetic Materials and their Derivatives?

A close perusal of the relevant legislation and case law reveals a consistency in the underlying principles for ceding of property rights in the human body, body parts, tissues, spleen, and genes, to businesses, following modification, preservation, or transformation of such body or body parts. At common law, this is otherwise known as the 'work and skill' exception to the general rule that there could be no property rights in the human body or body parts.

This trend arguably accommodates investments in the human body, and fuels the inexorable drive for commodification of the human body and genetic materials. However, while the law is quick to allocate property rights in the human body following the slightest modification or transformation from nature, there is no concrete legal arrangement to secure financial benefits for the donors of human genetic materials.

In this part, I will review the juridical and legislative methodology for property allocation in human genetic derivatives. I will highlight the flaw which denies donors of human genetic materials property and remunerative rights in human genetic derivatives. Although paragraph 132 of the Explanatory Report on article 21 of the Council of Europe Convention on Human Rights and Biomedicine concedes limited compensatory awards, I would argue that nothing short of adequate property and remunerative rights, as determined by market forces, would suffice.

Legal Perspectives on Ownership and Commodification of the Human Body, Body Parts, Tissues, Blood and Genes

Ownership of the human body and body parts is a recurring subject in contemporary bioethical debates, not least because of the increasing objectification and

---

been reportedly withdrawn following a spirited opposition from rights groups. See Dworkin, G. (1997), 'Should There Be Property Rights in Genes?' *Philosophical Transactions of the Royal Society Lond. B.* 352, 1077–86.

commodification of the human body, body parts, and genes in the global economy.[34] Despite its apparent prohibition in national and international laws, an illicit black market in the human body, body parts, tissues, and organs, continues to thrive underground in most countries.[35]

According to Nancy Scheper-Hughes, the human body is now a commodity object, routinely bartered and sold in the global marketplace, with the complicity of '… reproductive medicine, transplant surgery, bioethics and biotechnology …', in the new era of 'late modern cannibalism.'[36] The body as an object of commodification attracts players as diverse as grave robbers,[37] biotechnology companies,[38] museums, the medical profession, organ sellers and buyers, and so on.[39]

In law, the twin issues of commodification and ownership rights in the human body and body parts tend to receive separate treatment. While commodification of the human body and body parts is explicitly outlawed in most national and international laws,[40] the question of whether or not a person or their kinsman has proprietary rights in their body or body parts is not so settled in law.[41]

However, the general notion of ownership or property rights in tangible objects such as houses, cars, horses, and so on, connotes certain legal rights, duties and responsibilities that cannot be morally and legally extrapolated to the human body or body parts, except in slavery conditions. This arguably informs the preference of certain legal analysts for the relatively euphemistic terms of privacy and personal

---

34 See Scheper-Hughes, N. (2002), 'Bodies for Sale – Whole or in Parts', in Scheper-Hughes, N. and Wacquant, L. (eds), *Commodifying Bodies* (London: SAGE Publications Ltd) 1–8.

35 For instance, it is well documented that poor people in India, the Philippines and other countries around the world routinely sell kidneys and other body parts to feed their family. See Scheper-Hughes, op. cit., note 34. For example, property right in human body or body parts is forbidden in the United States. See Andre, J. (1998), 'Bodies for Sale', *Hastings Centre Report* (1 March). See also article 21 of the Council of Europe Convention on Human Rights and Biomedicine, and article 4 of the UNESCO Universal Declaration on the Human Genome and Human Rights.

36 See Scheper-Hughes, op. cit., note 34, 1.

37 For instance, the US authorities charged four people over bones theft in February 2006. The accused had allegedly looted bones and body parts from over 1,000 corpses and sold them for medical transplants. See BBC News (2006), 'Four Charges over US Bones Theft' (23 February) available at: http://news.bbc.co.uk/go/pr/fr/-/1/hi/world/americas/4742844.stm.

38 See Lock, M. (2002), 'The Alienation of Body Tissue and the Biopolitics of Immortalized Cell Lines', in Scheper-Hughes and Wacquant (eds), *Commodifying Bodies*, op. cit., note 34, 63–92.

39 See Cohen, L. (2002), 'The Other Kidney: Biopolitics beyond Recognition', in Scheper-Hughes and Wacquant (eds), *Commodifying Bodies*, op. cit., note 34, 9–29.

40 See, for instance, article 21 of the Council of Europe Convention on Human Rights and Biomedicine, op. cit., note 19. It states that the human body and its parts must not, as such, give rise to financial gains. It thus effectively prohibits the sales of organs, tissues, blood, and so on.

41 See Skene, L. (2002), 'Who Owns your Body? Legal Issues on the Ownership of Bodily Material', *TRENDS in Molecular Medicine* 8:1, 48–9.

integrity rights in the human body or body parts, rather than property or ownership rights.[42]

Privacy and personal integrity rights are often embodied in fundamental human rights, and are generally upheld by virtually all constitutional democracies. For instance, articles 10 and 11 of the Constitution of the Kingdom of the Netherlands respectively guarantee privacy and personal integrity rights.[43] Even then, such rights do not, stricto sensu, form a legal basis for any property or commodification rights in the human body and body parts. For instance, in the Netherlands, as in most countries, property rights in the living human body as a whole, as well as trade in body parts, are clearly prohibited.[44] However, the law does recognize property rights in the human body and body parts on certain conditions. The following paragraph will examine what those conditions are, and how they relate to the legal market in human genetic derivatives.

Commodification of the Human Body and Body Parts through Case Law

In common law jurisdictions, the law's stance on property rights in the human body is ambiguous at best. Prior to the abolition of slavery in the nineteenth century, the courts accepted that '... a portion of our fellow creatures may become the subject of property.'[45] However, judicial attitude soon changed, and property right in the human body was reportedly first denied in the 1614 *Haynes' case*.[46] However, the facts of the case do not appear to provide a basis for the 'no property right in human body rule,' as there was no actual theft of the human body. Rather, Haynes was charged with the theft of winding sheets used to wrap up four corpses in a graveyard. The apparent lack of a nexus between the facts of the case and the proposition has generated the view by analysts that the *Haynes case* did not actually establish the 'no property right in human body rule.'[47]

The *Haynes' case* was reportedly followed by the 1749 case of *Exelby v Handyside*,[48] where a lawsuit for a wrongful taking of still-born conjoined twins against Dr Handyside, a physician, was dismissed for a lack of property right in human corpses.[49] In 1998, the Court of Appeal in the UK categorically upheld the

---

42 See De Witte, J.I. and Welie, J.V.M. (1997), 'The Status of Genetic Material and Genetic Information in the Netherlands', *Social Science and Medicine* 45:1, 45–9.

43 See generally Chapter 1 of the Constitution of the Kingdom of the Netherlands, 2002, available at: http://www.minbzk.nl/contents/pages/6156/grondwet_UK_6-02.pdf. Last accessed on 22 April 2006.

44 See De Witte and Welie, op. cit., note 42, 45–9.

45 See *Gregson v Gilbert* (1783) 99 ER 629.

46 See *Haynes' Case* (1614) 12 Co. REP. 113.

47 For a discussion, see Magnusson, R. (1992), 'The Recognition of Proprietary Rights in Human Tissue in Common Law Jurisdictions', *Melbourne University Law Review* 18, 601–603.

48 See *Exelby v Handyside* (1749) 2 East PC 652.

49 Note, however, that it has been disputed that the *Handyside case* ever laid down the proposition that there was no property right in the human body. See, for instance, Matthews, P. (1983), 'Whose Body? People As Property', *Current Legal Problems* 193, 208.

'no property right in human body rule' in the *R v Kelly and Lindsay case*.[50] The proposition was, however, subject to the exception that proprietary right in body parts might exist if such body parts had been preserved or dissected through techniques, work and skill.

However, apart from the work and skill (investment or business) exception as re-affirmed in *Kelly's case*, the 'no property right in human body rule' is circumscribed by a host of other exceptions at common law. The first such exception is the theft exception, which forbids grave robbery or theft of body parts.[51] This rule was again exemplified in the case of *R v Kelly and Lindsay*. Kelly and Lindsay, who were artist and technician respectively, were charged with the theft of up to 40 anatomical specimens. The body parts were procured from the Royal College of Surgeons for Kelly by Lindsay, who worked there as a junior technician, at a fee of £400. Kelly's defense that he needed the body parts for his sculpture work was dismissed.[52]

Furthermore, at common law, property rights in the human body and body parts will be recognized on grounds of trespass, to protect against graveyard robbers. This is facilitated by the classification of the corpse as part of the soil. This is exemplified by *R v Sharpe*, where the defendant was found guilty of a misdemeanor for attempting to remove his mother's corpse from a protestant cemetery, and transfer it for burial in a catholic cemetery.[53] The trespass rule is ostensibly for the protection of the corpse rather than any purported commercial or financial interest of any family member in the corpse. Unlike the work and skill exception, the rule will not in any way ground any commodification or property rights in corpses of relatives.

Yet another exception to the 'no property right in human body rule' at common law is the 'next-of-kin exception.' It is similar to the trespass exception in its policy objective, as it is ostensibly designed to protect the interests of the deceased's relatives in the integrity of the bodies of their loved ones. The exception vests in the next-of-kin, a quasi-property right in the deceased's body, in order to facilitate a measure of control over what happens to the corpse.[54]

---

50 See *R v Kelly and Lindsay, Medical Law Review* (June 1998) p. 247. See also *Doodeward v Spence* (1908) 6 CLR 406. It was an earlier UK decision where the court held that the police had no right to seize a two-headed fetus preserved in a bottle filled with spirits. The appellant had bought the fetus from the estate of a medical doctor, and was displaying it for profits. The court found that sufficient work and skill had been expended on the fetus to render it the property of the appellant.

51 See, for example, the case of *R v Cundick* (1822) Dowl. & Ry N.P. 13. Mr Cundick, an undertaker, was found guilty of body theft. He took a body commissioned for burial to a surgeon's house where it was dissected and mutilated ostensibly for medical practice. The question remains, however, as to how the charge of theft of the human body could be sustained in the absence of property right in the same.

52 See *R v Kelly and Lindsay*, op. cit., note 50, 247.

53 See *R v Sharpe* (1856) Dears & Bell 159.

54 See *Smith v Tamworth City Council* (unreported) No. 4196 of 1996 (14 May 1997), cited in Taylor, R. (2002), 'Human Property: Threat or Saviour?' *E- Law, Murdoch University Electronic Journal of Law* 9:4, available at: http://www.murdoch.edu.au/elaw/issues/v9n4/taylor94.html.

This is exemplified by the US case of *Brotherton v Cleveland*. The plaintiff next-of-kin successfully sued the defendant for damages for unauthorized removal of the deceased relative's cornea.[55] However, such quasi-property right is no carte blanche for property rights or trading in the body parts of deceased relatives. Like the trespass exception, it is a policy meant solely for the protection of the corpse, rather than the deceased's relative's commercial interest in the body.

Another notable exception to the 'no property right in human body rule' is the medical experimentation exception. It is indeed a variant of the 'work and skill' exception in the context of biomedical experimentation. The rule vests property right in the human body or body parts on anyone who applies preservation techniques, dissects, or modifies the cadaver in any way.

In the 1998 *R v Kelly and Lindsay case* mentioned above, the British Court of Appeal held that the Royal College of Surgeons was in lawful control and possession of certain body parts, because they had applied preservation techniques and dissected the body. The body had therefore been substantially transformed from its original or natural state to ground ownership or property rights in recognition of the work and skill employed for its transformation.[56]

Significantly, unlike the next-of-kin and trespass exceptions to the 'no property right in human body rule,' the medical experimentation and work and skill exceptions do vest real property interests in the businesses or corporations responsible for the modification of the body or body parts.

The medical experimentation exception rule has arguably acquired a new significance and impetus with the advent of modern biotechnology, due mainly to the concomitant multi-million dollars of financial interests at stake. The landmark case that applied the medical experimentation exception to molecular biological experiment was the US case of *Moore v The Regents of the University of California.*[57] Due to the relevance of the decision to the central theme of this chapter, I will briefly review its facts.

Mr Moore was a leukemia patient at the University of California Medical Center. His physician noted that he had a unique cell which had great scientific and commercial advantages. He was asked to return to the hospital several times, ostensibly for treatment. During his numerous visits to the hospital, his tissues, spleen, and blood were repeatedly taken. He was never informed that he was a subject of scientific research. A cell line was eventually developed from his blood and spleen, and a patent was obtained for it. The cell line was useful for the treatment of leukemia patients, and it went on to become a successful multi-million dollar therapeutic product.

The courts found, inter alia, that there was no informed consent during the course of the research, but denied Moore any property rights in his cell line. If he had succeeded in his property claims, he could have been entitled to some of the profits accruing from the sales of his cell line. But it seemed the court and the scientific

---

55 See *Brotherton v Cleveland* 923 F 2d 477.

56 See *R v Kelly and Lindsay*, op. cit., note 50, 247.

57 See *Moore v The Regents of the University of California* 793 P 2d 479 Cal Sup. (1990).

communities were not prepared for property rights claims by donors of human genetic materials.[58]

The pertinent question is: is it morally right for the industry, as in the *Moore case*, to deny donors of genetic materials a share of the profits accruing from the commodification of their genetic derivatives? Again, this question will be answered in part three where the property allocation methodology in human genetic derivatives is subjected to ethical scrutiny.

Commodification of the Human Body and Body Parts via International Treaties and Conventions

Given the favorable antecedent stance of case law to vesting of property rights in the human body in corporations, researchers, businesses, and entrepreneurs, on evidence of investments or entrepreneurship, it does not come as a surprise that legislations are towing the same line. This is clearly exemplified by article 21 of the Council of Europe Convention on Human Rights and Biomedicine, which provides that 'The human body and its parts shall not as such give rise to financial gain.'[59] In other words, while trade in the human body, body parts or genes, as such, is disallowed, it is legal to deal in human blood, spleen, tissues, genes, cells,and so on, that had been worked on or invested in.

The point is put more explicitly by paragraph 132, an explanatory note on article 21 of the Convention, in the Explanatory Report to the Council of Europe Convention on Human Rights and Biomedicine:

> ... Under this provision organs and tissues proper, including blood, should not be bought or sold or give rise to financial gain for the person from who they have been removed or for a third party, whether an individual or a corporate entity such as, for example, a hospital. However, technical acts (sampling, testing, pasteurization, fractionation, purification, storage, culture, transport, etc.) which are performed on the basis of these items may legitimately give rise to reasonable remuneration. For instance, this Article does not prohibit the sale of a medical device incorporating human tissue which has been subjected to a manufacturing process as long as the tissue is not sold as such. *Further this Article does not prevent a person from whom an organ or tissue has been taken from receiving compensation which, while not constituting remuneration, compensates that person equitably for expenses incurred or loss of income (for example as a result of hospitalization).*[60]

It is instructive to note, however, that paragraph 132 cited above allows for a certain level of limited compensation for donors of organs, tissues, blood, and genetic materials. Remarkably, however, paragraph 132 sets out to deliberately limit the

---

58 See Dworkin, op. cit., note 33, 1077–86.

59 See article 21 of the Council of Europe Convention on Human Rights and Biomedicine, op. cit., note 19.

60 See Council of Europe Explanatory Report on the Convention for the Protection of Human Rights and Dignity of the Human Being with Regard to the Application of Biology and Medicine: Convention on Human Rights and Biomedicine, available at: http://conventions. coe.int/Treaty/EN/Reports/Html/164.htm. The emphasis is mine.

scope of compensation, while ruling out the possibility of remuneration. As shown in the above quote, it only allows for a sort of limited compensation '… for expenses incurred or loss of income (for example as a result of hospitalization).'[61]

The pertinent questions are: why is article 21, read in conjunction with paragraph 132, excluding donors from remuneration? It mentions equitable compensation, but even the nature of compensation allowable is questionable, since it is severely limited. Why limit compensation to mere out-of-pocket expenses, income loss and cost of hospitalization? Or rather, why compensation and not remuneration?

In other words, article 21, as read with paragraph 132, would appear to essentially support the scenario in the *Moore case*.[62] That is, if industry came up with a multi-million dollar therapeutic product, the donors should only be paid just enough to cover out-of-pocket expenses to and from the hospital and the costs of hospitalization.

Where then is the equity in that arrangement? What motivates such a disproportionate formula for benefits-sharing? In my opinion, this is no better than article 4 of the UNESCO Universal Declaration on the Human Genome and Human Rights (an in parimateria provision with article 21 of the Council of Europe Convention on Human Rights and Biomedicine), which is mute on the point of compensation, and makes no pretext at giving any form of financial awards to donors of human genetic materials.

It is patently clear that the drafters of paragraph 132 could hardly conceal their reluctance for a workable legal compensatory regime for donors of human genetic materials. In my opinion, paragraph 132 is no more than a legislative equivalence of the principle enunciated in the *Moore case*. It shows beyond doubt that the law is least concerned about the legal and ethical imperatives of adequate remuneration for donors of human genetic materials.

Commodification of the Human Body, Body Parts, and Molecules via the Patent Regime

It is pertinent to discuss the stance of the patent regime on the human body parts commodification process, as it is an integral part of the legal paradigm for property allocation methodology in the human body, body parts, and genome.

The patent regime allows for exclusive monopoly over any invention for a period of 20 years. For an invention to be patentable, it must be new, be inventive, and capable of industrial application.[63] The patent is generally perceived as an engine of innovation without which no one would invest their time, material resources and money into research and development.[64] The patent is especially crucial for

---

61 Ibid.

62 See *Moore v The Regents of the University of California*, op. cit., note 57.

63 See Warren-Jones, op. cit., note 27, 71–129; Dworkin, op. cit., note 33, 1080; Love, J. (2002), 'Access to Medicine and Compliance with the WTO TRIPS Accord: Model for State Practice in Developing Countries', in Drahos and Mayne, op. cit., note 13, 74; American Association, Council on Ethical and Judicial Affairs (1998), 'Ethical Issues in the Patenting of Medical Procedures', *Food Drug Law Journal* 53, 341.

64 See Mansfield, E. (1993), 'Unauthorized Use of Intellectual Property: Effects on Investment, Technology Transfer, and Innovation', in Wallerstein, M.B., Mogee, M.E.

continuing investments in biotechnology because of its capital intensiveness, and the promise of financial rewards for investments guaranteed through patent licensing and product commercialization.[65]

Since the 1980s when the first patent was granted on a non-human living thing (bacterium) in *Diamond v Chakrabarty*,[66] there have been hundreds of patents on life, including human genetic materials.[67] A good example is the patented cell line taken from the blood and spleen of Mr Moore, a leukemia patient, discussed above.[68]

Additionally, as noted earlier, a patent was granted for the cell line of a Papua New Guinean man for the treatment of T-lymphotropic virus type 1 in 1995.[69] It is estimated that at least 18.5 per cent of human genes are already covered by US patents.[70] In consequence, life patent has gained prominence in contemporary social, economic, religious, and academic discourses, while its ethical and legal proprieties have spawned innumerable literature.[71]

However, it is not the aim of this section to delve into the ethical propriety of patenting of life or human genetic products per se. The discourse is highly polemical, and has been well articulated in contemporary legal and moral philosophical literature.[72] My primary aim is to demonstrate the role of the patent regime in the exclusionary process of donors of human genetic derivatives from the remunerative scheme inherent in the human genetic derivative commodification paradigm.

The Nature and Scope of Patent Exclusivity in Human Genetic Derivatives

Patenting biotechnological inventions poses unique legal difficulties which are clearly beyond the remit of this discourse.[73] However, in order to obtain a patent, the applicant is required to fulfill the following basic requirements: have a patent claim which specifies the nature of his invention or improvement on a known invention. The invention or improvement on an existing invention can be a process or a product.

---

and Schoen, R.A. (eds), *Global Dimensions of Intellectual Property Rights in Science and Technology* (Washington DC: National Academy Press) 107; Frank, R. and Salkever, D. (1995), 'Pricing, Patent Loss, and the Market for Pharmaceuticals', *Southern Economic Journal* 59:2.

65 See *Pharmaceutical Industry Profile 2005* (Washington DC: PhRMA, 2005) pp. 2–3; Van Reekum, R. (1999), *Intellectual Property and Pharmaceutical Innovation: A Model for Managing the Creation of Knowledge under Proprietary Conditions* (The Netherlands: Capell, Labyrint Publications) 1.

66 See *Diamond v Chakrabarty*, op. cit., note 5.

67 See Resnik, D.B. 'DNA Patents and Human Dignity', *Journal of Law, Medicine and Ethics* (2001), 29: 2; King and Stabinsky, op. cit., note 30, 49–54.

68 See *Moore v The Regents of the University of California*, op. cit., note 57.

69 See Senituli, op. cit., note 33, 1–6.

70 See Pagan Westphal, op. cit., note 17.

71 See, for instance, Ida, R. (2004), 'Ethical and Legal Aspects of Biotechnology', in Brannigan, op. cit., note 6, 25–36; Oriola, T.A., op. cit., note 5, 450.

72 See, for instance, Ida, op. cit., note 71, 25–36.

73 For a discussion, see Warren-Jones, op. cit., note 27, 71–129; Wei, op. cit., note 22, 45.

The applicant for a patent will demonstrate how the invention or improvement works, show that the invention or improvement is replicable, and that the invention or improvement is new and inventive, and that it is capable of industrial application. This crucial information (patent claim) must be disclosed in what is known as a patent specification.[74]

Once granted, the patent owner has exclusive monopoly over the invention. With regard to genetic-related inventions, this would cover genetic information, the technique for the use of genetic invention, and so on. The subject matter of the patent could then be commercialized through patent licensing, or the sale of any resulting products or process. Hundreds of human genetic-related inventions have been so commercialized.

As a general rule, patents are granted only for inventions and not for mere discoveries or products of nature. It should be noted, however, that not all inventions are patentable.[75] In the context of genes patents, however, a loose interpretation of what constitutes an invention has led to numerous patents on mere genes discovery.[76] Besides, there is empirical evidence that life patents are impeding scientific research, and enclosing crucial scientific information, as well as hindering technology and knowledge transfer.[77]

The pertinent question is: how does the patent regime contribute to the exclusion of donors of human genetic materials from participating in the accruable profits incidental to human genetic derivatives commodification? I would argue that this is done indirectly, via the absence of a requirement in the patent law, that the source of human genetic materials or any genetic material for that matter be disclosed in patent claims or specifications. Without this crucial disclosure, donors would be in ignorance and would lack the means of tracing or linking to themselves any future commercial applications of genetic products based on their genetic materials.[78] This anomaly arguably facilitates the exclusion of donors of human genetic materials from claiming remuneration in any future commercial applications of the product or process based on their genetic materials.

---

74 For a discussion, see Warren-Jones, op. cit., note 27, 71–129.

75 Other conditionalities such as newness, novelty and industrial applicability must be satisfied. See Warren-Jones, op. cit., note 27, 76–80.

76 See Albright, op. cit., note 30, 29–39.

77 For a discussion, see King and Stabinsky, op. cit., note 30, 49–54.

78 This is an enduring subject of dispute mainly between developing and developed nations. Recently, a group of six developing countries led by India submitted a proposal to the World Trade Organization, suggesting changes to the WTO Trade-Related Agreement on Intellectual Property Rights to include the requirement of disclosure of source of biological materials in patent applications. See Gerhardsen, T.I.S. (2006), 'Developing Countries Propose TRIPS Amendment on Disclosure', *Intellectual Property Watch*, 1 June 2006, available at: http://www.ip-watch.org/weblog/index.php?p=323&res=1024&print=0. Although the primary focus of the proposal is the protection of the vast plant and animal genetic resources which predominate in the southern hemisphere, through the incorporation of the relevant text of the 1992 United Nations Biological Diversity Convention into the 1994 WTO TRIPS Agreement, it equally arguably resonates with the proposal for the recognition and disclosure of human genetic resources in patent applications.

Viewed from the foregoing perspectives, it is clear that the patent regime has clear rules for commercializing the human genes, via patent monopoly, without any provision for the recognition and disclosure of the source of human genetic materials. This anomaly arguably contributes to the difficulties of linking donors of human genetic materials to the commercialized genetic derivatives. In my opinion, this is the critical first step in the exclusion process that successfully alienates donors of human genetic materials from their genetic derivatives, and possible remunerative benefits accruable from its commercialization.

The stance of the patent regime is clearly consistent with juridical opinions and international conventions and treaties. In part three, I will assess the ethics of the legal methodology for property allocation which, in the main, fosters a non-inclusive market in human genetic derivatives, by excluding donors of human genetic materials from the inherent financial benefits and remunerative process.

The Ethics of Conferring Property and Remunerative Rights on Donors of Human Genetic Materials

It was noted earlier in this chapter how the law is skewed in favor of corporations, businesses, and entrepreneurs, and against donors, in its methodology for allocating property and remunerative rights in human genetic derivatives. The pertinent ethical questions are: is it fair or just to exclude donors from the market in human genetic derivatives as the law has done? Or more specifically, is it morally right to accord donors of human genetic materials remunerative and property rights in their genetic derivatives?

Although human genetic derivatives do not legally constitute human body or body parts per se, nevertheless, the ethical propriety of donors' remunerative and property rights in human genetic derivatives has great resonance with the highly polemical human body and body parts commodification discourse in contemporary literature. A fortiori, I will use familiar ethical principles on the human body commodification subject (human dignity, Kantianism, and justice) to appraise the rights and wrongs of proprietary and remunerative rights in human genetic derivatives.

As noted in the introduction, the choice of my ethical framework is arbitrary and non-systematic. This is consequent on the virtual impossibility of prescribing a definitive set of ethical theories for the resolution of any set of moral issues. It is trite that there cannot be a set of satisfactory ethical theories that would automatically, like a code or law, be applicable to a set of moral problems.[79] Besides, space constraint imposes a limitation on the range of applicable ethical theories that could be used to address the central ethical questions raised in this chapter. Moreover, my choice of ethical framework is a recurring feature in contemporary literature on human body commodification discourse.

---

79 See Rachels, J. (1998), 'Ethical Theory and Bioethics', in Kuhse, H. and Singer, P. (eds), *A Companion To Bioethics* (Oxford: Blackwell Publishing) 15–23.

Human Dignity Perspectives on the Proprietary and Remunerative Rights of Donors of Human Genetic Derivatives

In this section, the main question is whether or not conferring of proprietary and remunerative rights on donors of human genetic materials is compatible with the concept of human dignity? Human dignity has featured prominently in legislations and contemporary literature on the practical applications of modern bioscience in general, and on the propriety of the commodification of the human body and body parts in particular.[80]

For example, the Preamble to the Council of Europe's Convention on Human Rights and Biomedicine, inter alia, requires that member states should take measures that would safeguard human dignity and the fundamental rights and freedoms of the individual.[81] Moreover, outside of the bioscience or bioethics discourse, human dignity has a universal resonance in the human rights context, as exemplified by the post-World War II United Nations Universal Declaration of Human Rights.[82]

Ditto, many countries, such as Germany, consider the protection of human dignity imperative enough to enshrine it in their constitutions.[83] This is exemplified by section 10 of the Republic of South African Constitution, which enjoins that 'Everyone has inherent dignity and the right to have their dignity respected and protected.'[84]

Characteristically, modern democracies that are modeled after the Western ideals of individual liberty and freedom constantly strive to make human dignity protection the core and foundation of their nationhood. This they do partly by setting legal benchmarks for the protection of life, property, privacy, liberty, and so on.[85]

The pertinent question therefore is: what is human dignity? Theoretical conceptions of human dignity are as varied and contested as their applications in the fields of biomedicine, which range from embryo research and human cloning to genetic predictive diagnosis, human medical experimentation, and so on.[86] Thus

---

80 See, for instance, Beyleveld, D. and Brownsword, R. (2001), *Human Dignity in Bioethics and Biolaw* (Oxford: Oxford University Press) 1.

81 See the Council of Europe Convention on Human Rights and Biomedicine, op. cit., note 19.

82 Specifically, article 1 enjoins that 'All human beings are born free and equal in dignity and rights.' See the full text of the United Nations Universal Declaration of Human Rights of 1948, available at: http://www.un.org/Overview/rights.html.

83 See Simon, J. (2002), 'Human Dignity as a Regulative Instrument for Human Genome Research', in Mazzoni, C.M. (ed.), *Ethics and Law In Biological Research* (The Hague, London and New York: Martinus Nijhoff Publishers) 35–45.

84 Full text of the Constitution is available online at: http://www.info.gov.za/documents/constitution/1996/96cons2.htm.

85 See Balzer, P., Rippe, K.P. and Schaber, P. (2000), 'Two Concepts of Dignity for Humans and Non-Human Organisms in the Context of Genetic Engineering', *Journal of Agricultural Environmental Ethics* 13, 7–27.

86 See Simon, op. cit., note 83, 35–45; Oduncu, F.S. (2003), 'Stem Cell Research in Germany: Ethics of Healing vs. Human Dignity', *Medicine, Health Care and Philosophy* 6, 5–16.

there are different conceptual layers of human dignity ranging from the intrinsic worth and inalienable dignity of humans (from the Kantian perspective),[87] the dignity of moral stature of humans or virtue dignity,[88] the dignity of identity, to the dignity of merits.[89]

Viewed from the perspective of the varied theoretical nuances of dignity, an inflexible or a straight-jacketed application of human dignity to ethical issues such as property rights in the human body, body parts, human genome or human genetic derivatives, is bound to be problematic. Nevertheless, the varied theoretical conceptions of human dignity are, however, agreed on the imperatives of according respect to humans, as well as inviolability of the human person.

In his *Metaphysics of Morals*, Immanuel Kant conceived of human dignity in terms of respecting a person essentially because of his inherent humanity or intrinsic worth as a human being, including self-respect.[90] To Kant, human dignity is embedded in the inherent worth of all humans, which is intrinsic and universal, without necessarily having recourse to the rationality criterion.[91]

However, the intrinsic worth of all humans and the universality connotations of human dignity as espoused by Kant have been rejected by some critics who queried the inclusion of mentally impaired individuals, amongst others, or the non-inclusion of sentient non-humans on the list of those worthy of human dignity accolade.[92] Limited space and scope of subject hinder me from joining the fray. But I would nevertheless apply Kant's conception of respect for person as human dignity, because it resonates well with the main international treaties on biomedicine and human rights interface.[93]

The pertinent question is: how would Kant appraise the proposed donors' remunerative and property rights in human genetic derivatives? In the context of reciprocal respect for the person, and self-respect, I would argue that it is compatible with Kant's idea of human dignity to recognize property and remunerative rights in donors of human genetic derivatives.

My argumentation is premised on two grounds. First, a human genetic derivative is neither human body nor body parts as such, and therefore any property or remunerative rights would not contravene or undermine the concept of self-respect and reciprocal respect for the person, as conceived by Kant. Second, in my view, a denial of property and remunerative rights to donors would undermine donors' autonomy and, by extrapolation, their person and human dignity, which is central to

---

87 See Gregor, M. (ed.) (2000), *Kant: The Metaphysics of Morals* (*Cambridge Texts in the History of Philosophy*) (Cambridge: Cambridge University Press,) 209.

88 See Nordenfelt, L. (2004), 'The Varieties of Dignity', *Health Care Analysis* 12:2 (June) 59–81; Beyleveld and Brownsword, op. cit., note 80, 138.

89 See Nordenfelt, op. cit., note 88, 59–81.

90 See Gregor, op. cit., note 87, 209.

91 See Cutas, D-E. (2005), 'Looking for the Meaning of Dignity in the Bioethics Convention and the Cloning Protocol', *Health Care Analysis* 13:4, 303–13.

92 See, for instance, Balzer, Rippe and Schaber, op. cit., note 85, 7–27.

93 See the main texts of the Council of Europe Convention on Biomedicine and Human Rights, op. cit., note 19; and the UNESCO Universal Declaration on the Human Genome and Human Rights, op. cit., note 24.

the exercise of their will as human beings. This is premised on the proposition that it would be presumptuous to assume that donors would not be interested in property or remunerative rights in their genetic derivatives. Undoubtedly, there would be those donors who would not be. However, failure to give rights to those who might be interested in property and remunerative rights, however minute or insignificant their number might be, would, in my opinion, undermine their autonomy and dignity in Kantian terms.

On the other hand, Beyleveld and Brownsword espouse two practical conceptions of human dignity. The first is that of 'human dignity as empowerment,' while the second is 'human dignity as constraint.'[94] The empowerment conception of human dignity regards human rights as rooted in the intrinsic dignity of humans, and therefore calls for a respect for human autonomy.[95]

Conversely, the constraint conception of human dignity invokes a duty-driven paradigm which emphasizes human duties over human rights.[96] Beyleveld and Brownsword also postulate the notion of human dignity as a virtue in the context of societal disapproval for those who conduct themselves in an undignified manner.[97]

How would the proposal for property and remunerative rights for donors of human genetic materials fare under Beyleveld and Brownsword's conception of human dignity? I would argue that the empowerment conception of human dignity fits well with the argument for the recognition of property and remunerative rights for donors of human genetic materials in their genetic derivatives.

The basis of my argumentation is as follows: the empowerment conception of human dignity supports individuals' human rights in general and freedom and autonomy in particular. In this context, and like Kant's ideas of reciprocal respect for humanity, it is arguably empowering to facilitate property and remunerative rights for donors of human genetic materials. It is clearly compatible with the notions of freedom and autonomy, and to do otherwise would violate human dignity as conceived by Beyleveld and Brownsword.

What of the concept of 'human dignity as constraint?' Would it support the argument for property and remunerative rights in human genetic derivatives? Beyleveld and Brownsword noted that the constraint on human dignity is located in the new international instruments regulating bioethics such as the UNESCO Universal Declaration on the Human Genome and Human Rights.[98] The authors noted that the new international regulatory regimes on bioethics, by seeking to protect individuals from unauthorized interferences from others, (that is, via the informed consent rule) impose constraints which affect others as well as individuals themselves.[99]

Specifically, the authors noted article 21 of the Council of Europe Convention on Human Rights and Biomedicine, which prohibits the commercialization of the

---

94 See Beyleveld and Brownsword, op. cit., note 80, 1–68.

95 Ibid, 1.

96 Ibid.

97 Ibid, 2.

98 Ibid, 29–47.

99 Ibid, 33.

human body, as a self-restraining factor on the individual, with the aim of protecting human dignity.[100]

I would argue, however, that human genetic derivative is outside of the legal ambit of article 21 of the Council of Europe Convention on Human Rights and Biomedicine, because human genetic derivative is not human body as such. A fortiori, any award of property or remunerative rights to donors would not contradict the concept of dignity which the article seeks to protect.

However, I reject paragraph 132 of the explanatory note on article 21 of the Convention on Human Rights and Biomedicine, which prohibits remunerating donors of genetic materials, but supports limited compensatory awards such as out-of-pocket expenses and the costs of hospitalization.[101] In my opinion, this contradicts human dignity that article 21 seeks to protect. Human genetic derivative is not human body or body parts as such. It is a legally fungible object which is already legally commodified.

Again would remuneration or property rights in human genetic derivatives contravene human dignity as a virtue? Would any donor seeking remunerative and property rights in their genetic derivatives be perceived as conducting themselves in an undignified manner by society? This is largely a subjective question. I would, however, argue that there is nothing undignifyied in seeking such rights because human genetic derivative is not human body or body parts as such. A fortiori, donors who seek adequate remuneration are most unlikely to be subjected to societal opprobrium. Besides, and most importantly, big corporations, businesses and entrepreneurs are making fortunes out of a legal market in human genetic derivatives. What then is to preclude the individual donor?

In conclusion, I would argue that there is nothing in the general notion of human dignity to foreclose remunerating donors or according property rights in human genetic derivatives to donors of human genetic materials. The legal methodology for property rights allocation in human genetic derivatives allows for the complete exclusion of the donors from property and remunerative rights in human genetic derivatives. In my view, this compromises donors' autonomy, and undermines their self-worth and human dignity.

It is therefore imperative for authorities to reposition the law in order to accommodate donors' property and remunerative rights in their genetic derivatives. This is especially so since the market has failed to respond to such an obvious inequity. Therefore, if the market will not self-regulate for fair play, or create a level playing field, then the law should intervene. To the extent that the legal regime as it were fosters this atmosphere of inequity, it violates human dignity, in my view.

---

100 Ibid, 33.

101 See Council of Europe Explanatory Report on the Convention on Human Rights and Biomedicine, op. cit., note 60. See also my argument on the implications of the explanatory note in part two of this chapter.

Kantianism and Donors' Rights to Proprietary and Remunerative Rights in Human Genetic Derivatives

Immanuel Kant is credited with the renowned stricture that on no account should human beings be used merely as a means by others or by themselves. In his *Metaphysics of Morals*, he argued that:

> ... for a human being cannot be used merely as a means by any human being (either by others or even by himself) but must always be used at the same time as an end ...[102]

In essence, Kant's categorical imperative is that humanity should be treated as an end in itself, and never as a means only.[103] This proposition also embodies respect for humans and, by extrapolation, individuals' autonomy.[104] It is often invoked in bioethics debates to oppose the commodification of the human body and body parts.[105]

The pertinent ethical question is how might Kant view the legal exclusion of donors of human genetic materials from the market for human genetic derivatives? In other words, would Kant support the proposal for the recognition of property and remunerative rights for donors of human genetic materials?

I would argue that the exclusion of donors from the market in human genetic derivatives, as well as the absence of property and remunerative rights for donors, is tantamount to instrumentalizing or using human beings as a means only. In other words, it is compatible with Kant's stricture to vest property rights in donors and remunerate them in an all-inclusive market in human genetic derivatives. To the extent that the law fails to include donors in the market for human genetic derivatives, it acts outside of Kant's stricture, that humanity should not be instrumentalized or treated as a means only.

The Concept of Justice and Donors' Proprietary and Remunerative Rights in Human Genetic Derivatives

It is trite to say that justice is an elusive concept. As an ethical theory, it is susceptible to different interpretations, contingent mainly on which philosophical principle is employed. Thus there are libertarian, communitarian, utilitarian and egalitarian concepts of justice.[106] Justice is often defined in terms of fairness, desert, or entitlement by moral philosophers.[107] Traditionally the concept of justice deals with rights and duties, and the need to give a person their due in the absence of overriding

---

102 Gregor, op. cit., note 87, 209.

103 Ibid.

104 See Miyasaka, M. (2005), 'Resourcing Human Bodies: Kant and Bioethics', *Medicine, Health Care and Philosophy* 8, 19–27.

105 Green, R.M. (2001), 'What Does it Mean to Use Someone as "A Means Only": Rereading Kant', *Kennedy Institute of Ethics Journal* 11:3, 247–61.

106 See Beauchamp, T.L. and Childress, J.F. (2001), *Principles of Biomedical Ethics* (Fifth edition) (Oxford: Oxford University Press) 230–35.

107 Ibid.

moral justifications to the contrary. This is known as procedural justice, and very different from John Rawls' concept of justice.[108]

An assessment of justice as a concept can only be meaningfully carried out within the perimeters of the social–economic constructs of society. Social justice therefore provides the '… standard by which the distributive aspects of the basic structure of society are to be assessed.'[109] Additionally, social justice is often invoked to justify states' intervention and fair redistribution of rights and responsibilities amongst citizens.[110] Distributive justice thus '… refers to fair, equitable, and appropriate distribution determined by justified norms that structure the terms of social cooperation.'[111]

In the context of bioethical debates, distributive justice is a recurring principle. This is especially so in right to healthcare discourses vis-à-vis scarcity of goods and services, and responsibility and competition for same. Redistribution in this context would entail a reordering of rights, responsibilities and duties, some of which are already settled by law.

The pertinent question then is: how might the proposal for the recognition of property and remunerative rights in human derivatives for donors of human genetic materials fare under the principle of justice? I would argue that excluding the donors from the market, and denying them remunerative and property rights, is inequitable, unfair and unjust. An arrangement that allows corporations, businesses, entrepreneurs, and so on, to profit from human genetic derivatives, while excluding the donors, is plainly an unjust system of property allocation, and goes against the grains of justice.

In this part, I used the three principles of human dignity, Kantianism and justice, as a composite ethical framework to assess the fairness and justice of the legal exclusion of donors of human genetic materials from the market for human genetic derivatives. I noted that such exclusion was contrary to the principles of human dignity, Kantianism, and justice. Consequently, it is morally wrong in my opinion to so exclude donors, and deny them property and remunerative rights in human genetic derivatives.

Ethical and Legal Problematic of Conferring Property Rights in and Remunerating Donors of Human Genetic Derivatives

Conferring property and remunerative rights on donors of human genetic materials clearly has underlying ethical and legal implications. The following paragraphs will examine possible ethical and legal hurdles that could beset the proposal for the recognition of property and remunerative rights in donors of human genetic derivatives.

---

108 See Little, I.M.D. (2002), *Ethics, Economics and Politics: Principles of Public Policy* (Oxford: Oxford University) 55–73.

109 Ibid, 59.

110 Ibid, 60.

111 See Beauchamp and Childress, op. cit., note 106, 226.

The first practical problem is how to ascertain ownership rights in human genetic derivatives where there are multiple donors of genetic materials, not only within but outside of national boundaries. The potential for mixing up of genetic materials is real, and could complicate ownership issues. This is a practical problem but it is not insurmountable. Researchers could be obliged to keep all records relating to genetic materials and meticulously link them to research participants or donors. Since not all genetic materials taken would have useful or commercial applications, researchers again would be obliged to note whose genetic materials had useful commercial applications, to avoid unnecessary ownership disputes.

The second practical problem is the implication of positive identification of donors for remunerative and ownership purposes on their privacy and anonymity. With regards to genetic information, donors' relatives would also be at risk of being outed and losing their anonymity. This problem could, however, be overcome by devising a strategy that would simultaneously protect donors' anonymity, while positively linking them to their genetic materials for proprietary and remunerative purposes.

The third practical problem is the methodology for remunerating donors. In my argumentation, I maintain my preference for remuneration instead of limited compensation prescribed by paragraph 132 of the explanatory note on article 21 of the Council of Europe Convention on Human Rights and Biomedicine.[112] I would suggest that this should be left entirely to market forces. This would of course invariably depend on the market value of the genetic derivative in question, and what the parties agreed upon as adequate remuneration.

The fourth practical problem is the tendency for people to yield themselves to all sorts of medical experimentations, with an expectation of possible future financial benefits. There is thus a real possibility that research participants and donors of human genetic materials might be motivated solely by future monetary benefits rather than pure altruism. This would undermine individuals' autonomy, and such research would become ethically questionable. The potential for abuse is rife in this respect as this is an inherently human condition. The possible solution to this downside is rigorous regulatory oversight to pre-empt all forms of abuse that could undermine human dignity.

Conclusions

In this chapter, my primary aim was to generate a debate on the propriety of vesting of property and remunerative rights in donors of human genetic materials in their genetic derivatives. I reviewed the legal methodology for property allocation in human genetic derivatives. I noted that the legal regime is skewed in favor of businesses, entrepreneurs, and big corporations, who invest in the human body and body parts commodification process, and against the donors of human genetic derivatives.

---

112 See Council of Europe Explanatory Report on the Convention on Human Rights and Biomedicine, op. cit., note 60. See also my argument on the implications of the explanatory note in part two of this chapter.

The property allocation methodology in human genetic derivatives allows for the exclusion of donors from the legal market in human genetic derivatives, as well as denying them property and remunerative rights. I assessed this arrangement, using the ethical framework of human dignity, Kantianism, and justice. I take the stand that there is nothing in my composite ethical framework that ethically forbids remunerating donors, or accords them full property rights in human genetic derivatives.

I noted, however, the legal and ethical problematic of allocating property and remunerative rights in human genetic derivatives in donors. These range from practical problems such as tying genetic materials to donors where there are multiple donors, ascertaining remuneration payable, jeopardizing donors' anonymity, to the real danger of abuse, due to the possibility of submitting to biomedical research purely for financial gains. I recommended that these problems could be overcome by rigorous regulatory oversight, and diligence on the part of biomedical researchers.

Acknowledgement

The author thanks Professors Marcus Düwell and Frans Brom of the Insititute of Applied Ethics, University of Utrecht, Netherlands for their insightful comments on the original draft of this chapter. He however takes responsibility for all errors or shortcomings.

Chapter 14

4x4 Cars and the City: What are the Limits of Vehicle Manufacturer Responsibility?

Peter Wells

Introduction

Companies are social institutions, existing within dynamic situations in which cultural attitudes, norms and expectations shift over time. That which used to be acceptable as a business practice might become unacceptable, or activities previously frowned upon may become legitimate. Importantly, this is not simply a matter reducible to the law per se, though changes in the legal framework are often a feature of such transitions.

This chapter is about the consequences of the sale and use of large, four-wheel drive vehicles in urban areas. The main focus is on two issues: safety and environmental concerns. The chapter is derived from a document prepared for Greenpeace in relation to a campaign against so-called 4x4 vehicles in general, and Land Rover in particular. One starting point for this very 'live' social debate is perhaps that vehicle manufacturers, as custodians of engineering knowledge, have a responsibility to design and sell vehicles appropriate to the circumstances. Another is that if acting within the law, vehicle manufacturers simply offer their products to consumers and it is then up to those consumers to act responsibly.

Consumers are likely to seek to maximise their personal utility first, and be rather less concerned about the wider social costs. In this respect, the purchase of a large or heavy vehicle might (or might not) be logical as a means of maximising personal safety, even if it also potentially reduces the safety of other road users. In broad terms, the prevailing free-market assumption is that consumers should be able to purchase and use whatever vehicle they wish from those available on the market, regardless of the wider social and environmental costs (negative externalities) because these are matters handled by the government and by companies. In the contemporary era it is widely accepted that companies have a 'corporate social responsibility' towards society and to the environment by virtue of the concentration of knowledge and resources which the companies enjoy. The stance argued here is that this responsibility can and should involve more than mere compliance with regulatory controls and legal standards, but should also involve active leadership, enacting changes ahead of any such controls and standards, and using those resources to arrive at innovative solutions to social and environmental problems.

In addition there is a rather more complex problem to do with targeting and the conduct of campaigns of this type. On the one hand, Land Rover as a single company has for many years been associated only with vehicles with an off-road capability. Other companies may have other specialisations: Aston Martin is known for sports cars, for example. On the other hand, both of these two companies are in fact owned by a larger company, in this case Ford, with very diverse product ranges and market coverage. Moreover, Ford includes within its own product range a great many 4x4 models, particularly for the US market.

Defining the Terms of Debate

The problem with any virulent debate of this type is that in practice it is often difficult to arrive at a precise definition of the terms, even when in reality all parties to the discussion know what they are talking about.

There are various terms used somewhat interchangeably to refer to the type of vehicles represented by the two Land Rover models in question: the Discovery and the Range Rover. These terms are not defined by legal requirements arising from vehicle test and registration legislation, but are used by the automotive industry and in popular discourse to describe the vehicles and to place them within so-called 'segments' of the overall market. The main terms in common usage are:

- 4x4
- Sports Utility Vehicle (SUV)
- Off-road vehicle

A 4x4 vehicle is one that has (usually permanent) four-wheel drive. The majority of saloon cars, hatchbacks and other passenger cars sold in the UK are front-wheel drive only. Some are rear-wheel drive (BMW models, for example). Four-wheel drive vehicles are not necessarily endowed with specific off-road capability by design, and some vehicle manufacturers have introduced four-wheel drive versions of models that are more commonly found as front-wheel drive: Audi, for example, has for many years made available four-wheel drive variants of their A3, A4, A6 and A8 or antecedent models, sold with the Quattro designation. Subaru specialise in four-wheel drive models, only one of which could be described as being near the same market segment as the Land Rover Discovery or Range Rover. Sometimes the term 'all-wheel drive' is used. Generally speaking, the Land Rover models in question can be considered as large 4x4s, whereas the Land Rover Freelander model is an example of a medium 4x4.

A Sports Utility Vehicle is a description 'imported' from the US market. The term does not describe a sports car at all, but rather conveys the idea that the vehicles in question have a range of capabilities that cross between work (utility) and leisure (sport). This is a somewhat confusing term, because while the SUV segment does indeed capture the Land Rover Discovery and Range Rover, it is also used to embrace a wide range of vehicles that are distinctly different in terms of engineering, design and functional capability. It is worth noting, however, that the Land Rover models are classed as light trucks in the US market.

The term 'off-road vehicle' is used to describe a vehicle that has, to some degree, the capability to be used off-road. It does not mean that the vehicles are confined to off-road applications in the way that, for example, some very heavy-duty quarry lorries are so confined. The extent to which vehicles are able to go off-road is not precisely defined, and again a wide variety of vehicles may fall into this category. For example, quad-bikes are light-weight, single-seat off-road vehicles used both in work and leisure applications. As discussed below, designing a vehicle to be capable of off-road performance carries a significant efficiency and safety penalty when it is used on normal roads.

The Safety Issues

Deaths and injuries from road traffic accidents are a serious issue for public health with multiple causal factors and multiple agencies. One important factor is vehicle design, and hence one important agency is the vehicle manufacturer that designs and manufactures those vehicles. The safety issue may be divided into those matters concerning impacts between vehicles, and those concerning impacts with pedestrians.

While much has been made of the relatively good safety record in the UK, and while the vehicle manufacturers should get due recognition for the introduction of technologies and features to improve safety in the event of an accident, recent research has shown that a significant proportion of the improvement is attributable to better rescue and recovery systems operated by the emergency services.

In 2003, according to data from the UK Department for Transport, there were 3,508 people killed in road traffic accidents in the UK, 33,707 serious injuries, and 253,392 slight injuries. Of these there were 114 pedal cyclists killed, and 774 pedestrians killed with 7,159 seriously injured. That is, 22 per cent of deaths from road traffic accidents were pedestrians in 2003. In 2004 there were 3,221 deaths, of which 671 were pedestrians.

In order to gain Type Approval for sale in the European Union, all models must meet specified safety standards. These standards, however, pertain to the safety of the occupants. On 1 October 2005 the first EU pedestrian impact safety standards were introduced for all new models entering the market from that date. Standards such as these can be seen as minimum entry requirements.

Evidence from the US can be a useful starting point to understanding the relative safety performance of large 4x4 vehicles. In particular, the US data gives an insight into the consequences that arise when a large 4x4 is in collision with a car.

It is accurate to say that the US light truck segment upon which this data is based reflects a situation somewhat different to the UK – notably the 4x4s are heavier and occupants are less likely to wear seatbelts. On the other hand, these factors may be offset:

- US cars are also larger and heavier on average. There is of course a 'sub-compact' segment of the market, but no representation of European 'super-mini' cars (for example, Peugeot 206) or city cars (for example, Smart

ForTwo).
- US legal road speed limits are often lower than those in Europe or the UK, particularly in urban areas.
- US legal requirements at junctions are also different, for example, with the 'four-way stop' at crossroad junctions in urban areas.
- US driving styles tend to be more relaxed and slower, aided by the almost ubiquitous use of automatic transmission and power steering.

With respect to impacts with other vehicles, the main issues are the relative weight of the 4x4/SUV and the incompatibility of these vehicles with the impact structures found on cars. The greater weight means that for a given speed there is more energy to transfer to the other vehicle. The greater height of the 4x4 means that the point of impact tends to be higher than the bumpers or side-impact beams of the car, thereby allowing greater intrusion into the car or even riding up over the car. The stiffness of the SUV chassis means that it does not absorb the impact energy through progressive deformation, which is the way in which cars manage impacts via 'crumple zones', rather the chassis becomes the means by which energy is transferred to the other vehicle.

With these considerations in mind, the available US data clearly supports the view that 4x4/SUV vehicles are more dangerous to other road users than traditional cars in the event of an accident.

With respect to deaths and injuries caused to pedestrians, the implications for 4x4 vehicles are somewhat different. In the case of a normal front-engine car of typical height, the point of impact with the pedestrian is the bumper, which usually hits on the legs between the knee and the thigh. This primary impact then causes the pedestrian to rotate over the front of the car and results in secondary impacts, with the bonnet, windscreen frame or windscreen, to the head and upper body. The secondary impacts are more likely to result in death or serious injury. Further injury may be caused upon impact with the ground or other objects. Vehicle design improvements to reduce death and serious injury have concentrated on removing prominent features on the front of the car that could cause damage, and on managing the energy of the secondary impact. Such features can mitigate the effect of the impact on the pedestrian. Other concepts, such as external airbags, have been explored but not so far used.

With a typical 4x4 vehicle, the front of the vehicle is higher off the ground, and presents a 'wall' of steel, plastic and glass to the pedestrian. This has two consequences. First, the point of impact is higher, and more likely to be in the much more vulnerable torso region of the pedestrian. Second, the pedestrian cannot rotate over and onto the bonnet so there is a reduced opportunity to manage the impact forces.

From US data, pedestrians were two to three times more likely to die when struck by a light truck or van compared with a passenger car, and for a given impact speed the likelihood of serious head and thoracic injury is 'substantially' greater.

The Environmental Issues

A key target for the European automotive industry is that of an average of 140 g/km CO_2 emissions, the figure agreed to be reached between the European automotive industry representative body (ACEA) and the European Commission by 2008. In 1997, according to the Society of Motor Manufacturers and Traders (SMMT), the average figure for new cars sold in the UK was 189.8 g/km CO_2 emissions, falling to 172.1 g/km by 2003.

In 2003 the segment CO_2 emissions performance was as shown in the table below.

Table 14.1   Segment average and lowest CO_2 emitting models in each segment in the UK, 2003

Segment	Model	Fuel	CO_2 emissions g/km	Segment average CO_2 g/km
Mini	Smart	Petrol	113	138
Supermini	Citroen C2	Diesel	108	147
Lower Medium	Toyota Prius	Petrol/Electric	104	166
Upper Medium	Skoda Octavia	Diesel	138	181
Executive	Audi A6	Diesel	154	211
Luxury	Mercedes S320	Diesel	204	272
Sports	Honda Insight	Petrol/Electric	80	222
4x4	RAV4	Petrol	175	244
MPV	Peugeot Partner	Diesel	152	195

Source: SMMT

The performance of the Land Rover Discovery and Range Rover models is worse than the segment average. The basic data are shown in Table 14.2.

A Question of Responsibility

However, it is worth considering what Land Rover might have done in a technical sense, as a socially responsible company, to mitigate the situation by improving fuel economy. There are several technical options available. These include:

- Weight reduction
- Alternative fuels
- Cylinder de-activation
- Part-time 4x4
- Mild hybrid and stop/start cut-out systems
- Full hybrid

Table 14.2   The CO$_2$ emissions performance of the Land Rover Discovery and Range Rover models

Model	Variant	Engine	CO$_2$ emissions g/km
Discovery	V8 S	Petrol	354
	V8 SE	Petrol	354
	V8 HSE	Petrol	354
	TDV6 5st	Diesel	249
	TDV6 7st	Diesel	249
	TDV6 S	Diesel	249
	TDV6 SE	Diesel	249
	TDV6 HSE	Diesel	275
Range Rover	4.2 V8 Super	Petrol	376
	4.4 V8 SE	Petrol	352
	4.4 V8 HSE	Petrol	352
	4.4 V8 Vogue	Petrol	352
	4.4 V8 Vogue SE	Petrol	352
	TD6 SE	Diesel	299
	TD6 HSE	Diesel	299
	TD6 Vogue	Diesel	299
	TD6 Vogue SE	Diesel	299

Source: *What Car?*

The fuel economy measures outlined below would not contribute to an improvement in the safety performance of the vehicles.

Weight reduction offers some scope to improve fuel economy, but in the case of the Land Rover Discovery and Range Rover models, the scope for such reduction is limited by the technical choices made and by the simple reality of being large 4x4 vehicles. The models do employ aluminium in the body structure, but are still heavy vehicles by any standard. The maximum kerb weights are: for the TDV6 manual, 2,708 kg; the TDV6 automatic, 2,718 kg; and the V8 petrol, 2,704 kg. Many aspects of poor fuel economy derive from the design and market positioning of the vehicles and are the inevitable consequence of trying to match off-road performance with the levels of comfort and convenience expected by those that are in reality going to drive the vehicles in urban areas. A different design strategy, for example, with an aluminium frame and plastic composite body panels, could yield significant weight reduction that would in turn allow a weight reduction spiral, as other components and systems could also be reduced in weight.Alternative fuel vehicles offer some improvements in overall emissions performance according to the UK Vehicle Certification Agency.

Cylinder de-activation systems were first deployed in a 1981 Cadillac, but were withdrawn due to technical and reliability problems. With the advent of modern electronic control and engine management, the concept has been revitalised. In the

US, the cylinder de-activation technology concept has been applied to the largest of the 'light truck' vehicles produced by Chrysler and by General Motors (GM). The latest generation Dodge Ram 1500 pick-up truck, for example, has this technology, as does the Jeep Grand Cherokee (a large 4x4 similar to the Land Rover Discovery and Range Rover). Chrysler claim that by switching the V8 to a V4 configuration, fuel savings of up to 20 per cent are possible. Honda developed a 3.0 litre V6 with what the company termed 'Variable Cylinder Management' that is claimed to reduce pumping losses by up to 65 per cent. Honda made a more modest claim for 5 per cent improvement in fuel economy. Vehicles with this technology were launched in the US market and in Japan in 2003.

Mild hybrids and stop/start cut-out systems use electric assistance to accelerate a vehicle from rest. In the US, GM has been active in developing this technology that, in their application, is known as a Belt Alternator System (BAS). The first application will be an SUV, the Saturn VUE Green Line, to appear for the 2007 model year. Combined with regenerative braking and a modified four-speed automatic transmission, it is expected that the BAS will deliver a 12–15 per cent improvement in fuel economy over the basic model.

Part-time 4x4 is used to switch off the front-wheel drive element of a four-wheel drive vehicle when all-round traction is not required, by disengaging the front-wheel drive shaft. The approach is used in the 2006 Dodge Ram pick-up truck, for example. The fuel economy benefit, and hence CO_2 emissions benefit, depends upon the degree to which 4x4 drive is switched off. A reasonable estimate of the difference between a 4x4 version of a model and a two-wheel drive version is for 5–10 per cent lower CO_2 emissions from the two-wheel drive version.

Hybrid cars have entered the market in recent years, notably through the efforts of Honda and Toyota. Again, there is a significant benefit in terms of fuel economy. An example is the Lexus RX400h, a large vehicle that weighs up to 2024 kg and has a CO_2 performance of 192 g/km. This performance illustrates two points. First, that compared with the Land Rover Discovery and Range Rover models, it is possible to achieve between 23 per cent and 49 per cent lower CO_2 emissions. Second, that even with this technology, the fuel economy figure is still poor – nearly twice as much fuel is consumed as that achieved in the Toyota Prius that employs similar technology.

In a major US study, for example, it was estimated that a moderate package of measures, to include weight reduction, streamlining, low rolling resistance tyres and an integrated starter generator system, could yield an improvement of 70 per cent in fuel economy for a typical SUV (actually a Ford Explorer petrol engine V6) for a cost increase of just 4–7 per cent. A more aggressive approach with an 'advanced' SUV design, including direct injection petrol engines, could yield even greater improvements in fuel economy, with a price rise of about 10 per cent.

Conclusions

It is evident from the Land Rover corporate website, and from the promotional literature, that the go-anywhere promise of the models is the primary claim to distinction. Photographs of the models portray, almost universally, scenes bereft of other human features, with vehicles positioned within actual or stylised remote terrains. This is important because the emotional value of brands is often as crucial as the tangible content. In this respect, brands represent lifestyle statements for consumers; they are public statements for consumers wishing to establish to the wider social world their values and status.

In effect, the idea of the 'freedom of the open road' so often promised in mainstream car advertising has been replaced, a frank acknowledgement that our roads today are so congested that such a freedom is utterly unrealisable. Instead, these images offer the prospect of the 'freedom of the open countryside'.

In reality, Land Rover must know that many of these vehicles will not be used anywhere other than city environments, despite the host of inappropriate features that render these vehicles more dangerous and more resource-intensive than need be the case. Perhaps issues of 'responsibility' are not always distinct and clear, but what Land Rover and other companies need to realise is that the judgements are not made in a court of law, but in social discourse.

Chapter 15

From 'Jim Crow' to 'John Doe': Reparations, Corporate Liability and the Limits of Private Law

James Davey[1]

Introduction

A pattern of litigation is developing in the United States in which insurers, banks and other 'deep pocket' defendants are being sued for their role in facilitating the slave trade and other human rights abuses. This is not merely an issue for American lawyers, as British insurers and insurance markets are included for their part in the transportation of slaves from Africa.[2] Moreover, litigation in the United Kingdom remains a possibility, albeit an unlikely one.[3] This represents the latest generation of claims for black reparations, following attempts at the end of the American Civil War and again during the civil rights movement in the 1960s.[4] This gives the chapter its title. The initial struggle against segregation (the so-called Jim Crow laws) has been largely completed, but the political and legal battle for compensation continues. This is commonly pursued by the use of anonymised 'John Doe' claimants as representatives of the African American community.[5]

The claim for reparations is instinctively attractive: 'A great harm has been done'; 'Someone must pay'. However, the translation of these ideals into the everyday systems of private law is not straightforward. This chapter will consider a sample of the recent litigation to demonstrate some of the legal impediments to black reparations against insurers and other corporate bodies.

---

1 I am grateful to Richard Lewis, William Lucy and Annette Morris for their guidance on matters of tort law. The errors remain mine.

2 The Lloyds insurance market was recently sued (unsuccessfully) for its role in the provision of marine insurance for the 'middle passage' voyage from Africa to the West Indies.

3 See Shelton, D. (2002), 'Reparations for Human Rights Violations: How Far Back', *Amicus Curiae* 44, 3.

4 See Brophy, A.L. (2004), 'Reparations Talk: Reparations for Slavery and the Tort Law Analogy', *Boston College Third World Journal* 24, 81, 81–2.

5 See, for example, *In Re African-American Slave Descendants Litigation* (2005) 375 F. Supp. 2d 721.

A Natural History of Reparations Litigation

The claims for reparations to compensate the African American community are part of a continuum, which includes Holocaust and other Second and First World War claims.[6] The defendants in such actions have ranged from commercial entities operating inside Axis territory[7] to the United States government itself.[8] This chapter restricts itself to litigation in which one or more of the defendants were private corporations, rather than state entities.

The claims can be broadly categorised into two forms. The first approach sought the enforcement of some proprietary or contractual right that was expropriated or denied without compensation. These are generally founded on principles of property or contract law and are dealt with in part (a) below. The second form demands compensation for some tortious act, such as enforced labour. These are often presented as tort or unjust enrichment claims and are considered in part (b). Both types have been directed against the financial services industry. Either such companies are accused of having refused to honour banking and insurance agreements, or that they facilitated the exploitation of oppressed persons, by providing related financial services to the perpetrators.

(a) Deferred Enforcement: The Restoration of Property and Contractual Claims

The majority of claims settled to date related to Jewish assets held in occupied or Axis states during the Second World War. The settled claims listed in the survey by Bazyler and Everitt[9] now reach a total of approximately $1,447 million. The vast majority represented financial assets held by Swiss banks (some $1,250 million) but European insurers have also contributed for unpaid insurance policies to a sum of $131 million.[10] This latter fund, distributed under the auspices of the International Commission for Holocaust Era Insurance Claims, has been funded by major European insurance groups.[11] This claims process ended in December 2006.[12]

It is notable that these varied settlements represent the belated enforcement of established contractual and proprietary rights. They do not represent reparations for

---

6 One can imagine further developments, such as feminist reparations for recompense for the legal environment that denied women equal rights.

7 See Bazyler, M.J. and Everitt, G. (2004), 'Holocaust Restitution Litigation in the United States: An Update', *2004 ACLU International Civil Liberties Report* (ACLU) 4–5, available at: http://www.aclu.org/iclr/bazyler.pdf.

8 It has been suggested that a train loaded with Jewish valuables, sent out of Hungary ahead of the advancing Russian forces, was expropriated by US forces. See Bazyler and Everitt, op. cit., note 6, 8.

9 Ibid. The author has sought to update figures to September 2005 values, where available, and has converted all active currencies to US dollars at Reuters rates as of 27 October 2005. The Deutchsmark conversion above is that reported by Bazyler and Everitt at 1999 rates.

10 See: http://www.icheic.org .

11 These include the Generali Group, Allianz, AXA, Wintherthur and Zurich.

12 There has been criticism of the administration of the scheme. See Zabludoff, S. (2005), 'ICHEIC: Excellent Concept But Inept Implementation', *Jewish Political Studies Review* 17.

any separate tortious or criminal act in which corporations were active or passive participants.

The reclamation of property and contractual rights perhaps presents less of a problem for private law. As there are clear economic values for each, it is not difficult to see how past wrongs have affected current claimants. We are happy to see property rights as capable of easy transfer from generation to generation and can identify with a clear sense of unjustified enrichment of the Swiss banks and the account holders.[13] This is so even though the modern bankers and insurers did not themselves assist in such acts, although their companies did. Moreover, the defences raised by the defendants can appear as unnecessarily technical before the 'court of public opinion'. The existence of the Swiss banking secrecy laws was an unconvincing reason not to return looted and stolen property. Similarly, to refuse to pay on an insurance policy because of the inability of the relatives of murdered Jewish policyholders to provide death certificates (when the death camps did not provide any) is churlish. Just as public reaction demanded a relaxation of legal formality following the deaths in the 2005 Indian Ocean tsunami,[14] so legal technicalities feel 'wrong' when dealing with the broken promises of the Second World War. In law, the limitation periods for the pursuit of a contract and a tort claim are normally identical, but there does appear to be a difference in application to cases of historic importance, such as the Holocaust and slavery.

This is evidenced by the relative success of reparations litigation in restoring lost assets. However, this is in stark contrast to claims based in tort or unjust enrichment. There, the distance of time appears to weaken the desire to ensure full justice. This will be of concern to those seeking slavery reparations. The claims will not be for looted assets but for stolen lives. Can private law handle these claims as effectively as it made good stolen art and unpaid insurance policies? The indications from earlier cases are not promising. First, it is much more difficult to be precise in assessing the amount of loss. Second, the magnitude of compensation needed has made some suggest that it cannot be repaid. Estimates vary, but have reached $24 trillion.[15] Finally, there is evidence of a concern of over-compensation. This is not because the harm was not great, but because it was not suffered by those to whom the money is to be paid. The notion of a transgenerational tort claim appears to distort the systems of private law in a manner in which returning stolen property does not.

(b) Inherited Pain and Inherited Gain: Tort and Unjust Enrichment Claims

The settlement of litigation for the recovery of assets can be contrasted to the arrangements regulating compensation for the mass forced and slave labour conducted under German governance in Central and Eastern Europe. Such matters have largely

---

13 This is not meant in its technical legal sense.

14 See 'Legal Review for Tsunami Families in Limbo', *The Guardian* (London, 17 January 2005) 2.

15 The figures are often beyond comprehension, but $24 trillion is $24,000,000 million. See Fogarty, P.A. (2002–03), 'Speculating a Strategy: Suing Insurance Companies to Obtain Legislative Reparations for Slavery', *Connecticut Insurance Law Journal* 9, 211, 212, fn 2.

been resolved by international convention and in particular by the payment of DM10,000 million ($4,800 million at the time) by the German government in 2001. This was not merely recognition of state complicity, but also settled all past and future claims against private corporations involved in the exploitation of forced and slave labour. The international agreements by which compensation was paid to Holocaust era forced and slave workers are significant to those interested in slavery reparations. It is not only that they provided an initial payment of compensation ($7,500 for slave workers and $2,500 for forced labourers) but that the effect was also to bar claims in the US courts against the corporations involved.[16] This is not therefore an interim payment, but an imposed final settlement. Given that this applied to those who were actually enslaved in the Holocaust era, it is difficult to see a more generous scheme applied in favour of the *descendants* of African American slaves.

Even if we see black reparations as a new political paradigm, for which full tortious compensation should be awarded, there are legal obstacles. Attempts to sue private corporations for their role in the slave trade face at least three hurdles to overcome.[17] First, it must be shown that the claimants have standing to raise this issue before a court. Second, it will need to be demonstrated that these claimants are not barred by limitation periods. Finally, they will need to be recognised as a certifiable class, in order to bring a class action. It is the first element, of locus standi, that raises the most contentious points for the pursuit of reparations by court action.

The standing issue was considered expressly by Judge Norgle in the most recent suit in this area, *In Re African-American Slave Descendants Litigation*.[18] Though framed as a technical rule of law, it provided, in his view, the division between the proper legislative and judicial functions of the state. As he explained: 'without the doctrine of standing, the courts would be called upon to decide abstract questions of wide public significance even though other governmental institutions may be more competent to address the questions ...'[19]

On Norgle's analysis, the modern conception of standing is based upon three interrelated principles. First, that the claimant suffered an actual injury, which is 'concrete and particularised' and not 'conjectural or hypothetical'.[20] Secondly, there must be a causal link between the harm suffered and the actions of the defendant. Finally, the remedy sought must be likely to redress the wrong. These principles provide the limits of private law, as beyond this the matters are to be resolved by political and/or legislative means. The real battle before the court was showing that this was a matter for judicial rather than legislative resolution.

In such transgenerational actions, there is therefore a need for the current claimants to identify a loss that they have suffered personally. In the *African-American Slave Descendants case*, the claimants argued that they suffered as a result of their reduced economic opportunities as members of the African American community. They also

---

16 See *Deutsch v Turner Corpn (2003) 317 F.3d 1005*.

17 For a detailed analysis of these difficulties, see Fogarty, op. cit., note 14, 231–40.

18 *375 F. Supp. 2d 721 (2005)*.

19 Ibid, 745, quoting *Elk Grove Unified Sch Dist v Newdow* 542 U.S. 1 (2004).

20 Ibid.

suggested continuing 'psychological damage from the loss of their history, language and culture' and the loss of their true family names.[21]

Unsurprisingly, this was not successful. The claimants had failed to show that they had themselves suffered an injury that was justiciable. As Judge Norgle concluded:

> Plaintiffs cannot establish a personal injury sufficient to confer standing by merely alleging some genealogical relationship to African-Americans held in slavery over one-hundred, two-hundred, or three-hundred years ago.

Moreover, they were unable to show that any harm was caused directly by the actions of the particular defendants:

> In attempting to litigate the unopposed issue of slavery rather than their personal injuries, Plaintiffs also cannot satisfy the second requirement of constitutional standing – injury that is fairly traceable to the conduct of the defendants.

Given that these barriers to private law actions were predicted in advance, why were they still tested by the claimants in the *African-American Slave Descendants case*? On one view, this is merely 'sparring' as counsel raise arguments before the lower federal courts in order to gain access to the Supreme Court, where the novel nature of the issue might force a change in judicial attitudes to the doctrine of standing. A more convincing explanation is provided by Fogarty.[22] She identifies a common strategy of pursuing the reparations agenda by both judicial and legislative means. The litigation is a form of 'quasi-public' litigation in that it seeks redress on remedial terms, rather than seeking to correct an individual harm.[23] The existence of this litigation is likely to affect the shape of the legislative process. Whilst the nature of the litigation remains adversarial, it creates a community of interest in seeing the matter resolved legislatively. The claimants are able to use the increased public attention generated by the litigation to educate the public about the nature of their grievance. Moreover, the insurers and banks are able to forestall likely litigation, judgement and settlement costs by lobbying for a political, legislative resolution. The likely result is some form of institutional reform, a remedy beyond the scope of the courts to order. The role of the litigant is therefore, in part, to raise awareness of the issues beyond the confines of the courtroom, in wider social, legal and political fora.

It may be useful at this point to stop and consider what this tells us about the type of justice that is being sought in reparations litigation. This may help us to understand better the shifting nature of the limits of private law.

---

21 Ibid, 746.

22 See Fogarty, op. cit., note 14, 247–51.

23 This concept is derived, in part, from Chayes, A. (1976), 'The Role of the Judge in Public Law Litigation', *Harvard Law Review* 89, 1281.

Reparations and the Limits of Private Law

There are a number of perspectives from which we can consider the proper limits of private law, and whether they should encompass slavery reparations. If we take the utilitarian model of enterprise liability proposed by Calabresi,[24] there is a prima facie case for allowing recovery. Put simply, liability will be efficient if the costs of production of an item are properly reflected in the market price. If costs are externalised, then the product will be subsidised, and is likely to be over-consumed. This is likely to lead to an inefficient allocation of resources across society. During the slave era, part of the true costs of the production of sugar cane and other raw materials were excluded from the market price due to the forced nature of the labour. It would appear that this should be rectified. However, this provides us with a considerable difficulty. We are unable to affect the historic market price of sugar cane even by the imposition of liability on modern industry. We can make it more expensive today, but the question arises as to whether we should. If we consider that sugar cane was a subsidised product in the slavery era, we could adopt a long-term approach to pricing and impose costs so as to ensure that the industry bears the costs that it created, even if the subsidy and the corresponding liability are separated in time. A counter argument is that today's consumers and shareholders will ultimately bear the brunt of twenty-first-century liability. They had no control over the actions of the past, and ought not to be penalised for the actions of their predecessors.[25] We may talk of imposing liability on corporations, but the true effect will be felt more widely. We could therefore argue that the slavery era actions are too remote to be the proper domain of enterprise liability. However, this always raises the question of where to draw the line. It is not uncommon for industrial injuries to be undetectable until many years after cessation of the employment that caused it. If the inhalation of asbestos dust in a factory in the 1960s is not too remote to impose liability on the modern corporate entity,[26] why should slave actions of the 1760s be too distant? Does it matter if the insurer or bank in question had failed to make public its involvement in slavery?

One solution to this quandary is to consider the need for liability not only to influence the behaviour of the corporation, but to protect the injured party. Perhaps it is the inability of those injured persons to bring the claims in person that is the distinguishing factor. We can no longer compensate them, only their descendants. This leads naturally to the considerations of Aristotle's concepts of justice as discussed by Weinrib.[27] If we accept that corrective justice lies at the heart of tort and unjust enrichment, then we need an identifiable claimant and an identifiable defendant. Moreover, we need convincing proof of a causal link between the two. It is not normally enough to demonstrate that the defendant was engaged in the

---

24 Calabresi, G. (1961), 'Some Thoughts on Risk Distribution and the Law of Torts' *Yale Law Journal* 70, 499.

25 See Brophy, A.L. (2003–04), 'The Cultural War over Reparations for Slavery', *DePaul Law Review* 53, 1181, 1203.

26 We now prevent similar temporal anomalies by the imposition of compulsory insurance for employers, thereby imposing costs today in order to meet future liabilities.

27 Weinrib, E.J. (1991–92), 'Corrective Justice', *Iowa Law Review* 77, 403.

kind of activity that is culpable or deserving of the imposition of liability. Nor is it sufficient to show this claimant was harmed by similar acts. We need to demonstrate that this defendant harmed this claimant. In respect of slavery era activities, even if we are convinced that banks, insurance companies and railroads supported slavery, that does not show that they harmed particular individuals. Even if we can show, for example, that insurance policies were issued over named slaves, that does not demonstrate that harm was caused to the particular modern descendant.

The use of John Doe claimants as representatives of the African American community is significant. It is possible to state that slaves and the descendants of slaves were disadvantaged by actions carried out by latter day insurers and banks. If we are to provide a form of justice, it would appear that distributive justice,[28] of the kind used to compensate for Holocaust era slave labour, is more appropriate. A levy could be raised on those sectors of industry that benefited from slavery. The proceeds of this fund could be directed to individual claimants and to the wider community without the need to establish which 'defendant' was liable to which 'claimant'.[29] The breaking of the link between perpetrator and injured party may lead us to the conclusion that this is a matter to be resolved outside the domain of private law, by the imposition of liability directly from the state on a distributive basis.

The likely reason for claimants to prefer the individualised tort and unjust enrichment claim, at least in the reparations arena, is that the levels of compensation under such schemes have been extraordinarily low. It will be recalled that a slave worker was given a one-off settlement of $7,500 under the agreement between the US and German governments in 2001. The chief negotiator for the Clinton administration, Ambassador Stuart Eizenstat, recognised that the figure was a mere solatium, and not compensatory.[30] However, he rejected suggestions that this reduced the significance of the agreement. He identified three positive consequences of the agreement that went beyond the monetary sum. First, by gaining a public recognition of culpability from the German state and others.[31] Second, by creating the novel legal proposition that private corporations could be responsible for facilitating human rights abuses at home or overseas. Finally, by altering the nature of the negotiations in public international law agreements. This was not merely a process involving the states or their governments, but also included the corporations and other stakeholders. This is described as 'open' or 'democratised' foreign policy making.

---

28 'An exercise of distributive justice consists of three elements: the benefit or burden being distributed, the persons among whom it is distributed and the criterion according to which it is distributed.' See Weinrib, ibid, 408.

29 See Westley, R. 'Many Billions Gone: Is it Time to Consider the Case for Black Reparations', *Boston College Law Review* 40, 429, 470, who suggested a trust fund created out of general taxation.

30 Eizenstat, S. (2004), 'Imperfect Justice: Looted Assets, Slave Labour, and the Unfinished Business of World War II', *Vanderbilt Journal of Transnational Law* 37, 333, 342.

31 'Was it worth the effort? Survivors tell me it was, regardless of the numbers of zeros on their check, because at least at the end of the day, someone had been held accountable for their suffering.' Ibid.

In essence, the private litigation provided the backdrop, and much of the pressure, for the governmental resolution of the dispute. It may be that the recent slavery reparations cases will fulfil a similar function within national legislatures.

Conclusion

The quest for reparations for slavery is ongoing. The most likely mechanism for the legal resolution of this claim is legislative, as we have seen in many of the Holocaust cases to date. However, that will only provide a limited fund, and is likely to be rejected by many members of the African American community as insufficient compensation. If 'legal peace' and immunity from action was purchased from the actual victims of Holocaust era slavery for $2,500 per head,[32] it is difficult to imagine a greater sum being offered to those who are the descendants of those enslaved.

The fundamental difficulty for those who envisage a private law resolution is that these disputes are too large and yet too diffuse for private law actions to resolve. Proving the causal link, that this defendant harmed this claimant, is unachievable across such a wide community and timescale, and yet it is at the heart of our bi-polar private law system. The answer perhaps lies in Bazyler and Everitt's statement of what was achieved by legislative settlement of the Holocaust era cases.[33] They did not provide compensation, but they did impose 'legal peace'. Perhaps, ultimately, that is what can be provided by the current slavery claimants, and we should try and measure how much that is worth to the insurers, banks and other institutions at risk of litigation.

---

32 See text to note 15 above.
33 See note 6 above.

Chapter 16

A Crisis of Professional Self-regulation: The Example of the Solicitors' Profession

Mark Davies

Introduction

In recent years self-regulation by the solicitors' profession may be described as being in crisis. Failures can be seen at all levels, from the appropriate resolution of low-level complaints, to protecting the public from dishonest and other seriously miscreant solicitors. The Law Society has shifted its focus of attention in a variety of ways, but few of its efforts to date have made a significant difference. This chapter summarises some of the key issues which frame the crisis and attempts to resolve it.[1]

The History of Self-regulation

Self-regulation is one of the typically cited traits of professionalism, and the Law Society has always asserted this as a right of solicitors. A disciplinary committee can be traced back to the Solicitors Act 1888,[2] with the Solicitors Act 1974 largely governing the current position. Complaints handling has progressed through the stages of direct Law Society control, with a change in 1986 to the semi-independent Solicitors Complaints Bureau (SCB). A renaming and partial restructuring occurred in 1996, with the creation of the Office for the Supervision of Solicitors (OSS). This change was the Law Society's attempt to address sustained criticism from consumer interest groups, such as the National Consumer Council. The Council had found dissatisfaction rates by complainants to be as high as 60 per cent, and delays of two, three and even four years in the complaints handling process.[3]

Concerns were not assuaged by the changes implemented by the Law Society and criticism has continued into the current century. For instance, in 2004 the

---

1 The issues discussed in this chapter have been developed further in Davies, M., (2004) 'Regulatory Crisis in the Solicitors' Profession', *Legal Ethics* 6:2, 185–216; and Davies, M. (2005), 'Solicitors – the Last Twenty Years of Self-regulation?' *Professional Negligence* 21:1, 3–26.

2 Cranston, R. (ed.) (1995), *Legal Ethics and Professional Responsibility* (Oxford: Clarendon) 2–3.

3 National Consumer Council (1994), *Solicitors Complaints Bureau – A Consumer View* (London: MCC).

Consumers' Association found a significant dissatisfaction rate from the clients of solicitors, 40 per cent of whom had such little faith in the complaints and regulatory systems that they did not bother to make an official complaint.[4] During 2003–04, the Society again reorganised complaints handling, replacing the OSS with the Consumer Complaints Service (CCS). The CCS has delegated to it the significant disciplinary powers possessed by the Law Society.

The most serious disciplinary issues are dealt with by the Solicitors Disciplinary Tribunal (SDT). The SDT deals with applications in respect of solicitors relating to allegations of unbefitting conduct or breaches of the rules of professional conduct.[5] The main powers of the Tribunal are to strike a solicitor off the Roll, suspend the solicitor from practice or impose a fine.

External Elements of the Regulatory Process

An important external addition to the regulatory process occurred in the early 1990s, with the statutory introduction of the Legal Services Ombudsman (LSO).[6] The LSO oversees complaints handling by the Law Society, and it is intended that she should bring independent oversight to the self-regulatory process.

In 2002 the Law Society introduced the role of Independent Commissioner to monitor and audit complaints handling. As a non-lawyer, the Commissioner was to be independent of the Law Society, able to represent the views of the public and to give objective advice to the Law Society. However, it was far from clear how the Commissioner would add to existing oversight roles, notably the Legal Services Ombudsman. The Law Society may have recognised this, as only three years after the creation of the role, the Society announced that it was to be abandoned.

Should a legal professional body be deemed to be failing in its complaints handling, the Secretary of State is empowered to appoint a Legal Services Complaints Commissioner (LSCC).[7] In February 2004 this option was initiated with respect to the Law Society. The LSCC is empowered, inter alia, to investigate complaints handling by the Society; to set targets for improvements; and to impose fines if the Law Society fails to comply. In May 2005 the LSCC was reported to have found that complaints against solicitors were still subject to unacceptable delays. An audit of a random sample of complaints from mid-2004 had found average delays of almost six months in 70 per cent of cases.[8]

---

4 Baron, A. (2004), 'A Law unto Themselves', *Which*, July, 10–13, 13.

5 The Law Society, *The Guide to Professional Conduct of Solicitors*, para. 31.01. Online edition available at: http://www.guide-on-line.lawsociety.org.uk/.

6 Created by section 21 of the Courts and Legal Services Act 1990.

7 Access to Justice Act, sections 51 and 52.

8 Rose, N. (2005), 'Complaints Delays Slated', *Law Society Gazette* 102:20, 19 May, 3. The Law Society Chief Executive disputed the relevance of these findings, asserting that some of the audited cases were up to 18 months old, and that more recently 50 per cent of cases were resolved within three months.

Problems with Self-regulation by Solicitors

In June 1998 the Fabian Society called for regulation to be taken away from the Law Society, to be given to a lay-dominated independent body.[9] In March 1999 criticism by the Lord Chancellor culminated in the threat to seek powers to intervene in complaints handling by the profession.[10] This did not improve matters, and in December 2002 it was once again reported that the Lord Chancellor had serious concerns and was reviewing the future of complaints handling by the profession.[11]

In recent years the Legal Services Ombudsman has been critical of the Law Society for failing to meet public expectations for discipline and complaints handling.[12] In addition, the quality of decision making was also of concern, with close to 50 per cent of the complaints handled by the Law Society being dealt with unsatisfactorily. For example, significant delays have been of particular concern, in some instances for two years or more. Of particular concern are cases of this type which involve solicitors who already have a history of discipline problems.[13]

At a more fundamental level, the Law Society has also been slow to adapt its regulatory approach to an increasingly commercial approach to practice within the profession. Commercialisation may frequently occur at the expense of traditional notions of ethics. But by keeping any ethical debate largely free of the issue, the Law Society has allowed solicitors to slip further into the mentality of the market without having to consider the ethical or conduct implications of this.[14]

Dishonesty

Dishonesty will usually represent the most serious professional offence a solicitor can commit, yet the SDT has not always acquitted itself well when called upon to deal with such cases. Whilst low in number, there are examples of cases where a finding of dishonesty has not resulted in removal from practice. Notwithstanding the mitigation in such cases, it has to be questioned whether it is ever appropriate for a dishonest solicitor to remain in practice.[15]

---

9 Arora, A. and Francis, A. (1998), *The Rule of Lawyers*, Discussion Paper 42 (London: The Fabian Society) 14–15. It was suggested that the current Legal Services Ombudsman, who cannot be legally qualified (see Courts and Legal Services Act, section 21(5)), but who has legal support, could provide the foundations for the new regulatory system.

10 See *Law Society Gazette*, 14 April 1999, 14–15.

11 Rovnick, N. (2002), 'Lord Irvine Threatens Law Society's Disciplinary Role', *The Lawyer*, 2 December, 3.

12 See, for example, *Annual Report of the Legal Services Ombudsman 2001/2002*, HC940, 4 and 7.

13 See, for example, Davies, M. (1998), 'The Regulation of Solicitors and the Role of the Solicitors Disciplinary Tribunal', *Professional Negligence* 14:3, 143–73, 149–51.

14 See further Cranston, op. cit., note 2, 33.

15 For more detail and further examples, see Davies, op. cit., note 13, 143–73; and Davies, M. (1999), 'Solicitors, Dishonesty and the Solicitors Disciplinary Tribunal', *International Journal of the Legal Profession* 6:2, 141–74.

Similar concerns also arise from cases where the SDT has struck off a dishonest solicitor, but later has been persuaded to readmit him or her. In a few cases this decision has given the solicitor the opportunity to re-offend, sometimes with a severity equal to or greater than the magnitude of the offence which originally led to his or her striking off.[16]

Law Society Initiatives

During the 1990s the Law Society identified as the solution to its problems the devolving down to firm level many aspects of complaints handling. The Society would be left to concentrate on the more serious cases and to enhance prevention and education. However, a lack of engagement and commitment by some within the profession prevented this strategy from working, and by the early 2000s the Law Society reverted to a system of compliance visits to all firms. The attempt to ensure that complaints had been considered by the firm's internal complaints procedure before the OSS would consider them had failed to work effectively and had been criticised by the LSO and consumer interest groups. The strategy tended to ignore the likely power imbalance between solicitor and dissatisfied client, and also failed to enforce the requirement that all firms actually had a satisfactory internal complaints procedure.

The Law Society has also been criticised for attempting to both regulate and represent solicitors. Even though regulatory powers should not be used to inhibit competition, members will want their representative body to seek the best conditions possible, if necessary at the expense of competition.[17]

In recent years the Law Society has given consideration to this issue, no doubt anticipating the possibility that if it did not, the matter would be taken out of its hands. A Law Society Review Group[18] proposed that the Society's regulatory and representative functions should be separated. A new Regulatory Board, half of whose members would be non-lawyers, would take over responsibility for the Society's regulatory functions. In September 2004, the Law Society Council announced its plan to separate the functions of the Law Society in line with the principles recommended by the review group.[19]

The Legal Services Ombudsman has identified frequent changes in approach by the Law Society as confusing for those outside of the profession. She has also been critical of the Law Society for making important changes without prior communication with her office, or with other interest groups.[20]

---

16 See Davies, op cit, note 13, 143–73.

17 For discussion of this, see Sir David Clementi, *Review of the Regulatory Framework for Legal Services in England and Wales – Final Report*, December 2004, 29.

18 *Governance Review Group: Interim Report to the Law Society's Main Board and Council, May 2004*, cited in Sir David Clementi, op. cit., note 17, 38.

19 Hoult, P. (2004), 'Society Moves Closer to Power Shake-up', *Law Society Gazette*, 30 September (online edition).

20 *In Whose Interest?– Annual Report of the Legal Services Ombudsman for England and Wales 2003/2004*, HC 729, 50–51.

Modern Challenges to Self-regulation

Competitive pressures and the need to meet client demands may lead solicitors to adopt 'ethical tunnel vision'.[21] This may particularly be the case with large firms who, it has been said, are particularly vulnerable to subservience to clients at the improper expense of other parties and the wider social and legal system.[22]

The current self-regulation system is still built around the values of an older version of professionalism, involving service to individual, non-influential, clients rather than large, powerful institutional clients.

However, self-regulation remains an important means by which the solicitors' profession can resist external interference. This derives from the 'bargain theory of professions', according to which the profession receives, inter alia, autonomy from lay control, protection from competition, trust and high status in exchange for individual and collective self-control.[23] If the profession fails to keep its side of the bargain, the government may be quick to challenge self-regulation.[24] From the profession's viewpoint, self-regulation is relatively cheap compared with externally imposed regulation. Voluntary regulation therefore presents a sound business decision.[25]

The Future

Regulation

In July 2003 a Department for Constitutional Affairs report[26] concluded that the regulatory framework governing lawyers was excessively complex, and lacked transparency and accountability. Following this, Sir David Clementi was appointed to undertake a review of the regulation of legal services. His terms of reference included consideration of the type of regulatory framework which would best promote competition and innovation, as well as the public interest.

---

21 Nelson, R. (1985), 'Ideology, Practice and Professional Autonomy: Social Values and Client Relationships in the Large Law Firm', *Stanford Law Review* 37, 503.

22 Galanter, M. and Palay, T. (1995), 'Large Law Firms and Professional Responsibility', in Cranston, op. cit., note 2, 196. The experience of the accountancy profession following the Enron scandal in the US illustrates the dangers of situations in which independent professional judgement is overwhelmed by influential clients.

23 Rueschemeyer, D. (1973), *Lawyers and their Society: A Comparative Study of the Legal Profession in Germany and the United States* (Cambridge, Mass.: Harvard University Press) 13.

24 Events in the USA following the Enron and Worldcom scandals illustrate that governments can act speedily when self-regulation is perceived to have failed. The US government passed the Sarbanes-Oxley Act, described as probably the most radical redesign of federal securities law for 70 years.

25 See, for example, Maxwell, J.W., Lyon, T.P. and Hackett, S.C. (2000), 'Self-Regulation and Social Welfare: the Political Economy of Corporate Environmentalism', *Journal of Law & Economics* XLIII, 613–14.

26 *Competition and Regulation in the Legal Services Market*, July 2003.

Clementi issued a consultation paper in March 2004, and published his report on 15 December 2004. The consultation paper proposed three alternative models for regulation and complaints handling. Model A would remove all regulatory functions from the professional bodies and place these in the hands of a new, unified regulator, the Legal Services Authority (LSA). Advantages of this model would include: complete independence of the regulator from the regulated; clearer and simpler lines of responsibility because numerous regulators are replaced by a single one; and increased consistency. Possible disadvantages would include the risk of increased bureaucracy and a reduction of the sense of professional responsibility which should come with self-regulation.

The second model, Model B, would involve a super regulator, the Legal Services Board (LSB), overseeing individual professional bodies, which would retain regulatory functions. This model has the advantage of keeping regulation close to the heart of the profession.

The third model, Model B+, was a variant on the second model. Frontline regulation would remain in the hands of the professions, but in return the professional bodies would be required to separate their regulatory functions from their representative functions.[27]

The Legal Services Ombudsman favoured Model A, considering that profession-led regulation has lost all public legitimacy,[28] thus ruling out either of the other models. In contrast, in his final report,[29] Sir David Clementi concluded that Model B+ offered the best way forwards. This would build upon and strengthen existing regulatory systems, whilst also providing the oversight safety net in the form of the LSB.[30] Model B+ is also more likely than the others to find favour with government, as it avoids transferring any significant regulatory burden to the state.

Disciplinary Procedures

Surprisingly, in light of problems with the disciplinary system identified in academic research, the Clementi report found no major problems with the disciplinary processes relating to solicitors. Clementi recommended that in future the SDT would be required to report on an annual basis to the LSB, but otherwise there would be no notable changes.[31] These conclusions appear to have been reached without any significant research by Clementi. If this is the case, further consideration of the disciplinary process would be appropriate before it is given a clean bill of health.

---

27 Sir David Clementi, op. cit, note 17, 25.

28 *In Whose Interest?– Annual Report of the Legal Services Ombudsman for England and Wales 2003/2004*, HC 729, 10.

29 Sir David Clementi, op. cit, note 17.

30 Ibid, 49.

31 Ibid, 79.

Consumer Complaints

Whilst ultimately Clementi was content to leave significant responsibility for regulation in the hands of the professional bodies, the same was not true for complaints handling. Complaints handling, rather than regulation and discipline, had long been the focus of concern by bodies critical of the Law Society. The Legal Action Group, for instance, considered that consumer confidence in the ability of lawyers to deal adequately with complaints had been 'irreversibly undermined'.[32] The Legal Services Ombudsman was similarly critical, concluding that an independent complaints handling office would be the minimum acceptable outcome from the reform process.

Clementi therefore concluded that a single, independent, complaints handling body was the most appropriate way forward. Provisionally titled 'the Office for Legal Complaints' (OLC), the body would incorporate all of the current professional complaints handling bodies and the main oversight bodies. In an attempt to ensure a consumer focus, the OLC would have a lay-dominated managing board.[33]

The OLC would address individual complaints, but it would also have additional strategic roles. These might include, in co-operation with the LSB, target setting for the handling of 'in-house' complaints by practitioners, and overseeing indemnity insurance and compensation fund schemes.[34]

Future Business Structures

An additional key feature of the Clementi review was consideration of potential future business structures within which lawyers would be permitted to work. Clementi considered two alternatives, Legal Disciplinary Practices (LDPs) and Multi-Disciplinary Practices (MDPs). LDPs allow different types of lawyers, for example, solicitors and barristers, to work together. Non-lawyers would be permitted to own LDPs, subject to appropriate fitness criteria. Regulation would have to shift its focus from individual practitioners to the business unit as a whole. Regulatory focus would be upon the senior management within the practice. There would be a 'Head of Legal Practice' (HOLP), who would have overall responsibility for compliance with the regulatory rules.

MDPs would enable lawyers to practise with other professionals, for instance, accountants and surveyors. Each professional group within the MDP would practise together on equal terms.[35] From the regulatory perspective, a potential problem with MDPs is that of regulatory reach. For instance, the LSB would have no jurisdiction over non-lawyer professionals within MDPs. Clementi's solution would see the development of collaborative arrangements between regulators, including agreement as to which was to be the lead regulator for the business as a whole.[36]

---

32 Ibid, 59–60.
33 Ibid, 73.
34 Ibid, 68–9.
35 Ibid, 105 and 139.
36 Ibid, 134–5.

A Theoretical Alternative to the Current Regulatory Approach

Both the Law Society attempts to improve the regulatory process and the recent Clementi recommendations have focused upon relatively traditional models of regulation. In contrast, academic commentators have considered more radical alternatives. A key example of this is reflexive law. This focuses upon procedural norms, rather than formal rules.[37] Such norms concentrate upon the design and implementation of regulatory mechanisms; the aim is to achieve intended outcomes by aggregating individual self-regulatory decisions.[38] Reflexive law aims to mobilise the self-referential capacities of institutions, to enable them to best shape their own response to complex regulatory problems.[39] Legal control is therefore indirect, avoiding the need to directly regulate complex social areas. Instead, the system focuses upon controlling the regulatory structures and processes.

The emphasis is therefore on getting the structures and processes right. Some processes may be narrowly procedural, for example, the requirement that firms have compliance officers. Others may be in the form of legal rules, for example, senior members of firms being liable for the misconduct of junior members. The common theme is that regulation and compliance is delegated down to the level of the individual firm. This should ensure that management structures adapt so as to maintain issues of conduct and competence at the forefront of the firm's priority list.

Parallels can be drawn between reflexivity and the arguments employed in the nineteenth century to persuade the state to entrust regulation to professional bodies. Key amongst these was the argument that only the profession itself had the expertise to effectively regulate its members. As the profession has grown in numbers and the degree of specialisation increased enormously, similar arguments can now be applied within the profession. The Law Society is now in a similar position to the nineteenth-century state, subject to the problems of information complexity and deficiencies in analytical capacity when called upon to regulate highly specialist practices. Reflexivity would see the Society concentrating on the development of effective overarching regulatory structures, whilst regulation in practice would take place at a more local level.

Conclusions

The solicitors' profession is, perhaps for the first time in its long history, facing the serious risk of losing key aspects of its self-regulatory functions. If the recommendations of the Clementi review are adopted, key disciplinary and complaints functions will be taken over by lay-dominated external bodies. This would

---

37 See, for example, Teubner, G. (1983), 'Substantive and Reflexive Elements in Modern Law', *Law & Society Review* 17, 239, 254–5.

38 For further discussion, in the context of environmental law, see Fiorini, D. (1999), 'Rethinking Environmental Regulation', *Harvard Environmental Law Review* 23, 447.

39 See Orts, E. (1995), 'Reflexive Environmental Law', *Northwestern University Law Review* 89, 1227.

be particularly striking for consumer complaints, as all of the powers currently held by the Law Society would be taken over by the OLC. Further significant change is likely if solicitors are allowed to practise in LDPs or MDPs. Whilst Clementi makes recommendations intended to minimise the risk of regulator shopping by practices (firms attempting to fall under the auspices of the most benign regulator), complete success in this regard cannot be guaranteed. The Law Society could, therefore, find its role even further diminished if it loses regulatory reach over some solicitors, to the benefit of other legal regulatory bodies. The Law Society is currently pushing ahead with its latest plans to reinforce its regulatory and complaints handling systems. It remains to be seen whether it will be given the opportunity to put these to the test or, conversely, whether it has finally used up its chances to demonstrate that it can effectively regulate the profession.

PART IV
COMMENTARIES

Chapter 17

The National DNA Database: Why No Public Debate?

Mairi Levitt

Whereas the UK Biobank[1] has spawned years of public consultations, including at least eight official consultations between 2000 and 2003, and procedures only now being piloted, the National DNA Database (NDNAD) has quietly built up over 3 million samples. These include more than 750,000 from juveniles, age 10 to 17 years, and thousands from adults and children who have no criminal convictions. If you are arrested for a recordable offence, your DNA can be taken without consent (and without parental consent for children), stored on the database and the full sample retained. There has been no public consultation commissioned by the NDNAD, and questions about the database, contained in broader studies, indicate that most people support the taking of samples only for serious and violent crimes.[2] A qualitative study by the MRC and Wellcome Trust on public perceptions of the collection of human biological samples found that people were uneasy about the taking of biological samples from children, who were seen as different from adults and more vulnerable.[3] This was despite the fact that it was assumed parental consent would be required.

Discussion with parents of 10–12-year-old children found that most were unaware that children's samples could be taken without permission, expected them to be destroyed if the charges were dropped and to be kept for a limited time if the child was found guilty.[4] Statistically children age 10 to 17 are responsible for a disproportionate percentage of convictions (around 26 per cent in the UK) but most do not go on to be career criminals. Presumably, behind the special measures to deal with child criminals is the hope that most can be helped to 'grow out of it'. The

---

1 The UK Biobank website contains details of public consultations commissioned by the funding bodies; available at: www.ukbiobank.ac.uk.

2 Human Genetics Commission (2001), *Public Attitudes to Human Genetic Information*, Report prepared by MORI (London: HGC).

3 MRC/Wellcome Trust (2000), *Public Perceptions of the Collection of Human Biological Samples. Qualitative Research to Explore Public Perceptions of Human Biological Samples* (Report prepared by Cragg Ross Dawson for the Wellcome Trust and Medical Research Council) 40.

4 Levitt, M. and Tomasini, F. (2005), 'Bar-coded Children. An Exploration of Issues around the Inclusion of Children on the England and Wales National DNA Database', *Genomics, Society and Policy* 2:1, 41–56, available at: http://www.gspjournal.com/.

United Nations guidelines[5] on the prevention of juvenile delinquency warn against the danger of labelling children as deviant or delinquent and thus reinforcing their patterns of behaviour. Cases that have reached the press include a 13-year-old girl arrested in Ashford, Kent for throwing a snowball at a police car, and a 12-year-old ('S') who was included in a plea to the Court of Appeal over the retention of his DNA sample despite his acquittal. In the judgement rejecting the appeal, it was stated that those who have been acquitted are much more likely than the general population to offend in the future:

> Not all unconvicted people ... are equal from a policing point of view, even though they are from a legal one[6]

Looking at the two national DNA databases the UK Biobank is voluntary, only for mature adults, maintains the right to withdraw at any time and has an Independent Ethics and Governance Council. The National DNA database includes children, is not voluntary, has no right of withdrawal and samples are subject to continuous speculative searches and searches for family matching.[7] More recently it has been found, only through requests made under the Freedom of Information Act, that the database has been used for research. While it is generally accepted that criminals forfeit some of their rights due to their behaviour, it would not be acceptable to carry out medical research on criminals without consent, and the database includes the innocent and children. Should everyone be included at birth, as Alec Jeffreys, who invented DNA fingerprinting, has suggested as a way of preventing discrimination and stigma? Should children only be included for a limited time or for serious offences (as is the practice in other European countries)? Should those not convicted be automatically removed? Should the database be used for research? And, a fundamental question looked at by Genewatch, how effective is the database in solving crime and how should this be balanced against human rights?[8]

Some issues are coming to public attention. The MP, Grant Shapps, has a web-based campaign to help the innocent remove their DNA from the NDNAD,[9] and there has been media coverage of research into ethnic profiling from DNA. Given the current interest in genetic traits associated with violent and antisocial behaviour,

---

5 United Nations, *Guidelines for the Prevention of Juvenile Delinquency (The Riyadh Guidelines)*, adopted and proclaimed by General Assembly resolution 45/112 of 14 December 1990, available at: http://www.unhchr.ch/html/menu3/b/h_comp47.htm.

6 *R v Marper & S* (2002) [2002] EWCA Civ 1275. Court of Appeal (Civil Division).

7 Profiles, but not samples, are exported from Scotland for inclusion on the NDNAD; however, these profiles are removed from both the National and Scottish DNA databases if the case does not result in a court conviction.

8 GeneWatch UK (2005), *The Police National DNA Database: Balancing Crime Detection, Human Rights and Privacy* (Buxton: GeneWatch UK). Link from website: http://www.genewatch.org/; GeneWatch (2006), *The Police National DNA Database: An Update*, Human Genetic Parliamentary Briefing Number 6, July 2006. Link from website: http://www.genewatch.org/.

9 COND – Children off National DNA Database – website: http://www.grantshapps.org.uk/What%20is%20COND.aspx.

this could also be an area for future research. Any research would involve some sections of the UK population more than others; 37 per cent of black men already have profiles stored on the database compared with 10 per cent of white men.[10] At the very least there should be a public debate on the benefits *and* risks of the NDNAD and the arrangements for its regulation and governance.

The UK has a good record of public consultation and debate in the field of genetic research and applications, with bodies like the Human Fertilisation and Embryology Authority (HFEA) holding public meetings and providing extensive information on their decisions. The NDNAD is the largest in the world, but not perhaps the envy of the world, at least not among those who are concerned with civil liberty and child protection issues.

August 2006

---

10 Ibid.

Chapter 18

Can the Cell Nuclear Replacement Technique be Used to Overcome Genetic Disease?

Natasha Hammond

In his forthcoming book, *After Dolly: The Uses and Misuses of Human Cloning*, Professor Ian Wilmut advocates the use of human reproductive technologies to one day prevent the birth of a child with genetic diseases. He explains the use of the technique as such:

> One would take an IVF embryo with a hereditary defect, remove its stem cells, carry out a genetic correction, check that modification has worked, and then clone a defect-free cell to create a new embryo without the disease.[1]

Of course there are a wide number of genetic diseases which many argue would warrant the use of such a technique to overcome, including cystic fibrosis, Huntington's disease and haemophilia. I seek to argue that the cell nuclear replacement technique pioneered by Professor Ian Wilmut and his team at the Roslin Institute could legally and ethically be used to create embryos, and subsequent children, free from genetic diseases.

Gene therapy, genetic testing and human reproductive technologies have progressed rapidly in recent years and, combined with the discovery of the cell nuclear replacement technique, the possibilities of science correcting genetic defects has increased immensely. However, just because science may be able to correct genetic defects in embryos, thereby avoiding a life afflicted by disease, should we ethically be attempting to create genetic defect free children?

Many people in today's world are afflicted by genetic diseases and live full and happy lives; who are we to say that they would be living better lives if they were free of their genetic defects? And should we be calling such afflictions defects? Is it not something which makes each of us individual, both genetically and personally?

On the opposing side one could argue that although a person's genetic defect may be part of their personality, that it has helped them to be the person that they are, it is unethical not to help people to overcome their genetic defect if that is possible. The earlier in life that this is done, the better it is for the person. After all, are we not currently ethically obliged to provide help, support and care for those who are

---

1 'Be Careful with this Brave New World', *The Daily Telegraph*, 5 June 2006, 25.

afflicted by a genetic disease? If we are able to assist a person to be born free of genetic defects so that they are able to live a life free of hospital visits, treatments and prejudice, should we not be morally obliged to perform this work?[2]

Resource implications may also be quoted as a reason to perform such work. If we are able to ensure that a child is born free of a hereditary genetic defect, thereby avoiding costly hospital visits and care (besides the inconvenience and discomfort for the patient), and freeing resources for others who suffer from non-hereditary illnesses, should we not be obliged to do such work?

Of course the ethical debate on whether or not we should be genetically altering embryos prior to implantation will rage for some time, and ultimately it will be for the law to take a stance as it has done many times over the years. I suggest that the law will eventually seek a compromise, rather than a prohibitive stance, as I feel that it is inevitable that eventually the cell nuclear replacement technique, in conjunction with stem cells, will be used to correct genetic defects as Professor Wilmut advocates.

Could the process described by Professor Wilmut legally be used today to detect, correct and produce a genetic defect free clone? The Human Fertilisation and Embryology Act 1990 requires a licence to be obtained from the Human Fertilisation and Embryology Authority where embryos are to be created in vitro (either by in vitro fertilisation or by cell nuclear replacement).[3] The same Act prevents '… altering the genetic structure of any cell whilst it forms part of an embryo'.[4] However, the genetic alterations would be carried out on cells after they have been extracted from the embryo, so there is no apparent conflict here.

To perform the cell nuclear replacement technique, it is a legal requirement that a licence must first be obtained from the Human Fertilisation and Embryology Authority, so provided that the laboratory carrying out this work had the correct licence, it seems that they could then clone the genetically altered cells. The problem seems to arise with the proposal to implant the new genetic defect free embryo into a woman for implantation and development.

The Human Reproductive Cloning Act 2001 prohibits the placing in a woman of a human embryo which has been created otherwise than by fertilisation.[5] Whilst the genetic defect free embryo would have been created otherwise than by fertilisation immediately prior to implantation in a woman (through the use of cell nuclear replacement), it originally had been created by in vitro fertilisation. Therefore it is a unique genetic individual. The purpose of the Human Reproductive Cloning Act 2001 was to prevent the creation of genetically identical clones of people who already existed (either alive or dead).

---

2 Note the argument that the child is unable to complain about the situation as it is between actually being born genetically manipulated or not being born at all; raised in relation to sex selection in Harris, J. (2005), *No Sex Selection Please, We're British, Journal of Medical Ethics* 31, 286, 287.

3 Schedule 2, para. 1(1)(a) and (4), Human Fertilisation and Embryology Act 1990.

4 Schedule 2, para. 1(4), Human Fertilisation and Embryology Act 1990.

5 Section 1(1), Human Reproductive Cloning Act 2001.

If the cell nuclear replacement technique was used to create genetic defect free embryos, they would merely be creating clones of a unique genetic embryo created originally by in vitro fertilisation. Subsequent implantation would not defeat the purpose of the Human Reproductive Cloning Act, as the development and birth of one of these genetic defect free embryos would actually result in a unique genetic individual. The original defective embryo created by in vitro fertilisation would not also be implanted; there would not be clones in existence. It could of course be argued that both embryos could be implanted and still not defeat the purpose of the Act, as one would have the genetic defect and one would not, so they would not be identical genetically.

Human reproduction and embryology is a difficult and complicated area to legislate upon, as can be seen by the legal challenges which have occurred over the years. It can be difficult to foresee how the courts will analyse the legislation when faced with a new scientific method requiring interpretation of the relevant law. For example, refer to the *Quintavalle cases* [6] which challenged the legal definition of an embryo.[7] In light of this it may be possible that the courts would apply the strict letter of the law. The strict interpretation of the Human Reproductive Cloning Act would prevent the subsequent implantation of these embryos, after their genetic defect has been eradicated.

It would seem that if science does manage to progress to such a stage to allow the eradication of genetic diseases through the use of stem cell and cell nuclear replacement, then the law will need to be reformed to allow this work to progress to its conclusion, the birth of genetic defect free children.[8]

July 2006

---

6 *R (on the application of Quintavalle) v Secretary of State for Health* [2001] 4 All ER 1013, [2002] 2 All ER 625, [2003] 2 All ER 113.

7 For a full discussion of the cases, refer to Hammond, N. (2006), 'Revisiting *Quintavalle* – Knee Jerk Reactions and Illogical Judgments', *Medical Law Monitor* 13:6, 7, *Med. L. Mon* 13:7, 7.

8 Note for the reader: the HFEA recently granted a licence to the Centre at LIFE, Newcastle-upon-Tyne, to undertake research for mitochondrial disease. Although not undertaking all stages of the process as described by Professor Wilmut, the research licence permits the researchers to study possible methods of preventing the transmission of mitochondrial DNA disorders through the process of pronuclear transfer between zygotes. For further information, please refer to the HFEA website: http://www.hfea.gov.uk/cps/rde/xchg/SID-3F57D79B-E73F3EF8/hfea/hs.xsl/1075.html#Mitochondrial_DNA_Disorders_Is_there_a_way_to_prevent_transmission_R0153. Accessed on 26 October 2006.

Chapter 19

The Human Condition and the Pursuit of Perfection in Human Reproduction

Jennifer Gunning

It is probably true to say that every human being is flawed. We all carry errors in our genomes, but mostly these are balanced out by compensating normal alleles and we live our lives happily unaware of these defects. But modern reproductive biotechnology, the sequencing of the human genome and the identifying of specific disease-related genes have made us more aware of potential imperfections and the possibility of their eradication.

Now, of course, families carrying single gene disorders are only too aware of their implications. It is understandable that couples struggling to bring up a child with a severe and eventually fatal disorder such as Tay Sachs disease, Duchenne muscular dystrophy or β-thalassaemia should seek to ensure that their subsequent children are free from the disorder. Or that couples knowing that they are carriers of a disease should seek for their own children to be disease-free. Prenatal diagnosis offers couples such an opportunity. High-risk couples can be offered chorionic villus sampling (CVS) with genetic testing in the first trimester of pregnancy to detect whether their baby will have the disease or is a carrier. If the test is positive, the couple has the opportunity to terminate the pregnancy at an early stage. But even an early termination is not lightly undertaken and couples may suffer a series of affected pregnancies.

With the development of pre-implantation genetic diagnosis (PGD) such couples can now seek in vitro fertilisation and have the resulting embryos tested, having only 'normal' embryos returned to the womb. The number of diagnostic tests available has increased dramatically. In 1999 the European Society for Human Reproduction and Embryology reported referrals for PGD for some 24 genetic disorders;[1] by 2006 one American clinic was offering PGD for over 100 single gene disorders.[2] However, some countries, for instance, Germany, Austria, Italy and Switzerland, prohibit PGD but allow prenatal diagnosis, and couples in these countries preferring to seek PGD have to travel abroad in a form of genetic tourism.

So far so good; the elimination of severe progressive and fatal genetic disorders is commendable. But what about treatable genetic disorders or disorders that may become treatable? The other side of the biotechnological coin is that the more we

---

1 Gunning, J. (2000), 'Preimplantation Genetic Diagnosis', in Gunning, J. (ed.), *Assisted Conception: Research, Ethics and Law* (Aldershot: Ashgate Publishing Ltd).

2 http://www.reproductivegenetics.com/single_gene.html. Accessed in June 2006.

understand how individual genes operate, the more likely we are to be able to correct the effects of a malfunctioning gene product or to insert a correctly functioning gene. And stem cell therapy is a bright light on the horizon. PGD is already being offered for phenylketonuria (PKU), a disease which is normally detected through neonatal screening programmes and responds to dietary treatment, and for ocular albinism where sufferers may have some visual defects and lack of pigmentation, but for the most part can live normal, happy and useful lives. Is selecting out embryos carrying these genes a step down the slippery slope? Even now early diagnosis of cystic fibrosis means that, with appropriate treatment, an affected individual can live well into their thirties and have a worthwhile and productive life. So there is a dilemma. Should PGD and prenatal diagnosis be provided for any genetic disorder or should there be an agreed list of 'severe' disorders? If treatments should become available for certain disorders, should they then be removed from the list?

It has now become possible to identify genes which indicate a predisposition to disease. PGD is already offered for familial adenomatous polyposis (FAP), an autosomal dominant disorder where carriers of the gene have a 95 per cent chance of developing precancerous polyps in the colon by 35 years of age. This late onset disease can be controlled by early molecular genetic testing, surveillance and treatment, but carriers of the gene are at high risk of developing cancer of the colon. In approving a licence for this test in 2004, the UK Human Fertilisation and Embryology Authority (HFEA) said:

> FAP is a serious condition – prenatal diagnosis and selective termination of affected cases has been offered in the past. Families with the genetic condition have a 50 per cent chance of passing it on to their children, but using PGD can help these families have a healthy child.[3]

In May 2006 the HFEA announced that it would allow PGD for the BRCA1 and BRCA2 genes which are indicative of a predisposition for breast and ovarian cancer. Carriers of these genes have an 85 per cent risk of developing breast cancer by age 70, but there is some evidence that this form may be less aggressive.[4] Predisposition for ovarian cancer is 55 per cent for BRCA1 and 25 per cent for BRCA2. In announcing its decision, the HFEA said:

> ... the Authority agreed that we should consider the use of PGD embryo testing for conditions such as inherited breast, ovarian and bowel cancers that given the aggressive nature of the cancers, the impact of treatment and the extreme anxiety that carriers of the gene can experience. These conditions differ from those already licensed before because people at risk do not always develop cancer, it may occur later in life and some treatments may be available.

---

3 http://www.hfea.gov.uk/PressOffice/Archive/1099321195. Accessed in June 2006.
4 Pericay, C., et al. (2001), 'Clinical and Pathological Findings of BRCA1/2 Associated Breast Cancer', *Breast* 10:1, 46–8.

The inherited conditions suitable for PGD testing are very uncommon. This is not about opening the door to wholesale genetic testing. This is about considering a particular group of genetic conditions to be sufficiently serious to merit the use of PGD embryo testing.[5]

Nonetheless, choosing to implant only those embryos without the BRCA genes does not guarantee that these offspring will not suffer from the sporadic form of the disease. Moving from allowing the diagnosis of a genetic certainty to selecting out embryos which have a susceptibility for a late onset disease seems to represent a value judgement of a different order about the human condition.

In the UK, at least, it seems that couples are beginning to want to avoid any imperfection in their offspring. It has been reported that recent UK abortion statistics show that, following prenatal scans, women are aborting fetuses with treatable defects.[6] According to the latest statistics from the UK Office for National Statistics, between 1999 and 2004 20 women had late abortions of a fetus with club foot and a further four abortions were carried out where the fetus had an extra digit or webbed feet. All these conditions are treatable and are unlikely to result in serious handicap.

The progress in the identification of disease-related genes and the development of related diagnostic tests has provided incredible opportunities in the avoidance of severe and debilitating genetic diseases. However, the use of such technologies to avoid susceptibilities to disease or treatable diseases should be approached with caution. It is understandable that every couple wants a perfect child, but we all have imperfections, and when abortion becomes available for treatable physical deformities, the alarm bells begin to ring.

June 2006

---

5 http://www.hfea.gov.uk/PressOffice/Archive/1147269507. Accessed in June 2006.
6 http://www.timesonline.co.uk/article/0,,2-2201495,00.html. Accessed in June 2006.

Chapter 20

Drug Testing and the Use of Healthy Volunteers

Sam Salek

How are the Drugs Developed?

Discovery of New Molecules

Initially thousands of compounds are tested for their potential medicinal activity through combinatory chemistry in order to find one new active molecule. Following the discovery and initial testing, the new molecule is patented by the respective pharmaceutical industry with the patent office. The trade-off here for the company is gaining exclusivity for the discovery at the expense of making the details of the invention public.

Pre-clinical Safety Assessment

Special approval for this is normally sought from the relevant regulatory authority and by and large involves animal or animal models testing for the following:

- Toxicity effects on the following systems:
  ○ reproductive
  ○ genetic
  ○ immune
- Harmful effects:
  ○ causing cancerous activity
  ○ causing harm to foetus

Clinical Development

Having established the safety of the drug in animals and its lack of harmful effects on different organs of the body, the company will proceed to seeking approval from the relevant regulatory authority and ethics committees to take it into clinical development and test the drugs in humans for the intended condition. This path of drug development consists of a number of phases briefly described below.

Phase I

This phase is often referred to as 'first into man', conducted in normal, healthy volunteers to establish the following:

- Dose range tolerated for single/multiple doses
- What the drug does to the body
- What the body does to the drug

Recruitment of Healthy Human Volunteers for Phase 1 Clinical Trials

Pharmaceutical companies and other organisations conducting drug clinical trials rely heavily on healthy volunteers for their first into man studies. This by and large involves healthy young men who are on no medication and able to give written consent. Women are not generally considered at this stage of clinical development because of pregnancy or being on a birth control pill. Healthy human volunteers are recruited into clinical trials through the following methods:

- Advertising in local and national papers
- Community gazettes
- Phase I contract research organisation databases
- Radio
- University bulletin boards
- University student newsletters
- Poster display in universities
- Internet

By and large the focus of advertising would be written media, and university students are primary targets. The attraction for this group is that they are a younger group and largely on no long-term medication.

The use of healthy human volunteers for Phase I clinical trials is heavily regulated for ethical and safety issues and the participants are extensively protected through indemnity laws and the Declaration of Helsinki. Pharmaceutical companies and Phase I units strictly adhere to the following in recruiting healthy volunteers:

- The trial to be conducted only by scientifically qualified persons and the supervision of a clinically competent medical person
- A three-month wash-out period between taking part in one trial and volunteering for the next
- Availability of skilled medical help and hospital care with immediate effect if needed
- The health of the volunteers to be their first consideration
- Informed written consent
- Standard operating procedures for withdrawal of the volunteers from the trial
- Standard operating procedures to safeguard the volunteers' integrity

Use of serial volunteers is strongly discouraged on ethical and safety grounds. Sharing and transparency of information could prevent volunteers registering under several names in databases managed by the company.

The volunteers are not supposed to make money by taking part in clinical trials other than having their out-of-pocket expenses covered. The involvement of volunteers in such activities should be purely for altruistic motives to further scientific knowledge and to help suffering humans.

Phase II

This phase primarily focuses on establishing the efficacy of the drug in selected patients with the disease in question, with the following objectives:

- Assess the response of the disease to drug dose given
- Assess the effectiveness of the frequency of dosing
- Categorise type of patients
- Establish any other safety and efficacy issues

In addition, well-controlled studies to evaluate efficacy and safety in patients will be conducted. It is expected that this phase will provide early proof of clinical efficacy and represents the most rigorous demonstration of a drug's effect. It is because of this that studies of this nature in Phase II are referred to as pivotal studies. The size of studies in this phase range from a small pilot study of as few as eight patients to large studies of 300 patients. The following considerations are usually taken into account when conducting clinical trials of this nature:

- Need to establish proof of principle as soon as possible
- Small studies must be compatible with scientific rigour
- Consider use of placebo where possible
- Use of only single centre studies to ensure homogeneous populations
- Possibility of studying more than one indication at a time

Phase III

Clinical trials conducted in this phase are primarily confirmatory studies for efficacy and safety profiles of the drug. These are large in size and usually multi-centre, and often multi-country. The regulatory authorities favour active comparator to the investigational drug whenever possible and use placebo as a last resort. The regulatory authority recommendation is usually two studies per indication.

At the end of this phase, all the preclinical safety assessment and clinical development data are compiled and submitted to the regulatory authorities to obtain marketing authorisation.

Phase IV

This phase is often referred to as post-marketing surveillance, and the studies carried out in this phase are designed to monitor the safety of the marketed drug in society. What this really means is that the responsibility of the pharmaceutical company with respect to their drug does not end with obtaining marketing authorisation; in fact, the pharmaceutical industries are required to have a designated pharmacovigilance integrated into their daily activity.

It is important to appreciate that it takes an average of 12 years to bring a new drug from discovery to the marketplace and costs an average of $1 billion. Out of every ten drugs making it to clinical development (to be tested on patients), only one will make it to the marketplace. Putting things into perspective, it takes an average of eight years for a drug to peak sale.

What Went Wrong with TeGenero's Monoclonal Antibody Trial in Healthy Human Volunteers (TGN1412)?

TGN1412 is a new treatment for devastating illnesses such as leukaemia, rheumatoid arthritis and multiple sclerosis. It was developed in accordance with all regulatory and good clinical practice guidelines and standards. The drug was tested extensively in laboratories and on rabbits and monkeys. Therefore, in pre-clinical assessment studies TGN1412 was shown to be safe and did not show any harmful effects on any of the systems mentioned above. Because of its successful pre-clinical assessment, it was given approval by the Medicines and Healthcare products Regulatory Agency (MHRA) and the ethics committee to be taken to the clinical development phase for testing in humans.

The recent MHRA report concludes that side-effects seen with the six healthy human volunteers in Phase I clinical trials of TGN1412 were drug–related, and also confirms that the company was not at fault in observing standards, and that the pre-clinical safety testing did not show any sign of risk.

Therefore the side-effects reported in six of the eight volunteers were unexpected Serious Adverse Events (SAEs) related to the drug. It was reported that the six volunteers experienced a life-threatening incident of 'Cytokine Release Syndrome', which is a type of systemic inflammatory response to the substance released by activated T Cells. This is not common but it can happen depending on the animal species used in pre-clinical safety assessment. Undoubtedly there must have been compelling evidence about the effectiveness of TGN1412 to convince the regulatory authorities and the medical ethics committee to allow Phase I clinical trials to take place.

Phase I healthy volunteer studies are an essential part of the critical path of drug development, but it is universally accepted that it is not without its risks. No doubt with the tight regulations introduced in recent years and adherence to good clinical practice guidelines, the safety and rigour of Phase I clinical trials have tremendously improved and incidents such as those experienced with TGN1412 are extremely rare.

Looking on the bright side, in light of the recent incident, the announcement of the establishment of a new expert commission by the Secretary of State for Health to supervise future trials of monoclonal antibodies is most welcome. Nevertheless this poses new challenges to those in the biotechnology industry to rethink the way to develop such medicines in the future.

This new body will operate under the auspices of the Commission on Human Medicines which has, among its statutory duties, to advise the Secretary of State on matters affecting the safety of medicines. The proposed terms of reference for the Expert Group are:

1. To consider what may be necessary in the transition from pre-clinical to first in man Phase I studies, and in the design of these trials, with specific reference to:
    *   Biological molecules with novel mechanisms of action
    *   New agents with a high species-specific action
    *   New drugs directed towards immune system targets
2. To provide advice in the form of a report to the Secretary of State for Health for the future authorisation of such trials, with an interim report to be provided within three months.

Concluding Remarks

The recent incident with TGN1412 no doubt will have an impact on the future of drug testing with regard to issues such as challenges to regulators' abilities, animal testing, and the ethics of recruitment of volunteers.

May 2006

Chapter 21

The Assisted Dying Bill: 'Death Tourism' and European Law

John Coggon and Søren Holm

Introduction

Lord Joffe's Assisted Dying for the Terminally Ill Bill 2005 was aborted in 2006 following its second reading. Inevitably it raised controversy, with protagonists on all sides of the debate concerned about the likely effect of legalising physician-assisted suicide. The general debate on such legislation centres on the philosophical issues attached to the rightness or otherwise of 'mercy-killing', the proper limits that may be placed on the exercise of autonomy, the appropriate role of the medical profession in a system that allows 'assisted dying', and fears relating to 'slippery-slope' arguments. Necessarily, concessions were made in the Bill to avoid abuse of the proposed system; for example, it looked only to permit physician-assisted suicide and not euthanasia, and put in place elaborate procedural safeguards. Other clauses were drafted that made the Bill politically more viable; for example, the 'conscience clauses', which would have allowed practitioners and healthcare providers (such as hospitals and hospices) to avoid physician-assisted suicide altogether.

This chapter discusses the arrangement in the Bill designed to prevent the advent of 'death tourism' to England and Wales, and considers its compatibility with the law. 'Death tourism' is well publicised in the popular press, particularly with regard to UK citizens going to 'suicide clinics' in Switzerland. Furthermore, it has received what may be interpreted as a judicial nod and wink in the case of *Re Z*,[1] where Hedley J. found that a local authority had no right to restrain the husband of a competent woman suffering from cerebella ataxia, who intended to help her go to Switzerland to commit suicide.[2] To prevent an influx of 'death tourists', Lord Joffe's Bill required a 'qualifying patient' to have been registered for primary healthcare in England and Wales for at least one year,[3] essentially imposing a requirement of residence in the UK for at least one year. Whilst this may represent a desirable restriction, and may be pivotal for some people's maintained support of such legislation, it is not clear that it is lawful. There are good grounds for argument that it is contrary to human rights law and to European Community law.[4]

---

1 *Re Z* [2005] 1 WLR 959.
2 In contravention of the Suicide Act 1961, section 2.
3 Assisted Dying for the Terminally Ill Bill 2005, clause 13(1).
4 Our thanks to Professor Phil Fennell for suggesting this second line of argument.

Human Rights Arguments

Article 3 of the European Convention on Human Rights provides that '[n]o one shall be subjected to torture or to inhuman or degrading treatment or punishment'. Article 8, the right to respect for private and family life, has been found to include the right to respect for autonomy.[5] Both of these would provide a sound basis for a claim by a patient seeking to use assisted dying legislation, who was refused on the grounds that he or she had not been registered for primary healthcare here for 12 months. The protagonists of the Bill justify its very existence on the premise that for some patients, assisted dying will provide the only acceptable escape from suffering and indignity. If this is accepted – as it would be were a similar version of the Bill passed into law – then it is difficult to understand why the benefit of the 'treatment' provided by the Bill should be denied a person merely because of an arbitrary residence requirement. In the case of *D v UK*,[6] article 3 was successfully invoked by a patient who, in the advanced stages of AIDS, was to be deported to St Kitts. The deportation, though otherwise lawful, was not allowed because D would have received inadequate medical treatment in St Kitts, exposing him to a death in distressing circumstances. This could amount to inhuman treatment. If the use of the Assisted Dying legislation is the only means for some patients to avoid dying in distressing circumstances, it is submitted that they may raise a similar argument under article 3.

In the case of Dianne Pretty, it was accepted that the claimant's article 8 rights were engaged. In that case, of course, the European Court of Human Rights was able to deny Mrs Pretty the exercise of her right, because it found that the UK could justify an absolute prohibition on assisting suicide[7] in order to protect vulnerable individuals who would otherwise be at risk.[8] If the Assisted Dying Bill 2005 had become law, however, the same public interest arguments would no longer be applicable. And if assisted suicide were permissible for qualitatively identical patients, it is not evident how discrimination based on residence could be justified under article 8(2) of the Convention.

European Community Law Arguments

The second line of argument against the residence requirement comes under the European Community law relating to provision and receipt of services.[9] Although state-funded services do not fall within this, privately funded medical services do.[10]

---

5 *Pretty v UK* (2002) 35 EHRR 1.

6 *D v UK* (1997) 24 EHRR 423.

7 Suicide Act 1961, section 2.

8 Under article 8(2), European Convention on Human Rights.

9 Articles 49 and 50 EC (ex articles 59 and 60).

10 See Hervey, T.K. (1998), 'Buy Baby: The European Union and Regulation of Human Reproduction', *Oxford Journal of Legal Studies* 18, 207–33, 215.

The English Court of Appeal, in the case of Diane Blood,[11] held that the EC Treaty provided the right to receive medical treatment in another member state, and any interference with that right required justification. The case law suggests that a private medical practice offering assisted suicide in accordance with Lord Joffe's 2005 Bill would be providing a service, notwithstanding any arguments regarding the questionable morality of the practice.[12] According to Community law, there are two considerations relevant to the argument here:[13] first, that there is an inter-state element to the legal provision; second, that the services are provided for remuneration. Each of these would be met. It then falls on the member state to demonstrate the existence of any public policy reasons for restricting the provision of the service. To do this, the UK would have to demonstrate 'a clear, objective and proportionate imperative of public policy, public security or public health' as justification.[14] It is unlikely that a sense of disapprobation felt by UK residents to prospective 'death tourists' would be satisfactory justification.

The Law in the Netherlands and Belgium

Two EU member states currently allow some form of medical killing: the Netherlands and Belgium. Neither of these countries has a residence requirement built into its relevant legislation. However, both countries maintain that the procedural requirements in their legislation can only be fulfilled if there is a longstanding doctor–patient relationship, thereby limiting the possibility of 'death tourism'. The Dutch Ministry of Foreign Affairs, for instance, writes on its web pages concerning euthanasia:

Can people come from other countries to seek euthanasia in the Netherlands?

This is impossible, given the need for a close doctor-patient relationship. The legal procedure for the notification and assessment of each individual case of euthanasia requires the patient to have made a voluntary, well-considered request and to be suffering unbearably without any prospect of improvement. In order to be able to assess whether this is indeed the case, the doctor must know the patient well. This implies that the doctor has treated the patient for some time.

Granting a request for euthanasia places a considerable emotional burden on the doctor. Doctors do not approach the matter lightly. From this point of view too, longstanding personal contact between the doctor and the patient plays an important role.[15]

---

11 *Regina v Human Fertilisation and Embryology Authority, ex parte Blood* [1999] Fam 151.

12 See *The Society for the Protection of Unborn Children Ireland Ltd v Stephen Grogan and others* [1991] ECR I-4685, paragraphs 19 and 20.

13 See Morgan, D. and Lee, R.G. (1997), 'In the Name of the Father? *Ex parte Blood*: Dealing with Novelty and Anomaly', *Modern Law Review* 60:6, 840–56, especially 847–53.

14 Hervey, op. cit., 222.

15 http://www.minbuza.nl/default.asp?CMS_TCP=tcpPrintMinBuza2&CMS_ITEM=MBZ413299&CMS_PBG=A7462FBE98DF4DB380D4A19178A2BCF3X3X51010

It is not clear that these limitations are lawful: they are yet to be tested in the court in Strasbourg or in Luxembourg. But they do not impose any strict residence requirements, and the procedural requirements in the Dutch and Belgian laws can probably be fulfilled in considerably less than 12 months. Their existence does therefore not, of itself, support the inclusion of the 12-month requirement found in Lord Joffe's Bill. If any such attempt to limit the 'death tourism' problem is to be lawful, the legislators need to consider whether the restriction is (in EU law terms) proportionate, and look at the implications of the existing human rights law.

April 2006

X43. Accessed on 19 January 2006.

Chapter 22

Could Do Better? Hegemony and Freedom in Cyberspace

Ian Kenway

Several commentators have commented on the apparent 'irony' of Google's resolute determination on the one hand to resist the demands by the USA's Department of Justice (DoJ) to divulge millions of search records, and its willingness on the other to self-censor voluntarily its Chinese search engine in deference to the central authorities in that country. The cry of hypocrisy is easily made. But is it fair or, indeed, reasonably informed? Certainly the issues surrounding censorship and freedom of information are not always as straightforward as popularly imagined.

Google's corporate motto, 'Don't be evil', may at first sight seem high-minded, bordering on the theological, but is perhaps better, if less exotically, located in the idea of non-maleficence. The latter certainly finds a welcome home in the deontological ethics of W.D. Ross, which sought to relate prima facie duties to actual moral convictions in specific circumstances.

Google's apparent lack of consistency in its respective dealings with the DoJ and the Chinese authorities is itself complicated by its own corporate ambitions. The spectacular success of Google as a search engine has been well documented. Its pole market position, relative to Yahoo, MSN Search, Altavista, Jeeves and others, is already well established and likely to be enhanced by such diversifications as Gmail, Google Earth, Picasa and Book Search. This does not necessarily mean that there cannot be room for niche search engines or that a rival company is in any way constrained in developing a fundamentally different (that is, more intelligent or intuitive) search engine in the future. Nonetheless the future does look bright for Google as it has, like Microsoft, effectively cornered the market – at least for the foreseeable future. Moreover, technology is on its side with the inexorable advancement of higher capacity, and also cheaper, data storage, along with greater communication bandwidth.

Google's stated mission is 'to organize the world's information and make it universally accessible and useful'.[1] At first sight such a statement seems remarkably benign. However, we need to be mindful of the fact that privacy has in the past been secured not so much by legal entitlement, but rather by the relative *disorganisation* of information. It is difficult to gainsay that the gathering and indexation of data on a global basis poses real and substantial threats to personal privacy. Why should we feel less anxious about hegemonistic approaches to knowledge (as understood,

---

1 http://www.google.com/enterprise/whygoogle.html.

say, in Poppers 'World 3' sense) by large corporations than we would by national governments or perhaps international institutions?

The retention of personal data has profound implications. Notwithstanding substantial lobbying by civil society groups, including the European Digital Rights Campaign (EDRI), the EU Data Retention Directive, for example, was adopted by the European Parliament in December 2005. In February 2006 it was adopted by the Ministers of Justice and Home Affairs Council (JHA) – despite outright opposition by Irish and Slovakian representatives, as well as substantial parliamentary misgivings in the Netherlands and Finland.[2] In short the Directive requires all member states within the EU to introduce _mandatory_ data retention for telephony and internet data, for a period of between 6 and 24 months. Perhaps more significant is the fact that the directive is not limited to the 'fight against terrorism' and organised crime, but now embraces all serious crimes as defined by each individual member state. A few months earlier, the Report of the Tunis phase of the World Summit on the Information Society (WSIS) spoke about creating a 'global culture of cybersecurity'. Such a culture, according to WSIS, 'requires national action and increased international cooperation to strengthen security _while enhancing the protection of personal information, privacy and data_'.[3] It is not clear how the EU Data Retention Directive can be seen as taking to heart WSIS's desire for countries to take a principled approach in this particular area.

Google's resistance against the US government's subpoena had several strands. However, it is important to note in the first instance the specific context of the subpoena, namely the determination of the DoJ to effect the Children's Online Protection Act (COPA) passed by Congress in 1998. In particular, the DoJ was anxious to demonstrate that filtering technology was not effective in preventing children from reaching pornographic sites. Originally the DoJ requested all major internet service providers (ISPs) and search engines to submit 'all queries that have been entered into your company's search engine between June 1, 2005 and July 31, 2005'. Following resistance, it agreed to a more limited request that included a random sample of one million web addresses, together with a list of every search string during a one-week period. In January 2006, Yahoo, AOL and Microsoft indicated that they would comply with the DoJ's modified request. Google, however, decided that it ought to continue to resist the subpoena robustly on the basis that even the modified request raised sensitive issues concerning privilege, privacy and proprietary rights that would render compliance both unreasonable and oppressive. In March, the case was heard by District Judge James Ware who ordered Google to turn over a much smaller sample of search data – limited to 50,000 web addresses and 5,000 search terms – to the US government. According to Nicole Wong, an associate general counsel for Google, the ruling sends a clear message about privacy insofar as it indicates 'that neither the government nor anyone else has carte blanche when demanding data from internet companies'.[4]

---

2 European Digital Rights, EDRI-gram – Number 4.4, 1 March 2006.

3 _Report of the Tunis Phase of the World Summit on the Information Society_ (Tunis: Kram Palexpo) 16–18 November 2005, 13 [my italics].

4 http://googleblog.blogspot.com/2006/03/judge-tells-doj-no-on-search-queries.html.

In contrast, Google's full compliance with the request or wishes of the Chinese authorities means that it is now willing to block politically sensitive terms on its new China search site – Google.cn – and not provide e-mail, chat or blog publishing services as elsewhere. Previously it had only censored its news site in China by removing banned material, but had not taken the more draconian measures of its competitors of actually censoring its US-based search engine. According to co-founder Sergey Brin:

> The practical matter is that over the last couple of years Google was censored – not by us but by the government, via the 'the Great Firewall' ... France and Germany require censorship for Nazi sites, and the U.S. requires censorship based on the Digital Millennium Act. These various countries also have laws on child pornography.[5]

Such a policy shift, though essentially pragmatic, has inevitably attracted the ire of media libertarians. Reporters without Borders, for example, contends that the company's new policy is immoral and unjustifiable. In a statement it argues that:

> by offering a version without 'subversive' content, Google is making it easier for Chinese officials to filter the Internet themselves. A Web site not listed by search engines has little chance of being found by users ... The new Google version means that even if a human rights publication is not blocked by local firewalls, it has no chance of being read in China.[6]

Some claim, and with considerable passion, that the internet (which must not be equated *tout simple* with the World Wide Web) should remain an unlimited playground for the free exchange of ideas and information, an ideologically ramshackle world beyond hierarchical control.

Notwithstanding the phenomenal rise of blogging, the internet has become in recent years not so much a playground but rather a weary battleground in which ideologues and those with obvious vested interests seek practical influence and domination. The truth is that the Net not merely *reflects* certain social or geopolitical realities, but is now itself an extraordinarily powerful *instrument* in their actual constitution; in this sense the medium remains the message.

Clearly a case can be made for the Justice Department's subpoena in its determination to honour the intentions of Congress in passing COPA. Clearly a case can be made on behalf of the Chinese authorities who fear that the rapid adoption of Western-style forms of democracy might derail the country's current economic advance. Clearly a case can also be made for Google's desire to offer the public the most comprehensive and advanced approach to data gathering and indexation. However, in each instance, we are left with a profound, almost eerie, sense of unease.

The right to privacy and the right to information are more finely balanced than we frequently think. Neither child protection policies nor anti-terrorist strategies should become an alibi for defending any panoptical *folie de grandeur* on the part of

---

5 http://news.com.com/2100-1028-6031431.html.

6 http://www.rsf.org/article.php3?id_article=1626.

the state. Nor should the prospect of economic prosperity smother the concerns of those who wish to think or live 'differently' within society. Human rights language may have its problems, but the moral convictions to which it persistently refers are more often than not rooted in genuine human predicaments which require either redress or, at least, ameliorative action. Finally, neither technical ability nor commercial viability is an adequate substitute for proper moral debate when it comes to considering the collection, ownership and distribution of data. The *summum bonum* of the internet ultimately rests on the responsibility of all its participants to ask the critical question *'Cui bono?'* repeatedly when it comes to the collection, manipulation and maintenance of personal data.

March 2006

Chapter 23

Treatment in Time of Sudden Infectious Pandemic: The Need for a Proactive, Practical, Proportionate, Prophylactic Ethical Response to the Threat of Pandemic Influenza

Stephen Pattison and H. Martyn Evans

This chapter was first published as an article in early 2006. Since then, a number of important documents and policy initiatives have been issued. Readers are invited to reflect upon whether, and to what extent, the prognostications and concerns reflected in this chapter have proved to be valid.

Abstract

The threat of an avian flu pandemic focuses attention both on the extent of prior preparations on the part of governments to manage the social impact of a pandemic, and on the ethical and social acceptability of such preparations. In particular, the effectiveness of proposed policies, for prioritising those groups to whom limited vaccine supplies should be given, depends significantly upon the extent to which citizens believe that the policies have been described, explained and justified. Analogies with other emergency situations, including the behaviour of populations during time of war, suggests that people accept significant constraints provided that the rationale for them is clear and defensible. This chapter identifies a gap in ethical consultation in the preparation of relevant public policy, and argues the need for a compromise between the pragmatism and the elaborate ethical reasoning that are respectively found in two significant existing policy papers.

Introduction

Anxiety about the development of 'bird flu' into a humanly transmissible disease in the UK in the winter of 2005–06 brought flurries of people to general practitioners' surgeries asking to be vaccinated. Motives were various, ignorance was rife, and the currently available vaccines would not be effective against the virus because the development of vaccines is dependent on the emergence of particular viruses.

This preliminary ripple in the water, as the real or fantasised 'tsunami' of pandemic flu develops, is an appropriate moment to begin to think about the ethical principles and policies that might inform the distribution of effective treatment, were the rightly dreaded transformation of 'bird flu' into a humanly transmissible disease to take place. In ethics and policy, as in legal contracts, the time to think about evolving ethically defensible policies that are publicly discussed, agreed, understood and supported, is well in advance and in a calm atmosphere in which people's own vested interests and lives are not directly threatened. If there are no such publicly agreed and affirmed principles and policies, doctors and other health workers charged with distributing scarce resources will be put in an impossible position, as users and their families employ various strategies to lever out the resources that they feel they need. Immediately, this is likely to produce considerable personal aggression and ill feeling in healthcare relationships. In the longer term, it may help to create distancing and distrust between professionals and those they seek to serve.[1] This chapter calls for an examination of the policies underlying the use and distribution of effective treatments in the context of a pandemic medical emergency before such an emergency actually occurs. At the time of writing (March 2006), there appeared to be little specific commitment on the part of public health and policy experts to engage in ethical discussion much before the pandemic is upon us. Ethics, as so often, seems to be being conceived as an ancillary afterthought to more 'important' and practical matters.

This will not do. Clear policies that are both ethically justifiable *and acknowledged as such by the public* are essential. Health workers need a clear framework for action within an acknowledged set of rational public expectations, in order that they be able to deal with the public fairly and be seen to be acting fairly; it is essential for the maintenance of trust that members of the public understand that they are being dealt with justly and not on an *ad hoc* basis.[2] For the government and the body politic, it is essential that people be able to maintain their trust in government institutions including organised healthcare, at a time (such as a major disease pandemic) when social order is potentially under strain in both material and psychological terms.

In effect, political as well as physical health and morale will require in such circumstances the availability and use of ethical policies enjoying prior scrutiny and agreement. To make this possible, serious and detailed ethical debate and discussion about the distribution of treatment are needed now. They should be seen as an integral part of the prophylactic response to the threat of pandemic, and as a necessary protection for the body social and politic.

Background

An infectious pandemic threat is always the result of the emergence of new pathogenic viruses. Almost all flu viruses mutate gradually. Occasionally they undergo a much more radical change – giving rise to a new virus. The threat of a pandemic comes

---

1 O'Neill, O. (2002), *A Question of Trust: the BBC Reith Lectures 2002* (Cambridge: Cambridge University Press).

2 Ibid.

from the possibility that the virus will change in a way that enhances its ability to spread between humans and across species.

By definition a pandemic will affect many millions of individuals across the globe, testing even the most robust communities. It could overwhelm healthcare systems across the world; dealing with it will require more than new drugs and good infection control alone. The Severe Acute Respiratory Syndrome (SARS) crisis in 2003 exposed healthcare systems to rapidly emerging, difficult ethical choices. Dozens of healthcare workers were infected through their work, and some died. Others failed to report for duty to treat SARS patients out of fear for their own health or that of their family. A flu pandemic, where there may be no absolute protection or cure, would put far greater pressures on healthcare systems around the world.

There has not been a major flu pandemic in the world since 1968–69 when the 'Hong Kong' outbreak occurred. This was preceded by the 'Asian' flu pandemic in 1957–58. The most damaging flu epidemic of the last century was the 'Spanish' flu pandemic of 1918–19. This killed 250,000 people in the UK, and 20–40 million people worldwide – more than the entire number of people killed in the First World War.[3] Flu pandemics occur reasonably regularly. They have a devastating effect because there is no immunity to them amongst members of the population. Furthermore, effective vaccines cannot be properly developed until some time after the start of an infectious viral pandemic. The UK health departments estimate that each 'wave' of a pandemic is likely to affect 25 per cent of the population. Two or three 'waves' might occur. In Britain, about 50,000 deaths were anticipated in 2005 estimates.[4] There would be considerable disruption to all areas of national life, not least to the health services which would be enormously stretched.[5]

While flu pandemics since that of 1918–19 have not caused massive social discontent, there is always the possibility that the expected pandemic might be more severe than predicted. Furthermore, under the aegis of consumer choice and raised patient expectations, in a pandemic in 2006 or 2007, members of the public might expect more immediate access to care and treatment than was expected during previous pandemics.

The State of Ethical Debate and Discussion

If a pandemic were to occur, and limited amounts of effective vaccines were to become available in due course, who would be treated, in what order of priority, and according to which principles? The 2005 UK contingency plan acknowledges the need to determine the distribution of vaccines according to clear principles of priority and to have regard to equity and the 'management' of public expectations. However, significantly, it acknowledges that these principles and priorities still need to be worked out at some unspecified time and through some undefined process

3 United Kingdom Health Departments (2005), *Pandemic Flu: UK Influenza Pandemic Contingency Plan October 2005* (London: Department of Health).
4 Ibid.
5 Ibid.

before the pandemic occurs.[6] Beyond the mention of the need for some kind of equity, there do not appear to be any ethical principles enunciated in the plan, nor clear plans to involve ethicists in determining principles and priorities.

Any government hoping to deal with flu pandemic needs to have a strategy founded on commonly held ethical values. Policy makers need to engage with the public to agree in advance the rationale behind judgements such as the prioritisation of resources including hospital services and medicines, the extent of risk to be faced by front line healthcare workers, and the extent of support given to people under restrictions such as quarantine. Plans must reflect what most people will accept as fair, and good for public health. This point is well made by Peter Singer, Director of the Toronto Joint Center for Bioethics:

> A shared set of ethical values is the glue that can hold us together during an intense crisis, … a key lesson from the SARS outbreak is that fairness becomes more important during a time of crisis and confusion. And the time to consider these questions and processes in relation to a threatened major pandemic is now.[7]

There is little expertise to guide ethical reflection about treatment in the face of infectious flu pandemic. The most recent and most comprehensive guidance has come from the Influenza Pandemic Working Group at the University of Toronto Joint Center for Bioethics. In a report published in November 2005, *Stand on Guard for Thee*, the Working Group has recommended a 15-point ethical guide for pandemic planning, based in part on the experiences and study of the SARS crisis of 2003.[8]

The Toronto report wisely emphasises the importance of grounding public policy on transparency, inclusion, and 'widely held ethical values'. Unfortunately for public inclusion (and, paradoxically, for the virtues of transparency), the document identifies a full *fifteen* such values, ten of them 'substantive' and the other five 'procedural'. Although individual selections from these are made in the document in relation to its particular policy recommendations, it seems optimistic to suppose that pragmatic public policy – and intelligible public debate – can proceed on the basis of balancing the sometimes conflicting implications of such a range. The substantive values include obvious candidates such as the duty to provide care, respect for individual liberty, solidarity and so forth, but also more abstruse and even seemingly 'precious' values such as stewardship and reciprocity (denoting society's relations towards supporting healthcare workers facing the additional burdens and hazards of fighting a pandemic's consequences).

It is not that any of these values is un-*valuable*. The problem is that systematically working through them, consulting on them and so forth is probably too complex and unrealistic, particularly within the timescale available before a pandemic arrives. In the present circumstances the need is for a sustained, careful discussion that is realistic, practical, accessible and morally serious – something that is near to

---

6 Ibid, 44–5.

7 University of Toronto Joint Center for Bioethics, 2005, available at: http://www.utoronto.ca/jcb/home/news_pandemic.htm.

8 University of Toronto Joint Center for Bioethics, 2005, available at: http://www.utoronto.ca/jcb/home/documents/pandemic.pdf.

practice, but is also ethically reflective. This indicates a middle ground between the idealised abstractions of the Toronto report on the one hand and the sleeves-rolled-up, a-theoretical pragmatism of the Department of Health's guidance on the other. Neither of these documents really provides the basis for a realistic, inclusive debate that will engender public participation and trust. Nor does either of them really point towards a proportionate, practical, but credible, ethical response that embodies a middle distance realism about what is both possible and desirable – what might be called a proportionate ethical response.

What follows here is an attempt to make a preliminary case for necessary public discussion about the distribution of treatment resources for flu in terms that combine accessible abstraction with practical impact, and an acknowledgement of theory with an appeal to pertinent analogies. Getting the tone right is a necessary precursor to any public discussion credibly leading to consensus on the policy details concerning the distribution of vaccines (or, indeed, the restrictions on individual liberties).

The Problem

A disease pandemic is in some ways similar to other large-scale natural disasters; it arises from causes that are in a limited sense foreseeable, but in no sense entirely preventable. In other ways, chiefly concerning its adverse consequences, a disease pandemic can be compared to time of war, being a threat to nations and societies as corporate wholes, as well as to huge numbers of individuals. There are other parallels with times of war. For instance, if a pandemic occurs, it will constitute a major national emergency. Many of the same factors that call for hard practical decisions such as those taken in wartime would pertain. Seeking the public good would be to ensure the protection and survival of the population as a whole. It is significant that 'the population as a whole' is not the same thing as 'the whole population': the survival of the whole population implies the survival of every member of a population where plainly the survival of the population as a whole does not, and may well be inconsistent with it. As in wartime, planning for the survival of the population as a whole may require taking calculated risks involving foreseeable harms, even deaths, incurred by *identifiable* groups within the population.

When rational, population-level planning is paramount, individual choices and rights are likely to be necessarily curtailed or restricted. (The Toronto report suggests that with proper preparation and involvement, people are likely to regard accepting such restrictions as a civic duty.)[9] Resources would have to be rationed and strategically placed to ensure the long-term public good. So far, so unexceptionable – if unpleasant, uncomfortable and frightening. Clearly, this sort of situation is the kind of thing that governments plan for. It is right that they should devise effective strategies for maintaining the public health and social functionality and coherence; this is a matter of practical necessity. It also serves the principle of preserving human life in an undifferentiated sense in general terms.

---

9 Ibid, 13.

This way of framing overall response to a sudden disease pandemic is uncontroversial in public health terms. However, there must be a fundamental question about whether British health service users and providers, now used to the rhetoric of choice and consumption, will rapidly and willingly forgo their own rights and interests in the interests of the public good. Some individuals will almost undoubtedly try to ensure that they purchase vaccines privately and have these administered to themselves and their families. There is some anecdotal evidence that health workers are insisting that their families should also be immunised first in the case of an epidemic emerging. The concept of automatic public health altruism, 'Blitz spirit', if you like, may be problematic in the present climate of autonomy, individual rights and choices, consumerism and privatisation which puts the assumption of national 'health citizenship' in question.

Once one descends from overall principle to the distribution of treatment to groups, localities and individuals, it is less clear what principles should be followed, and how they might be justified. It is likely that in any pandemic, even if an effective vaccine or other treatment were available, it could not be given to all members of the population, and certainly not simultaneously; some kind of rationing or triage would have to take place. However, the basis on which this is conceived in the case of mass vaccination is almost certain to reflect two very strongly characteristic features of vaccines as a healthcare resource. First, the population-level benefit known as 'herd immunity' is likely to be achieved only by the most rapid and most widespread administration of vaccine to a critical – and perhaps unrealistically high – proportion of the population. Secondly, vaccination of *any* individual benefits not only that individual but also two other notionally identifiable groups of individuals, that is, all those other individuals who might otherwise have been exposed to infection from contact with an unvaccinated and infected person, and also all those other individuals who benefit from what the individual in question is able to do in the performance of their social or professional role. Key individuals in this sense not only derive personal benefit from vaccination but also 'multiply' the benefits to others of their own personal vaccination.[10]

Who, then, should be at the front of the queue? Should it be those whose individual survival will maximise the chances that the social order and function will survive? If this goal of seeking social survival is paramount, who, then, are those most vital to this? There are a number of candidates: for instance, politicians who have the democratic mandate to govern in the name of the people and so are empowered to make the necessary difficult decisions in time of crisis; senior civil servants who turn policy into practice and so can preserve order; the health workers who need to be there to administer treatments to, and care for, others; or, at a more basic level, drivers in the transport industry and supermarket managers whose roles ensure that the population can remain nourished and supplied and will neither starve nor riot. Alternatively, should those who embalm and bury the dead be the priority groups, to preserve the public health as well as public morale? Currently it has been argued that

---

10 We owe this point to Andrew Edgar.

Christian clergy should be among the first recipients of any effective flu vaccine, as they both bury the dead and comfort and care for the survivors.[11]

Moving beyond social functionality, what of the people who are not vital to the functioning of society in a state of national emergency? Should old people over a certain age simply be left to take their chances? Or, as particularly vulnerable people, should they be given priority as a mark of the civility and respect that is owed to those who have put so much into society in the past? Should children be a priority over middle aged people because they represent the future of our social order, or should they (as the Toronto report contemplates) be given *lowest* priority once over the age of two, on the grounds that they are statistically the age group best placed to survive the virus?[12] And what of the 'useless middle aged' – intellectuals, business people, unemployed people and journalists – whose contribution to society is not vital in terms of sheer survival, but whose loss might do much to demoralise and weaken the social fabric in the long term (not to mention leaving children and the elderly without adequate care)?

Perhaps we should just work on a principle of those who get ill first being treated first, whatever their age, status or social usefulness. If more needy people come along later when the vaccines have been used, too bad; a rough kind of arbitrary justice has been done. Or, less palatably, should we simply let those who are most wealthy, powerful, articulate, aggressive or insistent push themselves to the front of the list in the dubious Darwinian hope that thus we are helping the fittest to preserve themselves and so perpetuating the finest human stock? Perhaps the thing to do to be most fair would just be to vaccinate people on a random, pin-in-the-phone-book, basis, a kind of national lottery of misfortune.

There are no simple answers to these questions. Those who have to decide on principles, procedures and strategies have an unenviable job. In this context, they deserve the interest, respect and input of all of us at a time when pandemic is not yet imminent. How society handles issues like this is not just a matter of throwing the problem at emergency planners and asking them to arrive at technical solutions. We all have a part to play and some responsibility in both deriving 'best fit', proportionate, ethically justifiable principles that should govern any response to emergency, and then in acquiescing to, and supporting, the implementation of these principles if a pandemic emergency arises.

In some ways, this represents a particularly intense kind of ethical thought experiment in altruism and social contract where we have to put our own interests and needs behind a metaphorical 'veil of ignorance' (and then think about what would happen if we were to find ourselves in fear of our own individual lives or in need of treatment).[13] The question of mass vaccination involves as complex a form of detached rational prudence as is ever found behind the 'veil of ignorance'. Our individual prospects generally rely on whatever it takes to minimise the spread of pandemic disease and consequent social disruption; yet at the same time those prospects may be specifically at odds with *deliberate* policies necessary to contain

---

11 *Church Times*, 3 February 2006.

12 University of Toronto Joint Center for Bioethics, op. cit., 16.

13 Rawls, J. (1972), *A Theory of Justice* (Oxford: Oxford University Press).

the disease. The 'veil of ignorance' entails that we cannot know this, and must gamble on maximising the prospects for encountering minimal harm to ourselves when the 'veil' is lifted.

Starting the Ethical Debate

A starting point for informed debate would be to analyse further the government's operational plans for dealing with emergencies of this kind with a view to seeing what implicit and explicit ethical principles and insights inform it. Thereafter, it might be appropriate to begin to raise much more directly with government and public alike, in the media and other forums, the practical issues and ethical principles and dilemmas that are at stake here. Facts are generally more friendly than fantasy and we have to trust that ordinary people and citizens can often tolerate more reality than our paternalistic governors suppose.[14] People can tolerate even the recognition that they cannot always have what they want or need immediately (or, indeed, ever) if they understand and agree with the principles – whether ethical or pragmatic – upon which they are denied help. Generally, armed combatants accept the policy of battlefield triage as *prospectively* maximising the chances that they will survive, whilst knowing full well that in practice this will mean many individual cases of enduring acute suffering whilst others more likely to survive, or capable of being more speedily returned to active duty, are treated first.

Threat, chaos and crisis tend to bring out both the best and worst in people and groups. Those who survive any severe pandemic will learn a lot – both about themselves, and about the society and culture to which they belong. Sudden pandemics and the human reactions to them expose people and societies for what they are and reveal the nature of character and identity which have been formed. Such reactions reveal the depth – or lack of depth – at which are really rooted the ethical principles that are meant (or at least believed) to drive our conduct.

What structures could bring about this prior debate? We will not attempt specific suggestions here, but some general observations may be helpful, based on the distinction between, on the one hand, prior planning and, on the other hand, the concurrent administration of an emergency; the conduct of the latter should be guided, supported, but also constrained by the former.

One model might be drawn from the various regulatory authorities for ongoing matters of ethical contention (for instance, novel forms of organ transplantation, advances in human embryology and fertilisation, committees on euthanasia, the more general regulation of the activities of significant professions including medicine, education and the police) that embody elected or appointed lay representation to speak for the ordinary public as one of the principal 'stakeholders'. Admittedly, such regulatory bodies and their membership tend to address standing rather than ad hoc emergency concerns, but they exist in order to provide justified reassurance that the wider interests of the public, who after all are those upon whom the relevant professional activities are practised, are embedded in the establishment, regulation

---

14 Rogers, C. (1967), *On Becoming a Person* (London: Constable).

and monitoring of the activities concerned. These regulatory bodies also integrate what are taken to be relevant areas of expertise that are external to the immediate technical disciplines; so, for instance, law, ethics, theology, history and philosophy may be structurally available to the regulatory bodies concerned via their standing or co-opted membership, alongside the scientific and operational expertise. The parallel concern in terms of preparing for emergencies – what we might call prophylactic disaster planning – is that it provide the reassurance that representative democracy is reflected in relevant planning and operation during precisely those times of emergency when the ordinary processes of democratic rule might otherwise be in some respects under threat of restriction or suspension. Such reassurance can manifestly be provided only by processes that begin seriously in advance of the emergency itself, and that take visible and energetic account of lay representation and the input of 'external' professional perspectives.

Insofar as ethical discussion and discernment is intended to help us consciously shape who we are, where we are going and what we might like to become, it has an important part in helping all members of society to prepare for issues of treatment in time of pandemic. Prophylactic ethical debate may be one way of actually producing that elusive, if essential, component of social cohesion that we call moral fibre. By informing the process, outcomes and emergent policies of public debate about distribution of goods in time of emergency, ethics may be able to help us be better equipped, intellectually, emotionally, and practically. Amongst the immediate difficulties that it might help to avoid is the open hostility between health workers and the sick and their families that is likely to emerge if the former have to work as gatekeepers to resources without any perceived social or ethical framework or legitimacy. Thus ethical thought and argument have their own part to play both in preventive and reactive therapy – a role, of course, that stretches right back to the origins of philosophy, part of whose mission was precisely to help human individuals and societies to endure and make something of the terrible adversities and privations that are bound to afflict all living things from time to time.[15]

March 2006

---

15 Nussbaum, M. (1994), *The Therapy of Desire: Theory and Practice in Hellenistic Ethics* (Princeton NJ: Princeton University Press).

Chapter 24

Toy Stories, Horror Stories and Fairy Tales

Stephen P. Hogan

As the festive Christmas season approaches, the toy manufacturers are feeling anxious. With Christmas gifts accounting for over 50 per cent of all toys and games bought in the UK, this is the crunch trading period. With the challenges of a slowing retail market, pressure on prices and a falling number of children to be spent money on, the industry needs all the help it can get. Another regular hindrance, however, at this time of year is the media coverage of toys which, rather than extolling the technical wizardry of the new remote-controlled robot or the cunning ingenuity of the latest mind-bending game, has a habit of focusing on shock stories; the product with a potentially dangerous design or manufacturing defect found for sale in a street market; the trendy toy that has sold out in the shops and will lead to thousands of disappointed children on Christmas Day; the low wages or poor working conditions of toy workers in the developing world; or the ultimate horror story for parents, the exorbitant prices of this year's most popular toys and how much the average parent is spending on each of their children. Such stories led one toy company director to comment: 'I don't really know where journalists come from. There are very few journalists who write positive things about anything in truth!'

But does such coverage unfairly influence consumers' perceptions of the industry and, at a time when the moral issues about marketing to young children continue to be debated, is the media skewing the argument? David Lipman, the founder of JAKKS Pacific/Kidz Biz, a leading international toy company, contends that '... the public has a very bad perception of the toy industry and this needs to change. In most instances, this bad perception is actually driven by the media.'[1]

The purpose of this chapter is to objectively consider the role of the media in raising ethical issues, and is based upon some recent qualitative research carried out with senior managers in twelve leading international toy companies.

Ethical Issues in the Toy Industry

It is widely acknowledged that young children are particularly vulnerable as consumers,[2] that they need to be treated as a special group in different ways to

---

1 *Toy News*, January 2003, 55.

2 Paine, L.S. (1996), 'Children as Consumers: The Ethics of Children's Television Advertising', in Smith, N.C. and Quelch, J. (eds), *Ethics in Marketing* (New York: Primis

normal (adult) customers,[3] and that marketers have a special responsibility towards the vulnerable.[4]

The £2.1 billion traditional toy industry in the UK (which accounts for all children's toys and games sold except consoles/computer games) attracts regular adverse publicity in the media from some concerned parents, pressure groups and journalists who criticise its lack of morality in targeting young children directly and exploiting their limitations, in launching unsuitable products, and in bombarding them with advertising messages not only through television, but also through newer, more subtle and less regulated methods such as web sites, children's clubs, and in-school activities.[5] Toy companies also stand charged with encouraging pester power and contributing to playground peer pressure. What is clear is that, if toy companies are to gain the trust of parents in the face of such accusations, they need to demonstrate more clearly through their marketing behaviour that they are acting responsibly and considering the interests of others and not merely their own.

Although there is a strong body of counter arguments to such charges by both practitioners[6] and academics, the debate has attracted the attention of the European Union Commission and the national governments of many European countries, who have been reviewing the adequacy of their market controls in this area. The new 'Unfair Commercial Practices Directive' that comes into force in 2007 includes stricter controls on advertisements aimed at children, and bans any that include 'a direct exhortation to children to buy or persuade their parents or other adults to buy advertised products for them'.[7]

Toy Companies and Media Coverage

Most managers in the sample recognised that the media has a job to do and they were trying to work closely with journalists through personal contact, press packs and press releases. As one pointed out though, you cannot control what the media are ultimately going to say:

Custom Publishing (McGraw Hill)) 672–86; Mazis, M.B., Ringold, D.J., Perry, E.S. and Denman, D.W. (1992), 'Perceived Age and Attractiveness of Models in Cigarette Advertisements', *Journal of Marketing* 56, 22–37.

3 Brenkert, G.G. (1998c), 'Marketing and the Vulnerable', in Hartman, L.P. (ed.), *Perspectives in Business Ethics*, International edition (London: McGraw-Hill) 515–26.

4 Andreasen, A.R. (1975), *The Disadvantaged Customer* (New York: The Free Press); Goodin, R.E. (1985), *Protecting the Vulnerable* (Chicago: The University of Chicago Press).

5 Seaford, H. (1999), 'Should our Children be Spared Ronald?' *The Guardian*, 22 November, 8–9; Paine, L.S. (1996), op.cit.

6 Stanbrook, L. (2002), 'Public Policy Issues in Children's Advertising and Programming',
International Journal of Advertising and Marketing to Children 3:2, 63–8; Goldstein, J. (1999), *Children and Advertising: The Research, Advertising and Marketing to Children* (London: Advertising Association); Furnham, A. (2000), *Children and Advertising* (London: The Social Affairs Unit).

7 Browne, A. (2005), 'Ban on Adverts that Urge Youngsters to Pester their Parents', *The Times*, 25 February, 13.

Sometimes they might not write nice things about your toy but again in business those are the risks you take. We actively talk to them about what we're doing ... We've nothing to hide here. At the end of the day, we encourage them to write about what we are doing and if they don't like it, well they don't like it. And if they write they don't like it, that's their prerogative ...

A few managers saw the media's role as fair and sometimes even of benefit to the industry and particularly to responsible toy companies:

In principle, I think that our children do need protecting and I believe in freedom of the press and investigative journalism and if they find something, they should bring it out. And that's fine. I am all for toy companies that are unfairly exploiting children being exposed!

Other respondents, however, considered the media to be overly negative, arguing that it is headlines about the psychological and physical dangers of products rather than their play and educational values that tend to be the norm. Some considered that the industry was sometimes picked on because of its focus on children and the fact that toys and toy giving are still such an important part of Christmas:

I think it [the media coverage of toys] probably is unfair. At the end of the day, for children to learn, they have to play. There are lots of different ways children can play but a lot of play is through toys. It's always one of those emotive things that makes the headlines and will continue to do so. Many people have children, and even those that don't have an opinion, so it's an easy topic to target. But the toy industry does do an awful lot of good, whether it is directly in bringing the simple pleasure of playing with the toys to the work with charities, on child safety and everything else.

I think whenever we [the toy industry] have had bad press, it is because it has been what I call low news day. There is nothing else to talk about, so let's bring up this old chestnut. I can tell you now that on the sixth of December there will be a doll with a nail sticking out of it appearing on 'Look West' because if they haven't got anything happening on that day, the media will go down to the local Trading Standards to see what is happening there. The fact that three hundred people are killed on the road that day will completely pass everybody by. But it's just that it's topical, it's that time ...

Another manager believed that some journalists fabricated stories and referred to a claim that had been made in one newspaper in the United States that some of her company's products contained asbestos. There was no foundation at all to the story and the article created a lot of unnecessary disruption for the company concerned.

Inaccurate reporting in other ways could also have serious consequences for sales. An example was given of a children's ice cream maker, the 'McFlurry', that was featured on the BBC 1 consumer affairs programme 'Watchdog' in 2003. The presenters carried out a live demonstration of what they alleged to be the poor performance of the toy. It was claimed that the demonstration had been flawed as some ingredients had been mixed in a different order to the instructions, but the coverage devastated sales of the product.

A Responsible Role for the Media

Although there can be sympathy for the companies on some of the above issues, there is a seemingly important role for the media to play in exposing ethically dubious practices in children's markets. Raising such issues brings concerns into the open for debate and discussion and keeps companies on their toes. This perhaps contributed to the numerous comments from the managers that there is no hiding place for toy companies who must always therefore be seen to be doing 'the right things'.

There are a number of areas where the media might argue it has raised important issues about toys and toy company behaviour that are in the public interest and that have brought about change. The media has, for example, highlighted toys containing potentially hazardous materials such as lead in paint or phthalates in plastics, or reported on toys and games that could cause harm (such as the dangers of children playing unsupervised on toy trampolines). In 2003, it raised the initial concerns of some parents about the Yo-Ball, a Yo-Yo on an elastic string that potentially might have become wrapped around a child's neck. Creating awareness of the possible danger subsequently led the government to call for additional safety tests and resulted in the toy being banned, the first such incident for over a decade.[8] The media, more controversially, also raise concerns over what it deems to be unsuitable or distasteful children's products (for example, a Barbie doll dressed in lace lingerie or a range of licensed McDonald's toys), or over toys that might lead to aggressive boy's behaviour (toy guns) or an unhealthy obsession with wizardry (Harry Potter merchandise).

The media has reported on irresponsible and illegal toy company behaviour. Wide coverage was given to the substantial OFT fines handed down to one of the leading toy companies, Hasbro, and two retailers, Argos and Littlewoods, in 2003 for allegedly colluding over toy retail prices.[9] This has made the industry think very carefully about its pricing policies and the need to remain within the competition laws.

The media has exposed a number of abuses of toy workers. *Ethical Consumer* (2002)[10] cites reports by the US National Labor Committee of worker exploitation in toy factories in China by some of the leading brands including Mattel, Disney and Hasbro. More recently, there have been reports of strikes and protests over pay and conditions in China's Guangdong province that accounts for 70 per cent of global toy production.[11] The toy industry there employs almost one million people in 5,000 factories, many with barred windows, where workers are locked in for up to 18-hour shifts.[12] Other reports have highlighted seven-day working weeks, 360-day working years, and fines for non-attendance. Pay also seems low, with a minimum wage of 450 Juan per month, around £30.[13] It is perhaps such coverage that has contributed

---

8 Bird, S. (2003), 'Yo-Ball Toy Banned for Risk of Strangling', *The Times*, 25 April, 9.

9 Rankine, K. (2004), 'Two Toy Retailers Lose Price Fix Appeal', *The Daily Telegraph*, 15 December, 30.

10 *Ethical Consumer* (2002), 'Toying with their Lives', October/November, 10–15.

11 Spencer, R. (2004), 'Unseasonal Strife in Santa's Little Sweatshops', *The Daily Telegraph*, 22 December, 12.

12 August, O. (2003), 'Step Aside, Rudolph, Santa has Gone East', *The Times*, 19 December, 3.

13 Spencer, R. (2004), op. cit.

to the British toy industry signing up to the International Council of Toy Industries (ICTI) code in 2004, a global ethical manufacturing initiative designed to improve the pay and working conditions of toy workers in the developing world.[14]

Finally, the environmental credentials of the toy industry are regularly raised. With most toys made of plastic, concerns have been raised about the disposal of discarded toys. A 2005 report estimated that over 8.5 million working toys are thrown away each year in the UK, and although much of this waste can be blamed on consumers, the industry appears to have done little to date in incorporating more biodegradable materials into their production, other than in packaging, nor moving away from disposable batteries as the main power source of toys. This may change when the new European Waste and Electronic Equipment Directive comes into force in 2006, which will put the responsibility for toy recycling on manufacturers rather than consumers.[15]

Some Final Thoughts

So should we have some sympathy for toy manufacturers? Well, perhaps a little. Whilst the toy industry continues to target young children rather than their parents, there will always be a sense that they are being irresponsible, taking advantage, and yet there do appear to be areas where the industry is trying hard to address societal concerns and to become more trustworthy. The industry has a good record on toy safety, spends heavily on innovation and product development, and a feature of the industry is the many companies that have been producing and marketing children's toys for over 50 years. Unfortunately, in competitive markets where companies are fighting for their survival, the few companies that are tempted to push the boundary of what is ethically acceptable provide the media with its storylines and the legislators with the grounds to tighten regulation. Even one transgression seems to tarnish the whole industry and, like other industries, it suffers from many problems that are difficult for it to control. One in ten toys sold is counterfeit; three retailers account for over half of all toy sales, giving them enormous sway and buying power, and toys are losing out to other entertainment products as children abandon toys and games at ever-younger ages.

The media perform a valuable societal role in bringing important ethical issues to the attention of consumers, but it is also let down by the odd journalist who engages in writing fairy stories. The media are a strong voice with the power to influence opinion and consumer purchase behaviour. Most consumers seem to like being shocked by media horror stories, and the media might argue that it is these headlines that grab the attention. However, we could do with a little more cheer in the Christmas season and toy companies need, and perhaps deserve, a little more praise. So how about some more recognition for an industry that contributes so positively to giving our young people a happy childhood.

December 2005

---

14 *BTHA Handbook* (2004) (London: British Toy and Hobby Association).

15 Wallop, H. (2005), 'Brussels Lumps Teddies with Old Fridges in Waste Ruling', *The Daily Telegraph*, 29 January, 31.

Chapter 25

Herceptin in the Adjuvant Treatment of Breast Cancer

Daniela D. Rosa and Gordon C. Jayson

Breast cancer is the most frequently diagnosed malignant disease in women and the second-leading cause of cancer death after lung cancer. In women of 40 to 59 years old, it is the most frequent cause of cancer mortality. The lifetime risk for a woman to develop breast cancer is approximately 13 per cent. In the European Union, more than 191,000 new cases are diagnosed each year and more than 60,000 women will die from the disease.

Amplification (an excess number of gene copies) or overexpression (an excess of production) of particular proteins is associated with more aggressive behaviour by the affected cancer cell, including enhanced growth and proliferation, increased invasive and metastatic potential and stimulation of angiogenesis, the formation of blood vessels which is essential for tumour growth. Patients with breast cancer in which the HER2-neu growth factor receptor is amplified or overexpressed are likely to have poorly differentiated tumours with a high proliferative rate, positive axillary lymph nodes (glands in the arm pit) and decreased expression of oestrogen and progesterone receptors (markers of sensitivity to hormone-based drugs). These characteristics are associated with an increased risk of disease recurrence and death.[1]

Twenty to 30 per cent of women with early stage breast cancer have the expression of HER2-neu in their tumours.[2] Trastuzumab is a monoclonal antibody directed against the HER2-neu receptor that has been shown to improve outcomes, including survival, for patients with metastatic HER2-positive disease. Trastuzumab was first approved only for the treatment of metastatic disease; however, recent trials in the adjuvant setting (the term for a treatment given following removal of the primary tumour) indicated that the drug is even more beneficial if given earlier. The role of trastuzumab in adjuvant therapy for early-stage disease has been the subject of four large multicentre randomised controlled trials.

---

1 Slamon, D.J., Clark, G.M., Wong, S.G., Levin, W.J., Ullrich, A. and McGuire, W.L. (1987), 'Human Breast Cancer: Correlation of Relapse and Survival with Amplification of the HER-2/neu Oncogene', *Science* 235, 177–82.

2 Slamon, D.J., Leyland-Jones, B., Shak, S., Fuchs, H., Paton, V., Bajamonde, A., et al. (2001), 'Use of Chemotherapy Plus a Monoclonal Antibody against HER2 for Metastatic Breast Cancer that Overexpresses HER2', *New England Journal of Medicine* 344:11, 783–92.

The HERA (Herceptin adjuvant) trial,[3] that included more than 5,000 patients randomised from 478 institutions in 39 countries, compared one and two years of trastuzumab treatment with an observation arm in patients who had already completed their adjuvant chemotherapy and radiotherapy, when indicated. Two US trials were combined for analysis (National Surgical Adjuvant Breast and Bowel Project, B-31 and North Central Cancer Treatment Group trial, N9831).[4] In these trials, patients were randomised to receive trastuzumab concurrently or sequentially with adjuvant chemotherapy. The Breast Cancer International Research Group (BCIRG) trial, BCIRG006, is evaluating the use of two different chemotherapy regimens with or without concurrent trastuzumab.[5] Combined data from NCCTG N9831 and from NSABP B-31 showed a 52 per cent reduction in the risk of breast cancer recurrence and a 33 per cent survival benefit with the administration of trastuzumab therapy in the adjuvant setting. The HERA trial found a 46 per cent reduction in breast cancer recurrence and a 34 per cent survival benefit by giving trastuzumab as an adjuvant treatment.[6]

The BCIRG006 trial compared a standard adjuvant treatment arm of four cycles of doxorubicin and cyclophosphamide chemotherapy followed by docetaxel chemotherapy for six cycles (AC-T) to two regimens containing trastuzumab. One regimen included AC-T with one year of herceptin (AC-TH) and the other was a regimen of docetaxel plus carboplatin plus one year of trastuzumab (TCH). In the latter arm, trastuzumab was started concomitantly with chemotherapy (TCH). An interim analysis of more than 3,000 patients showed a relative reduction in the risk of breast cancer relapse of 51 per cent and 39 per cent for the AC-TH and TCH arms, respectively, compared to the AC-T control arm. There is insufficient information available at this moment to evaluate overall survival.

Severe congestive heart failure is a known side-effect of trastuzumab. The three-year cumulative incidence of class III or IV congestive heart failure or death from cardiac causes in the trastuzumab group was 0.5 per cent in the HERA trial, 4.1 per cent in the B-31 trial, and 2.9 per cent in the N9831 trial. In the BCIRG006 trial the proportion of protocol-defined cardiac events was 1.2 per cent, 2.3 per cent and 1.2

---

3 Piccart-Gebhart, M.J., Procter, M., Leyland-Jones, B., et al. (2005), 'Trastuzumab after Adjuvant Chemotherapy in HER2-positive Breast Cancer', *New England Journal of Medicine* 353, 1659–72.

4 Romond, E.H., Perez, E.A., Bryant, J., et al. (2005), 'Trastuzumab Plus Adjuvant Chemotherapy for Operable HER2-positive Breast Cancer', *New England Journal of Medicine* 353, 1673–84.

5 Breast Cancer International Research Group (BCIRG) (2005), 'Sanofi Aventis. Interim Analysis of Phase III Study Shows Docetaxel-based Chemotherapy Regimens Combined with Trastuzumab Significantly Improved Disease Free Survival in Early Stage HER2-positive Breast Cancer', press release, 14 September, available at: www.bcirg.org/Internet/Press+Releases/default.htm.

6 Smith, I.E., et al. (2006), 'Trastuzumab Following Adjuvant Chemotherapy in HER2-positive Early Breast Cancer (HERA Trial): Disease-free and Overall Survival after 2-year Median Follow-up', Scientific Special Session, American Society of Clinical Oncology (ASCO) Annual Meeting 2006.

per cent for the AC-T, AC-TH, and TCH arms, respectively. It should be noted that patients with a history of heart disease were excluded from all four trials.

The emergence of several targets and developmental agents in anticancer therapy has resulted in higher rates of success. Trastuzumab is the first monoclonal antibody to show a survival benefit as an adjuvant treatment for cancer. The implications of these novel treatments in oncology are important not only for patients but also for healthcare costs. The wide availability of information through not only specialised journals but also through the press has generated a strong pressure for the approval of trastuzumab by public healthcare systems all over the world. It is very important that this decision be made carefully after considering the totality of available scientific evidence. It should be noted that the follow-up period of studies of trastuzumab in the adjuvant setting has been relatively short, so there are as yet no long-term side-effect data. It is also unknown how long trastuzumab needs to be taken, and which is the longer interval of time that may be waited from the beginning of chemotherapy to the start of trastuzumab administration. Another barrier is the cost of testing for HER2 expression. Many centres offer HER2 testing to women with early disease, but this is by no means standard.[7] However, even with these limitations, it seems that trastuzumab is a revolutionary adjuvant treatment for the subgroup of patients with HER2-neu positive breast cancers.

November 2005

---

7 Dent, R. and Clemons, M. (2005), 'Adjuvant Trastuzumab for Breast Cancer: We Need to Ensure that Equity Exists for Access to Effective and Expensive Treatments', *British Medical Journal* 331, 1035–6.

Chapter 26

End of Life Decision-Making: The Implications of the Court of Appeal Decision in *Burke v General Medical Council*

Phil Fennell

Leslie Burke, aged 45, suffers from spino cerebellar ataxia, a progressively degenerative brain condition. There will come a time when he would be entirely dependent on others for his care. He would remain competent and able to communicate his wishes until the final days of his life. During his final days, he would lose the ability to communicate, although not at first awareness of his surroundings and predicament, before lapsing into a semi-comatose condition and then dying.

He was concerned that the General Medical Council Guidance *Withholding and Withdrawing Life Prolonging Treatment: Good Practice and Decision-Making* would mean that, when he lost capacity, medical staff might withdraw artificial nutrition and hydration (ANH) against his wishes, if they considered that this treatment was not in his best interests. He wished to ensure that ANH would not be withdrawn from him while he remained sentient.

He sought to achieve this by seeking judicial review of the GMC Guidance in the form of declarations that certain paragraphs of the Guidance were unlawful. The effect of granting the declarations sought would be that for the first time, a court was declaring that a capable adult could make an advance statement requesting a particular medical treatment which would be binding on the doctor. Hitherto, the accepted position has been that a doctor will be bound by a capable adult's advance directive *refusing* a specific medical treatment in specified circumstances, but will only be required to take into account an advance request for a particular treatment.

The reason why a patient has the right to refuse a particular treatment but not demand it is because of the principle that a doctor may not be required to give a treatment which is against his or her clinical assessment of the patient's best interests. This proposition was shaken by Munby J.'s judgement at first instance, suggesting that a patient's request for a treatment was determinative that the treatment was in the patient's best interests. As the Court of Appeal put it:

> A theme running through Munby J's judgment is that, provided that there are no resource implications, doctors who have assumed the care of a patient must administer such treatment as is in the patient's best interests and that, where a patient has expressed an

informed wish for a particular treatment, receipt of such treatment will be in the patient's best interests.[1]

The Court of Appeal did not accept this. Although autonomy conferred a paramount right on a capable adult to refuse even life-saving treatment, the court emphasised that the corollary did not follow:

> Autonomy and the right of self-determination do not entitle the patient to insist on receiving a particular medical treatment regardless of the nature of the treatment.[2]

The source of the doctor's obligation to provide treatment lay not in the patient's demand for the particular treatment, but in the common law duty to care, which comes into being once a patient is accepted into a hospital. The doctor's duty towards an incapable patient is to act in her or his best interests, and the Court of Appeal preferred an objective test of best interests.

The Court of Appeal considered that instead of going to law, Mr Burke could have addressed his concerns better by talking to his doctors and to the GMC to ascertain how the Guidance was likely to be applied in his case. Before embarking on its own analysis, the Court of Appeal found it necessary to re-define what Mr Burke's concerns actually were, taking the view that neither Munby J.'s summary nor Mr Burke's own statement 'sets out with clarity the precise nature of his concern'. In order to appreciate what his concern was, it was 'necessary to identify … the different circumstances in which … ANH might be withdrawn from a patient'.[3]

The first distinction to be made was 'between the withdrawal of ANH in circumstances where this will shorten life and the withdrawal of ANH where it will not have this effect because it is no longer sustaining life'. The court acknowledged that in practice this distinction might be very difficult to make, since the evidence showed 'that a patient may, as part of the process of dying, cease to eat or drink. In such circumstances the administration of ANH may delay, to some extent, the dying process.'

The court distinguished three situations where ANH might be withdrawn from:

1) a patient who is competent,
2) a patient who is sentient but not competent, and
3) a patient who is not sentient because, for instance, he is in a permanent vegetative state (PVS) or has lapsed into a coma at the end of a terminal illness.

Applying these distinctions, the Court of Appeal arrived at their own diagnosis of Mr Burke's concerns, and indicated firmly that he need not have gone to law to address them. According to the evidence, Mr Burke would remain competent until the final stage of his disease. Thus, so long as ANH was prolonging his life, he would be able, aided by a computerised device, to communicate his wish that ANH should

---

1 [2005] EWCA Civ 1003 para. 27.

2 Ibid, para. 31.

3 Ibid, para. 7.

be administered. He would lose competence 'in the final stages of his disease, first losing the ability to communicate while remaining sentient, and shortly thereafter lapsing into a coma'. During 'these final stages', as the court described them, ANH would 'cease to be capable of prolonging his life'.

The court therefore concluded that Mr Burke's fear was that ANH would be withdrawn before the final stages of his disease, and considered that 'there was no reason for him to have it':

> There are no grounds for thinking that those caring for a patient would be entitled to or would take a decision to withdraw ANH in such circumstances. Nor, as we shall show, did the Guidance suggest to the contrary. Had Mr Burke been well advised he would and could have sought reassurance from the GMC as to the purport of their guidelines and from the doctors who were treating him as to the circumstances, if any, in which ANH might be discontinued.[4]

Having decided what Mr Burke's concerns really were, the court went on to state that the six declarations granted by Munby J. went:

> far beyond the current concerns of Mr Burke in that (1) they deal with the position of an incompetent patient, when, on the evidence, Mr Burke is likely to remain competent until the final stages of his illness and (2) they address the effect of an advance directive, … , when Mr Burke has made no such directive.[5]

The court was aware that they had not addressed the position during the short period before Mr Burke lapses into his final coma when he will be sentient but unable to communicate his wishes. The court considered that the implications of withdrawal of ANH at that stage 'may depend critically on the effect, if any, that this will have on easing his final conscious moments'. In other words, if ANH was necessary to ease pain and suffering, it should not be withdrawn. The court considered that if Mr Burke's current concerns related to this stage, the court considered them premature. From all the information available, it seemed that what would happen when he lost capacity but not sentience was the very nub of Mr Burke's concern.

The court considered that it had never been open to doubt that the doctor providing care to Mr Burke would be obliged to provide ANH in accordance with his expressed wish, so long as the treatment was prolonging his life:

> Where a competent patient indicates her or his wish to be kept alive by the provision of ANH any doctor who deliberately brings that patient's life to an end by discontinuing ANH, will not merely be in breach of his duty but guilty of murder. Where life depends upon the continued provision of ANH there can be no question of the supply of ANH not being clinically indicated unless a clinical decision has been taken that the life in question should come to an end. That is not a decision that can lawfully be taken in the case of a competent patient who expresses the wish to remain alive.[6]

---

4 Ibid, paras 12–13.

5 Ibid, para. 22.

6 Ibid, paras 40 and 53.

Conclusion

The following general propositions flow from the Court of Appeal decision:

1) Where life depends on ANH, it may not be withdrawn if a competent patient has expressed the wish to remain alive. To withdraw it will be murder. A lot will of course depend on the assessment whether life depends on ANH, which will not always be clear cut.
2) Where the patient becomes incapable but remains sentient, ANH should be continued if it is necessary to keep the patient comfortable, unless the patient has expressly refused it.
3) A capable adult's valid advance directive refusing ANH in specified circumstances will bind the doctors.
4) A patient may not require a doctor to administer a treatment which is against that doctor's judgement of the patient's clinical needs.

Chapter 27

Does Nanotechnology Require a New 'Nanoethics'?

Søren Holm

Nanotechnology is the study, design, creation, synthesis, manipulation and application of functional materials, devices and systems through control of matter at the nanometre scale (1-100 nanometres, one nanometre being equal to 1×10^{-9} of a metre), that is, at the atomic and molecular levels, and the exploitation of novel phenomena and properties of matter at that scale.

The beginnings of the field can be dated relatively precisely to the 1959 speech by Richard Feynman entitled 'Plenty of Room at the Bottom', but it is only in the last ten to fifteen years that some kinds of deliberately produced nanotechnology have reached practical use (for example, Pilkington's self-cleaning window panes).[1]

Alongside the practical development of nanotechnology, ethical considerations have also begun to emerge, and it has been suggested that we need a new kind of ethics, 'nanoethics', to handle the ethical problems inherent in nanotechnology. Is this a reasonable suggestion? It is difficult to specify exactly what could make an area of technology so special that it needs its own ethics, but a minimal requirement must be that it either raises ethical issues that are not raised by other kinds of technologies, or that it raises ethical issues of a different (that is, larger) magnitude than other technologies. Is this the case for nanotechnology?

The Nano-dystopians

On one side of the debate about the implications of nanotechnology we find a group of commentators who hold a view which can be called 'nano-dystopian'. The development of nanotechnology will create great risks for society, and may in the end lead to the destruction of the human race. In the UK this view has gained prominence because it has been actively promoted by Prince Charles.[2] The most 'popular' doomsday scenario among nano-dystopians is the 'grey goo' scenario in which self-replicating nano-robots get out of control and devour all matter, turning the earth into a seething mass of grey goo. A slightly more refined version of this

---

1 Many traditional products can only be produced or work because of effects at the nano level (for example, many kinds of catalysts), but these were not previously achieved through deliberate manipulation at the nano level during production.

2 See, for instance, 'Spare Us All from Royal Nanoangst', available at: http://www. telegraph.co.uk/connected/main.jhtml?xml=/connected/2003/04/30/ecnano30.xml.

scenario, in which the nano-robots only devour organic material, forms the basis for Michael Crichton's 2002 novel *Prey*.[3]

Certain other uses of nanotechnology have also attracted particular negative attention. These are the use of nanotechnology for surveillance and the possible convergence of nanotechnology with a range of other technologies in a 'project' eventually leading to human enhancement.[4]

Nanosurveillance can be achieved by passive tagging of people or products with nanotransponders that can be read by an interested agent at some distance with the appropriate reader (in reality the transponders are currently and in the foreseeable future considerably larger than nanoscale); or it could perhaps in the future be achieved by active surveillance nanomachines. Other worries have focused not on the technology itself but on the forces that are shaping its development trajectory. It has, for instance, been noted that a lot of nanotechnology research is performed for and sponsored by the military.[5]

The Nano-utopians

On the other side of the debate we can find nano-utopians who predict that nanotechnologies are going to solve all our problems, and make us live forever. It is on this side of the debate that we find predictions about medical nano-robots that will clean up our clogged arteries from the inside, and generally repair all our ills, while other nano-robots will work tirelessly to clear up the environmental mess of the last 300 years of industrial society. This nano-utopian view has been promoted by the American writer Erich Drexler and his Foresight Institute since the 1980s.[6]

A specific strand of nano-utopianism focuses on a possible future convergence between nanotechnology, information technology, gene technology and cognitive science. This convergence is predicted to be the breakthrough that will finally allow effective cognitive enhancement of human beings (and presumably animals as well), and it is therefore highly popular among trans- and posthumanist thinkers.

A Plea for Nano-realism

As should be evident from the above, the author of this chapter thinks that both the nano-dystopians and the nano-utopians are far off the mark. Neither the dys- or the u-topian predictions are plausible, and even if they were, they would be at timescales much longer than those often bandied about. Predictors of technological developments seem to have an unfortunate attraction to either a three to five or a five

---

3 Crichton, M. (2002), *Prey* (New York: Harper Collins).

4 Khushf, G. (2004), 'Systems Theory and the Ethics of Human Enhancement: A Framework for NBIC Convergence', *Annals New York Academy of Sciences* 1013, 124–49.

5 See, for instance, the Swedish Defence Forces nanotech programme as an example of the military interest in the area: http://www.nanotek.se. Many other countries have military nanotech programmes, but few are as open as Sweden about the specific projects pursued.

6 Foresight Institute website: www.foresight.org.

to ten-year timeframe for the successful development of a new technology, and they are often completely resistant to revision of these estimates. But it is completely unlikely that we will see, for instance, functioning medical nano-robots within the next ten years.

This does not mean, however, that nanotechnology is not extremely important. The use of nanomaterials in consumer products does, for instance, raise new toxicological and environmental challenges. Some nanomaterials are completely new and have never before existed in nature. This is the case, for instance, for nanotubes and fullerenes. Their toxicological and environmental characteristics are therefore also unknown. But there are also new issues concerning nanosized particles of known materials. Because of their size, nanoparticles are dispersed differently in the environment and can gain access to other sites in the body than larger particles can, and partly because of their very large surface area to mass, they can have different chemical properties than larger scale particles of exactly the same material. This means that even though we know a certain chemical to be 'safe', this may no longer hold if it is formulated in nanosize particles. Health and safety issues related to nanomaterials and nanoparticles are, however, still in an early stage and, as a consequence, it seems premature to draw far-ranging conclusions regarding the potential hazards and risks related to exposure to these materials. The available data regarding the health hazards and risks of exposure to nanomaterials and nanoparticles are limited and there are no systematic investigations.

Recent data demonstrate that lung exposure to nanoparticles (<100 nm) produces greater adverse inflammatory responses compared with that of larger particles of the same composition and at equivalent mass concentrations.[7] The interaction of particles with cells and the consequence of surface area properties and free radical generation play an important role in nanoparticle toxicity. This effect is due to the high size-specific deposition of nanoparticles when inhaled as single particles rather than aggregated particles. It was concluded that surface area might play an important role in nanoparticle toxicity. It should be noted that size effects play an important role not only for the intensity of potential adverse effects (in the case of toxic materials), but also for the efficiency of nanoparticle-based drug delivery systems.

Why We Do Not Need a Specific Nanoethics

The strongest case for the need for a specific nanoethics could be made if either the predictions of the nano-dystopians or the nano-utopians are correct. So, let us for the sake of argument assume that these predictions are correct, and that nanotechnology has great destructive and other worrying potentials, or great beneficial potential (or perhaps even both at the same time). Is that enough to require us to create nanoethics as a separate field of inquiry? Probably not. There are plenty of extant technologies that could destroy the earth, or at least destroy the earth as we know it (for example,

---

7 Warheit, D.B., et al. (2004), 'Comparative Pulmonary Toxicity Assessment of Single-Wall Carbon Nano-tubes in Rats', *Toxicologist* 77:1, 117; Warheit, D.B., et al. (2003), 'Pulmonary Toxicity Studies with T_iO_2 Particles Containing Various Commerical Coatings', *Toxicologist* 72:1, 298.

atomic technology, the burning of fossil fuels), plenty of technologies that may be used for intensifying surveillance of citizens, and plenty of technologies where development is partially driven by military needs. At the same time the positive claims made for nanotechnology have over time been made for a range of other technologies, most recently, in the medical field, gene technology and stem cell therapies.

While there is thus a great need for an analysis of the many ethical issues raised by the different developments in nanotechnology, there is no need for a specific nanoethics. The toolbox developed in applied ethics during the last 35 years probably already contains the necessary tools for the analysis of nanotechnology.

August 2005

Chapter 28

Medically Assisted Procreation in Italy: The Referendum and the Roman Catholic Church

Norman Doe, Javier García Oliva and Cristiana Cianitto [1]

A referendum on medically assisted procreation, held on 12 and 13 June 2005, raised for Italian citizens some fundamental questions about society and the family: is the Italian understanding of the family still based on the traditional (Catholic) concept of marriage (that is, a union between one man and one woman for the procreation of children)? Is the embryo a human being with rights at the point of conception or do rights arise later? What rights does a mother have in relation to an embryo? To what extent should scientific research be subject to moral limits? The following outlines the successful intervention of the Roman Catholic Church in the referendum; it may be contrasted with two earlier referenda in which the intervention of the Church had failed: in relation to divorce in 1974 (Law 898/1970), when of the 87.7 per cent of the electorate voting, 59.6 per cent voted to preserve divorce, and abortion in 1981 (Law 194/1978), when of the 79.4 per cent of the electorate voting, 88.4 per cent voted to preserve the law on abortion.

Background

Prior to 2004 Italian legislation contained no provision as to medically assisted procreation. The matter was governed by medical practice, itself conditioned by common sense and respect for life, the human person and human rights. On 10 February 2004, Parliament approved law reform proposal 47A/2002, which became Law No. 40 of 19 February 2004. This legislation was approved by a very small majority (277 in favour; 222 against), though supported by political parties across the political spectrum. In brief, the law of 2004 provided for: (1) juridical equality for the mother, the father and the embryo; (2) a prohibition against implantation, following fertilization in vitro, of more than three embryos at the same time; (3) the requirement to implant the embryos in the womb of the mother; and (4) a prohibition against the creation or conservation of surplus embryos. Furthermore, pre-implantation diagnosis of the embryos was forbidden, even if a subsequent abortion

1 We are grateful to Dr Heather Payne, Consultant Paediatrician and Senior Lecturer, Cardiff University, for assistance with the medical aspects of the study.

was possible in accordance with Law 194/1978. As cryopreservation following artificial insemination was not permitted, so too was research into embryonic stem cells, with the prohibition against the creation of new embryos for express scientific purposes. Finally, heterologous insemination was not permitted.[2]

This legal framework produced heated debate. One criticism was that the regime was too close to the Roman Catholic view that the embryo becomes a juridical person at the point of conception. In Catholic teaching, at conception the embryo cannot be subjected to any manipulation, modification, or suppression.[3] The regime was understood to threaten the right to abortion.

Abrogative Referendum

In Italy, every law is open to review by the electorate if 500,000 voters so require.[4] Opponents to the 2004 law (including various womens' groups and law makers) collected four million signatures to subject those elements of the legislation described above to a referendum, the aim being to achieve relaxation of what medical biologists also regarded as excessively restrictive rules.[5] The opponents proposed five different possibilities to be considered in the referendum, from repeal of the law to its modification. The Constitutional Court, which under Italian law determines referendum questions,[6] did not admit the possibility of repeal and instead focused on the other four.[7]

In the referendum campaign, both the government and opposition parties were divided, and proceeded on the basis that the matter was one of conscience and therefore the subject of a free vote. Both the Prime Minister, Silvio Berlusconi, and the leader of the opposition, Romano Prodi, supported the 'No' campaign; that is, to maintain the law unmodified. The Minister for Equal Opportunities, Stefania Prestigiacomo, and her cabinet colleague, Carlo Giovanardi, publicly encouraged people to choose the 'Yes' option; that is, to modify the law to allow cryoconservation, heterosexual insemination, pre-implantation diagnosis, and not to require triple implantation.

---

2 For the bioethical issues and comment on the new law, see Santosuosso, F. (2004), *La procreazione medicalmente assistita – Commento alla legge 19 febbraio 2004, n. 40* (Milano: Giuffrè); Stanzione, P. and Sciancalepore, G. (eds) (2004), *Procreazione assistita – Commento alla legge 19 febbraio 2004, n. 40* (Milano: Giuffrè); Aramini, M. (2003), *Introduzione alla bioetica* (Milano: Giuffrè); and Camassa, E. and Casonato, C. (eds) (2005), *La procreazione medicalmente assistita: ombre e luci* (Trento: Universitá degli Studi di Trento).

3 Zanotti A. (1990), *Le manipolazioni genetiche e il diritto della Chiesa* (Milano: Giuffrè).

4 Article 75, Italian Constitution; on the use of referendum, see Rossi, E. (2005), 'Referendum e costituzione', *Il regno*, Documenti, 9/2005; see also Watkin, T.G. (1997), *The Italian Legal Tradition* (Aldershot: Ashgate Publishing Limited) 73–4.

5 Smoltczyk, A. (2005), 'Does Life Begin at Conception?' *Spiegel Online*, 6 June; Dolcini, E. (2004), 'Embrione, pre-embrione, ootide: nodi interpretativi nella disciplina della procreazione medicalmente assistita', *Rivista italiana di diritto e procedura penale*, anno XLVII, fasc. 2.

6 L. Costituzionale n. 1/1953.

7 The case was Corte Costituzionale n. 45/2005.

Implicit was the idea that the embryo does not have the same rights as the mother since conception.

The Position of the Roman Catholic Church

The Roman Catholic Church took an active part in this referendum campaign. The President of the Italian Episcopal Conference, Cardinal Ruini, declared its unequivocal opposition to the referendum: 'even if this law is not completely in line with the Catholic position, it does partially assure a sufficient level of respect for the essential principle of life and dignity of all the human beings from conception'. Accordingly, the Church advised its faithful 'to use all the different possibilities provided by the State framework to oppose' change to the law.[8] The Cardinal described the Catholic view as a 'Double No': no to the content of the four suggested alternatives, which it considered clearly worsened the law; and no to the use of a referendum for such an important matter with crucial human and social implications.[9] Consequently, and crucially, the Church exhorted abstention,[10] which would have had the effect of invalidating the referendum as, in Italian law, for a referendum to be valid, the turnout has to be above 50 per cent of the electorate.[11] Moreover, the Committee 'Science and Life', joined by academics, scientists, jurists, and ex-presidents of the Constitutional Court, advanced the same ideas as the ecclesiastical hierarchy.[12] Moreover, the members of the Committee were also successful in terms of making the public share their views about the suitability of an abstention from the referendum, which amounted in practical terms to a 'No' vote.[13]

The intervention of the Roman Catholic Church was successful: 74.1 per cent of Italian citizens abstained from voting. Of these it is estimated that about 30 per cent were unaffected by the exhortation of the Church (the so-called 'physiological abstention'). On 12 and 13 June, three out of four Italians did not vote in the referendum. However, of those who voted, the majority chose the 'Yes' option. The abstention and the result have been understood to indicate the profound influence of the Catholic Church (and the Catholic media) on Italians, not only active Catholics but also those Catholics who do not attend Mass on Sundays. The Church justified its intervention to defend life on the basis of natural law and its moral authority.

---

8 *Prolusione Consiglio Permanente 17 January 2005, Il Regno,* n. 3/2005.

9 Pope Benedict XVI implicitly supported the Italian bishops' efforts to block any relaxation of the law.

10 Rossini, S. (2005), 'Italian Referendum on Artificial Insemination', *Italy Magazine Online.* 9 June.

11 Article 75, Italian Constitution.

12 For the position of the Catholic Church, see Catechismo Chiesa Cattolica, Sez. II, Cap. II, art. 6, IV, available at: http://www.vatican.va/archive/catechism_it/index_it.htm.

13 Having said that, abstaining from taking part in the referendum represents, technically, a lack of choice: any person who abstains from voting does not give his/her opinion about it and is subject to the decision of the legislature, which is bound to maintain the piece of legislation in the first place, but that could suggest its modification after a deeper parliamentary debate in due course.

Some saw the Church as exercising its own right to freedom of speech (article 19, Italian Constitution), exercisable especially in relation to 'topical' issues. By way of contrast, others have argued that the intervention represents a violation of the separation of church and state enshrined in article 7 of the Constitution, and that the exhortation of Cardinal Ruini was a breach of the Concordat of 1984 (between the Italian state and the Holy See). In any event, in substance Cardinal Ruini succeeded in influencing the people in the exercise of their political and civil rights.

Conclusion

It seems to be a political fact that the Italian population appears to have acquiesced in the intervention of the Catholic Church in the legislative and political processes of the Italian state. Indeed, it has been understood by some commentators that the exhortation of Cardinal Ruini on this occasion is a prelude to intervention in other matters, such as cohabitation, gay marriages, limitations to divorce and abortion, and euthanasia. These events also raise important sociological questions about the *laicitá* (the secular nature or posture) of the state.[14] They might suggest a movement towards a restrictive interpretation of the concept of *laicitá*, and indeed of state neutrality towards religion, in which greater account is taken of the historical, social and numerical influence of Catholicism. In this sense, the referendum seems to highlight a crisis of Italian politics and its failure to deal systematically with matters of conscience. In this respect, this successful intervention by the Church might be linked to the collapse of the *Democrazia Cristiana*, which until the 1990s was the political expression of Catholicism in Italy. Nowadays the Catholic hierarchy itself assumes a function formerly performed by *Democrazia Cristiana*. Today the Church is not associated exclusively with any one political party and it addresses directly the faithful who belong to many different political groups. Even Catholics in Communist-inspired parties vote pro-Church on matters related to life, marriage, and so on. And in contemporary Italy, no institution seems to have the will to oppose the goals of the Church.

Recently, the law on medically assisted procreation has been upheld in the Constitutional Court,[15] suggesting a contrast between article 13 of the Law,[16] and articles 2, 3 and 32 of the Italian Constitution. In the case, the claimants asked for a pre-implantation diagnosis in accordance with the general principle of abortion law, which allows abortion when there is a danger to the mother's health. The woman had had an abortion after a previous in vitro insemination because the foetus was discovered to be affected by beta-thalassemia. This was a stressful event for the mother, who asked not to be subjected to this again through pre-implantation diagnosis. The court decided that in Italy: (1) no right to a healthy child exists; 2) in Law n. 40/2004 the veto against pre-implantation diagnosis was intended to avoid the risk of genetic selection of people; 3) in the balance between the health of the

---

14 See, for example, Zagrebelsky, G. (2005) 'Gli atei clericali e la fonte del potere', *La Repubblica*, 5 July 2005, available at: www.Italialaica.it.

15 The case is Corte Costituzionale, ordinanza n. 369/2006.

16 Article 13 states the prohibition of pre-implantation diagnosis of the embryo.

mother and that of the embryo, there is no evidence that the health of the mother is increased through an assurance that the embryo is free from genetic imperfections; 4) the general principle of Law n. 40/2004 is that the mother's, father's and embryo's rights are perfectly equivalent, so no pre-implantation procedure is allowed if it is not directed to preserve the embryo's health. The petition was rejected. Therefore, up to now, the law has not been modified by the Constitutional Court, which tries to preserve coherence within the law. This necessity for coherence also surfaces in a recommendation of the Italian *Senato*,[17] which binds the government to support medical research, including stem cells not derived from embryos. This recommendation came after the disclaimer of the ethical declaration that Italy made in July 2001with other European nations.[18] In sum: at the moment in Italy there is no significant movement against the position set out in Law n. 40/2004.

July 2005

---

17 Risoluzione Senato della Repubblica, 19 July 2006.

18 This ethical declaration was made in relation to the debate in the European Parliament concerning the draft of the 7th Framework Programme (2007–13). In this document, Italy was asking the Framework Programme to avoid supporting research in which embryo's derived stem cells were going to be used.

Chapter 29

From Fridge Mountains to Food Mountains? Tackling the UK Food Waste Problem

Samarthia Thankappan

Introduction

Saving food from going to waste – New figures show about a third of food grown for human consumption in the UK ends up being thrown away.[1]

Unused food: What a waste – Britain throws away £20bn worth of unused food every year – equal to five times our spending on international aid and enough to lift 150 million people out of starvation.[2]

These are but a few headlines that hit our daily newspapers. What can be done to reduce this excessive waste?

According to United Nations estimates, the amount (£20 billion) Britain throws away as unused food would be required per year until 2015 to stop the 150 million people in Africa suffering from starvation.

The food and drinks sector accounts for a substantial amount of the UK's annual commercial waste, especially if the food chain is taken in its entirety from farm to fork. There is limited information available on the amount of waste generated by the agricultural sector and similarly the waste generated by the retail food and drinks sector has not been accurately determined. The food manufacturing sector has an annual turnover of about £68 billion and employs over half a million people in about 7,500 businesses,[3] and by the end of the 1990s this sector was estimated to generate over eight million tonnes of waste annually.[4] A number of studies have also drawn attention to the high proportion of food-related waste present in municipal solid waste.[5]

---

1 Allen, L. (2005), 'Saving Food from Going to Waste', BBC News, 14 April.

2 Milmo, C. (2005), 'Unused Food – What a Waste', *The Independent*, 15 April.

3 Atari, G. (2004), 'Food Waste as a Resource', *Biogas – How to Sustain Output from Today's Number One Renewable*, Renewable Power Association Conference, December 2004, London.

4 Food Processing Faraday (2003), *Waste Minimisation, Reuse and Recycling Strategies for the Food Processor*, Technical Report.

5 Craig, A. (2005), Personal Communication.

Britain is striving hard to reach its target to cut by almost half the 22.5 million tonnes of domestic waste, including 3.4 million tonnes of waste food, it sends to landfill sites in the next five years. The current level (22.5 million tonnes) of domestic waste sent to landfill sites must be reduced to 6.4 million tonnes by 2020, requiring a dramatic increase in the use of composting methods.

Landfilled waste from food production has been estimated at 2.7 million tonnes per annum.[6] The majority of this is organic matter that decomposes within the landfill to produce methane, a powerful greenhouse gas contributing to climate change, and leachate, a toxic capable of considerable groundwater pollution. The waste strategy for England and Wales published in 2000 sets clear targets for commercial waste, including food waste that is disposed of in landfills. Diversion of all organic wastes away from landfills is fundamental to all future waste management strategy.

We are faced with several ethical issues when it comes to food consumption. Ethical food consumers demonstrate social and/or environmental responsibility by their food choices. There is a growing recognition of some of the ethical issues of food consumption amongst a small section of consumers, for example, environmental sustainability, localism, human rights/working conditions and fair trade, animal welfare, genetically modified foods, and so on. However, consumers still have not caught up with the food waste aspect of ethical food consumption. Consumers have not yet grappled with the concept of not wasting food and using only what one needs. Food takes energy and natural resources to produce, so wasted food wastes these resources.

It ultimately falls to individual households to cut down on waste to meet an EU target, already achieved by most Scandinavian countries, of recycling 45 per cent of waste by 2020.

There are no indications so far as to whether the UK's throw-away society is showing any signs of changing course; but definitely the waste mountain that is being created is now starting to spill out of its landfill sites. As there is a decrease in landfill space, the cost of landfilling our waste will continue to grow, ultimately being passed on to businesses and residents in the form of high disposal fees. The focus of waste management in the United Kingdom so far has been on waste disposal at a minimal cost, with relatively few measures to protect the environment. Over the last decade this stance has changed significantly, with powerful directives from both the European Union and national governments instilling greater awareness and recognition of the negative impacts of waste on the wider environment. The aim of this communication is to introduce the extent of the food waste problem in the UK. The chapter moves forward by presenting a brief overview of the UK waste strategy, highlighting the need for more focus on tackling food disposal rates. The chapter then discusses alternate ways of handling the issue of food waste.

---

6 Biffa (2003), 'Future Perfect: An Analysis of Britain's Waste Production and Disposal Account, with Implications for Industry and Government for the Next Twenty Years', Report published by Biffa Waste Services Ltd, UK, 105pp.

UK Waste Management Policy

The amount of waste that the UK produces, particularly in the domestic sector, is growing exponentially, with little sign of this growth being brought under control. Over the last decade, the UK's waste management infrastructure has come under increasing pressure and this situation is likely to deteriorate quickly as new legal requirements restrict access to landfill sites. In some areas we are literally running out of room in landfills – existing capacity is only expected to last another five to ten years.

The Framework Directive on Waste (75/442/EEC, as amended by Directive 91/156/EEC) requires that member states of the EU produce a National Waste Strategy setting out their policies on the disposal and recovery of waste. In part the Directive is implemented in the UK by the Environment Act 1995, which sets out the objectives of the UK National Waste Strategy. These are:

- to ensure that waste is recovered or disposed of without endangering human health and without using processes or methods that could harm the environment;
- to establish an integrated and adequate network of waste disposal installations, taking account of the best available technique not entailing excessive costs (BATNEEC)
- to ensure self sufficiency in waste disposal
- to encourage the prevention or reduction of waste production and its harmfulness
- to encourage the recovery of waste by means of recycling, reuse or reclamation, and the use of waste as a source of energy (Environment Act, 1995).

Following the adoption of the strategy requirements, the UK government published a strategy proposal in December 1995 for the sustainable management of waste in England and Wales, entitled *Making Waste Work*.[7] This document set out the government's waste management policies by building upon the ideas set out in the government's Sustainable Development Strategy (published in January 1994). The proposed strategy adopted three key objectives:

- to reduce the amount of waste produced;
- to make the best use of what waste is produced;
- to choose waste management practices that minimise the risk of immediate and future environmental pollution and harm to human health.[8]

In January 1998, the Minister for the Environment announced a review of the objectives set out in *Making Waste Work* and issued a consultation document in June 1998 called *Less Waste: More Value*. The aim was to establish a public view on the management of waste. Responses to *Less Waste: More Value* were used to

---

7 Department of the Environment and Welsh Office (1995), *Making Waste Work: A Strategy for Sustainable Waste Management in England and Wales* (London: HMSO).
  8 Ibid.

inform and direct the development of a draft Waste Strategy for England and Wales. This draft strategy, called *A Way with Waste*,[9] was published in June 1999, and set out various non-mandatory goals for future waste management within England and Wales.

During 2000 and 2001, a finalised waste strategy was published for England and Wales, as well as separate strategies for Scotland and Northern Ireland. These were produced after consultation documents about objectives were released, such as *Less Waste: More Value*. The status of waste management strategies for each region is shown in Table 29.1.

Table 29.1   Status of waste management strategies in the UK

Country	Status
England	Waste Strategy 2000 for England and Wales launched May 2000.
Wales	Managing Waste Sustainably, a consultation paper produced July 2001. Consultation to this document will end on 5 October 2001.
Scotland	National Waste Strategy for Scotland launched October 1999, after consultation in May 1999.
Northern Ireland	Waste Strategy launched 20 March 2000.

A Way with Waste stresses that the National Assembly for Wales retains its ability to choose a separate or joint strategy with England, and the feasibility of a separate strategy is still being considered. Proposals suggest that a Welsh strategy would set out the options for Wales, but also link overarching strategies to Waste Strategy 2000 for England and Wales.

The main themes of the UK National Waste Strategies have developed from the concept of sustainable development. The way in which waste is managed can impact on the degree to which the aims of sustainable development can be achieved.[10] The National Waste Strategies have sought to provide a policy framework that can address the concept of sustainable development, and therefore promote a more sustainable and integrated approach to waste management.[11] All of the National Waste Strategies acknowledge common key principles, which should be considered in taking waste management forward in a sustainable way. These principles are outlined below in Table 29.2.

The landfilling of waste has been recognised by the European Union as unsustainable and is the option of last resort in the waste hierarchy. The waste hierarchy (Figure 29.1 below) prioritises waste management techniques in order of their environmental impact. At the top of the hierarchy is prevention of waste

---

9 –Department of the Environment, Transport and the Regions (DETR) (1999), *A Way with Waste: A Draft Waste Strategy for England and Wales* (London: HMSO).

10 Ibid.

11 Williams, P. (1998), *Waste Treatment and Disposal* (Chichester: John Wiley and Sons); Scottish Environmental Protection Agency (SEPA) (1999), *National Waste Strategy – Scotland: Draft for Consultation* (Stirling: SEPA).

Table 29.2   Waste Strategy principles and strategies

Principles	Strategies
Sustainable development	Resource productivity
Waste hierarchy	Waste elimination-led strategy
Proximity	Innovative product design
Self-sufficiency	Development of recycling markets
Local community-based solutions	Development planning for the creation of a waste management infrastructure
Integration/partnership	Sustainable transportation
Tackling social disadvantage	Access to better waste data

production, whilst disposal in landfill is at the bottom. The landfilling of waste is unsustainable because it uses up valuable land space, and potential resources are lost, which increases the depletion of virgin materials. In addition, it causes air, water and soil pollution, and discharges carbon dioxide and methane into the atmosphere and chemicals and pesticides into the earth and groundwater.

The final principle is integration and partnership, which in fact work hand and hand with a number of the outlined strategies. This principle requires an integrated approach to waste management needing a number of interested parties to work in close association. It includes a mix of options including public, private and voluntary organisations working together and a life cycle approach to the environmental impacts of a product.

Categories and Sources of Waste

According to the Environment Act 1995, waste is defined as 'any substance or object which the holder discards or intends or is required to discard'. There are various terms used in waste management; listed below are various types of waste:

Estimates show that the UK produces around 400 million tonnes of waste annually, of which 29.3 million tonnes is municipal solid waste (MSW), most of which is disposed of in landfill. Table 29.4 gives the latest estimates of waste produced in the UK.[12]

Though MSW may seem a small proportion of the total waste produced, recycling levels for municipal waste are often much lower than for other types of waste. For example, about 40 per cent of industrial and commercial waste is recycled or recovered compared to 17 per cent of MSW.[13] Recovery, which includes recycling, is the use of waste to replace other materials, thereby conserving natural resources.

---

12 Department for Environment, Food and Rural Affairs (DEFRA) (2001), *Environmental Protection Group Research Newsletter* 2001–02 <http://www.defra.gov.uk/environment/research/2001/pdf/eprn0102.pdf>

13 Department of the Environment, Transport and the Regions (DETR) (2000), *Waste Strategy 2000 for England and Wales* (London: HMSO).

Table 29.3   Types of waste

Waste	**Controlled waste** Covered by EPA (Environmental Protection Act 1990) and COPA (Control of Pollution Act 1974)	Household waste	From domestic premises, civic amenity sites, street sweeping, prisons, campsites, household hazardous waste, household clinical waste, school waste
		Special/hazardous waste	Controlled waste of any kind that may be dangerous to treat – covered by the Special Waste Regulations 1995
		Industrial waste	From hospitals, laboratories, workshops, dredging noxious waste from certain processes, e.g. dry cleaning and paint mixing, waste oil, scrap metals, waste from ships, aircraft, commercial garages, premises for animals, nuclear waste
		Commercial waste	From offices, hotels, clubs, showrooms, private garages, markets, government departments, council offices, parks and gardens, courts, corporate bodies
		Sewage sludge	When landfilled or incinerated
	Uncontrolled waste Covered by separate legislation	Agricultural waste	Manure, slurry, crop residues, animal treatment dips, packaging
		Mining and quarrying waste	
		Explosive waste	
		Sewage sludge	When spread on agricultural land

Source: http://www.swpho.org.uk/waste/

Incineration of waste with energy recovery would be included in this figure. This is demonstrated in the hierarchy shown in Figure 29.1 below.

'The Soggy Lettuce Report' from Prudential[14] showed in 2004 that the average person throws away £424 of food. It revealed that over half of people in the UK throw away lettuce, bags of salad, loaves of bread and fruit every week simply because they did not have a chance to eat them before they went off or exceeded the sell-by date. Also regularly wasted were pints of milk, cooked meat, packet foods, cheese, prepared meals and unfinished bottles of wine. The following food disposal rates by commercial generators were derived from an industrial waste survey conducted in 2003 in Wales.

---

14 Prudential (2004), 'Soggy Lettuce Report: Are We a Nation of Wasters?', available at: http://www.assurre.eu/uploads/documents/13-1-soggy_lettuce_report_2004.pdf.

Table 29.4   Estimated waste production in the UK, by sector

	Million Tonnes	Percentage Of Total	Date Of Estimate
Mining & Quarrying	118	28	1997
Agriculture	87	20	1999
Demolition & construction	72	17	2000
Industrial	50	12	1998/99
Dredged material	41	10	1997
Municipal	30	7	1999/2000
Commercial	25	6	1998/99
Sludge	1	<1	1998/99
Total	424		

Note: A number of these estimates are for England and Wales only.

Source: Department for Environment, Food and Rural Affairs (DEFRA) (2002), Digest of Environmental Statistics

Table 29.5   Commercial food disposal rates in Wales

Type Of Food Waste Generators	Average Tonnes Of Waste Generated Annually	Sample Size
Food manufacturers	1881.59	132
Hospitality & leisure (hotels & restaurants)	93.86	364
Other business activities	156.46	112
Hospitals & nursing homes	376.91	85

A survey of the waste from a multi-occupied office block in the City of London concluded that each employee generated 0.74 kg of waste each day or 192 kg per year. The total percentage of paper contained in the waste was 91 per cent.

It is not just food waste that is costing us money. Up to £470 is spent each year by households purely on food packaging – it makes up over 40 per cent of the waste ending up in our bins. That amounts to 4.5 million tonnes per year, the vast majority of which ends up in landfill sites or, increasingly, incinerators. A report, commissioned by the charity Crisis, stated that the £350 million worth of wholesome but 'close to sell-by date' food ending in landfills or incinerators each year is enough to feed 270,000 homeless people.

How are we Managing Waste Currently?

There are significant differences in the management of MSW in the UK. The North West had the highest rate of landfill in England in 2000–01 (94 per cent). The West

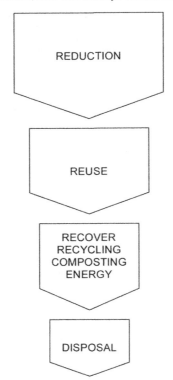

Figure 29.1   Waste hierarchy

Source: DETR, 2001

Midlands had the lowest level of landfill (58 per cent) and the highest percentage of waste incinerated (31 per cent). Rates of recycling/composting varied from 7 per cent to 18 per cent. National levels are given in Table 29.6 below.

In the UK, the most common disposal method is landfill. Incineration, anaerobic digestion and other disposal methods are also used.

Each year approximately 111 million tonnes, or 57 per cent, of all the UK's controlled waste (household, commercial and industrial waste) are disposed of in landfill sites. Some waste from sewage sludge is also placed in landfill sites, along with waste from mining and quarrying. The UK has valuable minerals that are mined extensively for industry. The extraction of these minerals produces large holes in the ground, which need to be filled in and landscaped. The use of these sites for the burial of waste seems a convenient solution. The UK has ideal underlying geology in many places, making landfill a cheap waste disposal option. In 1994 there were approximately 4,000 landfill sites in the UK.

Incineration is the second largest waste disposal method in most countries. In the UK, approximately 5 per cent of household waste, 7.5 per cent of commercial waste, and 2 per cent of industrial waste is disposed of by incineration. When burning waste, a large amount of energy is given off. Modern incinerators use this energy to generate electricity and hence prevent energy from being wasted. The UK

Table 29.6   Management of municipal solid waste in England, 1996/97 and 2000/01

Method	1996/97		2000/02	
	Thousand tonnes	Percentage of total	Thousand tonnes	Percentage of total
Landfill	20631	83.9	22055	78.3
Recycled/ composted	1750	7.1	3454	12.3
Incineration with EfW	1446	5.9	2479	8.8
Incineration without EfW	614	2.5	20	0.1
RDF manufactured	147	0.6	67	0.2
Other	0	0.0	75	0.3
Total	24588		28150	

EfW – Energy from waste   RDF – Refuse derived fuel

Source: Municipal waste management statistics 2000/01, DEFRA

houses numerous types of incineration plants, ranging from large-scale, mass-burn and municipal waste incinerators to clinical waste incinerators. However, emissions from the burning of hazardous hospital waste were said to be too high under the Environmental Protection Act of 1990.

Diversion from Landfill: the Government's Targets

Article 5(2) of the Landfill Directive sets targets for the amount of biodegradable municipal waste (BMW) that is sent to landfill. The Directive defines municipal waste as 'waste from households, as well as other waste which, because of its nature or composition, is similar to waste from households', and biodegradable waste as 'any waste that is capable of undergoing anaerobic or aerobic decomposition', including food and garden waste, and paper and paperboard. BMW represents about two-thirds of all municipal waste. The targets are expressed as a percentage of the amount of waste that was landfilled in 1995. The UK has taken advantage of the derogation, which is available under the Directive, allowing member states which had previously landfilled more than 80 per cent of BMW to postpone meeting the targets by up to four years. Its targets are set out in Table 29.7 below. Given that municipal waste has been continuing to rise at a rate commonly quoted at around 3 per cent (although it varies significantly between authorities), these targets present a daunting challenge to the government, and the country as a whole.

Current trends in municipal waste show that the total amount of waste has continued to rise, although the proportion of that waste being recycled or composted has also risen. The amount incinerated with energy recovery has remained roughly

Table 29.7   The UK's targets for diversion of BMW from landfill

	2010	2013	2020
Proportion of BMW allowed to be landfilled compared to 1995 amounts	75%	50%	35%

Source: DEFRA, Ev 47

constant. For the first time in recent years, the actual tonnage of municipal waste landfilled has registered a slight decrease, from 22.3 million tonnes in 2001–02 to 22 million tonnes in 2002–03.[15]

The government has implemented various measures to meet the national targets. These include a tax on landfill, funding for schemes to stimulate waste minimisation, reuse and recycling, additional funding for local authorities, most recently through the Waste Implementation Programme (WIP), statutory recycling and composting targets for local authorities, and a system of tradable landfill allowances for local authorities.[16]

The other main driver introduced by the government to influence local authorities is the Landfill Allowances Trading Scheme (LATS). Under the scheme, each waste disposal authority is allocated a certain amount of BMW that it is allowed to landfill in each year from 2005–06 to 2019–20. Authorities will be able to trade allowances with other authorities, save them for future years or use some allowances in advance.

Table 29.8   Waste management technologies for municipal solid waste

Treatment	Definition
Biological Processes	
Anaerobic Digestion	Biodegradable wastes are decomposed by bacteria in the absence of air, under elevated temperatures in much the same way as organic waste degrades in landfill sites to produce methane, but under accelerated controlled conditions. This leads to the production of a 'digestate' containing bio-solids that may be suited for application to land and/or a liquid, and a methane-rich 'biogas' which can be used as a fuel to produce electricity. Can be used to deal with certain high organic content industrial or agricultural wastes.

---

15 DEFRA (2002), *Independent Risk Assessment on Suitable National Standards*, available at: www.defra.gov.uk/animalh/by-prods/cater/comprisk.htm.

16 Ibid.

Treatment	Definition
Centralised Composting	Green wastes (and sometimes kitchen waste or the biodegradable fraction of MSW, e.g. cardboard) are composted in a centralised facility. Where kitchen waste is involved, this requires in-vessel or enclosed systems. The process is tightly controlled to achieve and maintain specific temperatures to facilitate bacteria/pathogen destruction to satisfy the provisions of the Animal By-products Order. Produces a compost or soil conditioner which may have a market value. May also accept certain commercial wastes, e.g. catering waste, due to be banned from landfill under ABPO.
Vermiculture	Vermiculture, or worm composting, is another option, where worm colonies are deliberately introduced to help compost concentrated organic materials such as food waste. It is particularly suitable for domestic application, but operations on a municipal scale reported by Warmer Bulletin include those at La Voulte, France (15 tonnes per day of organic household waste); and Bombay, India (4 tonnes per day of slaughterhouse waste).

Thermal Processes

Conventional Incineration with Energy Recovery (EfW)	Combustion of mixed waste under controlled conditions, to reduce its volume and hazardous properties, and to generate electricity and occasionally heat. It uses a wide variety of combustion systems developed from boiler plant technology and also more novel systems such as fluidised bed. Principal residues produced are: bottom ash, which is non-hazardous and can generally be recycled as an aggregate; metals which can be recovered for recycling; and fly ash, which is classed as hazardous and requires specialist treatment/disposal.
Gasification	A high temperature (800–1200^{0}C) thermal process, similar to pyrolysis but involving breakdown of hydrocarbons into a gas via partial oxidation under the application of heat. Some outputs (syngas) can be used as a fuel to produce electricity, some may find a use as a chemical feedstock but may require disposal if no markets are available. May be used in combination with combustion of syngas.
Pyrolysis	A thermal process (400–700^{0}C) where organic-based materials are broken down under the action of applied heat in the absence of oxygen to produce a mixture of gaseous and liquid fuels and a solid char fraction (mainly carbon). Most technologies prefer a homogenised feedstock containing limited non-organics. The outputs may be used as a fuel to generate electricity, while others may require disposal or additional processing for recycling/energy recovery. May be combined with gasification to maximise production of 'syngas'.

Hybrid Processes

Mechanical Biological Treatment (MBT)	A generic term covering a range of technologies for the processing of MSW using the combination of mechanical separation and biological treatment. In its simplest form MBT bio-stablises the mass of residual waste to be landfilled. Normally the processing of the incoming waste stream permits the extraction of fractions of the waste stream with end purposes in mind, with biological processing of the residual waste. Some systems use in-vessel composting or anaerobic digestion to process the residual biodegradable elements of the waste. Most systems generate a material suitable for use as a refuse derived fuel (RDF). MBT is extensively used in Germany, Austria and Italy.

Treatment	Definition
Mechanical Heat Treatment	Using mechanical and thermal processes to separate/prepare mixed waste into more usable fractions and/or render it more 'stable' for deposit into landfill. An example is the application of steam and pressure to a mixed waste stream in a sealed vessel (autoclave) to initially degrade the waste. The remaining material may be sorted, depending on the available applications.

Source: *Beyond Waste* (2006) Waste Management Sector Waste Development Framework Engagement Report for Kent County Council, UK

How Can the Targets be Met?

To meet the targets for diversion of waste away from landfill, it is necessary to reduce the amount of waste being produced, and to reuse or recycle a greater proportion of the waste which is subject to disposal. The government has done a great deal to assist businesses to find ways of minimising waste and reusing materials, for instance, through the funding of the Waste Implementation Programme (WIP), the Waste and Resources Action Programme (WRAP) and Envirowise. The government is also continuing to provide funding for local authorities to further develop household recycling and similar projects. Financial instruments like the Landfill Tax and the LATS also have an important role. An important factor in diversion from landfill, the adequacy of treatment capacity for existing and future waste streams, therefore needs to be addressed.

There is a range of treatment methods for municipal waste; these are set out in Table 29.8 above.

The best way to eliminate food waste, however, is to not create it. This can be accomplished by streamlining processes and using resources more efficiently. Grocery shoppers can buy produce in quantities that can be used before they spoil, despite the sale price. At restaurants, diners can ask about portion sizes and be aware of included side dishes with entrees. With the popularity of all-you-can-eat buffets, we can help by only taking what we can eat, having regard to food waste prevention and appropriate nutritional needs.

Preventing Food Waste

As discussed in the earlier sections, food waste constitutes the largest single proportion, accounting for an average of 21 per cent of total commercial waste arising. Food preparation and consumption involves a large number of natural resources along the supply chain. Much of the food consumed today has been processed, packaged and transported extensively before it reaches the end consumer. These activities themselves are often associated with the generation of large amounts of waste. A number of UK organisations today promote sustainable food consumption. Sustain, the Alliance for Better Food and Farming, uses the following criteria as the definition for sustainable food:

Proximity – originating from the closest practicable source or the minimisation of energy use

Healthy – as part of a balanced diet and not containing harmful biological or chemical contaminants

Fairly traded – between producers, processors, retailers and consumers

Non-exploiting of employees in the food sector in terms of pay and conditions
Environmentally beneficial or benign in its production (for example, organic)

Accessible both in terms of geographic access and affordability

High animal welfare standards in both production and transport

Socially inclusive of all people in society

Encouraging knowledge and understanding of food and food culture

Packaging used to protect foods during transport contributes significantly to the waste generated by catering activities. Minimising packaging waste is therefore a major concern when purchasing food, and catering contractors can do so by specifying to suppliers that:

Packaging is kept to the minimum necessary to protect the goods in transit

Maximum use is made of recycled and recyclable materials (that is, materials for which facilities exist for collection and recycling) in the manufacture of crates, pallets, and so on

Take-back schemes, operating for reusing packaging or, less preferably, recycling any crates, pallets and other larger items of packaging, are made use of wherever possible

Encouraging catering contractors to minimise packaging; for example, items such as sandwiches can be wrapped in grease-proof paper rather than in plastic boxes

Educate staff about the environmentally preferable lunch options, those with less packaging, and packaging which can be recycled.

Conclusions

The food processing industry is a major contributor to industrial waste. According to the Environment Agency, the UK's food and drink sector produces between seven and eight million tonnes of waste per year, and consumes approximately 900 megalitres of water each day (enough to supply almost three-quarters of all customers' needs daily in London alone). Processors must now operate under amended laws that will see less scope for waste in the industry. In addition, incineration and landfill are the waste management options with most potential for negative environmental effects, for example, on soil, air and water quality. Incineration releases more nitrous oxides, hydrogen chloride, dioxins and furans than any other waste option. It is also an important source of particulates.

Action needs to be, and is being, taken. There is a drive to take organic waste out of landfill, largely because of methane emissions – a major factor in global warming. This change in waste management is having a knock-on effect on the food production industry. Although commercial landfills are not covered, there are now targets in municipal landfills to reduce organic matter. This means there is less space for waste coming from food processing operations. This is also affecting the packaging industry. There is a growing move away from the use of plastic and towards starch and other biodegradable materials. But with organic matter being taken out of landfill in the UK, both the food processing and packaging industries need to think carefully about waste management.

Requirements for source separation

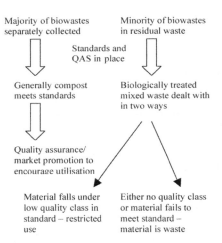

No requirement for source separation

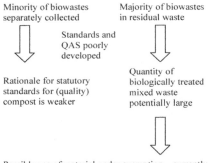

Figure 29.2 Contrasting policy frameworks for bio-wastes

Source: WRAP (2002) *Comparison of Compost Standards within the EU, North America and Australasia*, Report published by The Waste and Resources Action Programme (WRAP) UK

The role of mechanical-biological treatment in waste management is increasing and represents something of an evolution from earlier periods where not-so-dissimilar techniques were considered as 'composting'.

The emerging trend is for source-separation systems to aim to minimise, as far as possible, the biodegradable fraction, or better still, the capability of residual waste to ferment. Source-separation of food waste is the primary step for achieving this reduction.

Only intensive schemes tackling food waste (such as the ones run in some regions in Italy and recently under development in Catalunya) can, on their own, reach the targets of the Landfill Directive. Consequently, both countries with long-running source-separation systems for bio-waste, and those with more recently implemented intensive schemes, have set in place legislation concerning the landfill of waste in order to try to achieve the requirements of the Landfill Directive.

Figure 29.2 depicts the contrast in approach between countries which target source separation (left-hand side), and the current situation in the UK (right-hand side). Were a Bio-waste Directive to be passed in its current form, the UK would immediately be required to transform itself into a country of the type represented on the left-hand side of the figure.

Minimising the volume of food waste at both pre- and post-production points is vital to producers. Throughout the food chain the opportunity to adapt waste management in order to minimise inputs, reduce the potential for waste, and to consider re-engineering or creation of co-products to add value, will have to be an essential business objective.

There are no quick fixes for the challenges facing society on waste. Identifying and securing the necessary changes in behaviour to achieve any vision is an ongoing, iterative process that must be based upon robust evidence and thorough analysis of that evidence. In developing policies and specific measures to support those policies that may emerge following agreement on the strategic approach to waste, it must be ensured that they are both environmentally and economically rational, with realistic timescales to allow for the planning of investment by businesses and public authorities.

Public attitudes to waste treatment are fundamental to the successful achievement of the landfill diversion targets, given that waste minimisation and reuse cannot in themselves ensure that the targets are reached. Even the more 'acceptable' treatments of waste, such as recycling and recovery of materials, will require the development of more facilities. The public has to recognise and accept that, while society continues to produce more waste, more and different waste treatment methods will be required. Central to public acceptance, it will be the government's role to ensure that the public has confidence in the systems put in place to treat waste.

June 2005

Chapter 30

A Gain for Autonomy and Reproductive Choice: The Issue of 'Saviour Siblings' Resolved

Jennifer Gunning

On 28 April 2005 the House of Lords dismissed the appeal of *Quintavalle (on behalf of Comment on Reproductive Ethics) v Human Fertilisation and Embryology Authority*. This brought to an end the long drawn out legal battle as to whether it was permissible under the Human Fertilisation and Embryology Act (1990) to allow the tissue typing of an embryo to detect whether it would be suitable as a tissue donor for a sick sibling. The five Law Lords concerned were unanimous in their judgement that the scope of the Act was sufficiently broad to allow tissue typing.[1]

The story goes back to the year 2002 when the Human Fertilisation and Embryology Authority (HFEA) gave permission to the fertility clinic treating Raj and Shahana Hashmi to carry out pre-implantation genetic diagnosis (PGD) including tissue typing. The Hashmis have a son, Zain, who suffers from the blood disorder beta thalassaemia. This is a life-threatening disease which requires Zain to have regular blood transfusions and his life expectancy is short unless a suitable tissue donor can be found. None of his three elder siblings was tissue compatible and a fourth sibling, conceived after Zain's birth, was also incompatible. In another pregnancy the fetus was also found to have the same disease and Mrs Hashmi underwent an abortion. It appeared that in vitro fertilisation with PGD to eliminate the chance of beta thalassaemia, together with tissue typing to ensure compatibility with Zain, was the only option. No sooner had the HFEA permission been given than Josephine Quintavalle, on behalf of the pro-life pressure group Comment on Reproductive Ethics (CORE), brought judicial review proceedings of the decision and the procedure was stopped.

Meanwhile, the HFEA refused to allow tissue typing to another couple, Michelle and Jayson Whitaker, hoping to undergo fertility treatment to try for a tissue-matched sibling for their son Charlie, who suffered from the equally life-threatening disease Diamond Blackfan anaemia (DBA). The Authority's reasoning in this case was:

> Although some children with DBA inherit this genetic condition from carrier parents, most cases arise as a result of a sporadic mutation. In such cases, where neither parent can

---

1 www.parliament.the-stationery-office.co.uk/pa/ld200405/ldjudgmt/jd050428/quint-1.htm.

be demonstrated to be a carrier, the risks of having a further affected child are considered relatively low. PGD would only be applicable when parents were carriers and where the mutation could be tested in the embryos.

The HFEA License Committee was informed that, in this particular case, neither parent appeared to be a carrier of the genetic mutation, the existing child's condition was likely to be a sporadic case, and that embryos conceived in the future by these parents would not be at significantly greater risk of DBA than embryos conceived by the general population. Therefore it could not be argued that PGD was necessary to select embryos free from the condition.[2]

In other words they would not allow PGD for tissue typing on embryos that were likely to be normal. By that time PGD combined with tissue typing was already well established in the United States and the Whitakers went abroad for their treatment.

The judicial review of the Hashmi case was undertaken by Maurice Kay J.[3] Ms Quintavalle claimed that the HFEA had no power under the Human Fertilisation and Embryology Act (HFE Act) to authorise tissue typing. Mr Justice Kay supported this claim but an appeal was allowed. He took a narrow view of the Act and the interpretation of the term 'suitable', as in 'practices designed to secure that embryos are in a suitable condition to be placed in a woman or to determine whether embryos are suitable for that purpose' in Schedule 2 of the Act, setting out activities that the Authority may license.

The case then moved to the Court of Appeal. In April 2003, the Master of the Rolls, Lord Phillips of Worth Matravers, and Lord Justices Schiemann and Mance unanimously upheld the appeal.[4] As summarised in the Law Report, the Court of Appeal took a broader view of the intentions of the HFE Act and found that:

When the object of the treatment was to enable a woman to bear a child with a tissue type that would enable stem cells to be provided to a sick sibling, an embryo would only be suitable for the purpose of being placed within her if it would lead to the birth of a child with the tissue type in question. Accordingly, the authority was right to decide that the Act authorised it to licence IVF treatment with PGD for the purpose of tissue typing subject to such conditions as it considered appropriate. IVF treatment could help women to bear children when they were unable to do so by the normal process of fertilisation. Screening of embryos before implantation enabled a choice to be made as to the characteristics of the child to be born with the assistance of the treatment. Whether and for what purposes such a choice should be permitted raised difficult ethical questions. Parliament had placed that choice in the hands of the authority.[5]

---

2 http://www.hfea.gov.uk/PressOffice/Archive/43573563.

3 http://www.hmcourts-service.gov.uk/judgmentsfiles/j1474/quintavalle_v_human_ fertilisation.htm.

4 *R (Quintavalle) v Human Fertilisation and Embryology Authority (Secretary of State for Health Intervening)* [2003] EWCA Civ 667.

5 'Tissue-typing of Human Embryos formed in vitro – Whether treatment services "for the purpose of assisting women to carry children"', *R (Quintavalle) v Human Fertilisation and Embryology Authority (Secretary of State for Health Intervening)* [2005] 2 WLR 1061. www.lawreports.co.uk/civmayc0.5.htm.

The Hashmis found themselves free to continue with their attempt, albeit unsuccessfully, to have a tissue-compatible sibling for Zain, and Quintavalle, on behalf of CORE, appealed to the House of Lords. The House of Lords has now upheld the decision of the Court of Appeal which found in favour of the HFEA. Lord Phillips referred back to the White Paper of which he said:

> The intention was ... to define the functions of the Authority in very broad terms. To ensure that the legislation was flexible enough to deal with 'as yet unforeseen treatment developments which may raise new ethical issues', the Bill would:

> 'contain powers to make regulations (subject to the affirmative resolution procedure) to add to or subtract from the range of matters coming within the regulatory scope of the [authority].' (Para. 14).

He further went on to say that:

> It could be said that the Act made no reference to HLA typing because neither the Warnock Committee nor Parliament in 1990 foresaw it as a possibility. But there was intense discussion, both in the report and in Parliament, about selection for sex on social grounds. If ever there was a dog which did not bark in the night, this was it. It is hard to imagine that the reason why the Act said nothing on the subject was because Parliament thought it was clearly prohibited by the use of the word 'suitable' or because it wanted to leave the question over for later primary legislation. In my opinion the only reasonable inference is that Parliament intended to leave the matter to the authority to decide. And once one says that the concept of suitability can include gender selection on social grounds, it is impossible to say that selection on the grounds of any other characteristics which the mother might desire was positively excluded from the discretion of the authority, however unlikely it might be that the authority would actually allow selection on that ground.

In July 2003 Jamie Whitaker was born, a perfect tissue match for his sick brother Charlie. In this case the embryo screening had taken place in the USA and a successful cord cell transplant was subsequently carried out. In July 2004 the HFEA changed its mind about allowing tissue typing in the case where a familial genetic disorder was not involved. The reason given was that the Authority had:

> ... now carefully reviewed the medical, psychological and emotional implications for children and families as well as the safety of the technique. There have been three further years during which successful embryo biopsies have been carried out, both in the UK and abroad and we are not aware of any increased risk.[6]

It is not clear that in three years the number of PGDs carried out would have made a statistically significant difference to the safety of the procedure. But the decision at least meant that reproductive tourism to avoid restrictions in the UK could be avoided in the context of embryo screening. The Authority still reviews applications on a case-by-case basis but, subsequent to their change of decision, permission has

---

6 www.hfea.gov.uk/PressOffice/Archive/1090427358.

been given to another family, the Fletchers, with a Diamond Blackfan child, to have embryo screening for tissue type.[7]

The principal discussions in all this have been on interpretations of the law rather than the ethical issues involved; issues such as autonomy in reproductive choice, the commodification of the donor child and its welfare versus the welfare of the family as a whole. One might question the motives of CORE, which hampered the potential treatment of a sick child over a period of two and a half years, in trying to pick holes in the HFE Act. As a well-funded pro-life organisation, it seems to have attempted to steamroller individual choice in pursuit of the right to life of the embryo. There is nothing in the law to stop a couple conceiving in the natural way and having prenatal diagnosis to establish the tissue type of the fetus and, where genetic disease is involved, aborting the affected fetus. But this resort, and one which the Hashmis tried, is a lottery which may result in killing a fetus rather than disposing of an early stage embryo.

The House of Lords decision will not open the floodgates for applications for embryo screening. The HFEA, very rightly, regards pre-implantation tissue typing as a last resort. Other sources of stem cells exist and umbilical cord cell banks now hold over 230,000 cord blood units worldwide,[8] a number which is growing annually. These sources should be explored before the 'saviour sibling' route is tried.

May 2005

---

7 www.shef.ac.uk/bioethics-today/archives/files/PGDcomm.htm.

8 http://www.bmdw.org/index.php?id=number_donors. Accessed on 15 March 2007.

Chapter 31

Human Rights and Gypsies: It is Time for a Rethink

Luke Clements

Once more the tabloid press is full of vitriol and hate speech. Once more it is aimed at Gypsies (now referred to euphemistically as 'travellers'). If one is to believe what one reads, Gypsies are now the single greatest threat to the peace and security of the United Kingdom. And again, if we are to believe what we read, the reason why this threat exists is because of 'human rights'. As *The Sun* and the *Mail* now proclaim 'human rights have gone too far' – these stealers of our children and despoilers of our countryside are getting away with their despicable acts, because of 'human rights'.

It takes little to provoke the tabloid press and generally there is no shortage of politically intemperate remarks. These are not of course confined to the local press and local councillors. In the 2005 General Election campaign the Conservatives published a full-page advertisement[1] directed at Gypsies and other travelling people arguing that 'too many people today seem to think they don't have to play by the rules and they are using so-called human rights to get away with doing the wrong thing'. This fed into a *Sun* newspaper campaign – with its front-page banner headline 'SUN WAR ON GIPSY FREE-FOR-ALL', with the newspaper asking its readers to 'tell us your gipsy stories'. Gypsies are a recognised ethnic group under UK law:[2] just re-read the above, substituting 'Jewish' for 'Gipsy'.

The Tories are not the only party to provide kindling to spark the tabloid furnaces. Take, for instance, Jack Straw, the Leader of the House, who has recently been so keen to portray himself as a moderate and reasonable man in his debate concerning the wearing by Muslim women of the full veil.[3] Compare this with his 1999 comments concerning 'so-called travellers' as people who 'think it's perfectly OK for them to cause mayhem in an area, to go burgling, thieving, breaking into vehicles, causing all kinds of trouble including defecating in the doorways of firms and so on'.[4] One trembles to think what he would have said if a Gypsy had planted a bomb on the underground.

---

1 The *Independent*, Sunday, 20 March 2005.

2 *Commission for Racial Equality v Dutton* [1989] QB 783.

3 In his weekly article he voiced his unease about the full veil, referring to 'the apparent incongruity between the signals which indicate common bonds', *The Lancashire Telegraph*, 3 October 2006.

4 Jack Straw, interview with Annie Oathen, Radio West Midlands, 22 July 1999.

Such comments invariably ignite a tabloid inferno. As a UNESCO report noted almost 30 years ago,[5] the restraints that generally operate 'on the coverage of race [do] not apply in the case of travelling people'; and some sections of the media freely 'portrayed travellers as dirty, criminal, alien, etc., giving rise to communal tension'.

These vile outpourings – demonising Gypsies – are periodic occurrences. When new scapegoats fail (for example, asylum seekers, Central European benefits scroungers, single mothers, paedophiles) then the traditional ones resurface. Gypsies seem to fulfil this requirement admirably; they are one of the few racial groups that no one seems to complain about if you incite people to hate them.

Curiously there is virtually nothing to stop the press behaving this way. The race relations legislation does not touch newspapers, the Press Complaints Commission's remit does not cover generalised hate campaigns of this nature[6] and virtually no one is ever prosecuted for incitement to commit racial hatred. The Traveller Law Research Unit at Cardiff Law School once convened a meeting of newspaper editors (with the help of the Commission for Racial Equality) and asked them why they said such foul things about Gypsies – and why did they not say equally despicable things about Jews or Black people. One of the editors explained. The reason was simple: if they wrote an equivalent story about Jewish people or Black people, then their offices would be burned down. Such a frank admission may explain the 'restraint' shown by the tabloids in not publishing the cartoons depicting the Prophet Muhammad in 2005.[7]

The present batch of anti-Gypsy stories pedalled by the tabloids have about as much truth as did the abominable anti-Jew and anti-Gypsy stories peddled by the German press in the Nazi days. Yes, Gypsies are occupying land without planning permission[8] – and thereby causing upset to neighbouring landowners; yes, some Gypsies behave badly. Yes it is quite understandable to feel sympathy for those we understand – the landowning 'settled people'. What is seldom heard (because it requires thought) is that Gypsies are victims too. Far from being rich wheeler-dealers, they are the most deprived of all ethnic groups in the UK.[9] They have the highest infant mortality rates of any such group and the highest illiteracy rates. Over a third have absolutely nowhere lawful to live – of those that do, over 50 per cent

---

5 UNESCO (1977), *Ethnicity and the Media*, cited in Morris, R. (2000), 'Gypsies, Travellers and the Media: Press Regulation and Racism in the UK', in *Communications Law* 5:6, 213—19, 218.

6 As Rachel Morris states: 'The Press Complaints Commission supervises a code of practice which makes reference to racial offence but only considers complaints to be within its scope when the offensive words are used in relation to an identified individual who then themselves complain. Effectively this means that the PCC never upholds any complaints on grounds of racial offence', in Morris, op. cit., 214.

7 Twelve cartoons published on 30 September 2005 by the Danish newspaper *Jyllands-Posten*, which depicted the Muslim Prophet Muhammad.

8 Generally, however, it is land that they themselves own.

9 Gypsies and travellers constitute the single largest category of people (numerically) deemed to be 'at very high risk of social exclusion', in *Breaking the Cycle: Taking Stock of Progress and Priorities for the Future. A Report by the Social Exclusion Unit* (London: Office of the Deputy Prime Minister, September 2004) para. 1.61.

live on official sites that are in environmentally harmful locations (for example, sited next to motorways or major roads, rubbish tips, industrial sites or sewage works).[10]

The Traveller Law Research Unit at Cardiff, in common with many others, predicted that the 1994 repeal of the duty on local authorities to provide sites (via the Criminal Justice and Public Order Act) was a recipe for future chaos. Gypsies are now being punished for the inevitable consequences of the Major government's narrow minded, bigoted policy; a policy described by the Police Federation as 'knee-jerk' and opposed by the Country Landowners Association, the National Farmers Union, all the Local Authority Associations and countless others. If Gypsies have nowhere legal to live, then what are they supposed to do: evaporate? Historically, their hopes of getting planning permission are slim: until the recent reforms they had a 90 per cent refusal rate compared to the 80 per cent success rate for other communities.[11]

It would of course be relatively simple to solve their problem. There are probably only 4,000 or so Gypsy families in need of accommodation assistance. If, each year, every local planning authority (of which there are about 450) provided a few more planning permissions, then within a relatively short period of time the problem would be resolved. This is essentially what the government has suggested – and hence the tabloid hysteria.

How is it that the press can get away with this frenzy of racial hatred? The irony, of course, is that it is 'because of human rights'. The press repeatedly rely on the Human Rights Act 1998. Any attempt to curtail their intrusions or output is met with by a bevy of lawyers cantering off to court to trot out their impassioned references to human rights.

The European Convention on Human Rights was drafted as a legal bulwark to guard against any reoccurrence of the excesses that blighted the lives of minorities during the Second World War;[12] excesses that led to the extermination of over a million Gypsies; excesses that were presaged by a constant stream of vicious fictions criminalising the Jewish and Gypsy peoples. Curiously, however, although article 10 of the Convention protects the right to free speech, it contains no fundamental prohibition against hate speech. For almost all other European states, this omission is of little consequence since the victims of hate speech in these states have access to two effective procedural rights. Under the International Covenant on Civil and Political Rights,[13] complaints can be made to the UN Human Rights Committee in Geneva about a state's failure to take reasonable measures to protect individuals from hate speech. Although the UK was one of the first states to ratify the Convention,

---

10 ODPM Housing, Planning, Local Government and the Regions Committee, for their inquiry into Gypsy and Traveller Sites, HC 633-II, published 17 June 2004, para. 4.11, available at: www.publications.parliament.uk/pa/cm200304/cmselect/cmodpm/633/633we02.htm.

11 Column 1132, 7 June 1994, House of Lords, Hansard, Per Lord Irvine of Laird.

12 Kenrick, D. and Puxon, G. (1972), *The Destiny of Europe's Gypsies* (London: Chatto).

13 Article 20(2) provides that 'Any advocacy of national, racial or religious hatred that constitutes incitement to discrimination, hostility or violence shall be prohibited by law'.

it alone of the 25 European Union members does not recognise the right to take individual complaints to the Human Rights Committee.

Likewise almost all other European nationals can seek the protection of the UN Convention on the Elimination of All Forms of Racial Discrimination, article 4 of which requires states to prosecute bodies (including newspapers) that disseminate racial hatred and to criminalise propaganda activities which promote and incite racial discrimination. However, the UK has entered a reservation to this provision – in effect exempting the media.[14]

Ironically, the tabloids also get special pleading under section 12 of the Human Rights Act 1998. Section 12 applies when a court is considering whether or not to grant an injunction or compensatory damages against a newspaper. The House of Lords have held[15] that this provision provides enhanced protection for the media – over and above that which existed prior to the Act coming into force.[16]

If there is a category for irresponsible freeloaders at large in our society, then I for one would have no hesitation in nominating the tabloid press for its pole position. They are uniquely privileged, having been given (by successive governments) immunity from virtually every human rights treaty. They personify everything that is antipathetic to the communitarian view of human rights; they believe that they have the absolute right to do what they like; rights without an iota of responsibility.

So *The Sun* and the *Mail* and their wretched followers have for once hit the nail on the head – human rights have gone too far. If the Press Complaints Commission cannot curtail this appalling hate campaign, then it is time for the government to look again at the justification for giving the UK press the unique legal privileges that they enjoy.

April 2005

---

14 Article 4(a) requires, amongst other things, that states make it illegal to disseminate ideas based on racial hatred, and article 4(b) requires that states prohibit activities which promote and incite racial discrimination. The UK reservation applies a restrictive interpretation to this duty, stating: '[I]t remains the UK's view that Article 4 requires a party to adopt further legislative measures in fields covered by sub-paragraphs (a), (b) and (c) of Article 4 only if it considers, with due regard to the principles embodied in the Universal Declaration of Human Rights (in particular the right to freedom of opinion and expression and the right to freedom of peaceful assembly and association) that any additional legislation is necessary to meet those ends. The interpretative statement is a useful clarification, which puts beyond doubt that the principle of proportionality applies and ensures an appropriate balance between the rights to freedom of expression and association and protecting individuals from violence and hatred.

15 *Cream Holdings v Banerjee* [2004] UKHL 44.

16 The test then being determined by *American Cyanamid Co v Ethicon Ltd* [1975] AC 396.

Chapter 32

Forgetting to be Nice: The National Institute for Clinical Excellence's Preliminary Recommendations Concerning Drugs for the Treatment of Alzheimer's Disease

Søren Holm

At the beginning of March 2005 the National Institute for Clinical Excellence (NICE) published an appraisal consultation document concerning the use in the National Health Service in England and Wales (NHS) of the four drugs that are registered for the treatment of Alzheimer's disease (AD). Like all of NICE's appraisal documents, this contains a review of the evidence concerning the effectiveness and cost-effectiveness of the drugs, and the preliminary conclusions of the Appraisal Committee.

In 2001 NICE had appraised the same group of drugs and recommended their use in the NHS for certain clearly defined groups of patients with AD. As the result of this recommendation, the use of the drugs has increased, and with it the cost to the NHS. All of NICE's recommendations include a recommendation for when the recommendations should be reviewed, and the current appraisal is the first scheduled review after the initial 2001 appraisal.

The preliminary recommendations in the consultation document have raised significant concern and anger among patients, carers and professionals, since NICE is now recommending that none of these drugs should be used in the treatment of AD, although patients already receiving one of the drugs '... may be continued on therapy ... until it is considered appropriate to stop'.[1] NICE further recommends that the newest drug, which is the only drug for use in moderate to severe AD, can be prescribed as part of clinical trials to generate further evidence concerning the effectiveness of this drug.

Given that NICE recommendations very strongly influence what NHS organisations do, the effect of the implementation of the recommendations will be that very few patients will be prescribed these drugs in the NHS in the future.

---

1 National Institute for Clinical Excellence (2005), 'Appraisal Consultation Document – Donezepil, Rivastigmine, Galantamine and Memantine for the Treatment of Alzheimer's Disease', 1.3. <http://www.nice/org.uk/page.aspx?o=245908>

Cost and Consistency

The rationale for the change in recommendations is mainly economical. There is, for all of the drugs, evidence that they are effective against some of the manifestations of AD, and that they can delay the progression of the disease to some extent. This is, however, achieved at a cost per quality adjusted life year gained of approximately £40,000–50,000, although it is evident from the document that these figures are extremely sensitive to minor changes in the model used to calculate them. Based on these calculations, the Committee concludes that it '... put the AChE (acetylcholinesterase) inhibitors [three of the four drugs] outside the range of cost effectiveness that might be considered appropriate for the NHS'.[2]

This is slightly surprising. NICE officially maintains that it uses a cut-off of about £20,000–30,000 per quality adjusted life year gained,[3] but analysis of previous NICE decisions shows that the cut-off is variable and that it is really closer to £35,000–£40,000.[4] If the drugs are outside the range, they are just outside the range, and NICE has previously recommended the use of treatments that are even more outside the range. This clearly raises significant problems of consistency in NICE recommendations, if the preliminary recommendations become final.

Forgetting to be Nice

But apart from the likely inconsistency in the justification of NICE's preliminary recommendations, there are other, and perhaps even more important, ethical considerations that NICE ought to have taken into account.

AD is not a nice disease to have for most patients, and caring for someone with AD is not easy. It is frightening to literally lose one's mind, and it is a cause of great sorrow to see this happen in a spouse, partner or parent whom one has lived with or known for years, as illustrated in the Oscar winning film *Iris*. In the NICE document, this aspect of AD is not sufficiently recognised. NICE writes:

> People with AD lose the ability to carry out routine daily activities ... and, as a result, many of them require a high level of care. Often, this is provided by an elderly relative, whose own health and quality of life can be seriously affected by the burden of care provision. Behavioural changes in the person such as aggression are particularly disturbing for carers.[5]

But this is an over-objectified and sanitised version of the reality of living with AD as a patient or carer.

---

2 Ibid.

3 Rawlins, M.D. (2001), 'The Failings of NICE. Reply from Chairman of NICE', *British Medical Journal* 322:7284, 489.

4 Devlin, N. and Parkin, D. (2003), 'Does NICE have a Cost-effectiveness Threshold and What Factors Influence its Decisions? A Discrete Choice Analysis', unpublished manuscript.

5 NICE (2005), op. cit., 2.3.

The drugs that NICE now recommends should not be prescribed are the only ones shown to be effective in AD, and by preventing people from getting them prescribed in the NHS essentially removes one of the only sources of hope available to the patients and their carers (those who can afford to pay will, of course, still be able to get the drugs).

If the drugs had been hugely expensive, way outside of the NICE cut-off for cost-effectiveness, this could have been justified, but given that the drugs are not that far from the threshold, the decision is difficult to justify. NICE seems to have forgotten one of the central values in healthcare, the value of compassion. Among the many patient groups that suffer and die, only a few could make a stronger claim on our compassion than those who suffer and die from AD.

Or to put it in simpler terms, NICE has forgotten that it is not enough to be effective, one also need to be compassionate and nice.

Conclusion

There can be no doubt that clinical excellence must include ethical excellence. An organisation that only promoted clinical excellence in a narrow technical sense would be seriously deficient and morally at fault. NICE ought, therefore, to re-think its recommendations in the light of the truly horrific experiences of patients with AD and the people who care for them.

March 2005

Further reading

Purtilo, R. and ten Have, H.A.M.J. (eds) (2004), *Ethical Foundations of Palliative Care for Alzheimer Disease* (Baltimore: The Johns Hopkins University Press).

Index

Made in the USA
Monee, IL
10 August 2021

75390803R00188